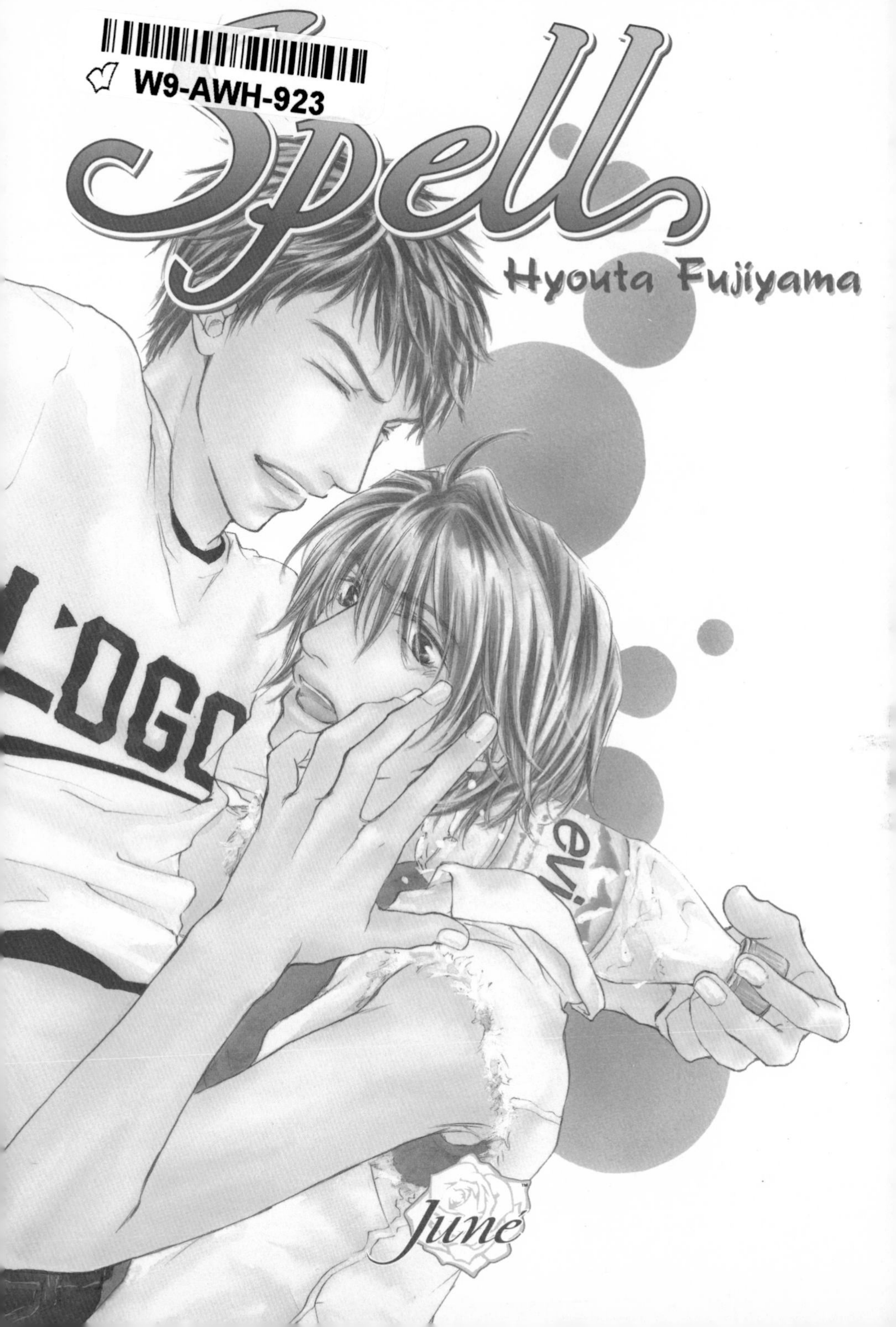
Spell
Hyouta Fujiyama
Juné

Spell

Translation   Vivian Chien
Lettering   Studio Takomanga
Graphic Design   Wendy Lee/Fred Lui
Editing   Wendy Lee
Editor in Chief   Fred Lui
Publisher   Hikaru Sasahara

English Edition Published by
DIGITAL MANGA PUBLISHING
A division of DIGITAL MANGA, Inc.
1487 W 178th Street, Suite 300
Gardena, CA 90248

www.dmpbooks.com

First Edition: September 2007
ISBN-10: 1-56970-806-1
ISBN-13: 978-1-56970-806-4

1 3 5 7 9 10 8 6 4 2

Printed in China

スペル
word.1
Spell

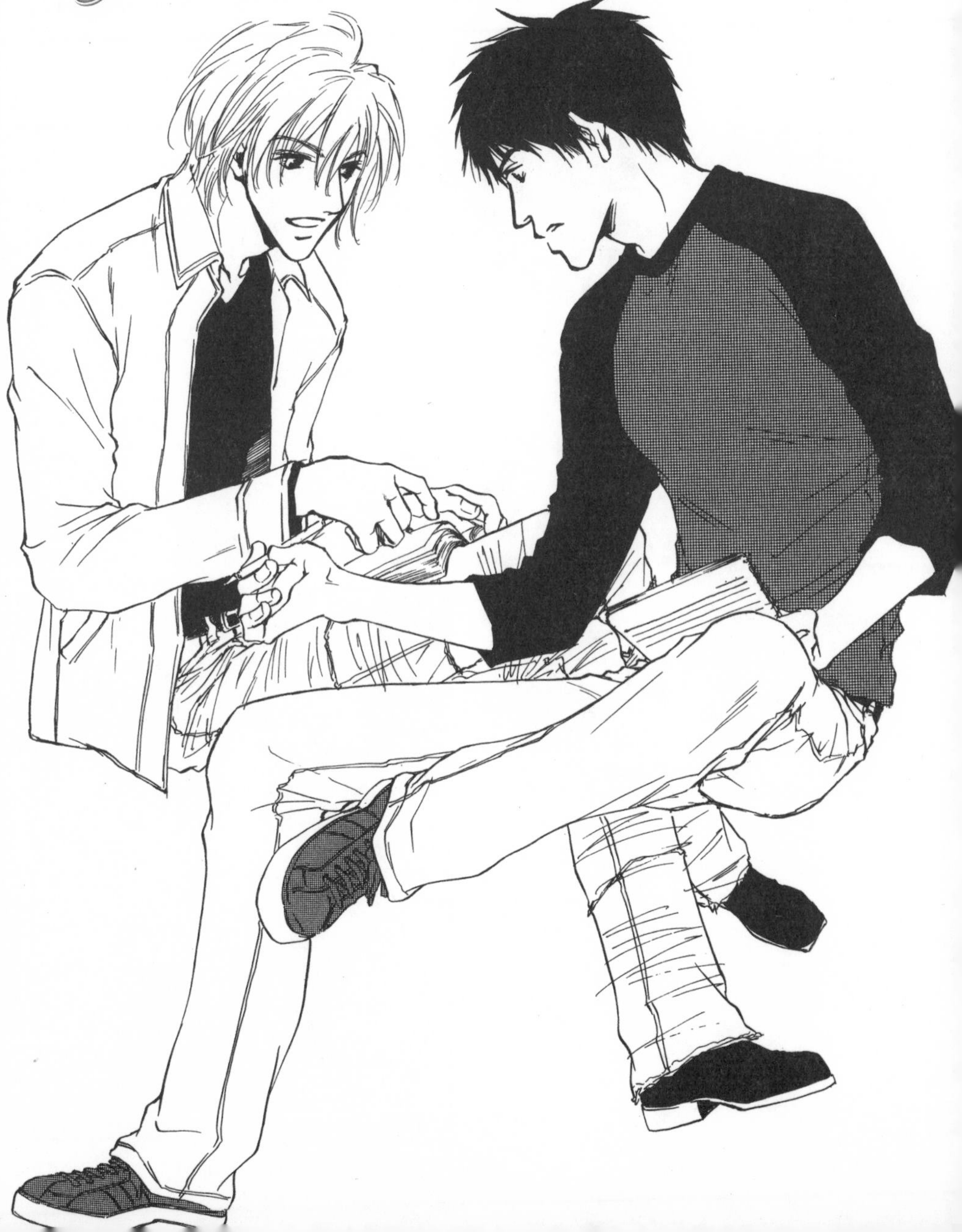

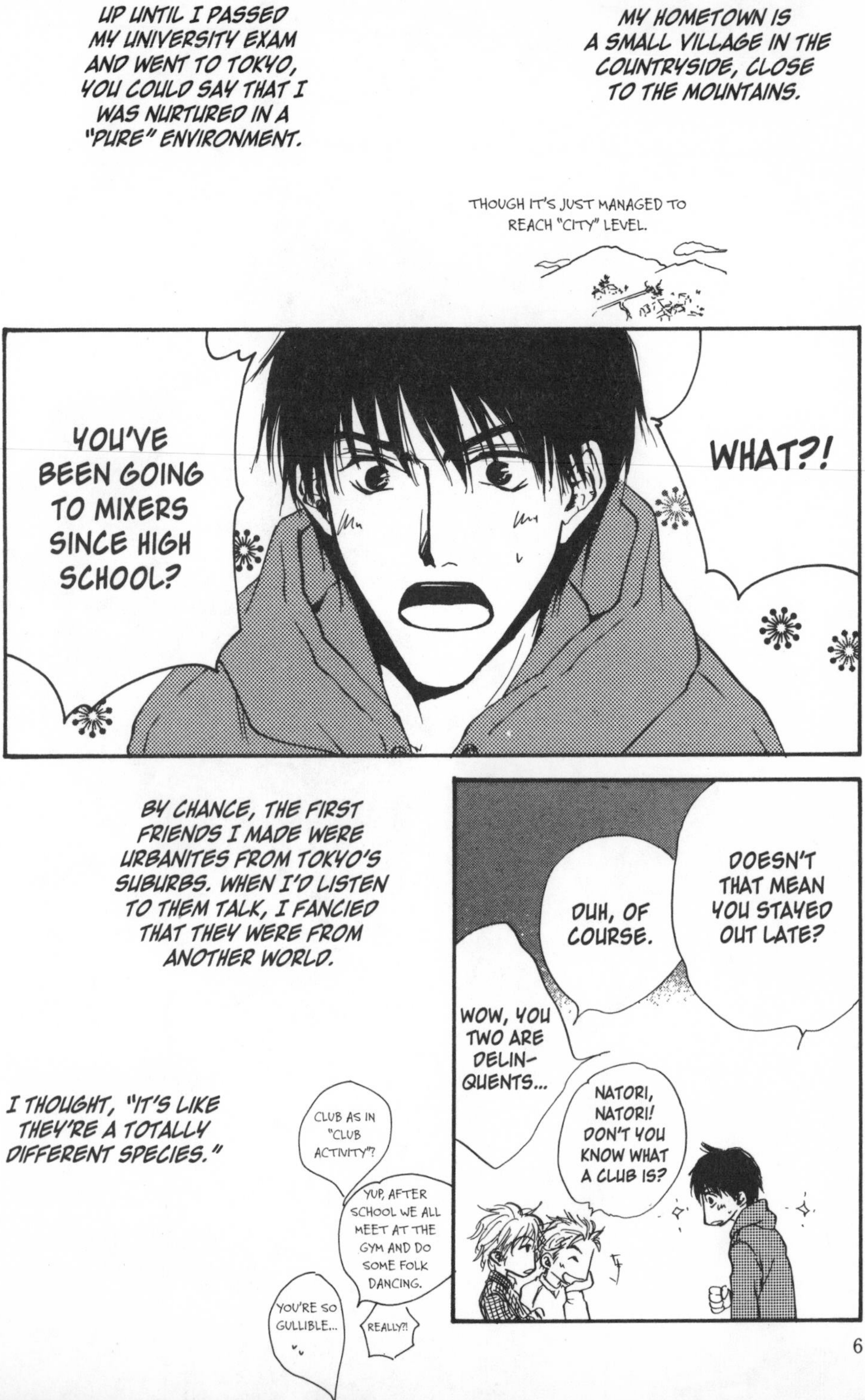
MY HOMETOWN IS A SMALL VILLAGE IN THE COUNTRYSIDE, CLOSE TO THE MOUNTAINS.
THOUGH IT'S JUST MANAGED TO REACH "CITY" LEVEL.
UP UNTIL I PASSED MY UNIVERSITY EXAM AND WENT TO TOKYO, YOU COULD SAY THAT I WAS NURTURED IN A "PURE" ENVIRONMENT.
WHAT?!
YOU'VE BEEN GOING TO MIXERS SINCE HIGH SCHOOL?
DOESN'T THAT MEAN YOU STAYED OUT LATE?
DUH, OF COURSE.
WOW, YOU TWO ARE DELIN-QUENTS...
NATORI, NATORI! DON'T YOU KNOW WHAT A CLUB IS?
CLUB AS IN "CLUB ACTIVITY"?
YUP, AFTER SCHOOL WE ALL MEET AT THE GYM AND DO SOME FOLK DANCING.
REALLY?!
YOU'RE SO GULLIBLE...
BY CHANCE, THE FIRST FRIENDS I MADE WERE URBANITES FROM TOKYO'S SUBURBS. WHEN I'D LISTEN TO THEM TALK, I FANCIED THAT THEY WERE FROM ANOTHER WORLD.
I THOUGHT, "IT'S LIKE THEY'RE A TOTALLY DIFFERENT SPECIES."

THAT WAS THEN. NOW...

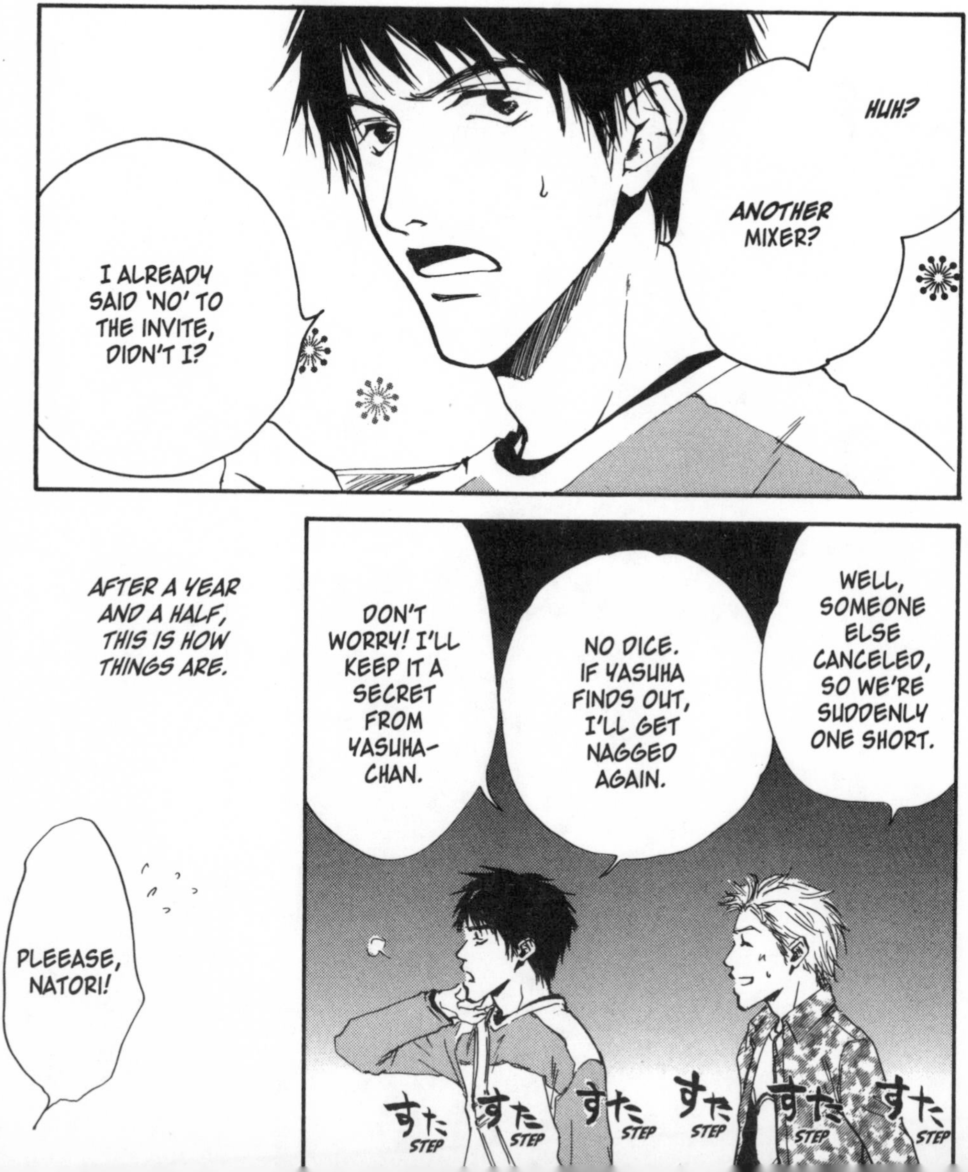
HUH?
ANOTHER MIXER?
I ALREADY SAID 'NO' TO THE INVITE, DIDN'T I?
WELL, SOMEONE ELSE CANCELED, SO WE'RE SUDDENLY ONE SHORT.
NO DICE. IF YASUHA FINDS OUT, I'LL GET NAGGED AGAIN.
DON'T WORRY! I'LL KEEP IT A SECRET FROM YASUHA-CHAN.
AFTER A YEAR AND A HALF, THIS IS HOW THINGS ARE.
PLEEASE, NATORI!
すた STEP
すた STEP
すた STEP
すた STEP
すた STEP
すた STEP

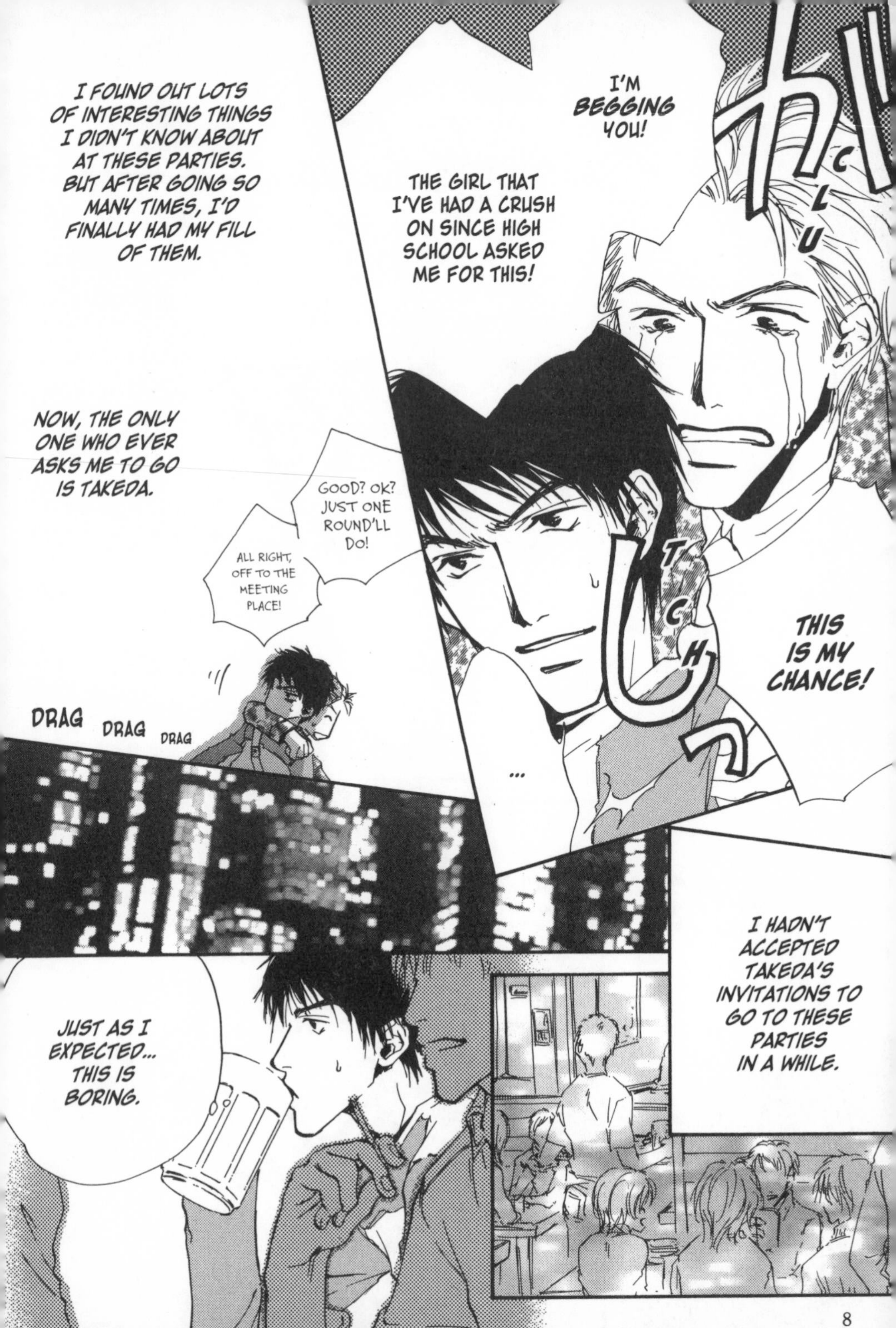
I'M BEGGING YOU!
THE GIRL THAT I'VE HAD A CRUSH ON SINCE HIGH SCHOOL ASKED ME FOR THIS!
CLUTCH
THIS IS MY CHANCE!
...
I FOUND OUT LOTS OF INTERESTING THINGS I DIDN'T KNOW ABOUT AT THESE PARTIES. BUT AFTER GOING SO MANY TIMES, I'D FINALLY HAD MY FILL OF THEM.
NOW, THE ONLY ONE WHO EVER ASKS ME TO GO IS TAKEDA.
GOOD? OK? JUST ONE ROUND'LL DO!
ALL RIGHT, OFF TO THE MEETING PLACE!
DRAG DRAG DRAG
I HADN'T ACCEPTED TAKEDA'S INVITATIONS TO GO TO THESE PARTIES IN A WHILE.
JUST AS I EXPECTED... THIS IS BORING.

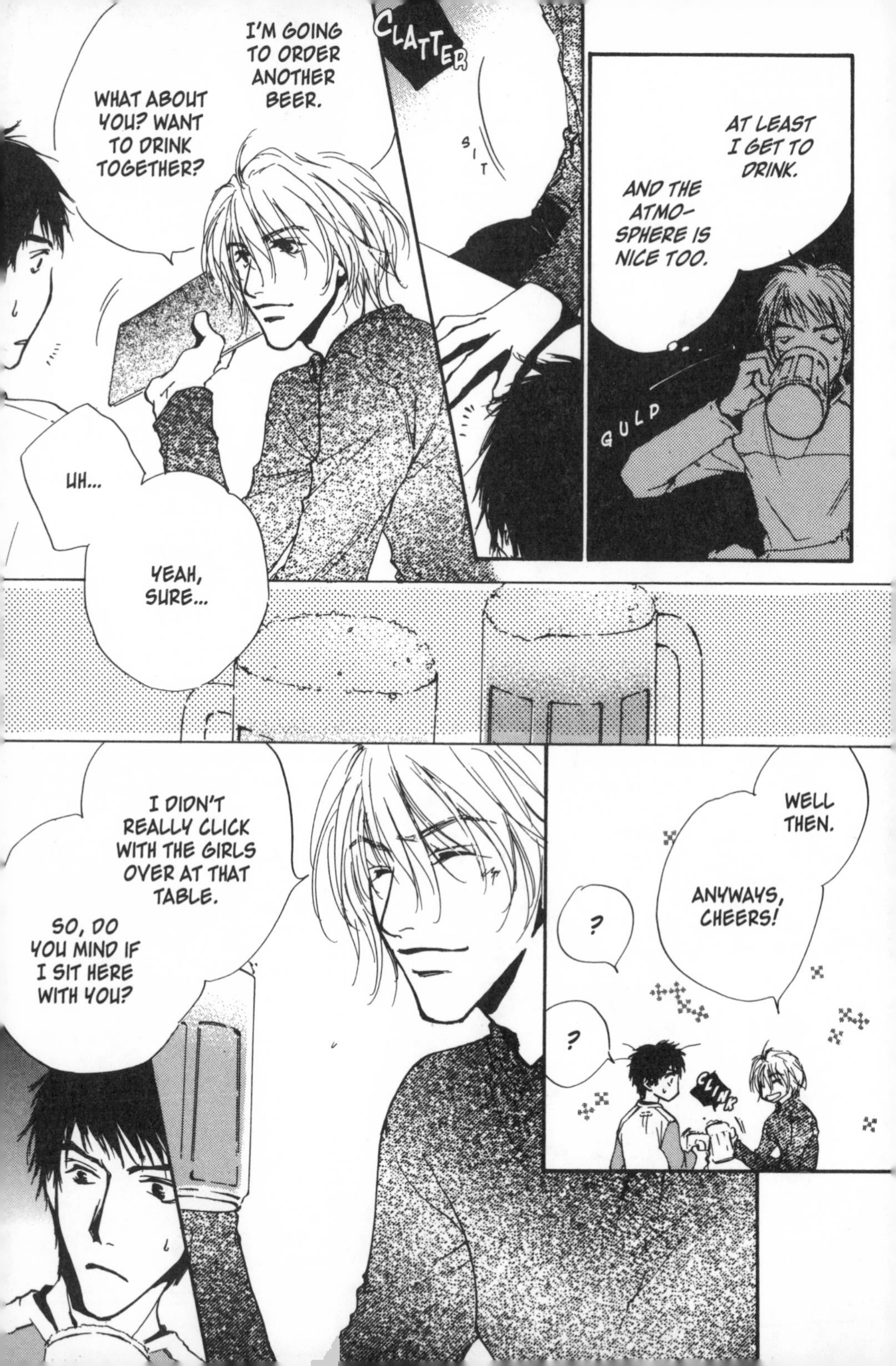
AT LEAST I GET TO DRINK.
AND THE ATMOSPHERE IS NICE TOO.
GULP
CLATTER
SIT
I'M GOING TO ORDER ANOTHER BEER.
WHAT ABOUT YOU? WANT TO DRINK TOGETHER?
UH...
YEAH, SURE...
WELL THEN.
ANYWAYS, CHEERS!
?
?
CLINK
I DIDN'T REALLY CLICK WITH THE GIRLS OVER AT THAT TABLE.
SO, DO YOU MIND IF I SIT HERE WITH YOU?

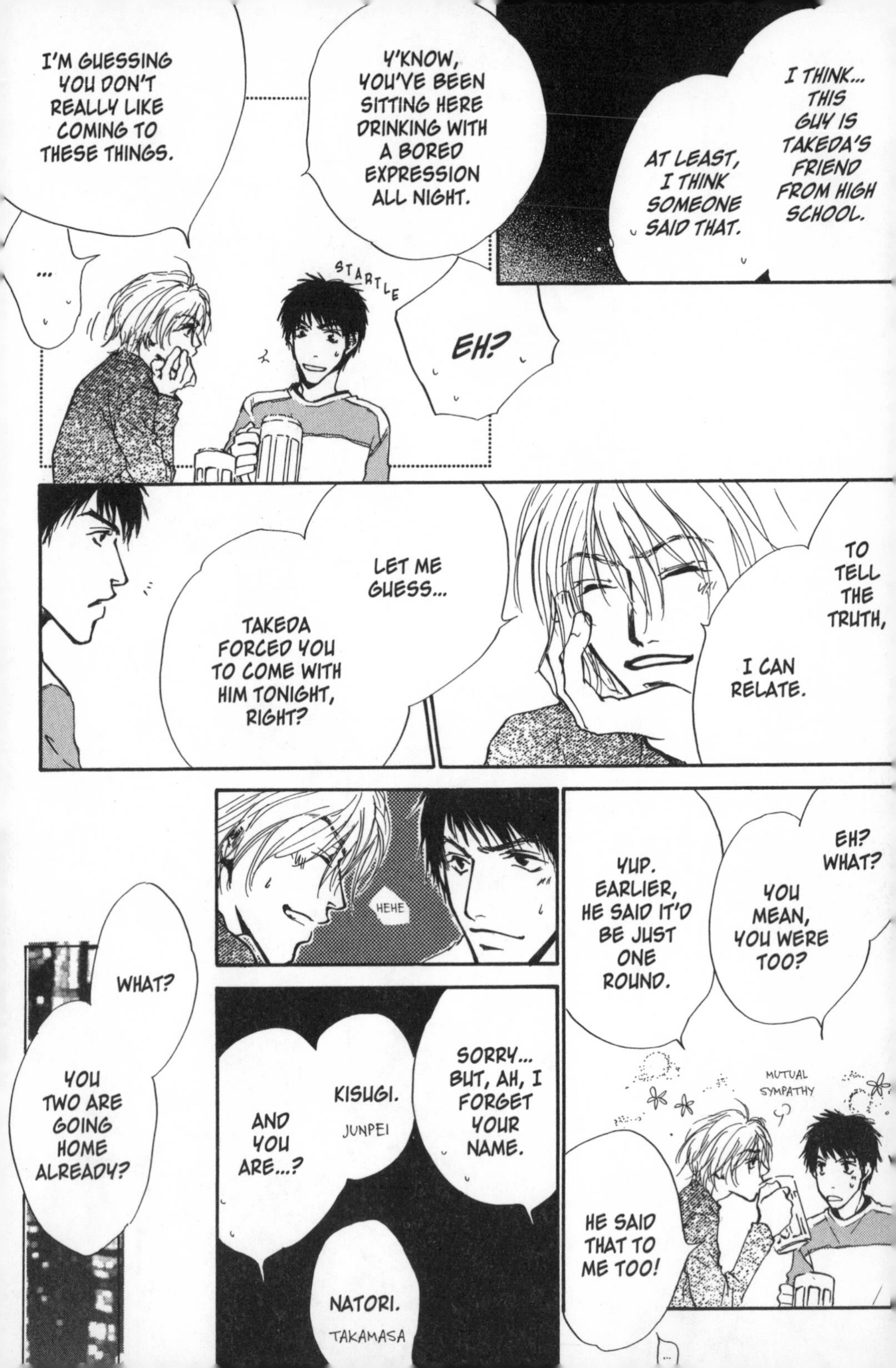
I THINK... THIS GUY IS TAKEDA'S FRIEND FROM HIGH SCHOOL.
AT LEAST, I THINK SOMEONE SAID THAT.
Y'KNOW, YOU'VE BEEN SITTING HERE DRINKING WITH A BORED EXPRESSION ALL NIGHT.
I'M GUESSING YOU DON'T REALLY LIKE COMING TO THESE THINGS.
STARTLE
EH?
...
TO TELL THE TRUTH,
I CAN RELATE.
LET ME GUESS...
TAKEDA FORCED YOU TO COME WITH HIM TONIGHT, RIGHT?
EH? WHAT?
YOU MEAN, YOU WERE TOO?
YUP. EARLIER, HE SAID IT'D BE JUST ONE ROUND.
MUTUAL SYMPATHY
HE SAID THAT TO ME TOO!
...
HEHE
SORRY... BUT, AH, I FORGET YOUR NAME.
KISUGI.
JUNPEI
AND YOU ARE...?
NATORI.
TAKAMASA
WHAT?
YOU TWO ARE GOING HOME ALREADY?

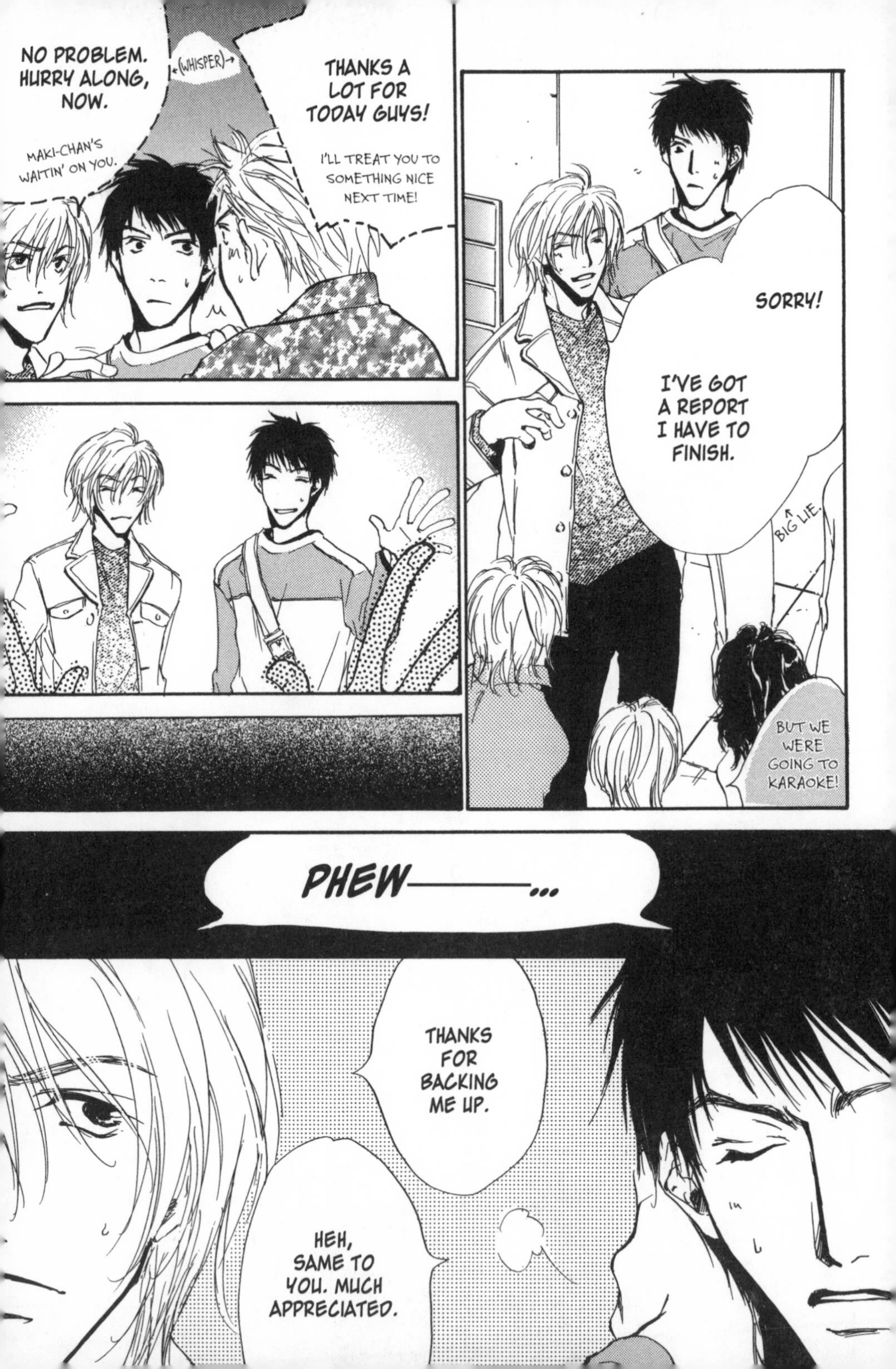
SORRY!
I'VE GOT A REPORT I HAVE TO FINISH.
BIG LIE.
BUT WE WERE GOING TO KARAOKE!
THANKS A LOT FOR TODAY GUYS!
I'LL TREAT YOU TO SOMETHING NICE NEXT TIME!
(WHISPER)
NO PROBLEM. HURRY ALONG, NOW.
MAKI-CHAN'S WAITIN' ON YOU.
PHEW———...
THANKS FOR BACKING ME UP.
HEH, SAME TO YOU. MUCH APPRECIATED.

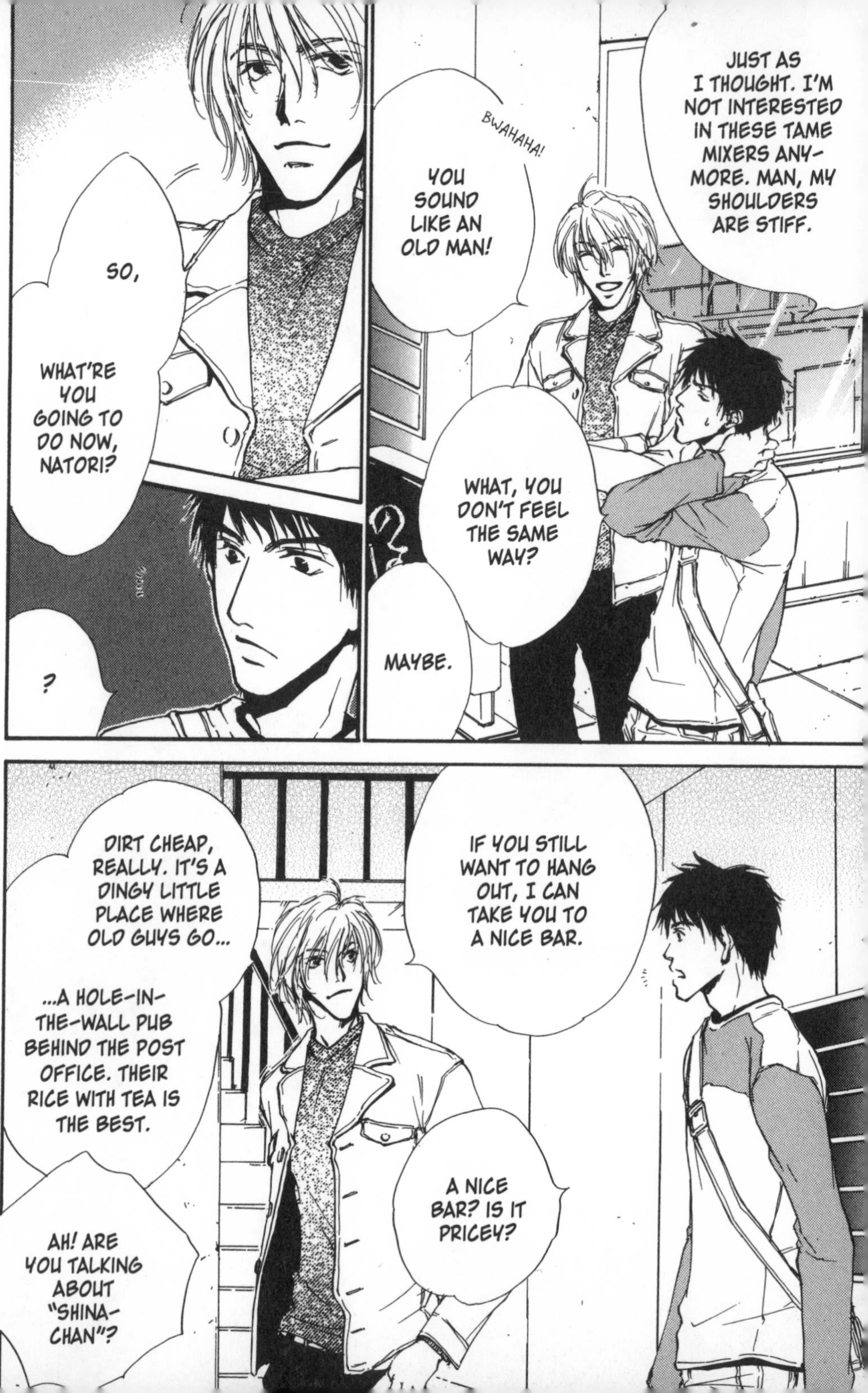

JUST AS I THOUGHT. I'M NOT INTERESTED IN THESE TAME MIXERS ANY-MORE. MAN, MY SHOULDERS ARE STIFF.
BWAHAHA!
YOU SOUND LIKE AN OLD MAN!
WHAT, YOU DON'T FEEL THE SAME WAY?
MAYBE.
SO,
WHAT'RE YOU GOING TO DO NOW, NATORI?
?
IF YOU STILL WANT TO HANG OUT, I CAN TAKE YOU TO A NICE BAR.
A NICE BAR? IS IT PRICEY?
DIRT CHEAP, REALLY. IT'S A DINGY LITTLE PLACE WHERE OLD GUYS GO...
...A HOLE-IN-THE-WALL PUB BEHIND THE POST OFFICE. THEIR RICE WITH TEA IS THE BEST.
AH! ARE YOU TALKING ABOUT "SHINA-CHAN"?

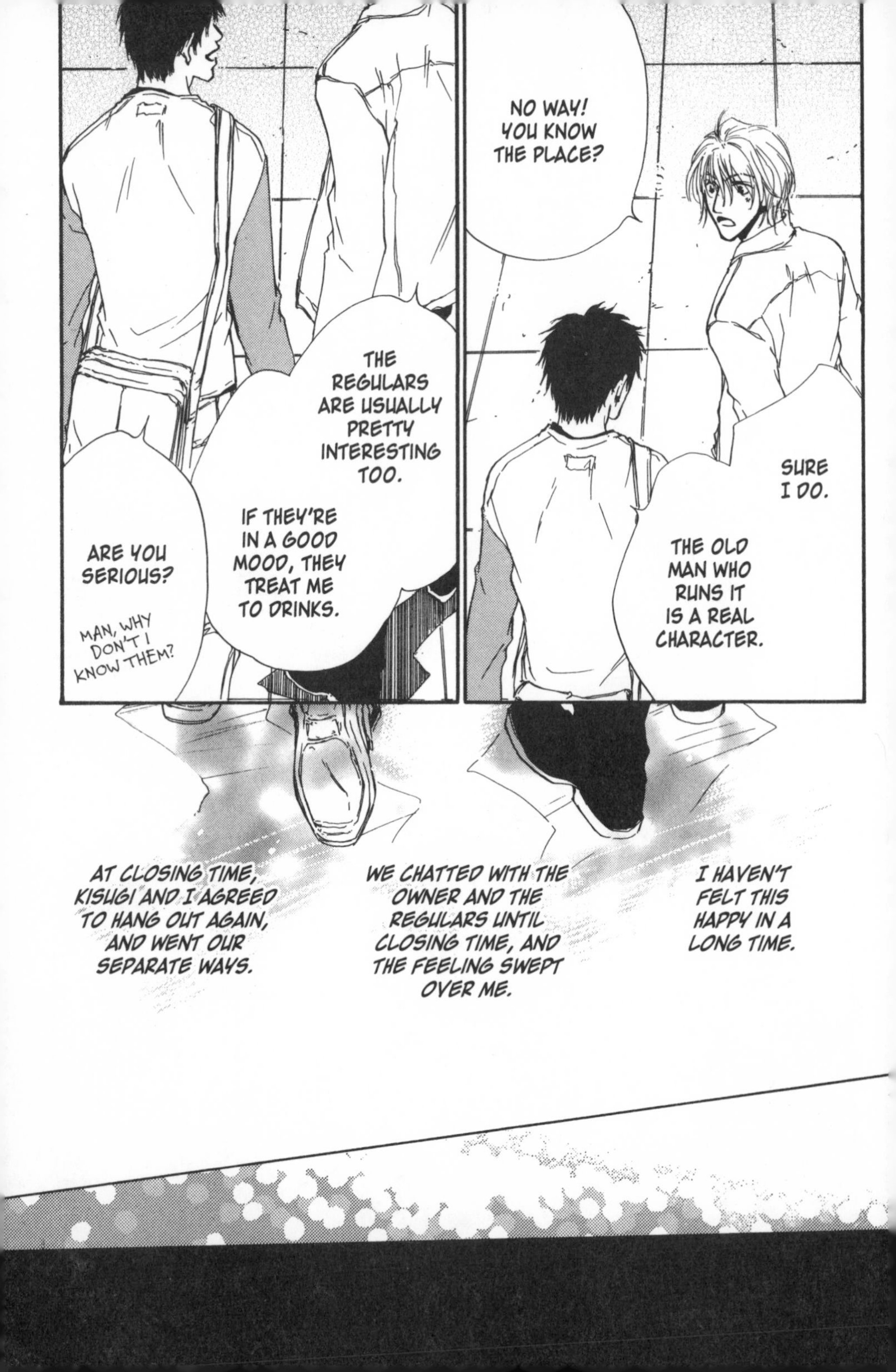
NO WAY! YOU KNOW THE PLACE?
SURE I DO.
THE OLD MAN WHO RUNS IT IS A REAL CHARACTER.
THE REGULARS ARE USUALLY PRETTY INTERESTING TOO.
IF THEY'RE IN A GOOD MOOD, THEY TREAT ME TO DRINKS.
ARE YOU SERIOUS?
MAN, WHY DON'T I KNOW THEM?
I HAVEN'T FELT THIS HAPPY IN A LONG TIME.
WE CHATTED WITH THE OWNER AND THE REGULARS UNTIL CLOSING TIME, AND THE FEELING SWEPT OVER ME.
AT CLOSING TIME, KISUGI AND I AGREED TO HANG OUT AGAIN, AND WENT OUR SEPARATE WAYS.

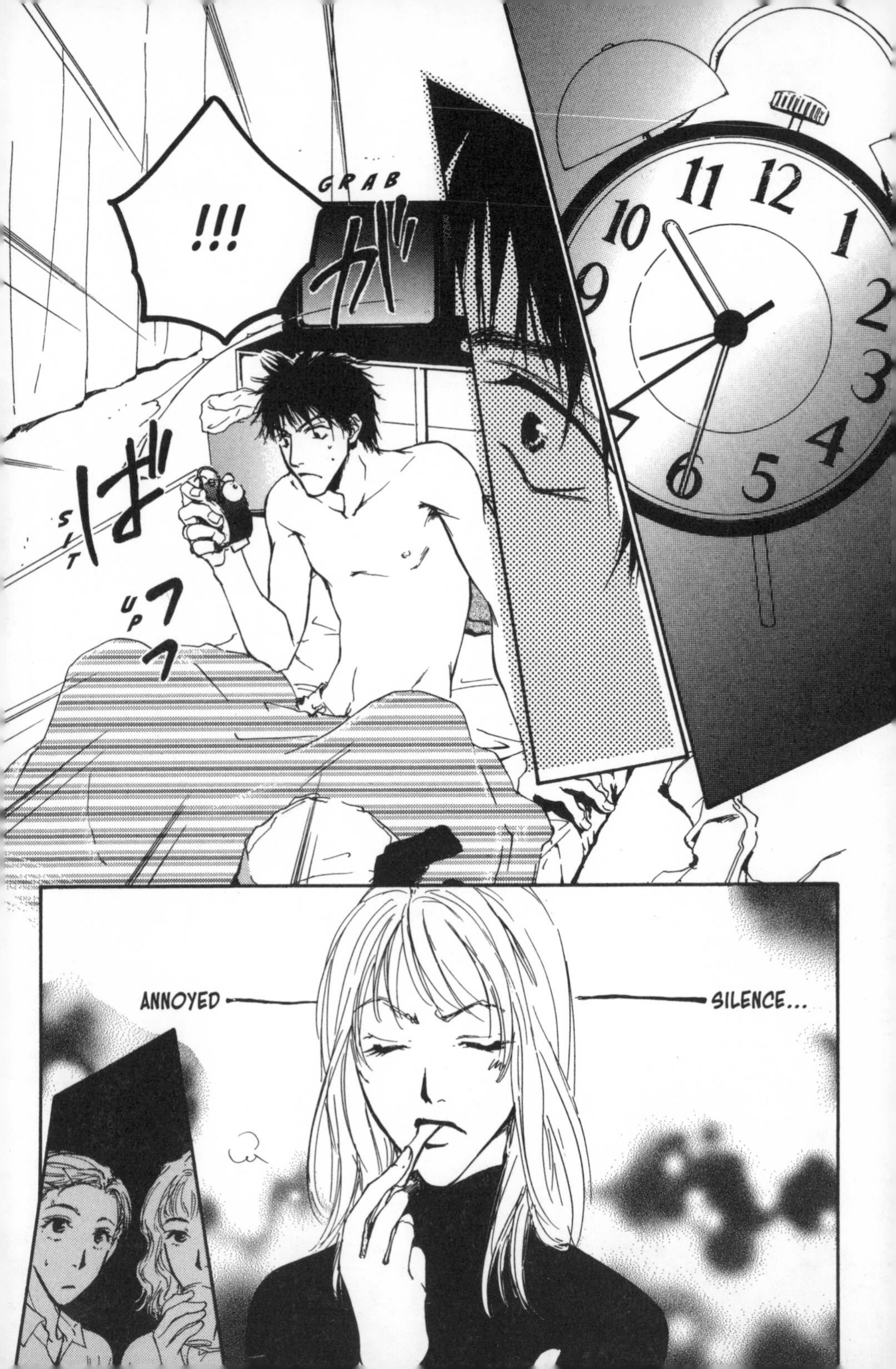
GRAB
!!!
SIT
UP
ANNOYED
SILENCE...

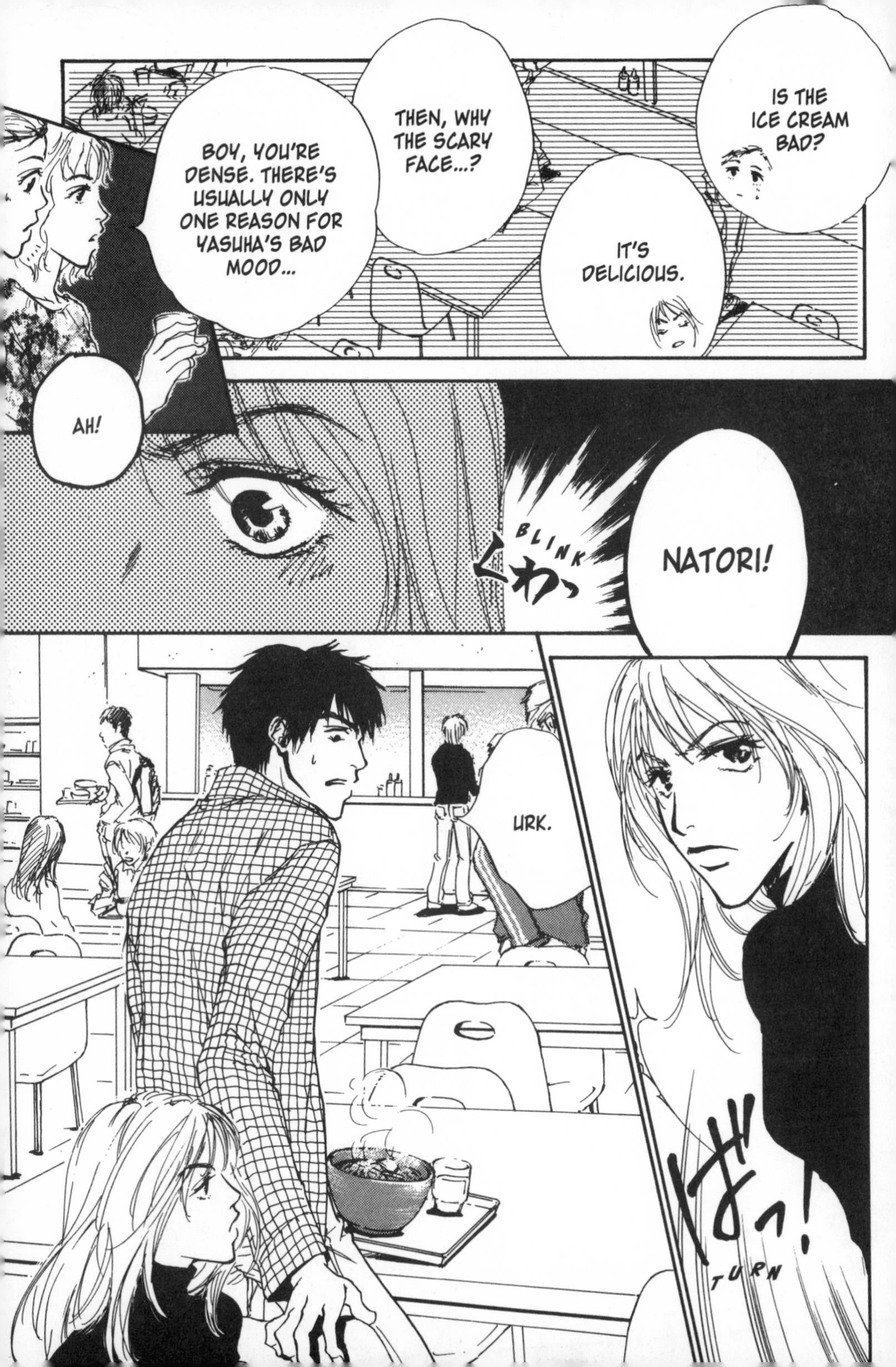
IS THE ICE CREAM BAD?
IT'S DELICIOUS.
THEN, WHY THE SCARY FACE...?
BOY, YOU'RE DENSE. THERE'S USUALLY ONLY ONE REASON FOR YASUHA'S BAD MOOD...
AH!
BLINK
NATORI!
TURN
URK.

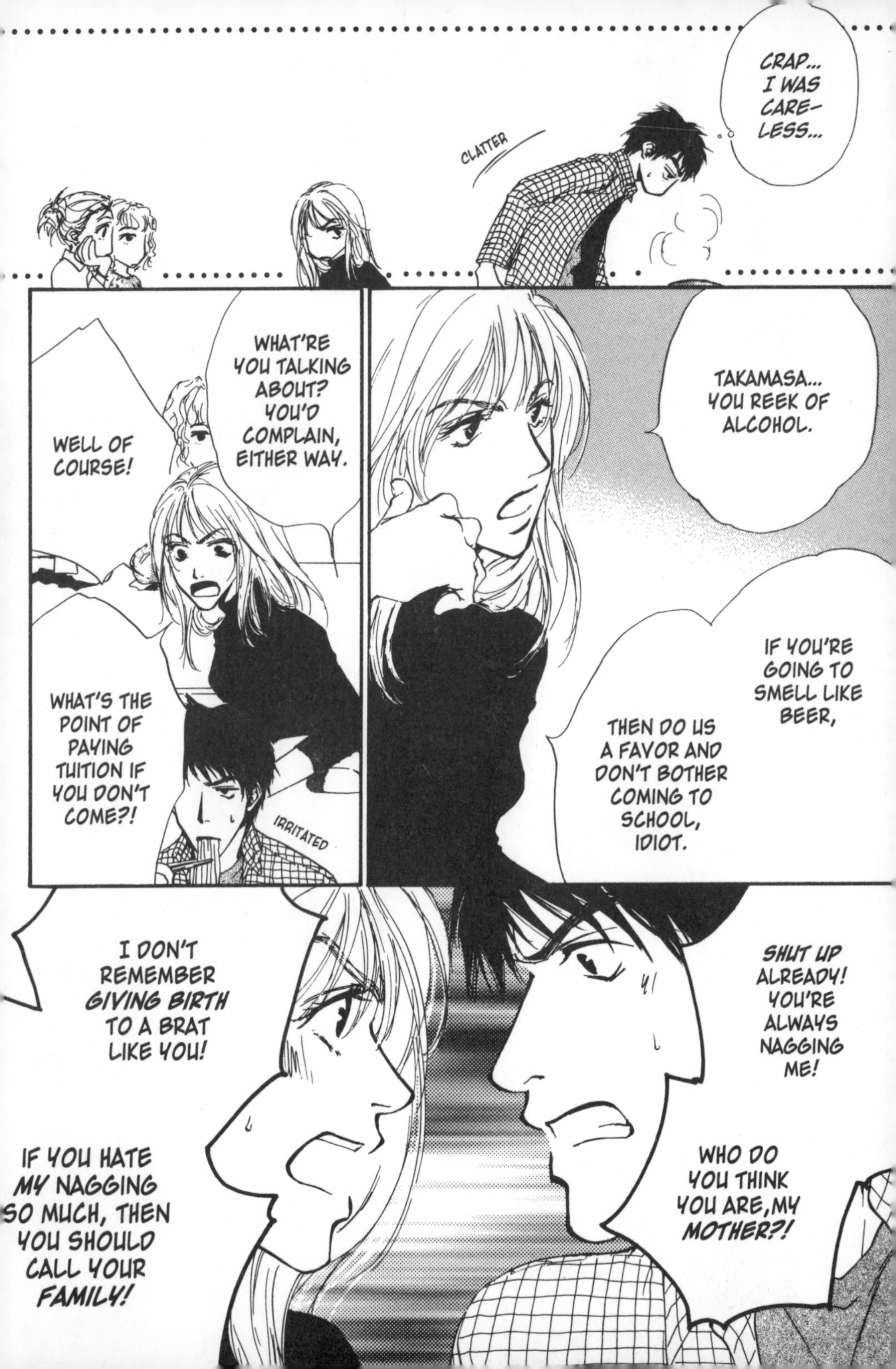
CRAP... I WAS CARE-LESS...
CLATTER
TAKAMASA... YOU REEK OF ALCOHOL.
IF YOU'RE GOING TO SMELL LIKE BEER,
THEN DO US A FAVOR AND DON'T BOTHER COMING TO SCHOOL, IDIOT.
WHAT'RE YOU TALKING ABOUT? YOU'D COMPLAIN, EITHER WAY.
WELL OF COURSE!
WHAT'S THE POINT OF PAYING TUITION IF YOU DON'T COME?!
IRRITATED
SHUT UP ALREADY! YOU'RE ALWAYS NAGGING ME!
WHO DO YOU THINK YOU ARE, MY MOTHER?!
I DON'T REMEMBER GIVING BIRTH TO A BRAT LIKE YOU!
IF YOU HATE MY NAGGING SO MUCH, THEN YOU SHOULD CALL YOUR FAMILY!

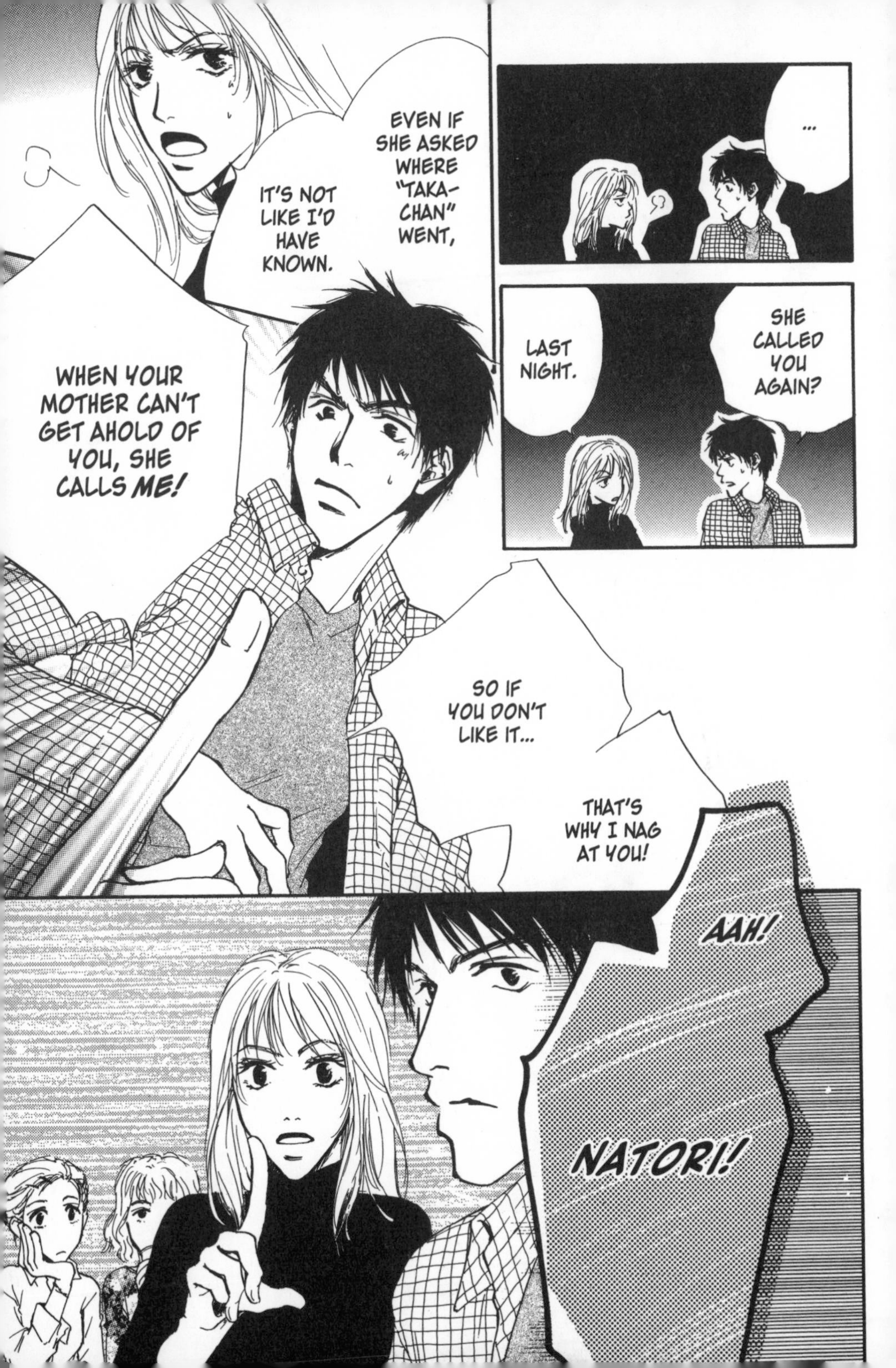
...
SHE CALLED YOU AGAIN?
LAST NIGHT.
EVEN IF SHE ASKED WHERE "TAKA-CHAN" WENT,
IT'S NOT LIKE I'D HAVE KNOWN.
WHEN YOUR MOTHER CAN'T GET AHOLD OF YOU, SHE CALLS *ME!*
SO IF YOU DON'T LIKE IT...
THAT'S WHY I NAG AT YOU!
AAH!
NATORI!

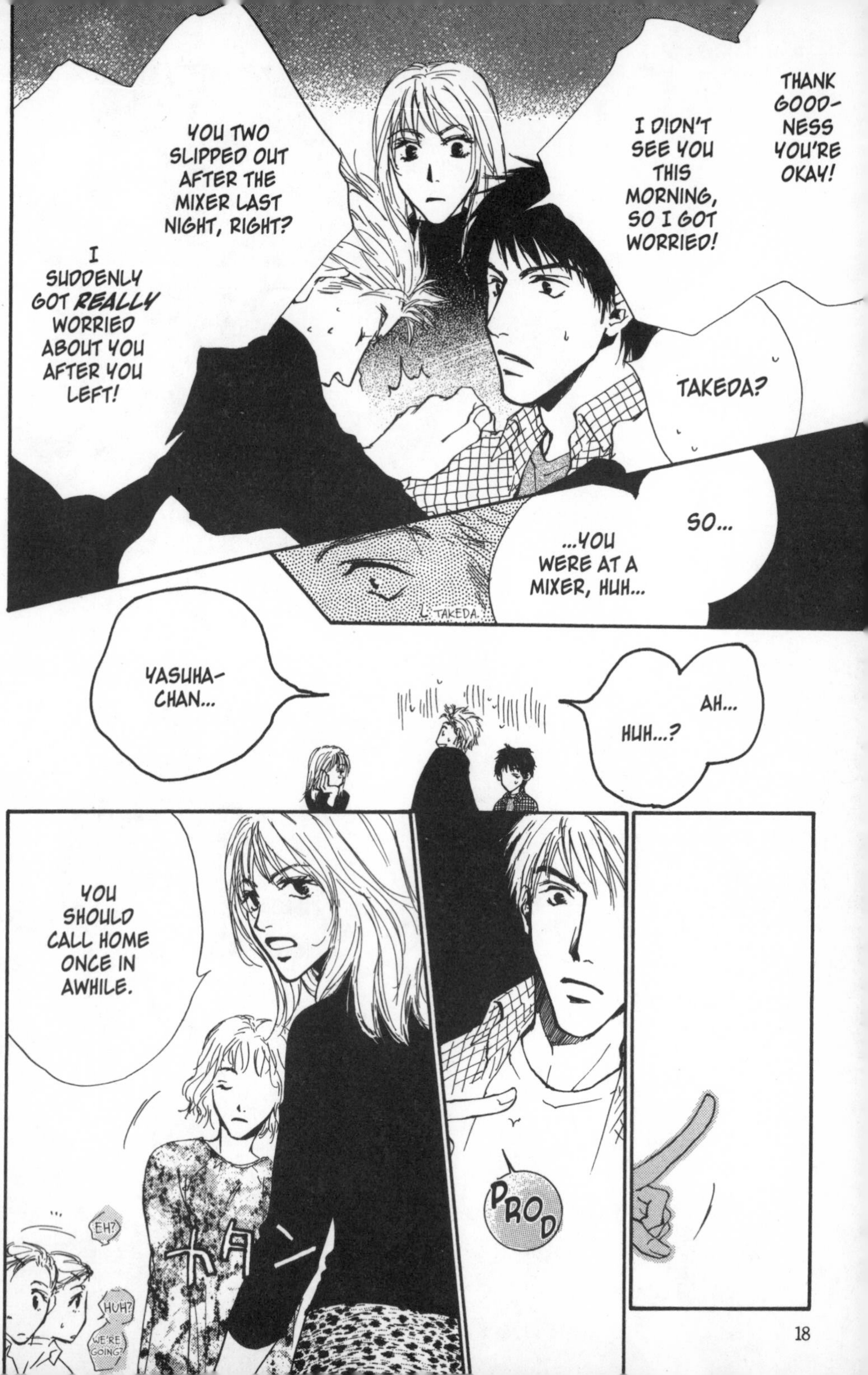
THANK GOODNESS YOU'RE OKAY!
I DIDN'T SEE YOU THIS MORNING, SO I GOT WORRIED!
YOU TWO SLIPPED OUT AFTER THE MIXER LAST NIGHT, RIGHT?
I SUDDENLY GOT **REALLY** WORRIED ABOUT YOU AFTER YOU LEFT!
TAKEDA?
SO...
...YOU WERE AT A MIXER, HUH...
TAKEDA
AH...
HUH...?
YASUHA-CHAN...
PROD
YOU SHOULD CALL HOME ONCE IN AWHILE.
...
EH?
HUH?
WE'RE GOING?

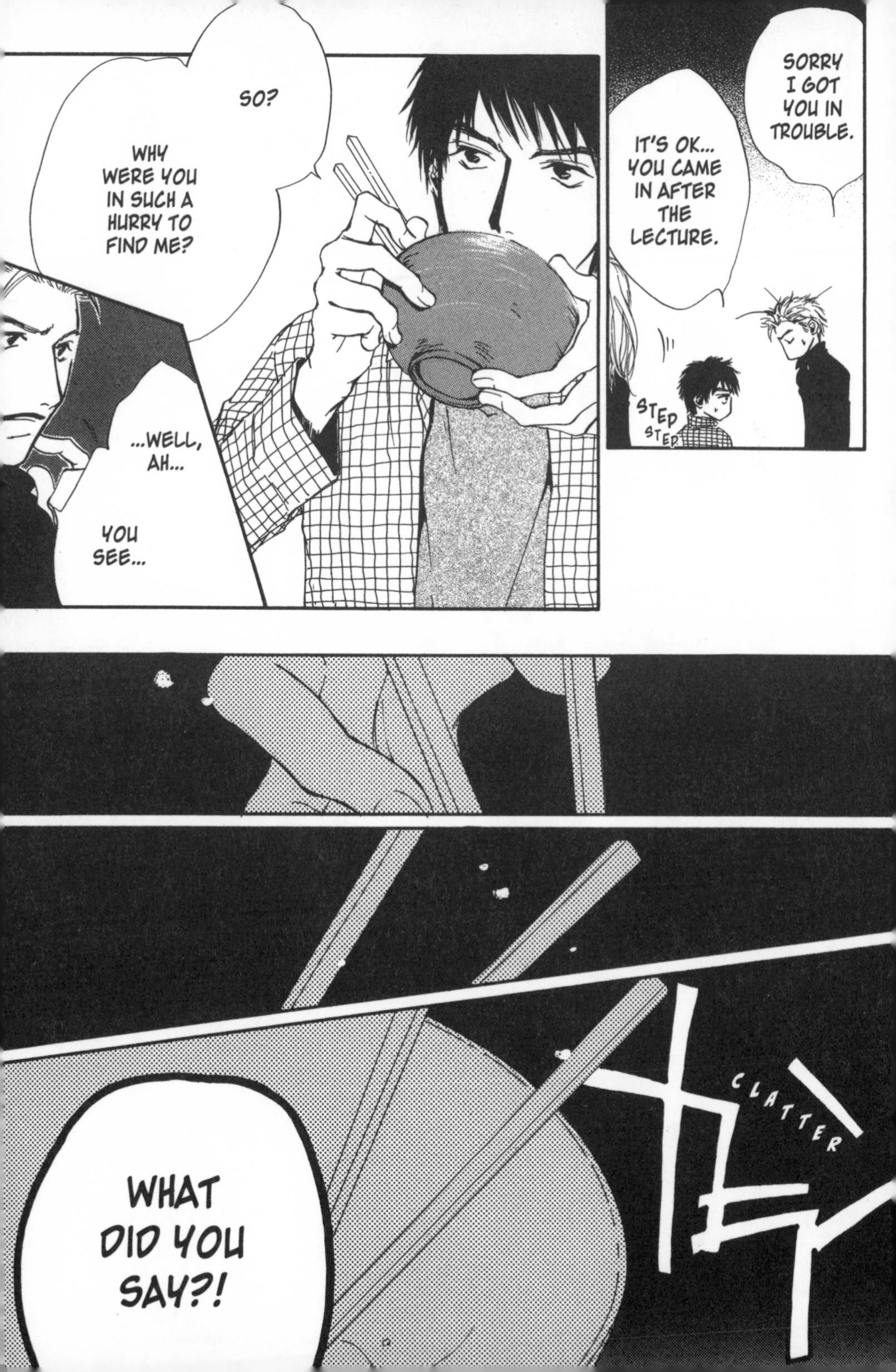
SORRY I GOT YOU IN TROUBLE.
IT'S OK... YOU CAME IN AFTER THE LECTURE.
STEP STEP
SO?
WHY WERE YOU IN SUCH A HURRY TO FIND ME?
...WELL, AH...
YOU SEE...
CLATTER
WHAT DID YOU SAY?!

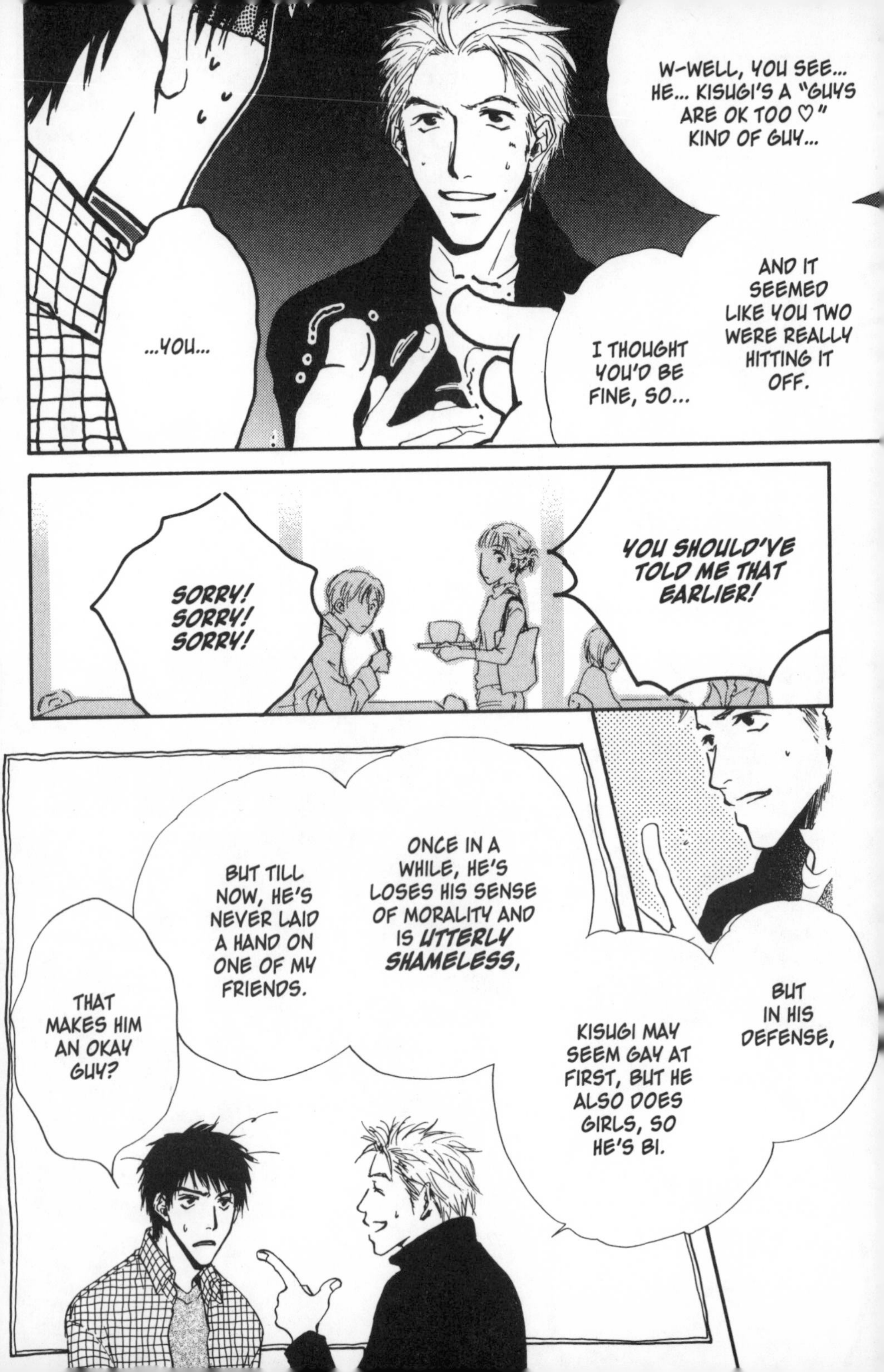
W-WELL, YOU SEE... HE... KISUGI'S A "GUYS ARE OK TOO ♡" KIND OF GUY...
AND IT SEEMED LIKE YOU TWO WERE REALLY HITTING IT OFF.
I THOUGHT YOU'D BE FINE, SO...
...YOU...
YOU SHOULD'VE TOLD ME THAT EARLIER!
SORRY! SORRY! SORRY!
BUT IN HIS DEFENSE,
KISUGI MAY SEEM GAY AT FIRST, BUT HE ALSO DOES GIRLS, SO HE'S BI.
ONCE IN A WHILE, HE'S LOSES HIS SENSE OF MORALITY AND IS UTTERLY SHAMELESS,
BUT TILL NOW, HE'S NEVER LAID A HAND ON ONE OF MY FRIENDS.
THAT MAKES HIM AN OKAY GUY?

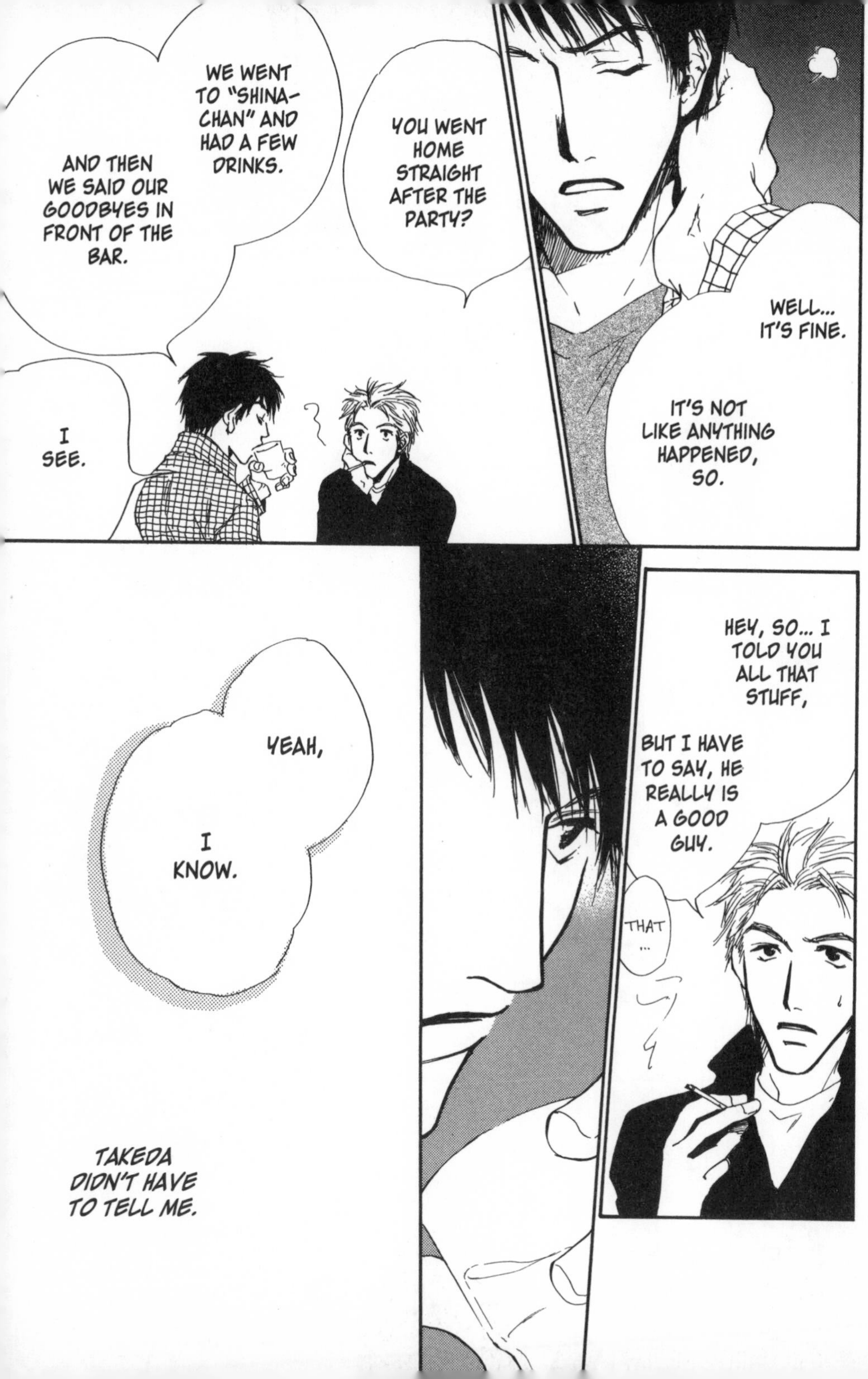
WELL... IT'S FINE.
IT'S NOT LIKE ANYTHING HAPPENED, SO.
YOU WENT HOME STRAIGHT AFTER THE PARTY?
WE WENT TO "SHINA-CHAN" AND HAD A FEW DRINKS.
AND THEN WE SAID OUR GOODBYES IN FRONT OF THE BAR.
I SEE.
HEY, SO... I TOLD YOU ALL THAT STUFF,
BUT I HAVE TO SAY, HE REALLY IS A GOOD GUY.
THAT ...
YEAH,
I KNOW.
TAKEDA DIDN'T HAVE TO TELL ME.

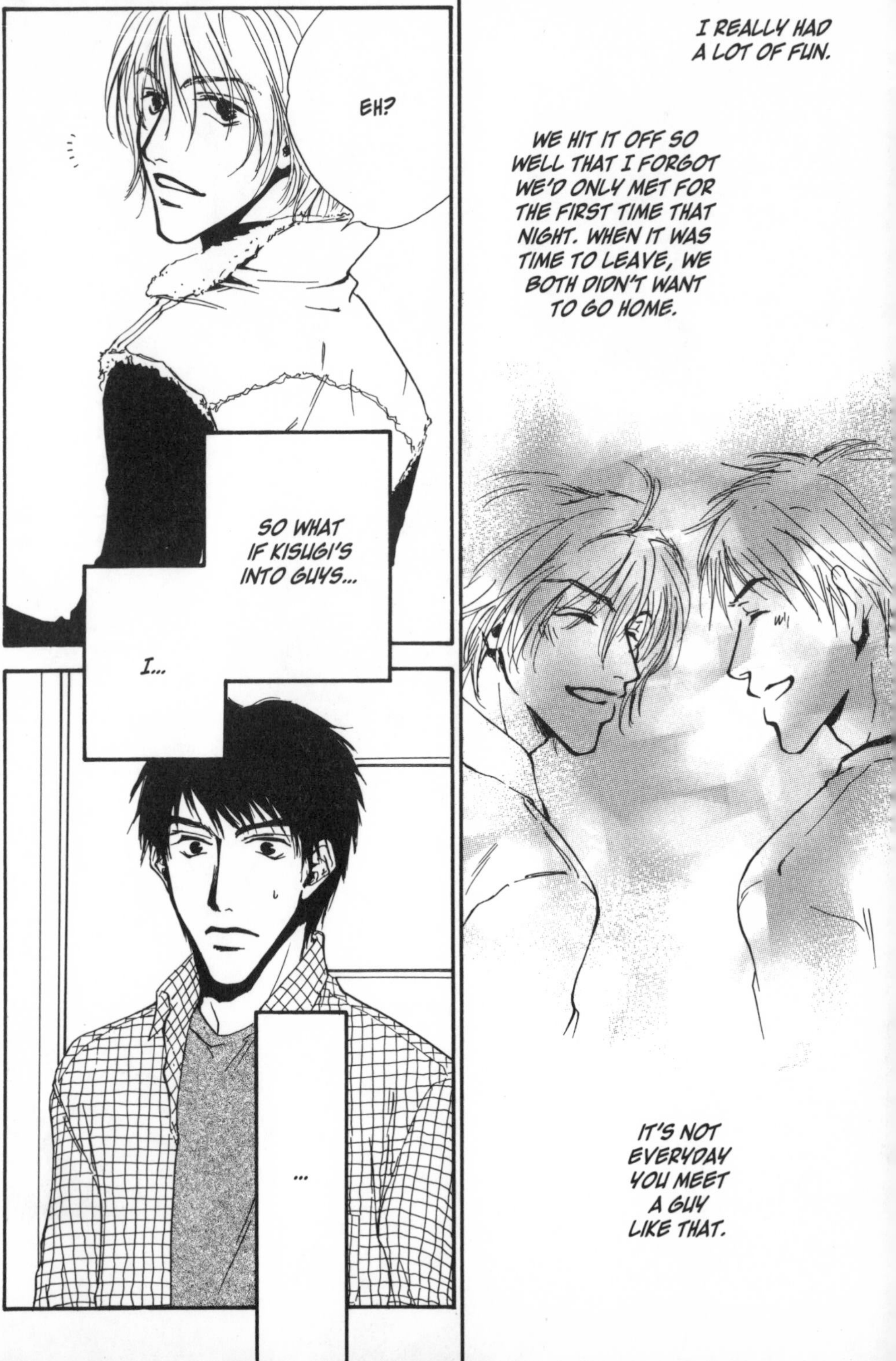
I REALLY HAD A LOT OF FUN.
WE HIT IT OFF SO WELL THAT I FORGOT WE'D ONLY MET FOR THE FIRST TIME THAT NIGHT. WHEN IT WAS TIME TO LEAVE, WE BOTH DIDN'T WANT TO GO HOME.
IT'S NOT EVERYDAY YOU MEET A GUY LIKE THAT.
EH?
SO WHAT IF KISUGI'S INTO GUYS...
I...
...

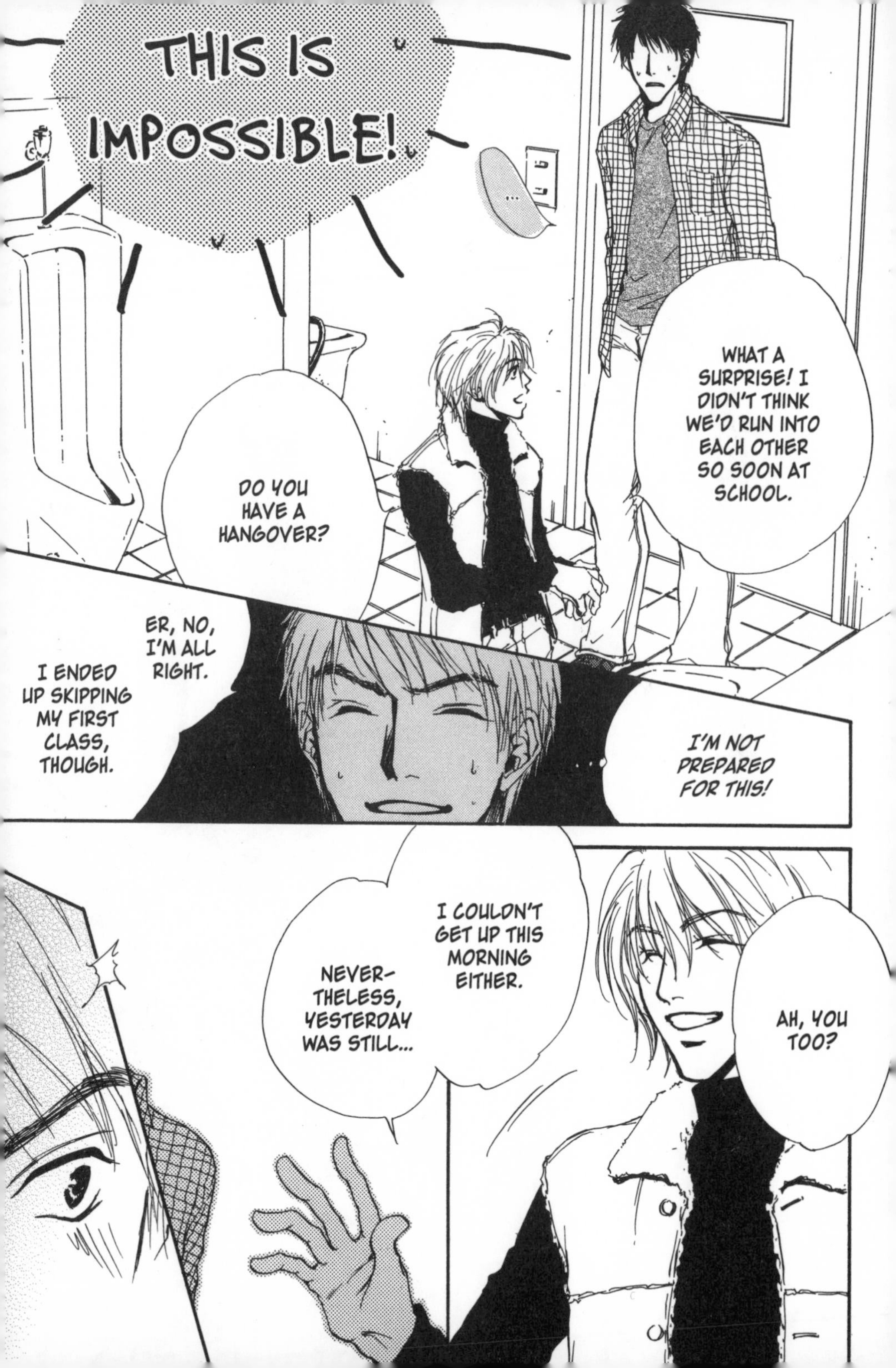
THIS IS IMPOSSIBLE!
...
WHAT A SURPRISE! I DIDN'T THINK WE'D RUN INTO EACH OTHER SO SOON AT SCHOOL.
DO YOU HAVE A HANGOVER?
I'M NOT PREPARED FOR THIS!
ER, NO, I'M ALL RIGHT.
I ENDED UP SKIPPING MY FIRST CLASS, THOUGH.
AH, YOU TOO?
I COULDN'T GET UP THIS MORNING EITHER.
NEVER-THELESS, YESTERDAY WAS STILL...

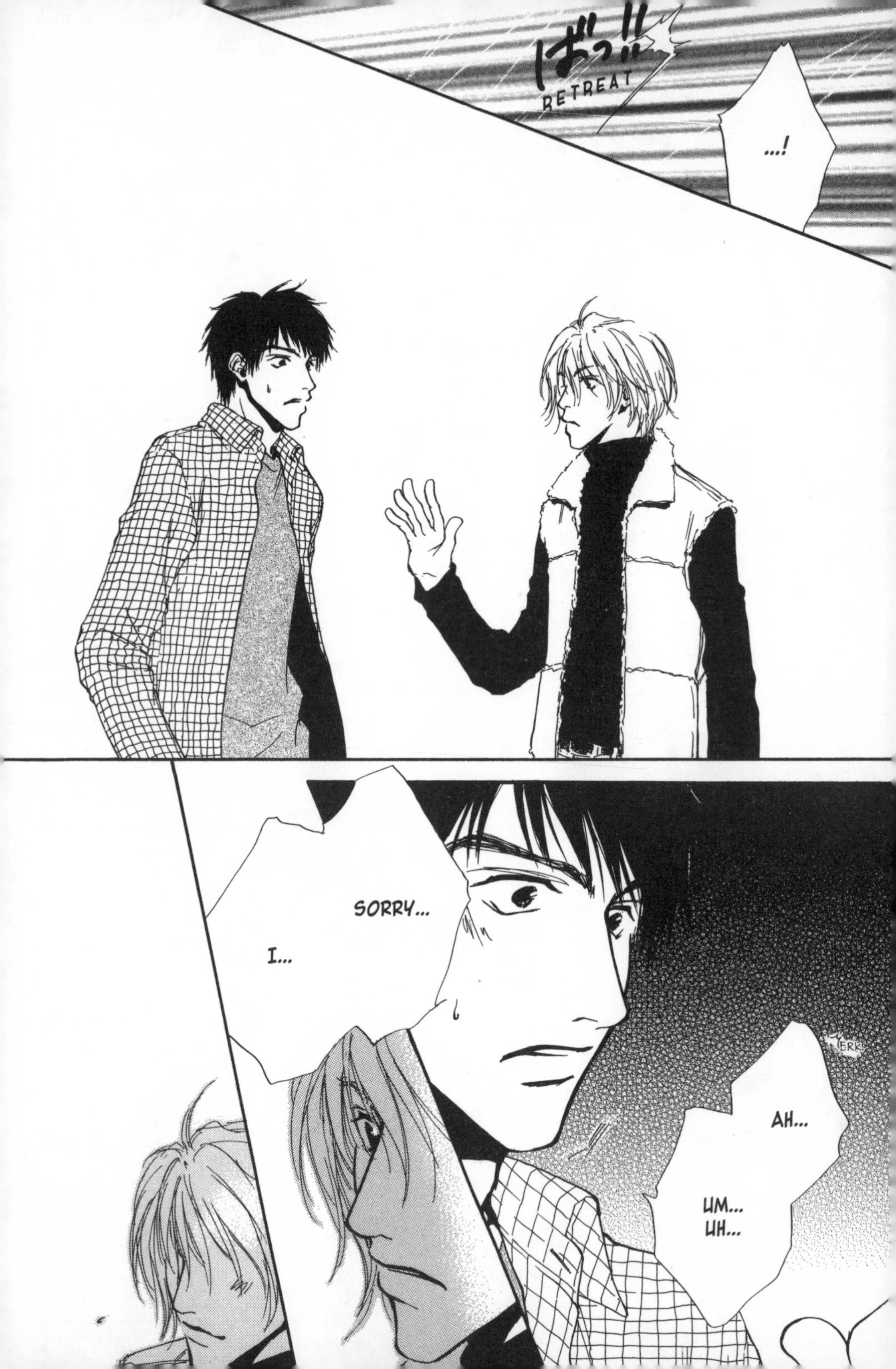
ばっ!!
RETREAT
...!
ERK
AH...
UM...
UH...
SORRY...
I...

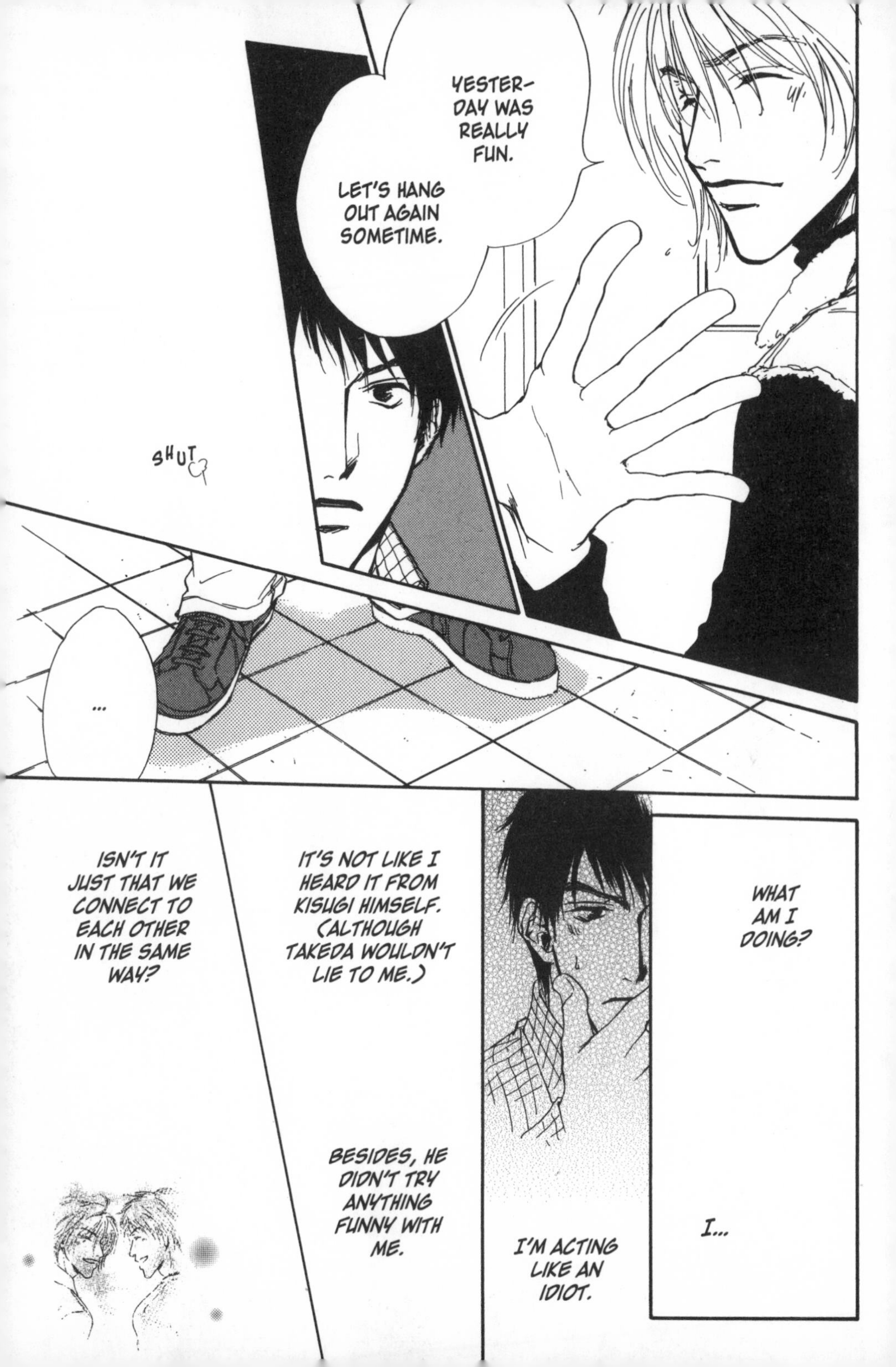
YESTER-DAY WAS REALLY FUN.
LET'S HANG OUT AGAIN SOMETIME.
SHUT
...
WHAT AM I DOING?
I...
I'M ACTING LIKE AN IDIOT.
IT'S NOT LIKE I HEARD IT FROM KISUGI HIMSELF. (ALTHOUGH TAKEDA WOULDN'T LIE TO ME.)
BESIDES, HE DIDN'T TRY ANYTHING FUNNY WITH ME.
ISN'T IT JUST THAT WE CONNECT TO EACH OTHER IN THE SAME WAY?

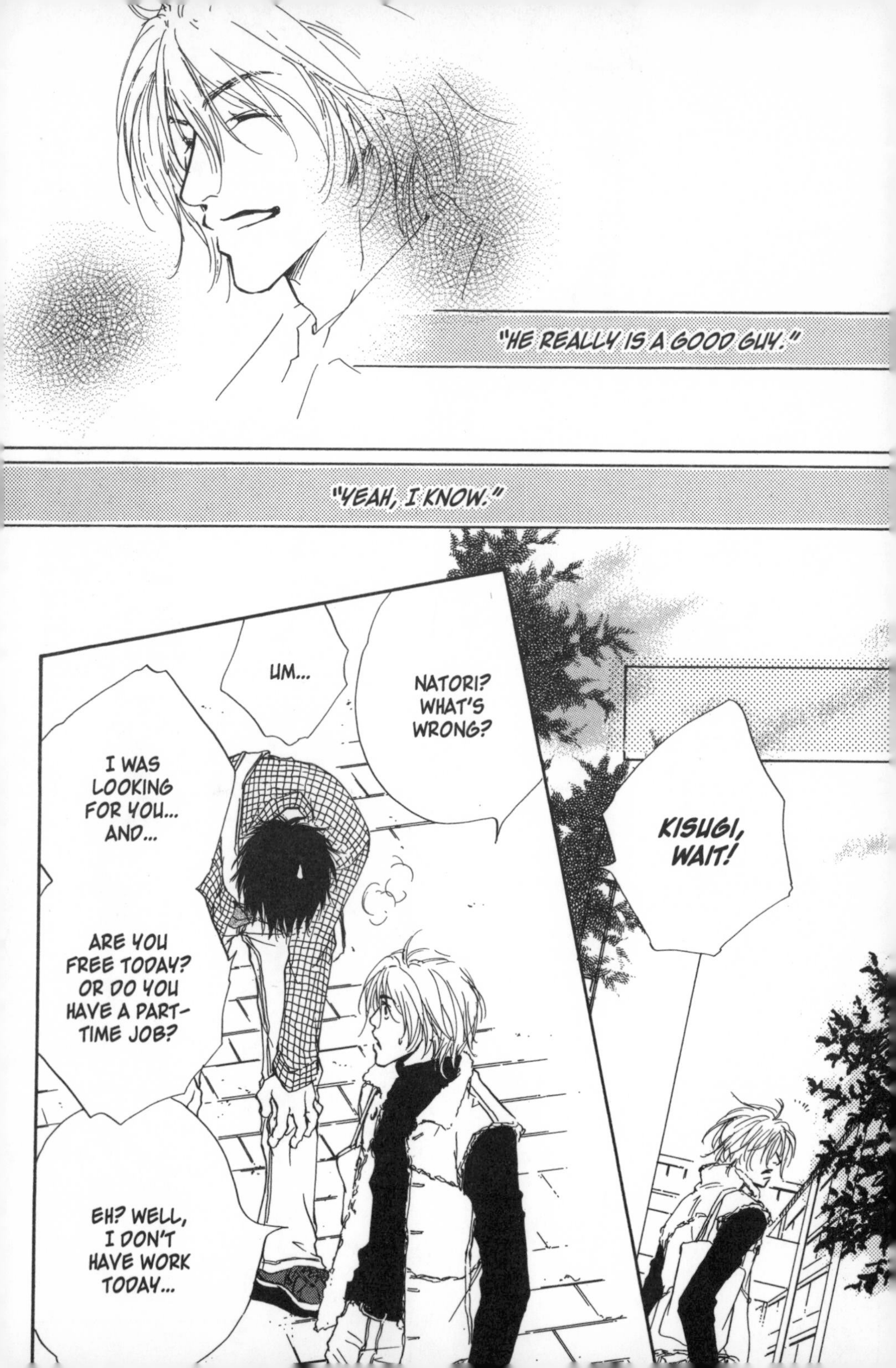
"HE REALLY IS A GOOD GUY."
"YEAH, I KNOW."
KISUGI, WAIT!
NATORI? WHAT'S WRONG?
UM...
I WAS LOOKING FOR YOU... AND...
ARE YOU FREE TODAY? OR DO YOU HAVE A PART-TIME JOB?
EH? WELL, I DON'T HAVE WORK TODAY...

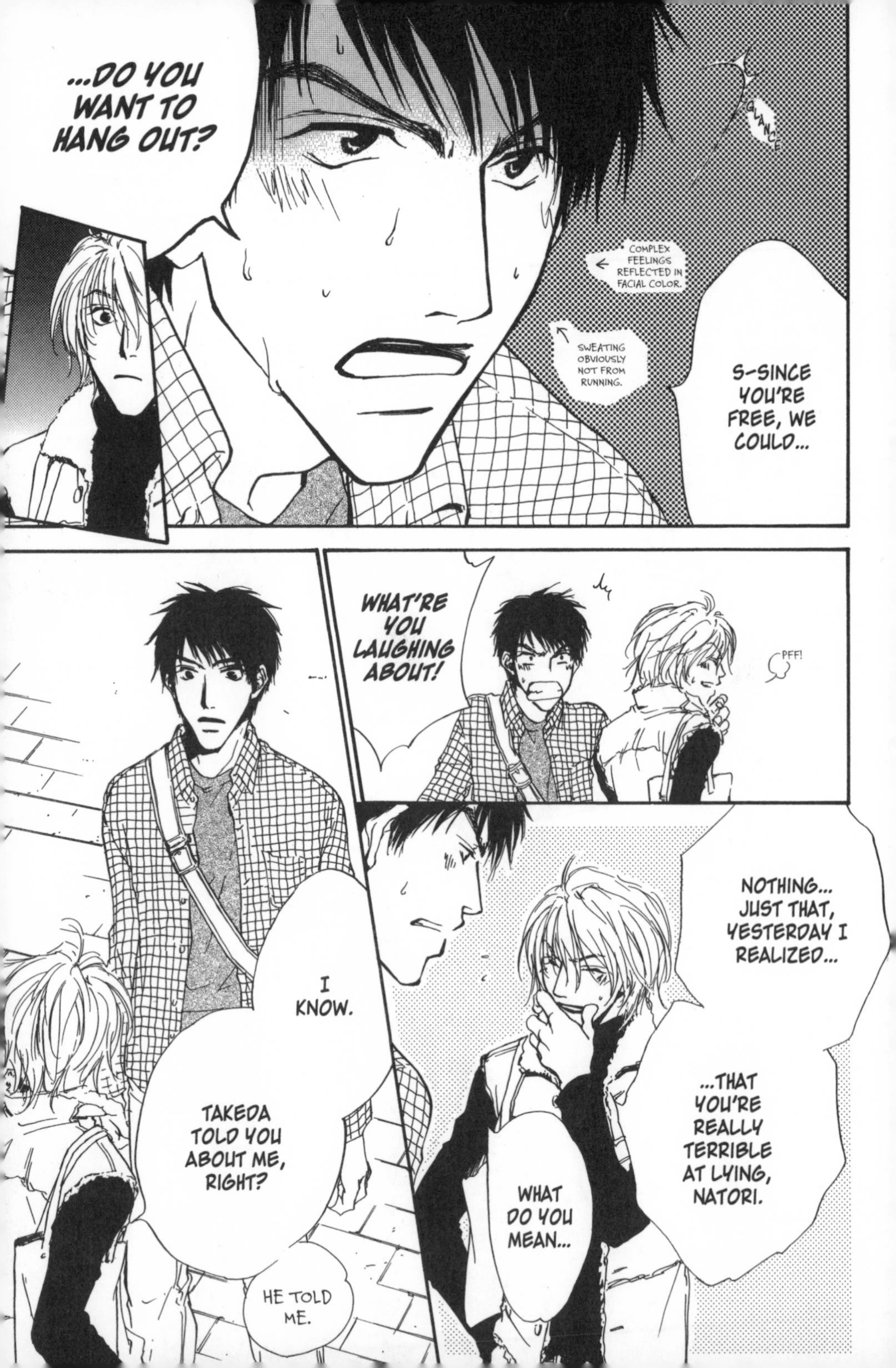
GLANCE
S-SINCE YOU'RE FREE, WE COULD...
COMPLEX FEELINGS REFLECTED IN FACIAL COLOR.
SWEATING OBVIOUSLY NOT FROM RUNNING.
...DO YOU WANT TO HANG OUT?
PFF!
WHAT'RE YOU LAUGHING ABOUT!
NOTHING... JUST THAT, YESTERDAY I REALIZED...
...THAT YOU'RE REALLY TERRIBLE AT LYING, NATORI.
WHAT DO YOU MEAN...
I KNOW.
TAKEDA TOLD YOU ABOUT ME, RIGHT?
HE TOLD ME.

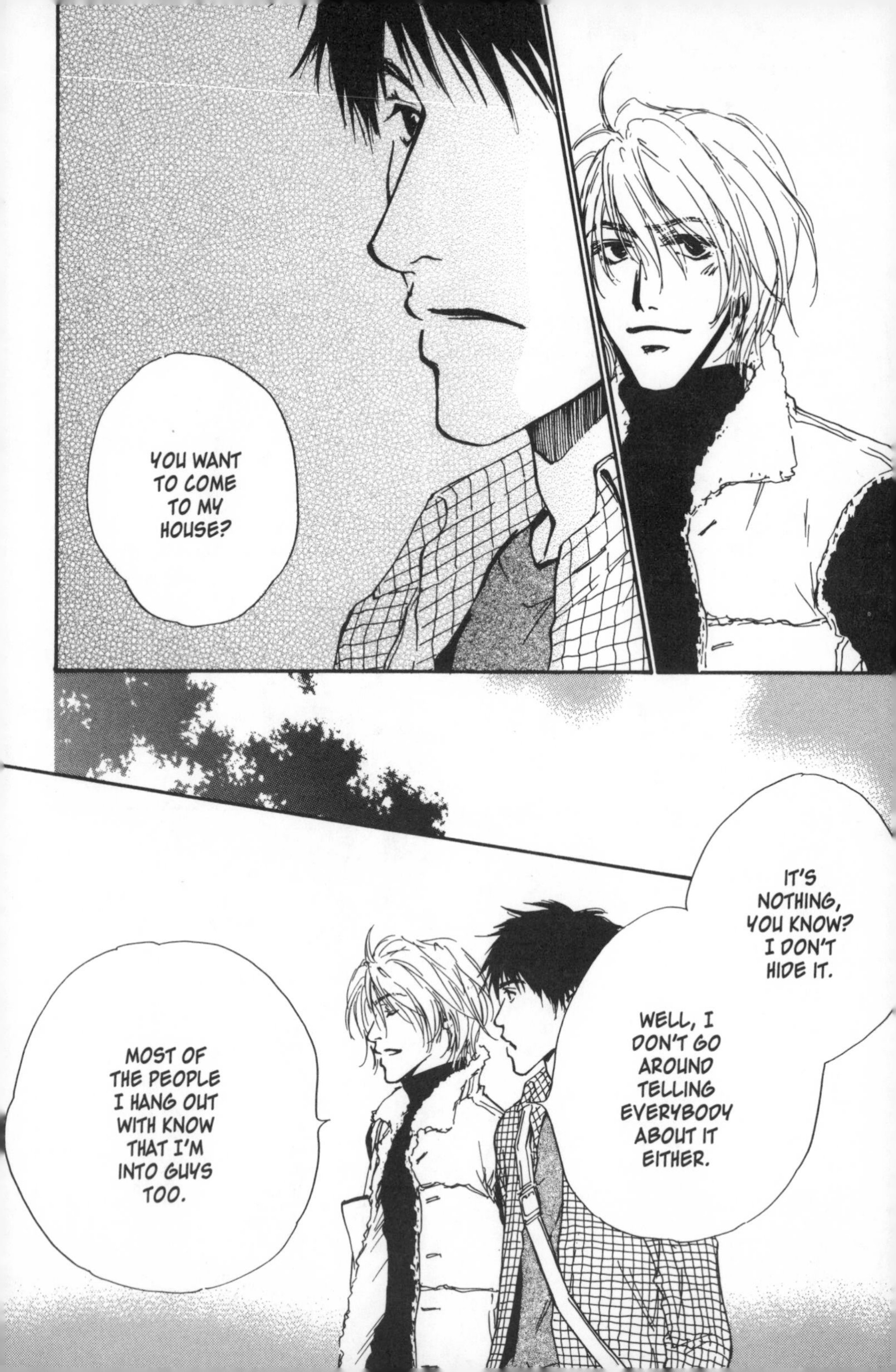
YOU WANT TO COME TO MY HOUSE?
IT'S NOTHING, YOU KNOW? I DON'T HIDE IT.
WELL, I DON'T GO AROUND TELLING EVERYBODY ABOUT IT EITHER.
MOST OF THE PEOPLE I HANG OUT WITH KNOW THAT I'M INTO GUYS TOO.

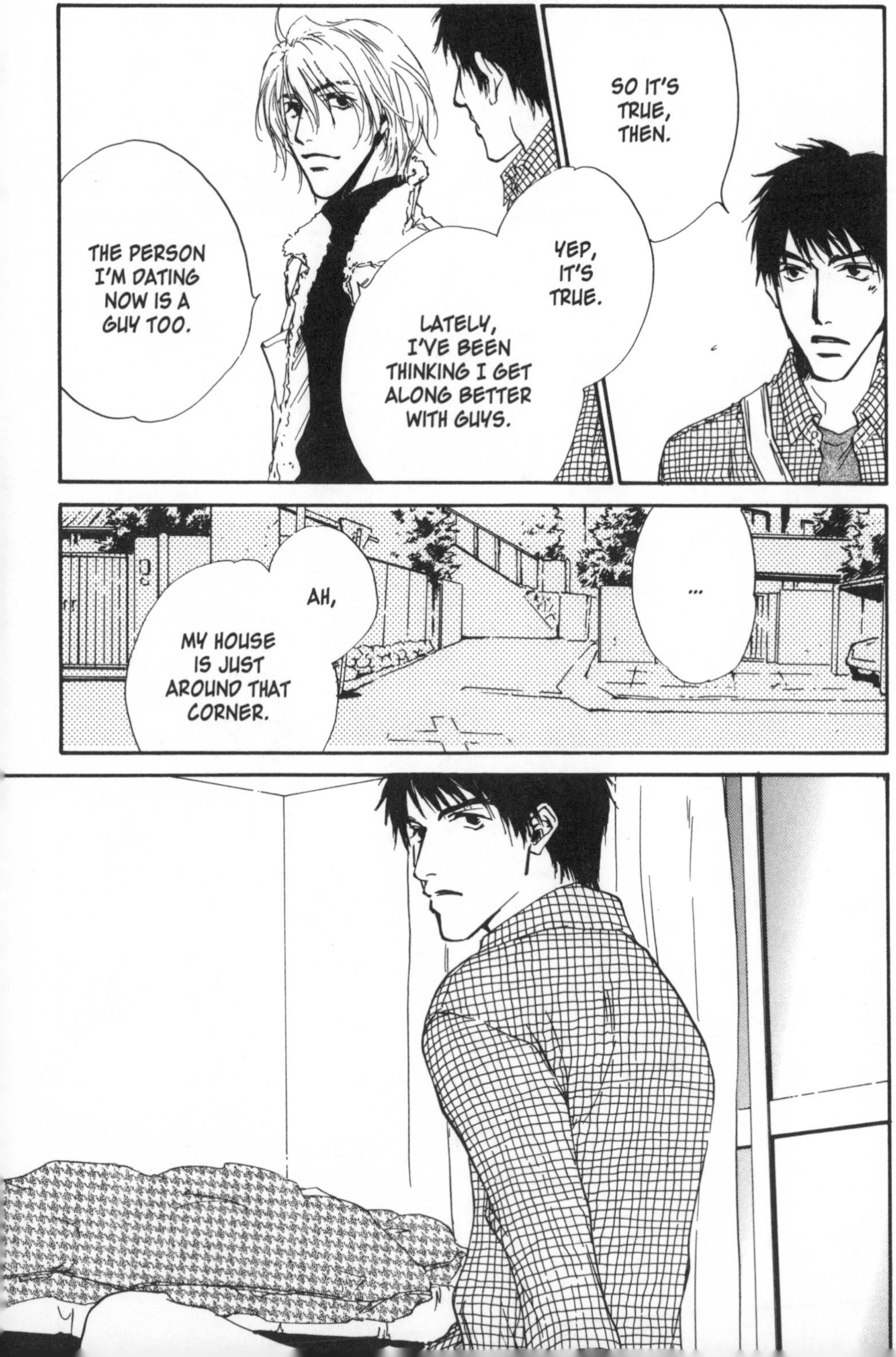
SO IT'S TRUE, THEN.
YEP, IT'S TRUE.
LATELY, I'VE BEEN THINKING I GET ALONG BETTER WITH GUYS.
THE PERSON I'M DATING NOW IS A GUY TOO.
...
AH,
MY HOUSE IS JUST AROUND THAT CORNER.

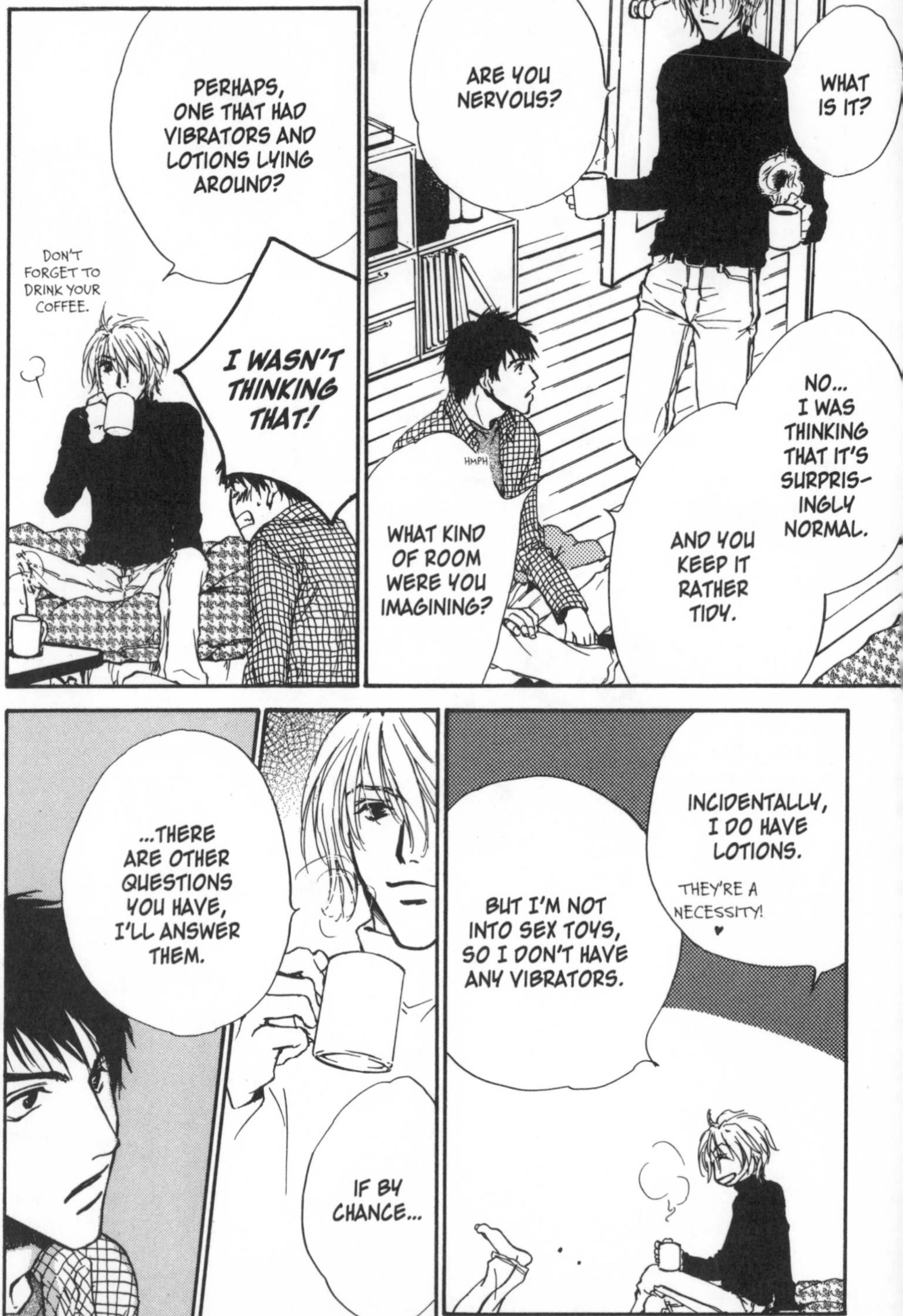
WHAT IS IT?
ARE YOU NERVOUS?
NO... I WAS THINKING THAT IT'S SURPRISINGLY NORMAL.
AND YOU KEEP IT RATHER TIDY.
HMPH
WHAT KIND OF ROOM WERE YOU IMAGINING?
PERHAPS, ONE THAT HAD VIBRATORS AND LOTIONS LYING AROUND?
I WASN'T THINKING THAT!
DON'T FORGET TO DRINK YOUR COFFEE.
INCIDENTALLY, I DO HAVE LOTIONS.
THEY'RE A NECESSITY! ♥
BUT I'M NOT INTO SEX TOYS, SO I DON'T HAVE ANY VIBRATORS.
IF BY CHANCE...
...THERE ARE OTHER QUESTIONS YOU HAVE, I'LL ANSWER THEM.

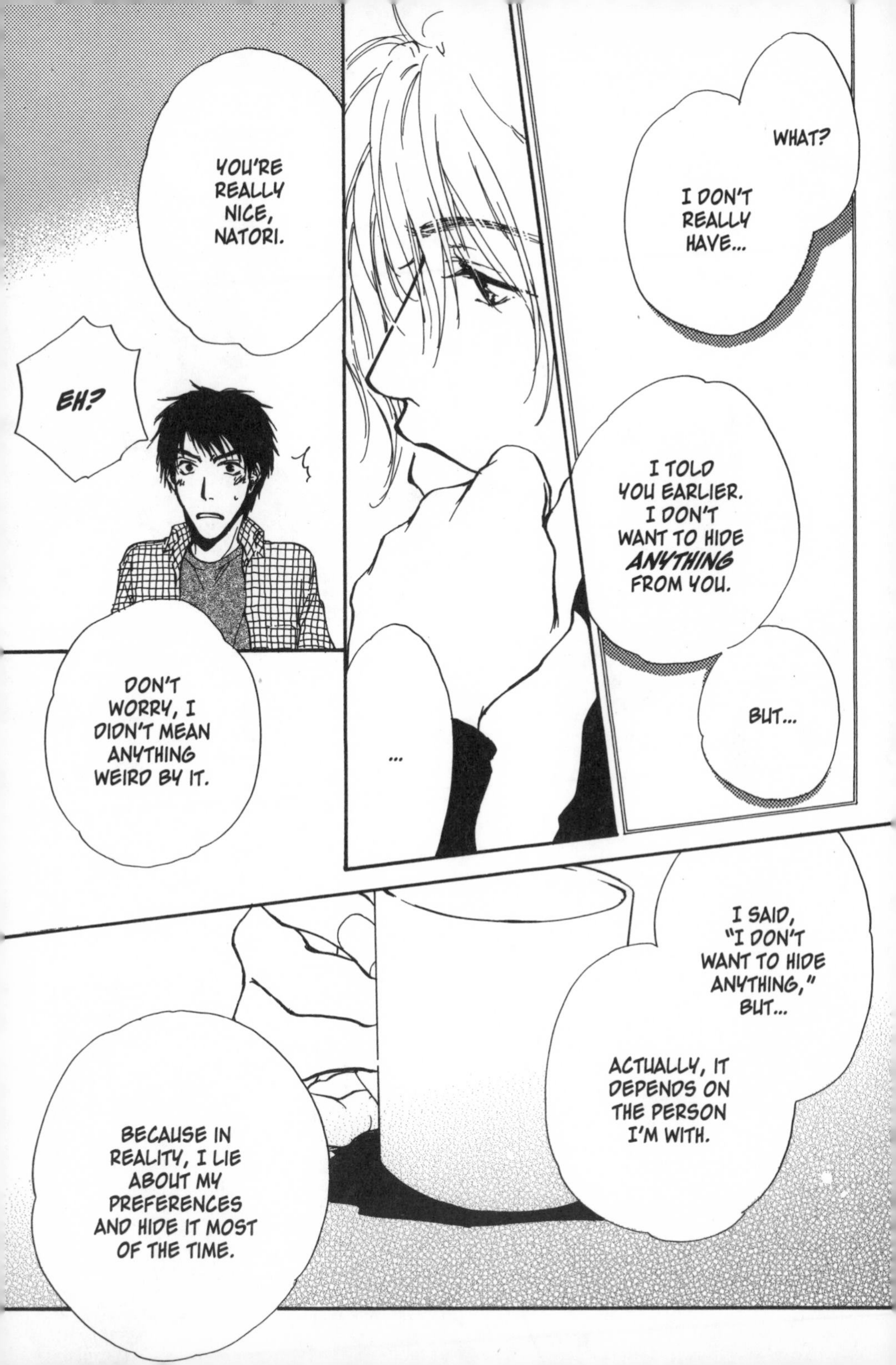
WHAT?
I DON'T REALLY HAVE...
I TOLD YOU EARLIER. I DON'T WANT TO HIDE *ANYTHING* FROM YOU.
BUT...
...
YOU'RE REALLY NICE, NATORI.
EH?
DON'T WORRY, I DIDN'T MEAN ANYTHING WEIRD BY IT.
I SAID, "I DON'T WANT TO HIDE ANYTHING," BUT...
ACTUALLY, IT DEPENDS ON THE PERSON I'M WITH.
BECAUSE IN REALITY, I LIE ABOUT MY PREFERENCES AND HIDE IT MOST OF THE TIME.

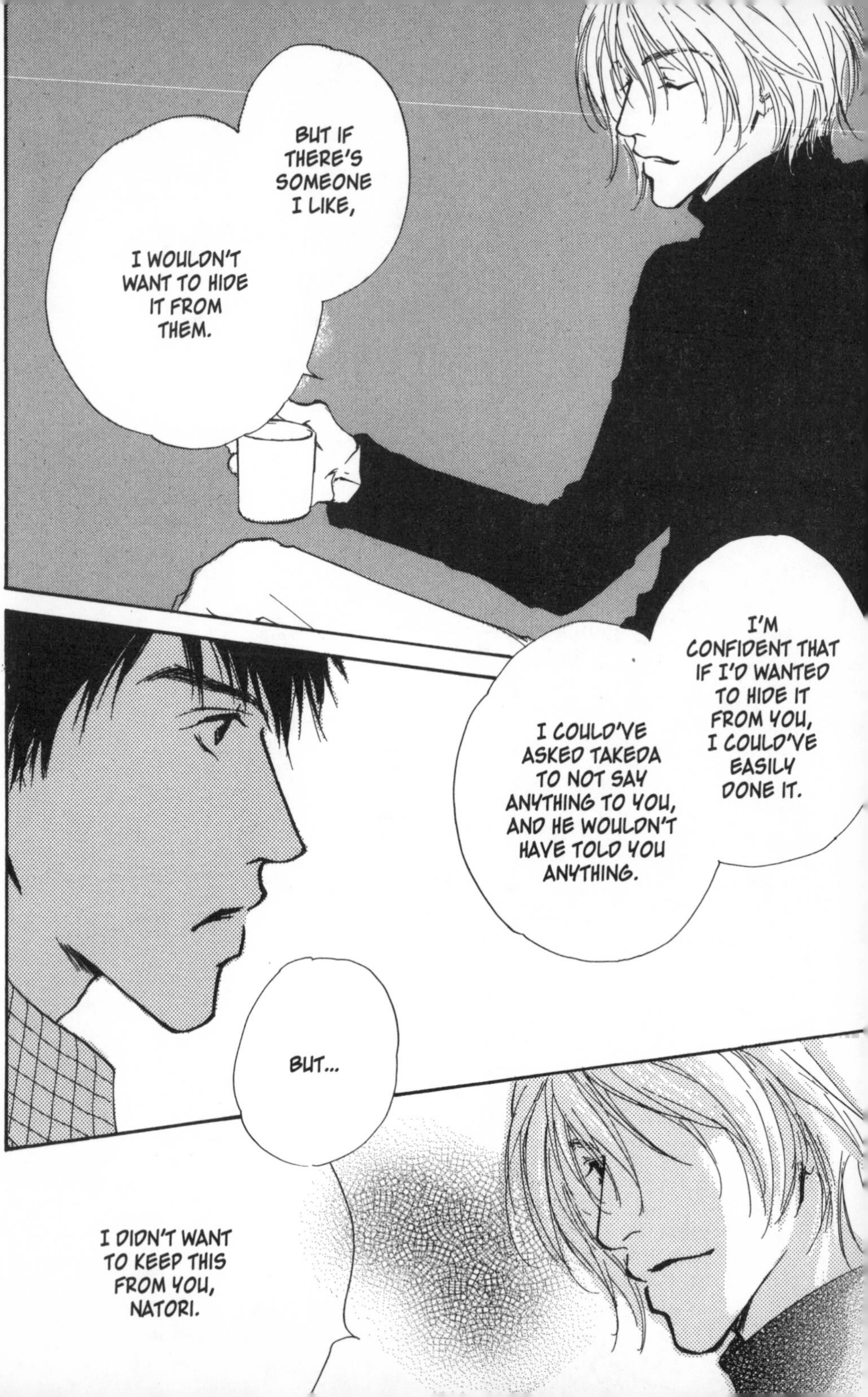
BUT IF THERE'S SOMEONE I LIKE,
I WOULDN'T WANT TO HIDE IT FROM THEM.
I'M CONFIDENT THAT IF I'D WANTED TO HIDE IT FROM YOU, I COULD'VE EASILY DONE IT.
I COULD'VE ASKED TAKEDA TO NOT SAY ANYTHING TO YOU, AND HE WOULDN'T HAVE TOLD YOU ANYTHING.
BUT...
I DIDN'T WANT TO KEEP THIS FROM YOU, NATORI.

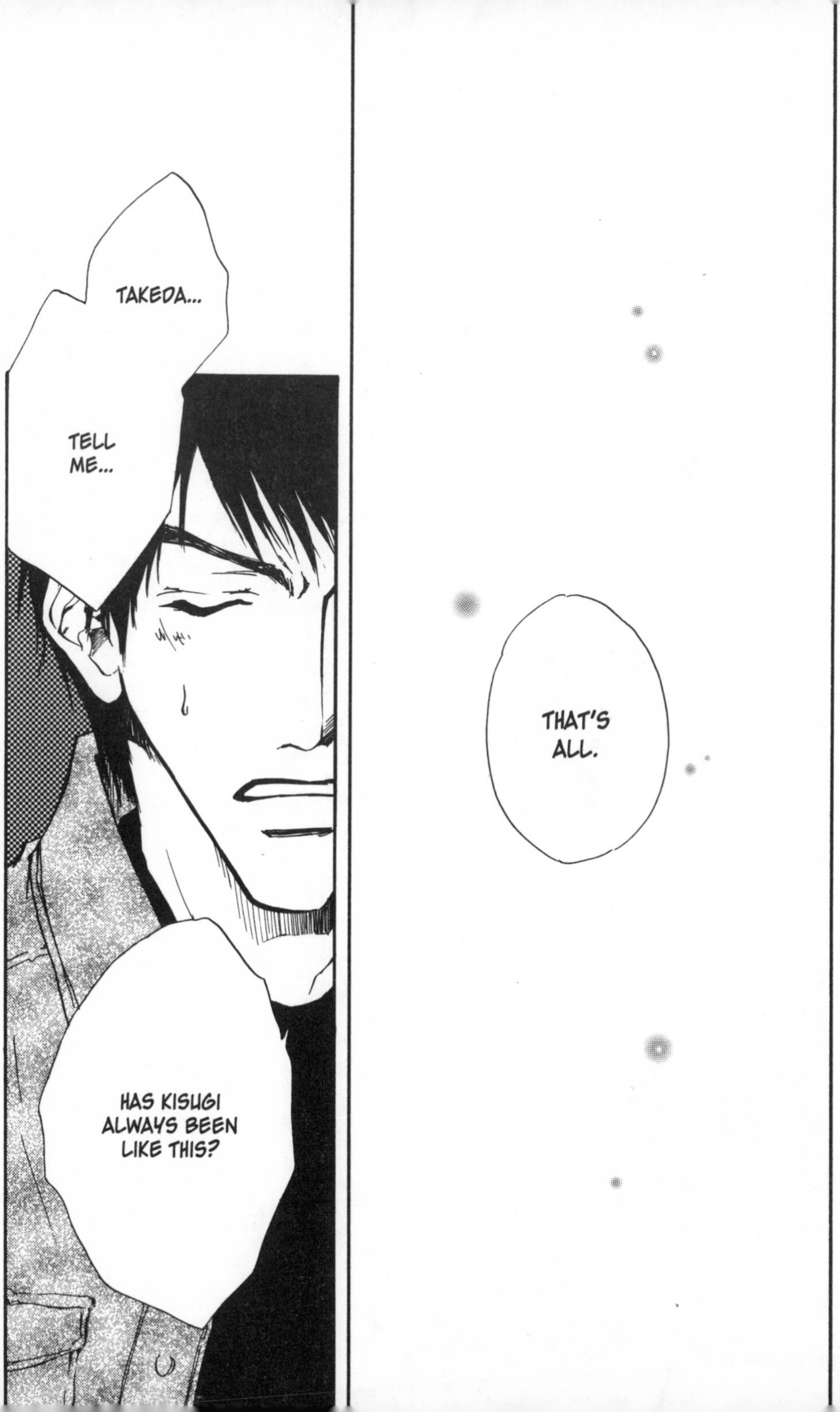
THAT'S ALL.
TAKEDA...
TELL ME...
HAS KISUGI ALWAYS BEEN LIKE THIS?

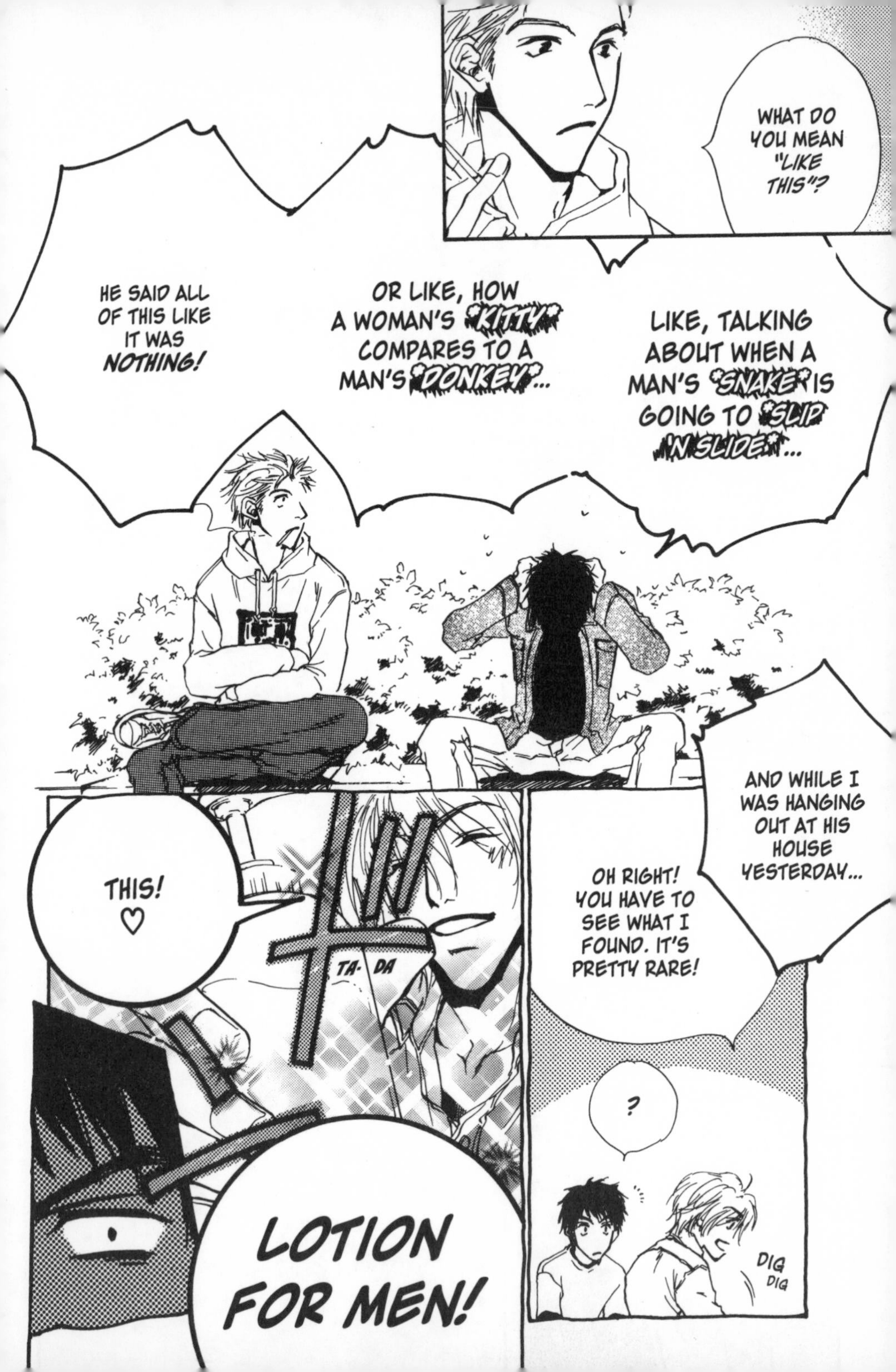
WHAT DO YOU MEAN "LIKE THIS"?
LIKE, TALKING ABOUT WHEN A MAN'S *SNAKE* IS GOING TO *SLIP 'N SLIDE*...
OR LIKE, HOW A WOMAN'S *KITTY* COMPARES TO A MAN'S *DONKEY*...
HE SAID ALL OF THIS LIKE IT WAS NOTHING!
AND WHILE I WAS HANGING OUT AT HIS HOUSE YESTERDAY...
OH RIGHT! YOU HAVE TO SEE WHAT I FOUND. IT'S PRETTY RARE!
?
DIG DIG
THIS! ♡
TA-DA
LOTION FOR MEN!

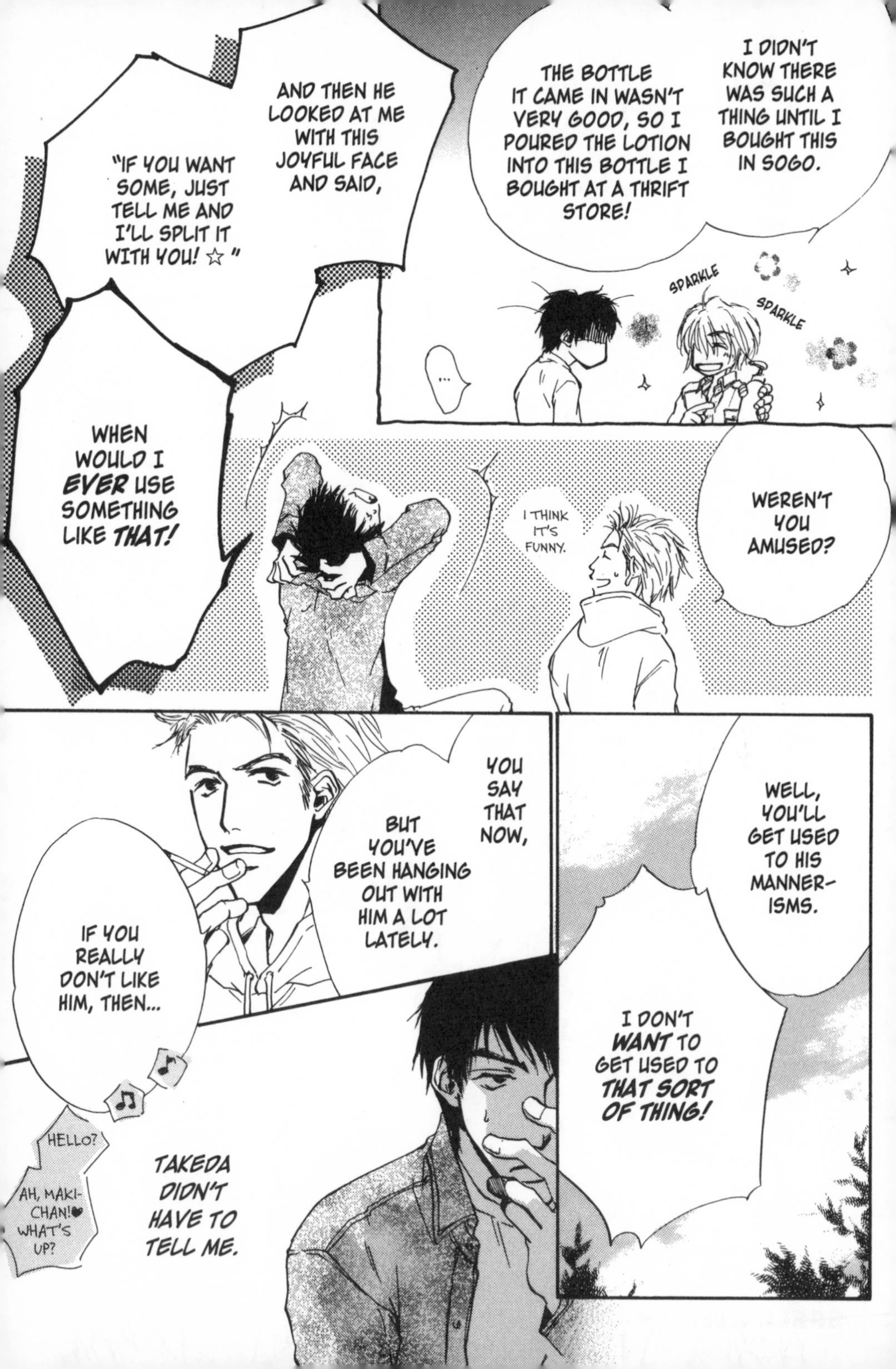
I DIDN'T KNOW THERE WAS SUCH A THING UNTIL I BOUGHT THIS IN SOGO.
THE BOTTLE IT CAME IN WASN'T VERY GOOD, SO I POURED THE LOTION INTO THIS BOTTLE I BOUGHT AT A THRIFT STORE!
SPARKLE
SPARKLE
...
AND THEN HE LOOKED AT ME WITH THIS JOYFUL FACE AND SAID,
"IF YOU WANT SOME, JUST TELL ME AND I'LL SPLIT IT WITH YOU! ☆"
WEREN'T YOU AMUSED?
I THINK IT'S FUNNY.
WHEN WOULD I **EVER** USE SOMETHING LIKE **THAT!**
WELL, YOU'LL GET USED TO HIS MANNER-ISMS.
I DON'T **WANT** TO GET USED TO **THAT SORT OF THING!**
YOU SAY THAT NOW,
BUT YOU'VE BEEN HANGING OUT WITH HIM A LOT LATELY.
IF YOU REALLY DON'T LIKE HIM, THEN...
TAKEDA DIDN'T HAVE TO TELL ME.
HELLO?
AH, MAKI-CHAN! WHAT'S UP?

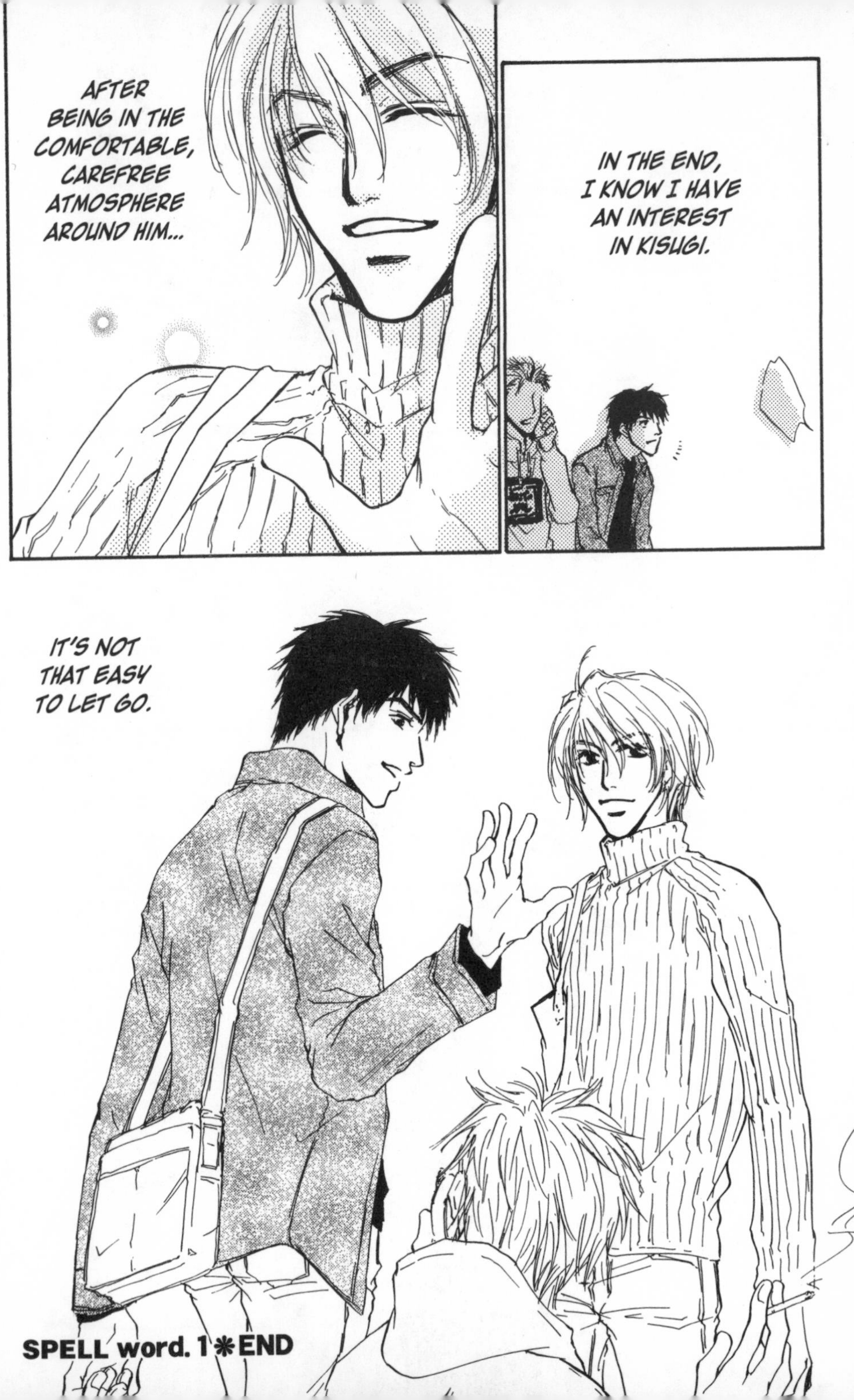
AFTER BEING IN THE COMFORTABLE, CAREFREE ATMOSPHERE AROUND HIM...
IN THE END, I KNOW I HAVE AN INTEREST IN KISUGI.
IT'S NOT THAT EASY TO LET GO.

SPELL word. 1 ✱ END

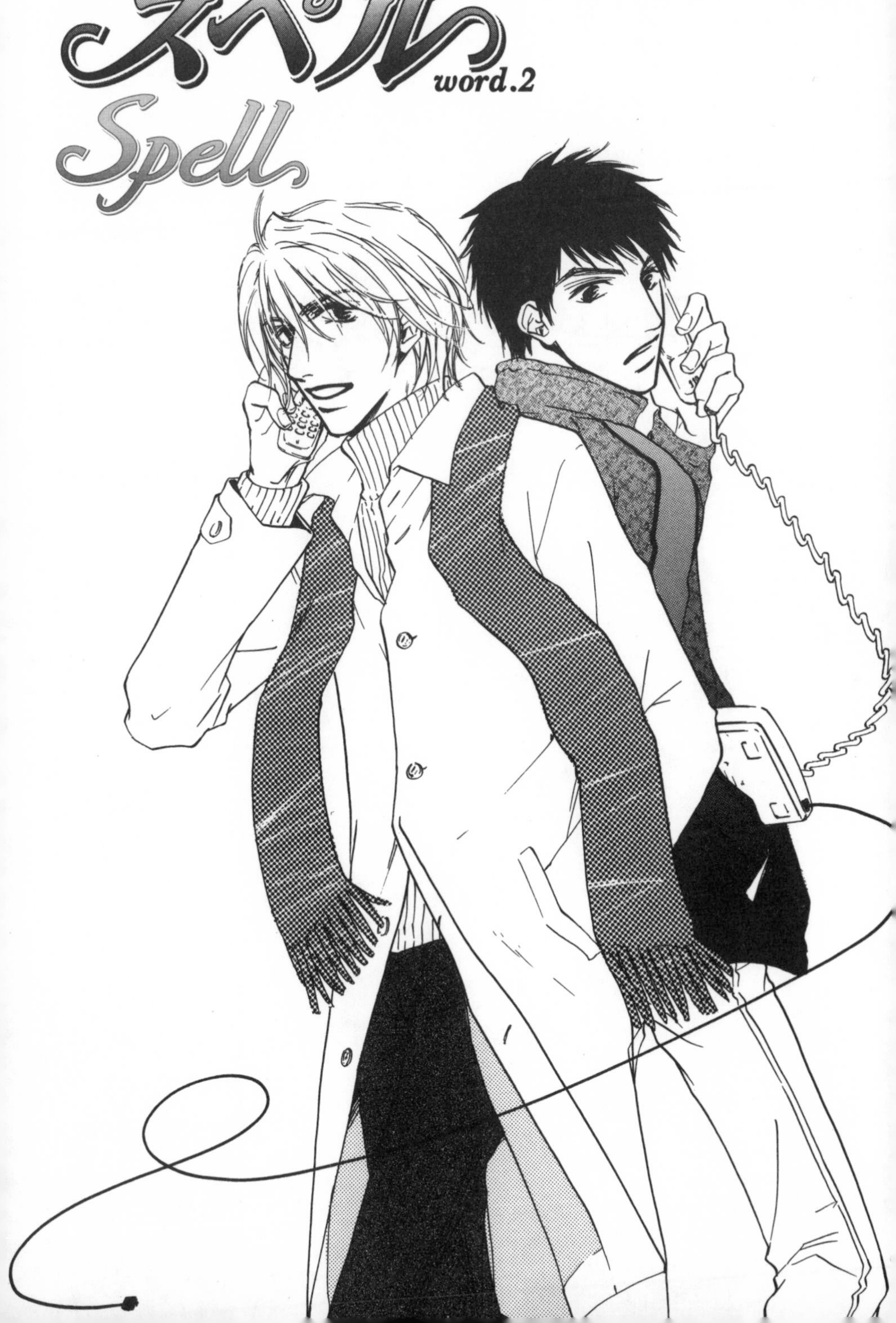
スペル
word.2
Spell

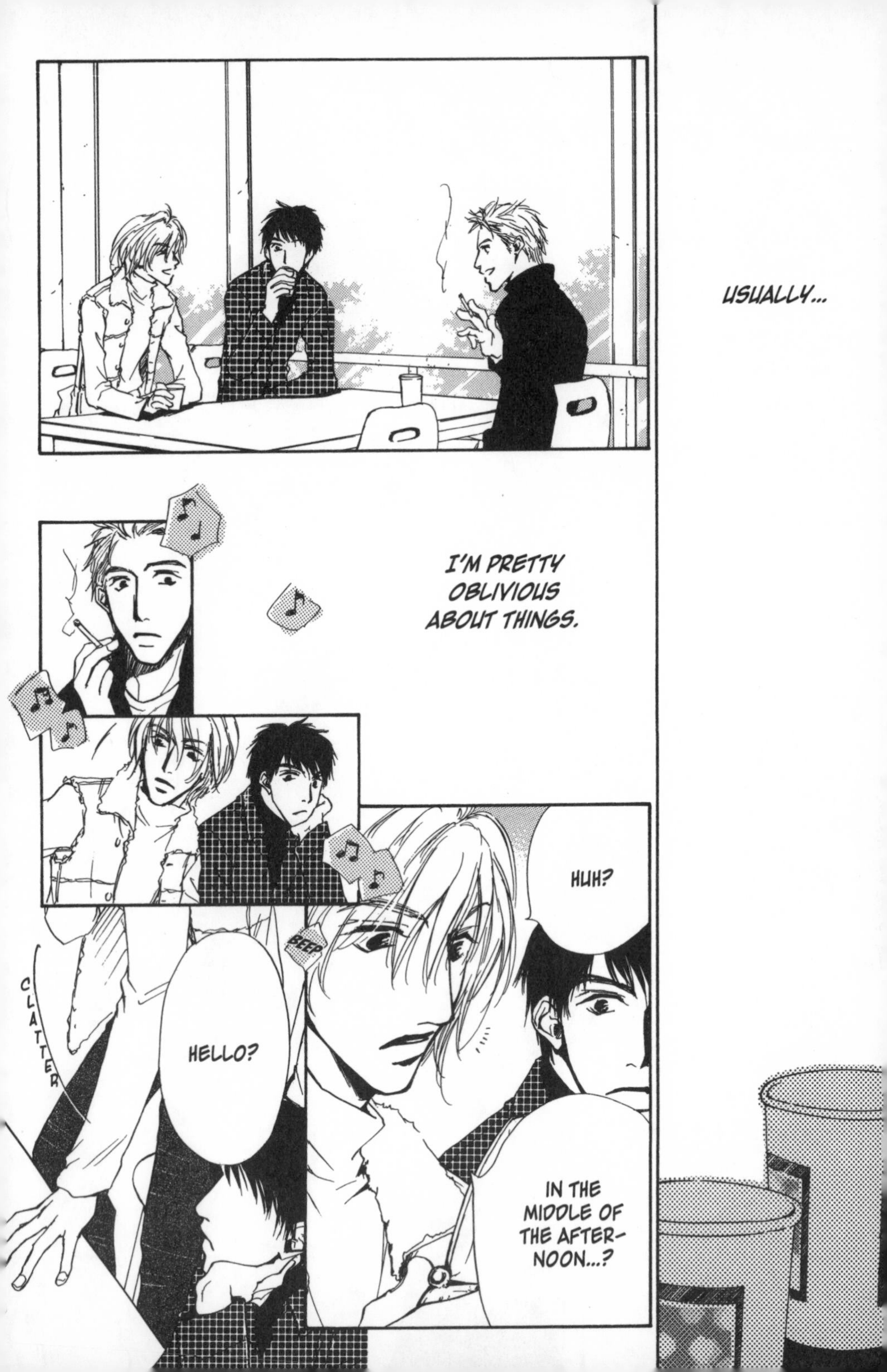
USUALLY...
I'M PRETTY OBLIVIOUS ABOUT THINGS.
HUH?
BEEP
IN THE MIDDLE OF THE AFTER-NOON...?
HELLO?
CLATTER

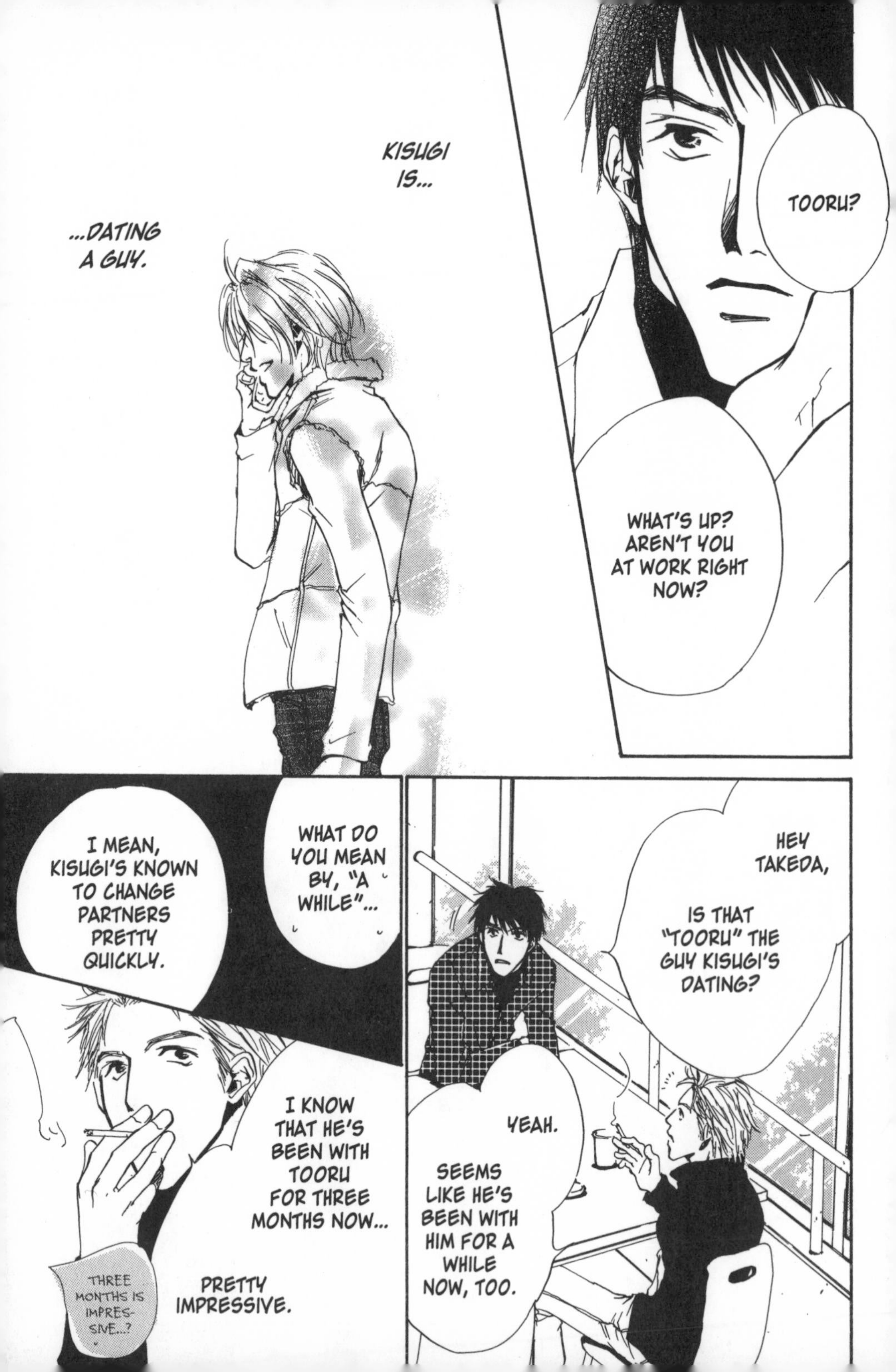
TOORU?
WHAT'S UP? AREN'T YOU AT WORK RIGHT NOW?
KISUGI IS...
...DATING A GUY.
HEY TAKEDA,
IS THAT "TOORU" THE GUY KISUGI'S DATING?
YEAH.
SEEMS LIKE HE'S BEEN WITH HIM FOR A WHILE NOW, TOO.
WHAT DO YOU MEAN BY, "A WHILE"...
I MEAN, KISUGI'S KNOWN TO CHANGE PARTNERS PRETTY QUICKLY.
I KNOW THAT HE'S BEEN WITH TOORU FOR THREE MONTHS NOW...
PRETTY IMPRESSIVE.
THREE MONTHS IS IMPRES-SIVE...?

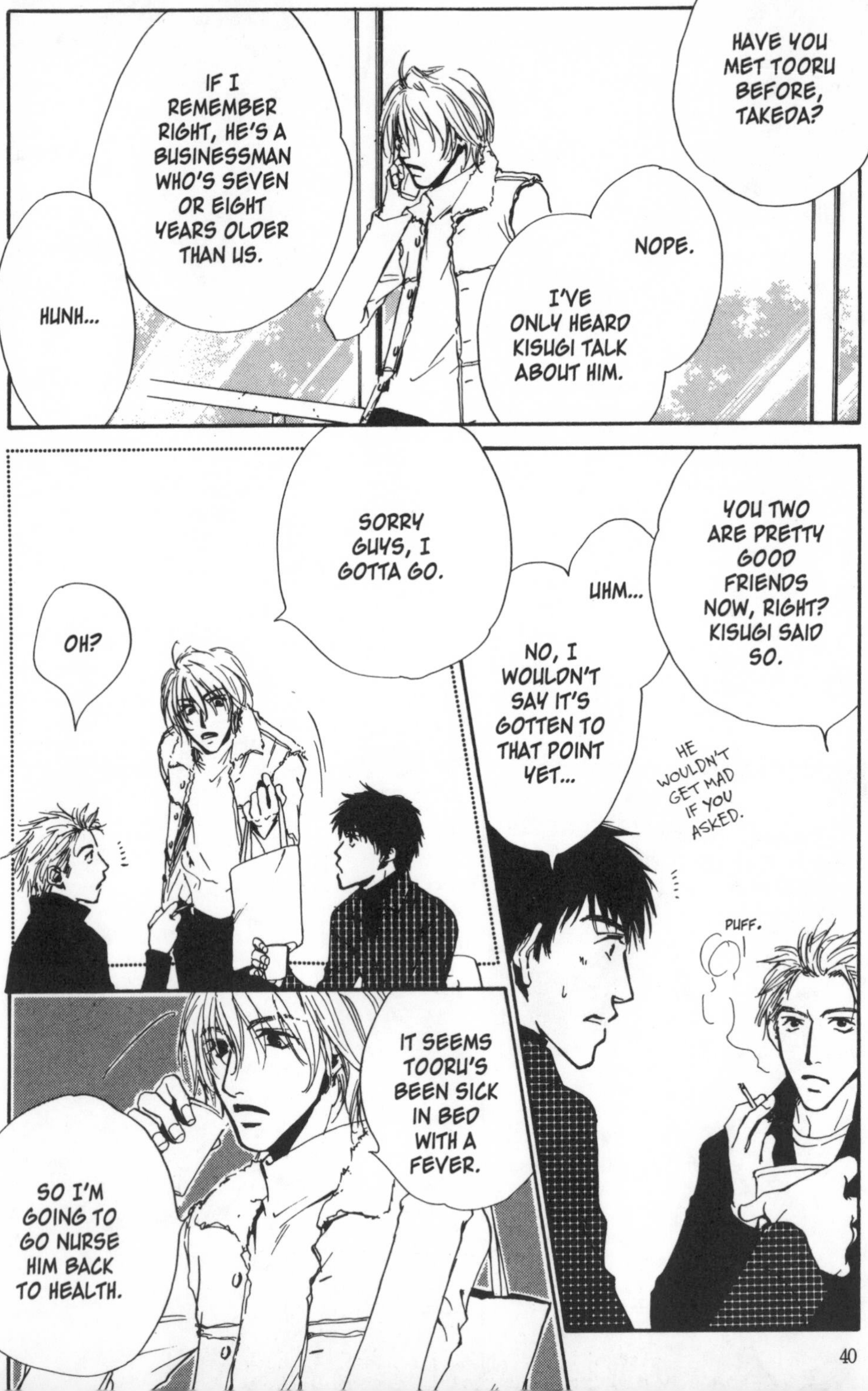
HAVE YOU MET TOORU BEFORE, TAKEDA?
NOPE.
I'VE ONLY HEARD KISUGI TALK ABOUT HIM.
IF I REMEMBER RIGHT, HE'S A BUSINESSMAN WHO'S SEVEN OR EIGHT YEARS OLDER THAN US.
HUNH...
YOU TWO ARE PRETTY GOOD FRIENDS NOW, RIGHT? KISUGI SAID SO.
UHM...
NO, I WOULDN'T SAY IT'S GOTTEN TO THAT POINT YET...
HE WOULDN'T GET MAD IF YOU ASKED.
PUFF.
SORRY GUYS, I GOTTA GO.
OH?
IT SEEMS TOORU'S BEEN SICK IN BED WITH A FEVER.
SO I'M GOING TO GO NURSE HIM BACK TO HEALTH.

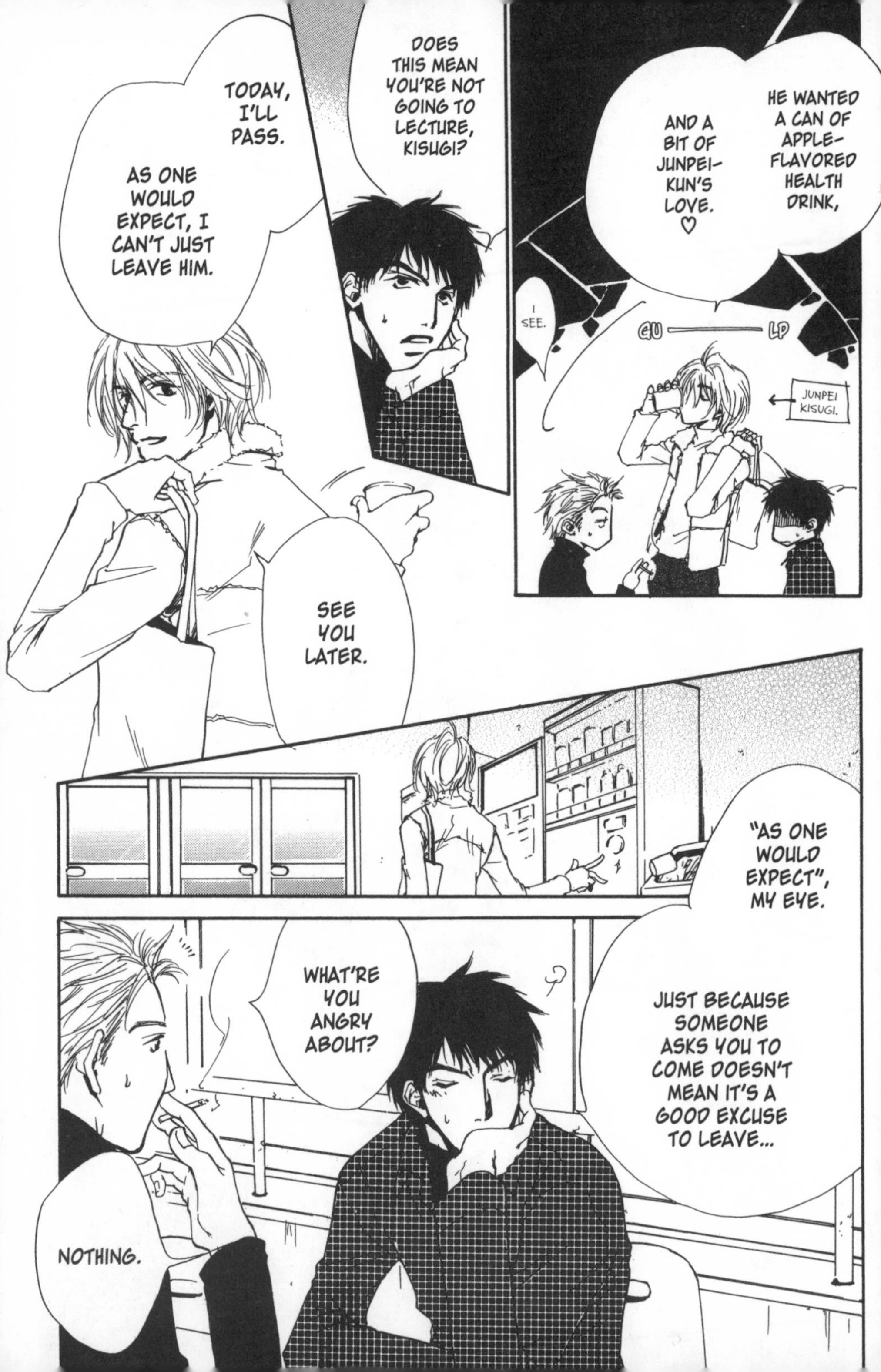
HE WANTED A CAN OF APPLE-FLAVORED HEALTH DRINK,
AND A BIT OF JUNPEI-KUN'S LOVE. ♡
I SEE.
GU —— LP
JUNPEI KISUGI.
DOES THIS MEAN YOU'RE NOT GOING TO LECTURE, KISUGI?
TODAY, I'LL PASS.
AS ONE WOULD EXPECT, I CAN'T JUST LEAVE HIM.
SEE YOU LATER.
"AS ONE WOULD EXPECT", MY EYE.
JUST BECAUSE SOMEONE ASKS YOU TO COME DOESN'T MEAN IT'S A GOOD EXCUSE TO LEAVE...
WHAT'RE YOU ANGRY ABOUT?
NOTHING.

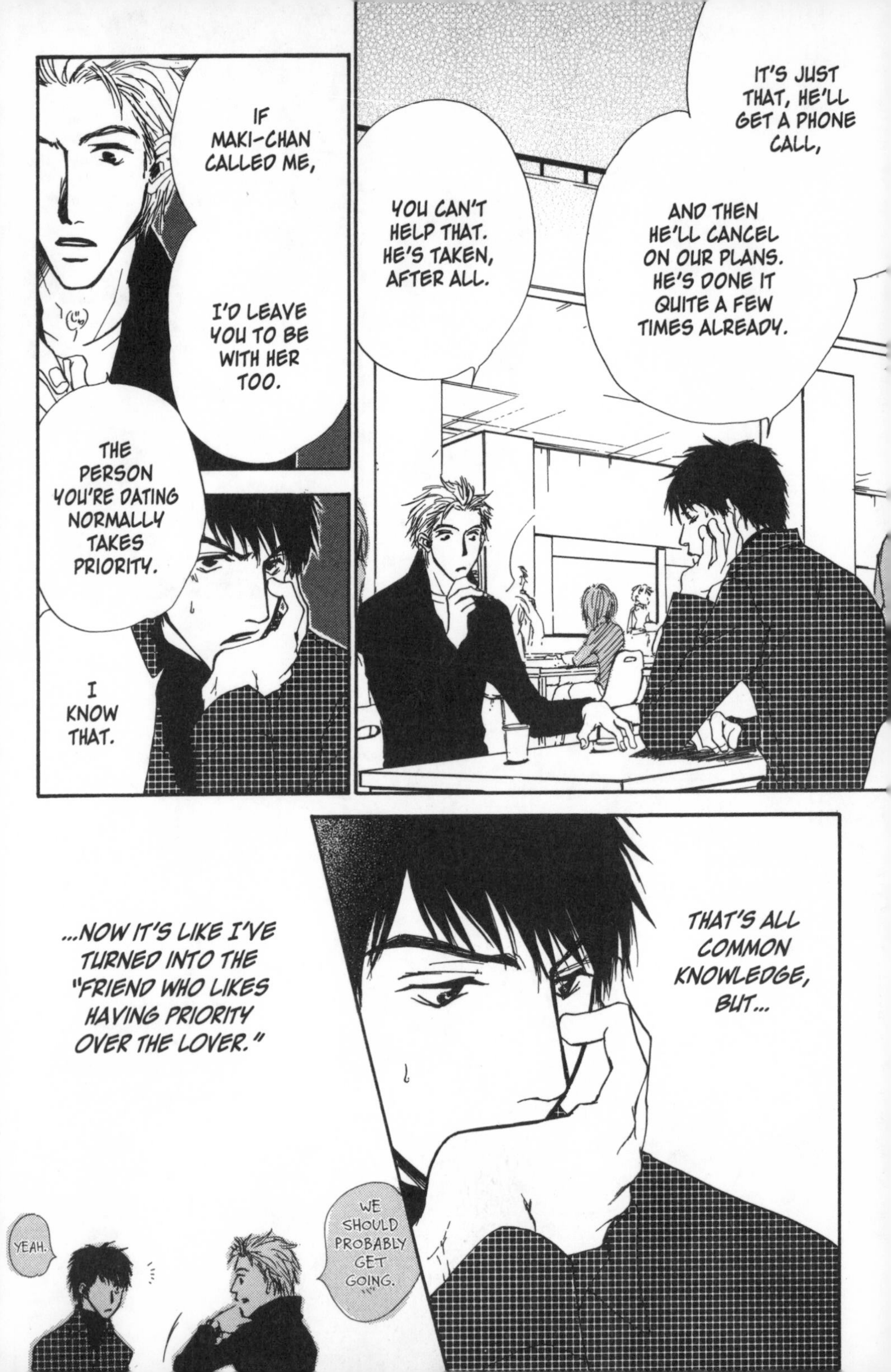
IT'S JUST THAT, HE'LL GET A PHONE CALL,
AND THEN HE'LL CANCEL ON OUR PLANS. HE'S DONE IT QUITE A FEW TIMES ALREADY.
YOU CAN'T HELP THAT. HE'S TAKEN, AFTER ALL.
IF MAKI-CHAN CALLED ME,
I'D LEAVE YOU TO BE WITH HER TOO.
THE PERSON YOU'RE DATING NORMALLY TAKES PRIORITY.
I KNOW THAT.
THAT'S ALL COMMON KNOWLEDGE, BUT...
...NOW IT'S LIKE I'VE TURNED INTO THE "FRIEND WHO LIKES HAVING PRIORITY OVER THE LOVER."
WE SHOULD PROBABLY GET GOING.
YEAH.

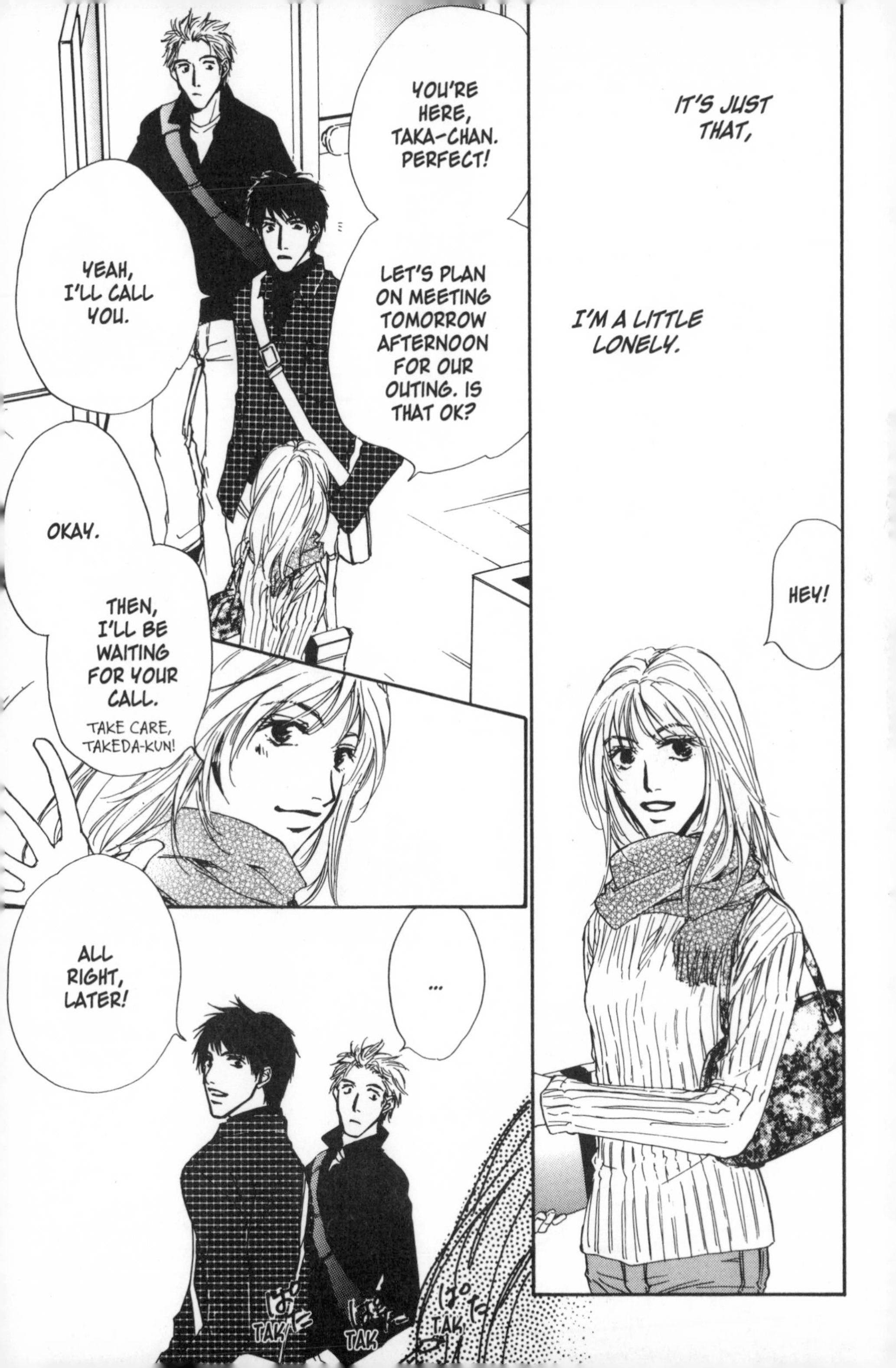
IT'S JUST THAT,
I'M A LITTLE LONELY.
HEY!
YOU'RE HERE, TAKA-CHAN. PERFECT!
LET'S PLAN ON MEETING TOMORROW AFTERNOON FOR OUR OUTING. IS THAT OK?
YEAH, I'LL CALL YOU.
OKAY.
THEN, I'LL BE WAITING FOR YOUR CALL.
TAKE CARE, TAKEDA-KUN!
...
ALL RIGHT, LATER!
TAK
TAK
TAK

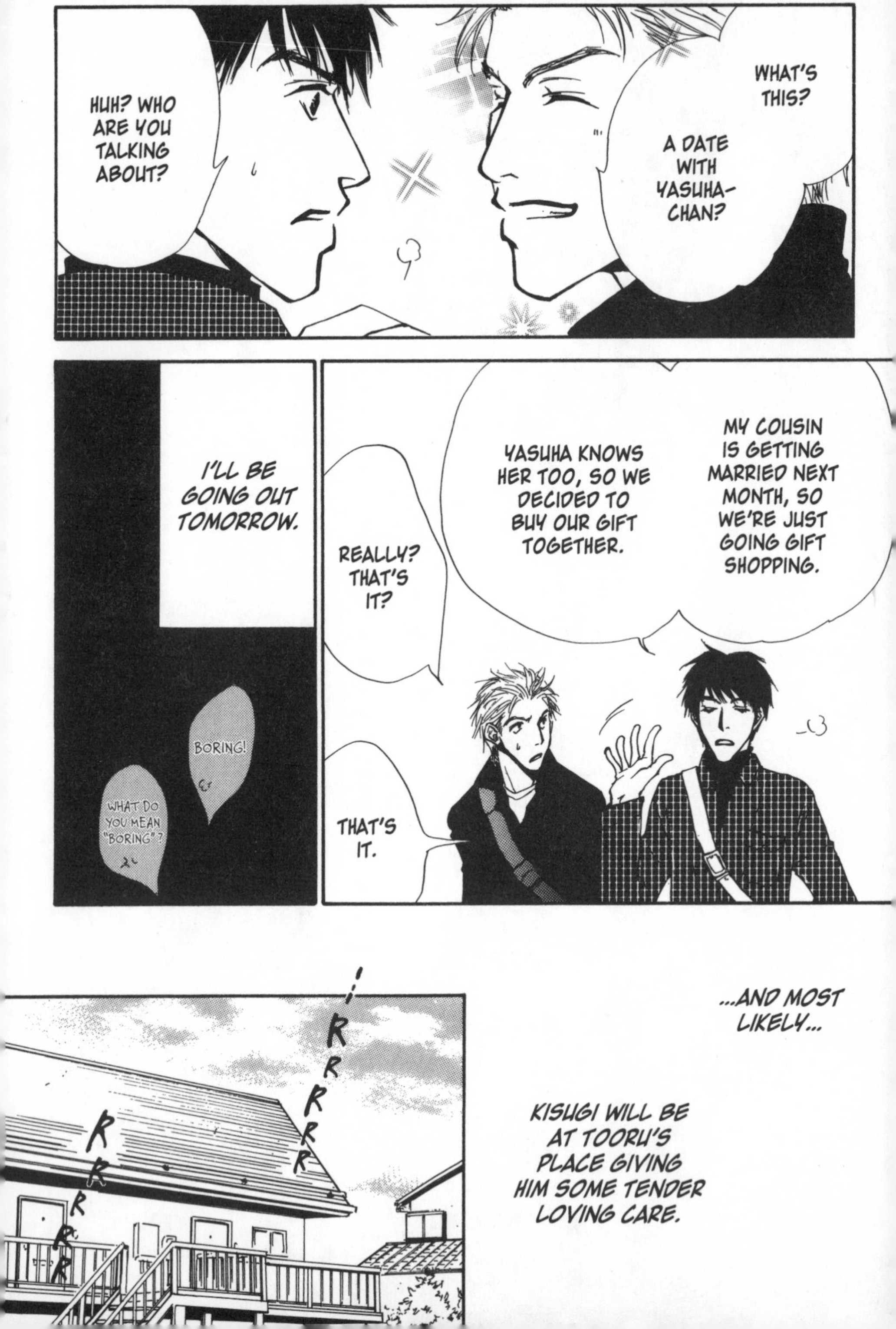
WHAT'S THIS?
A DATE WITH YASUHA-CHAN?
HUH? WHO ARE YOU TALKING ABOUT?
MY COUSIN IS GETTING MARRIED NEXT MONTH, SO WE'RE JUST GOING GIFT SHOPPING.
YASUHA KNOWS HER TOO, SO WE DECIDED TO BUY OUR GIFT TOGETHER.
REALLY? THAT'S IT?
THAT'S IT.
I'LL BE GOING OUT TOMORROW.
BORING!
WHAT DO YOU MEAN "BORING"?
...AND MOST LIKELY...
KISUGI WILL BE AT TOORU'S PLACE GIVING HIM SOME TENDER LOVING CARE.
RRRRRRRRRR!!

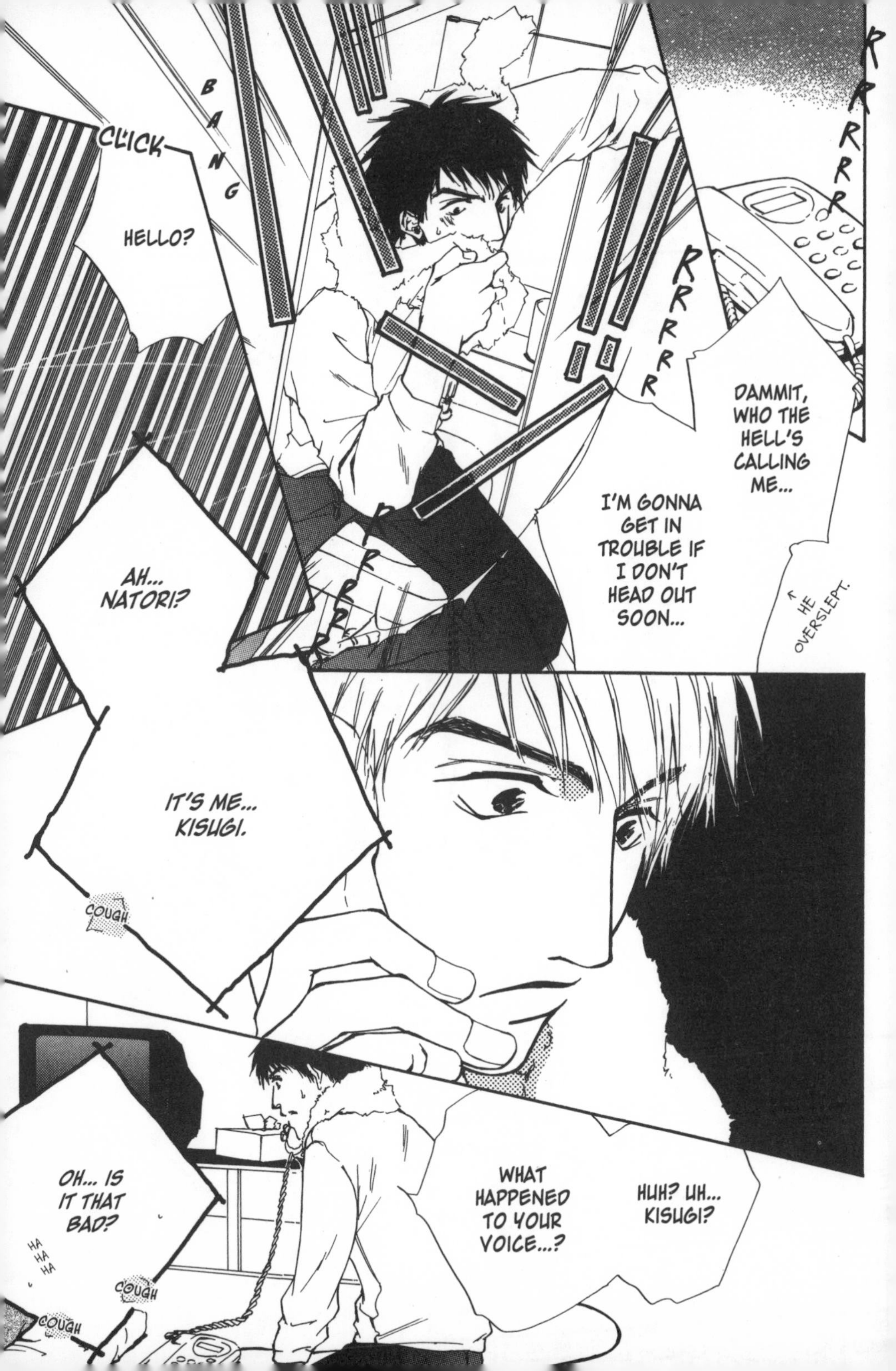
RRRRRR
RRRRRR
DAMMIT, WHO THE HELL'S CALLING ME...
HE OVERSLEPT.
I'M GONNA GET IN TROUBLE IF I DON'T HEAD OUT SOON...
RRRR
BANG
CLICK
HELLO?
AH... NATORI?
IT'S ME... KISUGI.
COUGH
HUH? UH... KISUGI?
WHAT HAPPENED TO YOUR VOICE...?
OH... IS IT THAT BAD?
HA HA HA
COUGH
COUGH

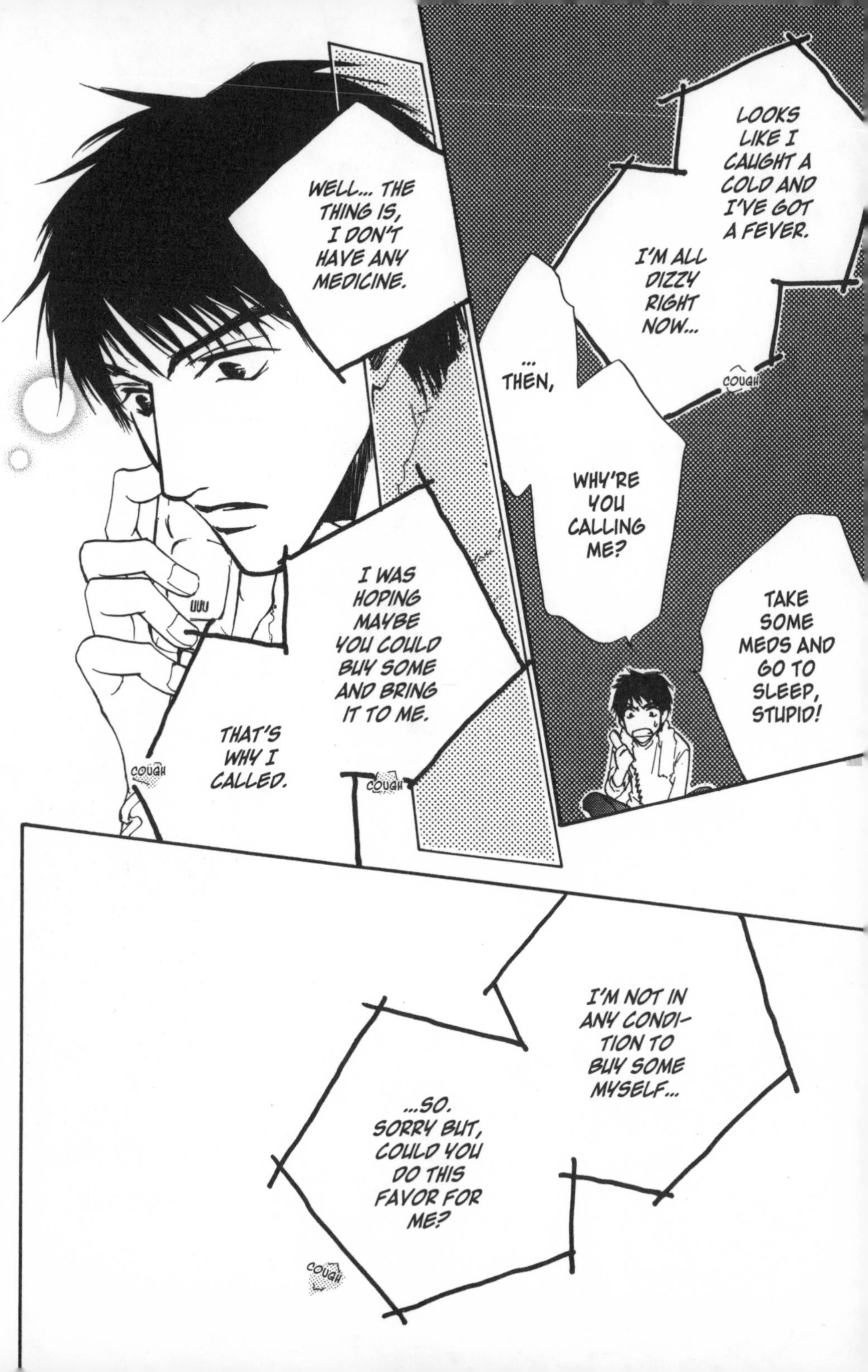
LOOKS LIKE I CAUGHT A COLD AND I'VE GOT A FEVER.
I'M ALL DIZZY RIGHT NOW...
COUGH
... THEN,
WHY'RE YOU CALLING ME?
TAKE SOME MEDS AND GO TO SLEEP, STUPID!
WELL... THE THING IS, I DON'T HAVE ANY MEDICINE.
I WAS HOPING MAYBE YOU COULD BUY SOME AND BRING IT TO ME.
COUGH
UUU
THAT'S WHY I CALLED.
COUGH
I'M NOT IN ANY CONDI-TION TO BUY SOME MYSELF...
...SO. SORRY BUT, COULD YOU DO THIS FAVOR FOR ME?
COUGH

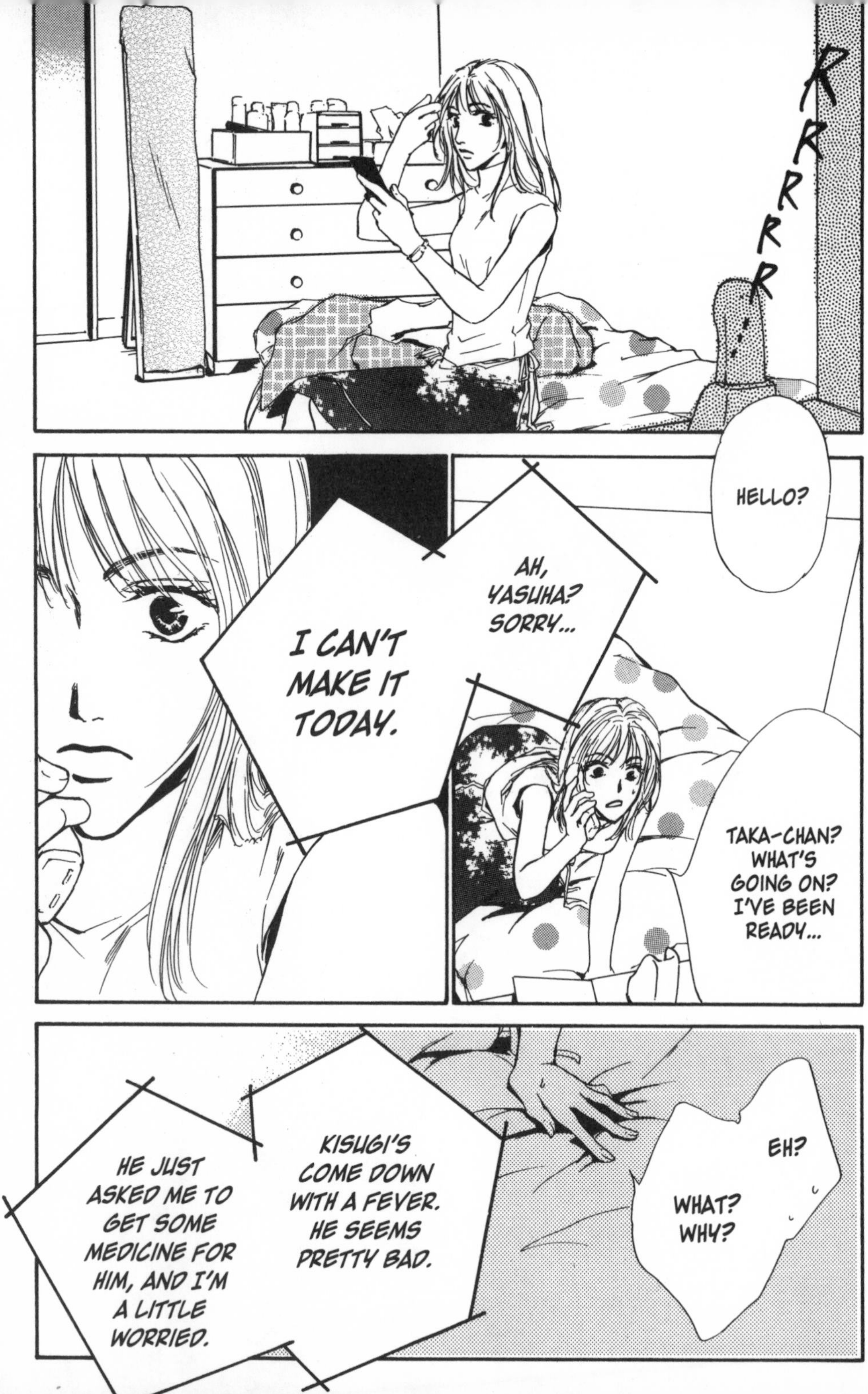
RRRRRR...
HELLO?
AH, YASUHA? SORRY...
TAKA-CHAN? WHAT'S GOING ON? I'VE BEEN READY...
I CAN'T MAKE IT TODAY.
EH?
WHAT? WHY?
KISUGI'S COME DOWN WITH A FEVER. HE SEEMS PRETTY BAD.
HE JUST ASKED ME TO GET SOME MEDICINE FOR HIM, AND I'M A LITTLE WORRIED.

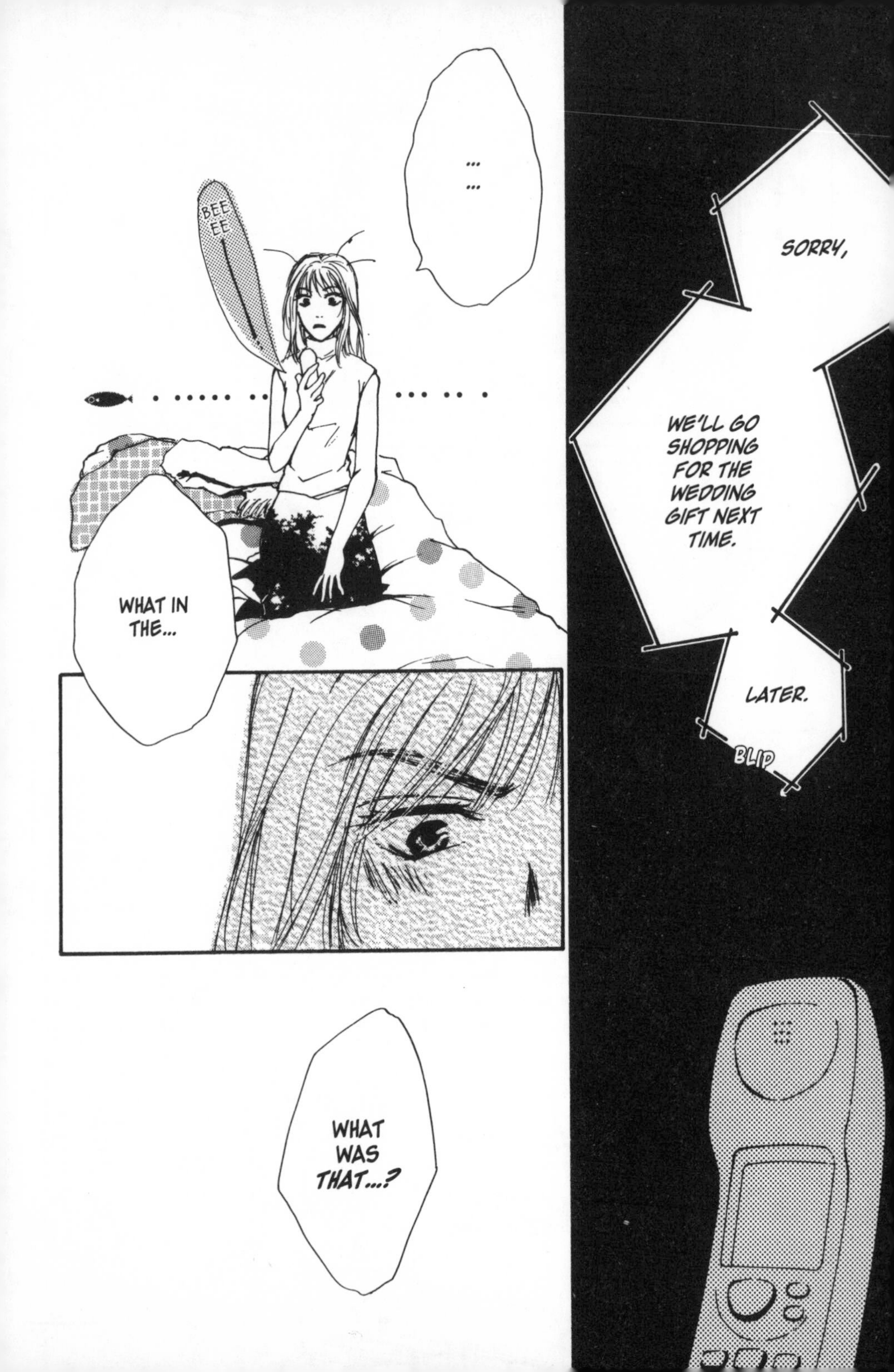

SORRY,
WE'LL GO SHOPPING FOR THE WEDDING GIFT NEXT TIME.
LATER.
BLIP
...
...
BEEE EE
WHAT IN THE...
WHAT WAS THAT...?

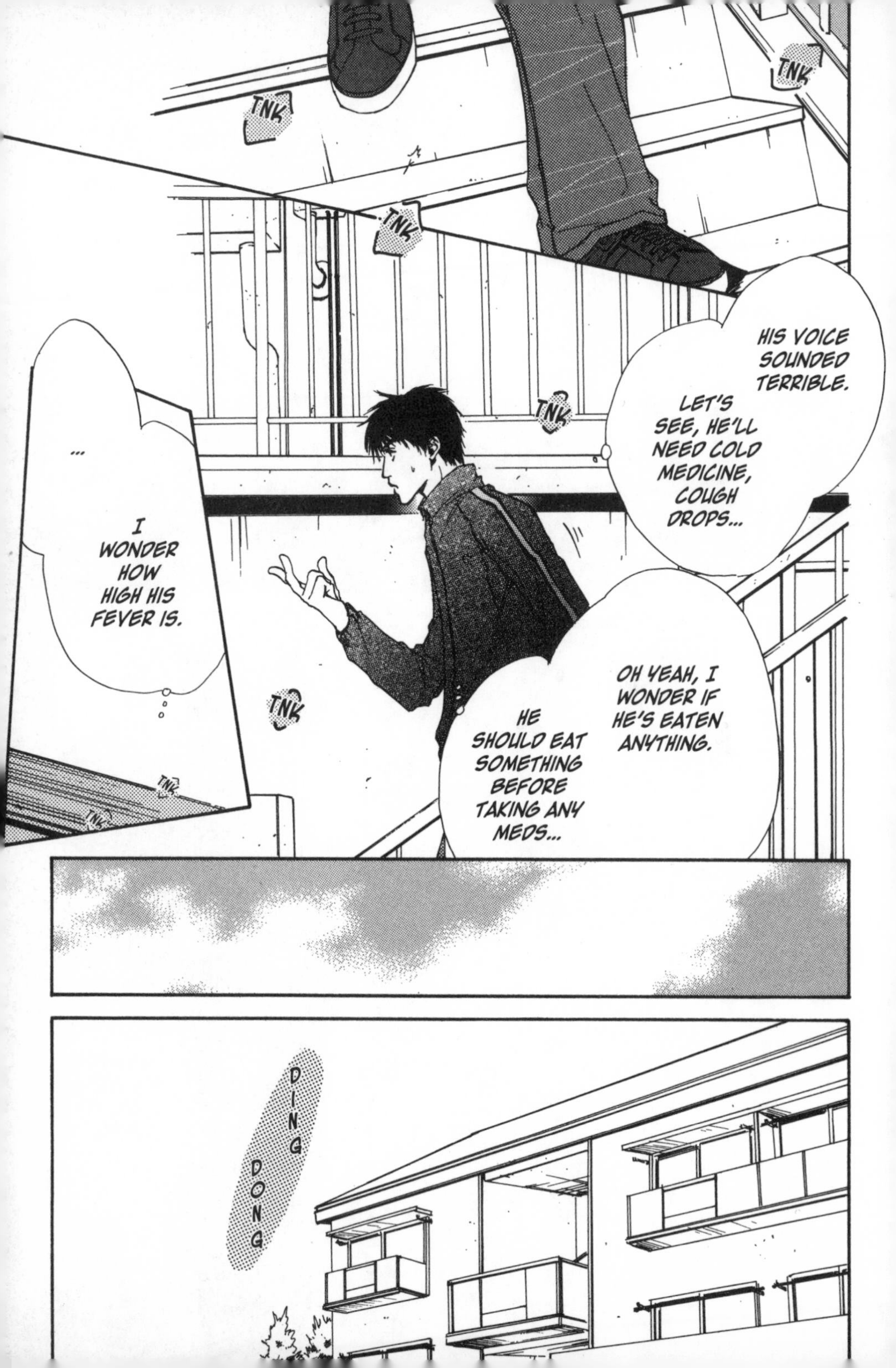
TNK
TNK
TNK
TNK
HIS VOICE SOUNDED TERRIBLE.
LET'S SEE, HE'LL NEED COLD MEDICINE, COUGH DROPS...
...
I WONDER HOW HIGH HIS FEVER IS.
TNK
OH YEAH, I WONDER IF HE'S EATEN ANYTHING.
HE SHOULD EAT SOMETHING BEFORE TAKING ANY MEDS...
TNK
TNK
DING DONG

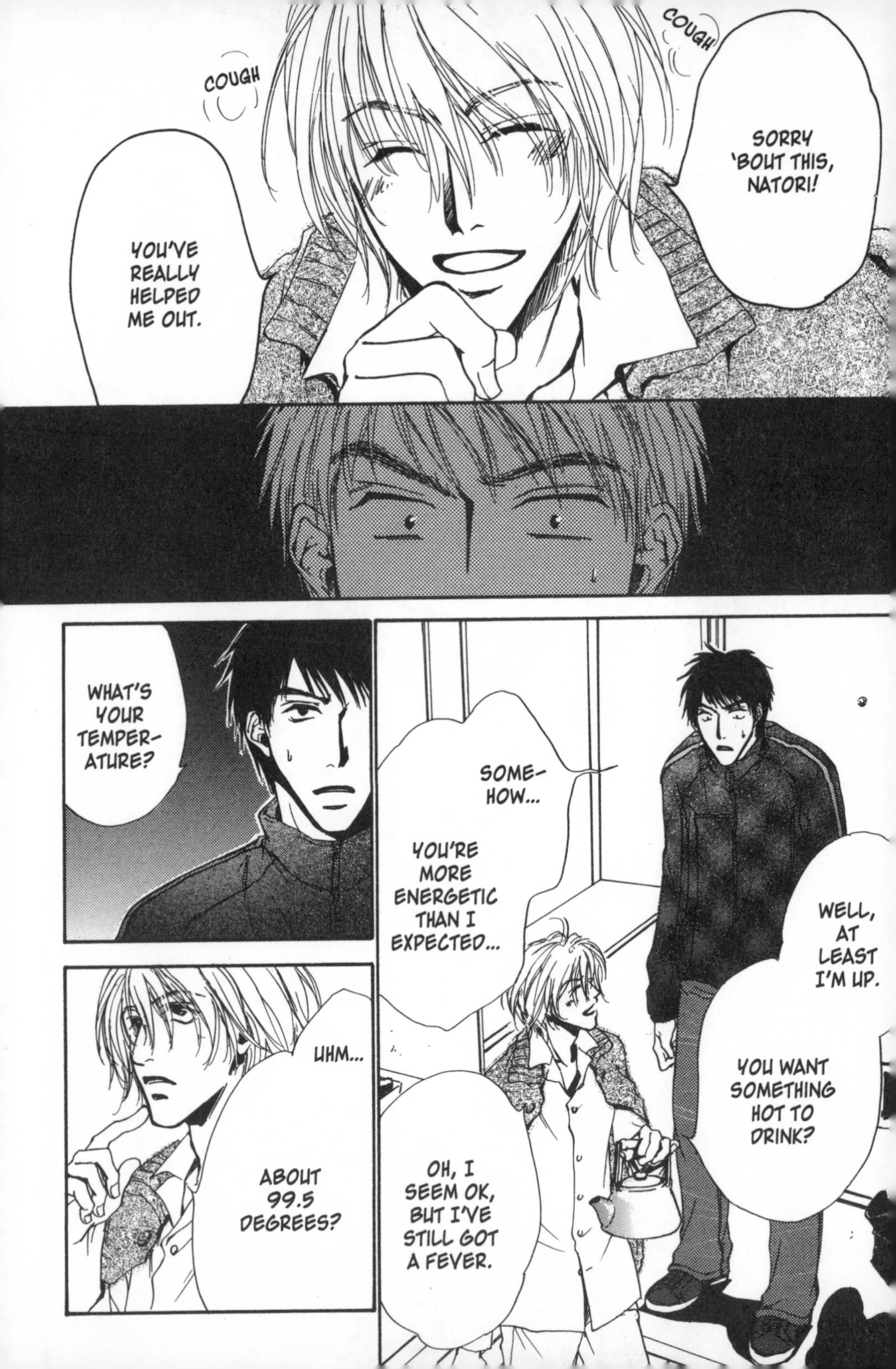
COUGH
SORRY 'BOUT THIS, NATORI!
COUGH
YOU'VE REALLY HELPED ME OUT.
WELL, AT LEAST I'M UP.
YOU WANT SOMETHING HOT TO DRINK?
SOME-HOW...
YOU'RE MORE ENERGETIC THAN I EXPECTED...
OH, I SEEM OK, BUT I'VE STILL GOT A FEVER.
WHAT'S YOUR TEMPER-ATURE?
UHM...
ABOUT 99.5 DEGREES?

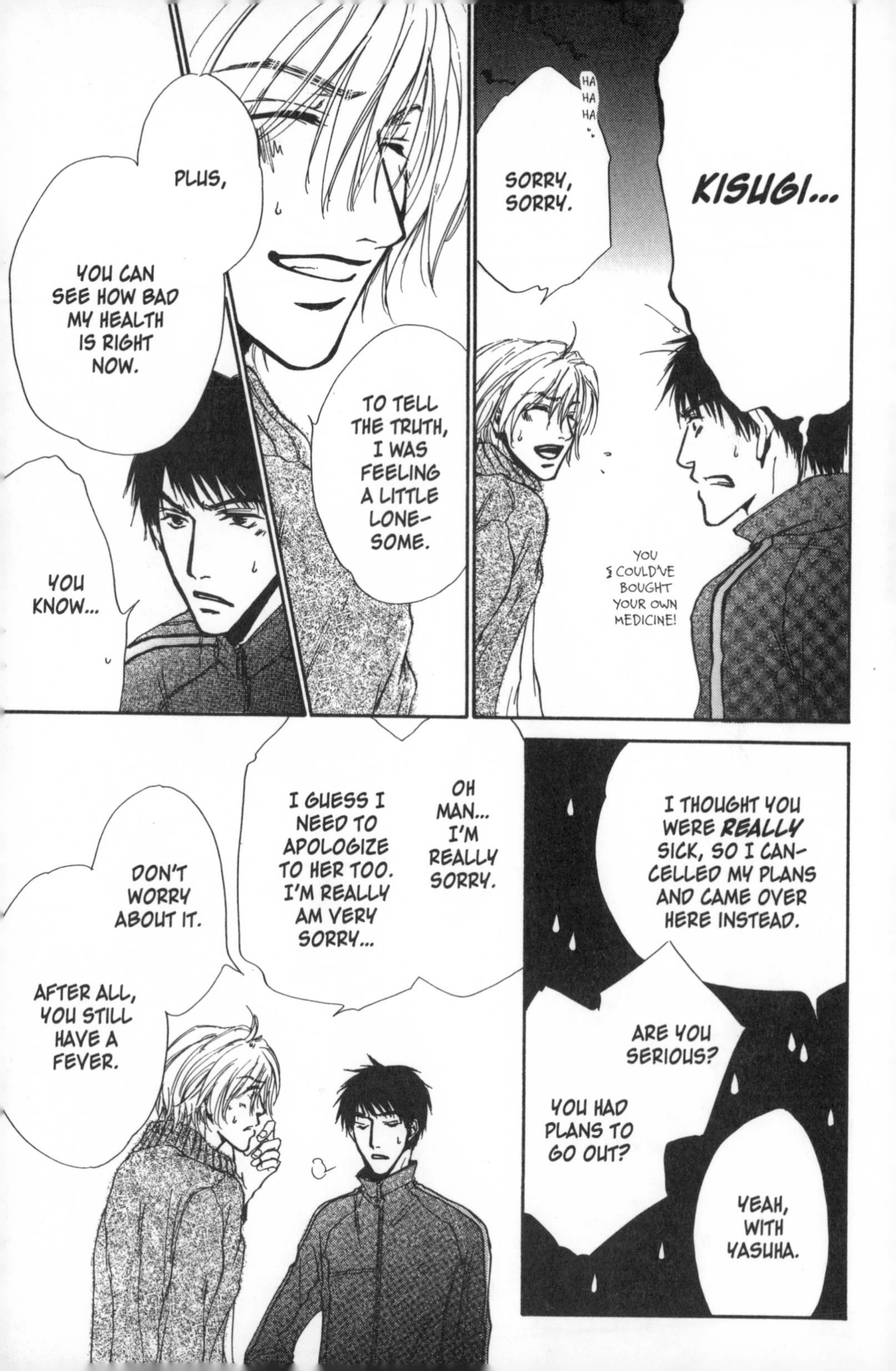

HA HA HA
SORRY, SORRY.
KISUGI...
YOU COULD'VE BOUGHT YOUR OWN MEDICINE!
TO TELL THE TRUTH, I WAS FEELING A LITTLE LONE-SOME.
PLUS,
YOU CAN SEE HOW BAD MY HEALTH IS RIGHT NOW.
YOU KNOW...
I THOUGHT YOU WERE ***REALLY*** SICK, SO I CAN-CELLED MY PLANS AND CAME OVER HERE INSTEAD.
ARE YOU SERIOUS?
YOU HAD PLANS TO GO OUT?
YEAH, WITH YASUHA.
OH MAN... I'M REALLY SORRY.
I GUESS I NEED TO APOLOGIZE TO HER TOO. I'M REALLY AM VERY SORRY...
DON'T WORRY ABOUT IT.
AFTER ALL, YOU STILL HAVE A FEVER.

SO, JUST WAIT. THIS'LL BE READY IN A LITTLE BIT.

ONCE YOU TAKE THIS MEDICINE, YOU'LL BE GOOD AS NEW.

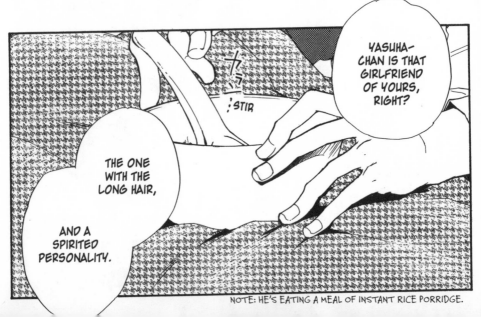

YASUHA-CHAN IS THAT GIRLFRIEND OF YOURS, RIGHT?

THE ONE WITH THE LONG HAIR,

AND A SPIRITED PERSONALITY.

:STIR

NOTE: HE'S EATING A MEAL OF INSTANT RICE PORRIDGE.

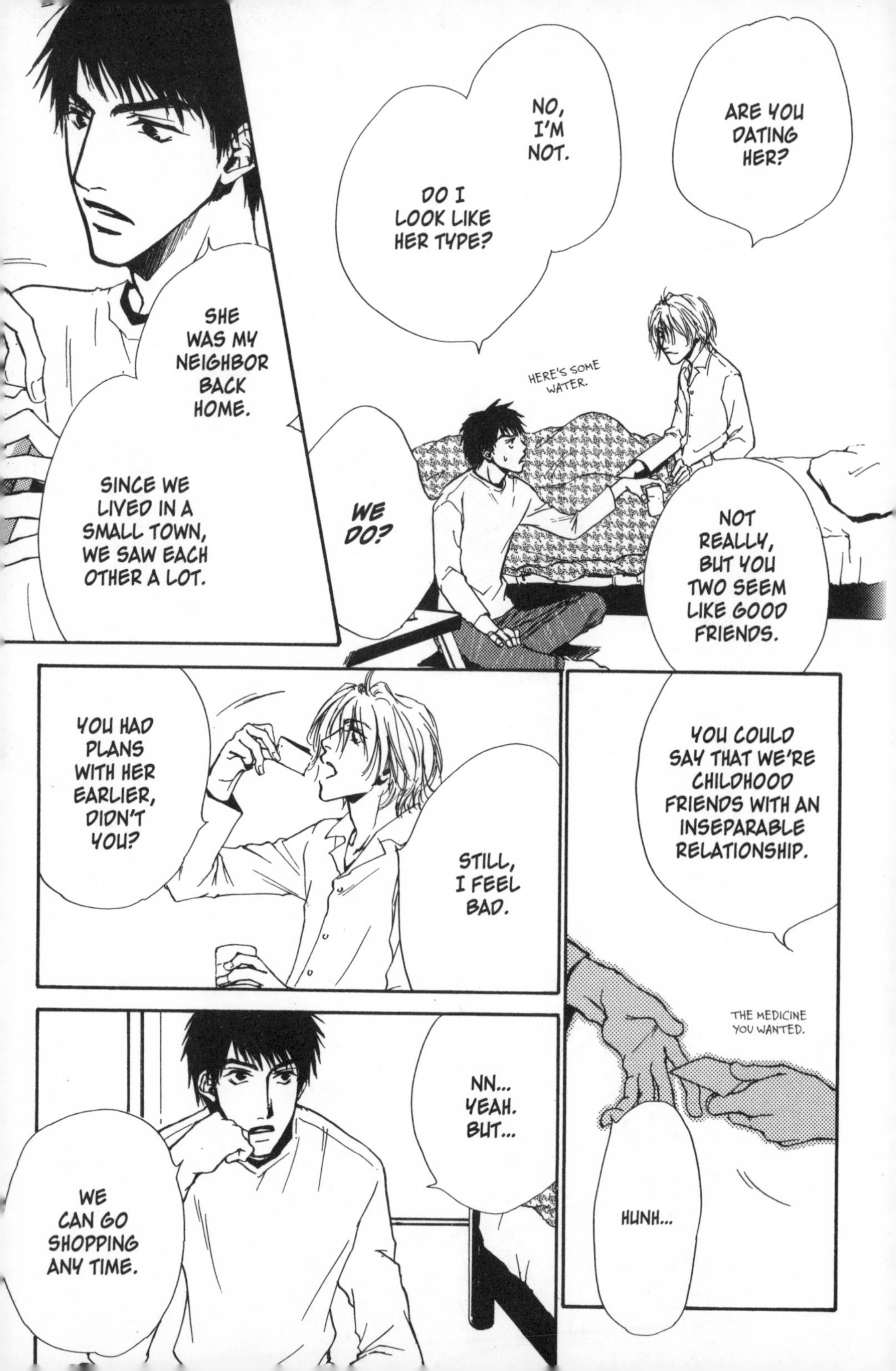
ARE YOU DATING HER?
NO, I'M NOT.
DO I LOOK LIKE HER TYPE?
HERE'S SOME WATER.
NOT REALLY, BUT YOU TWO SEEM LIKE GOOD FRIENDS.
WE DO?
SHE WAS MY NEIGHBOR BACK HOME.
SINCE WE LIVED IN A SMALL TOWN, WE SAW EACH OTHER A LOT.
YOU COULD SAY THAT WE'RE CHILDHOOD FRIENDS WITH AN INSEPARABLE RELATIONSHIP.
THE MEDICINE YOU WANTED.
HUNH...
YOU HAD PLANS WITH HER EARLIER, DIDN'T YOU?
STILL, I FEEL BAD.
NN... YEAH. BUT...
WE CAN GO SHOPPING ANY TIME.

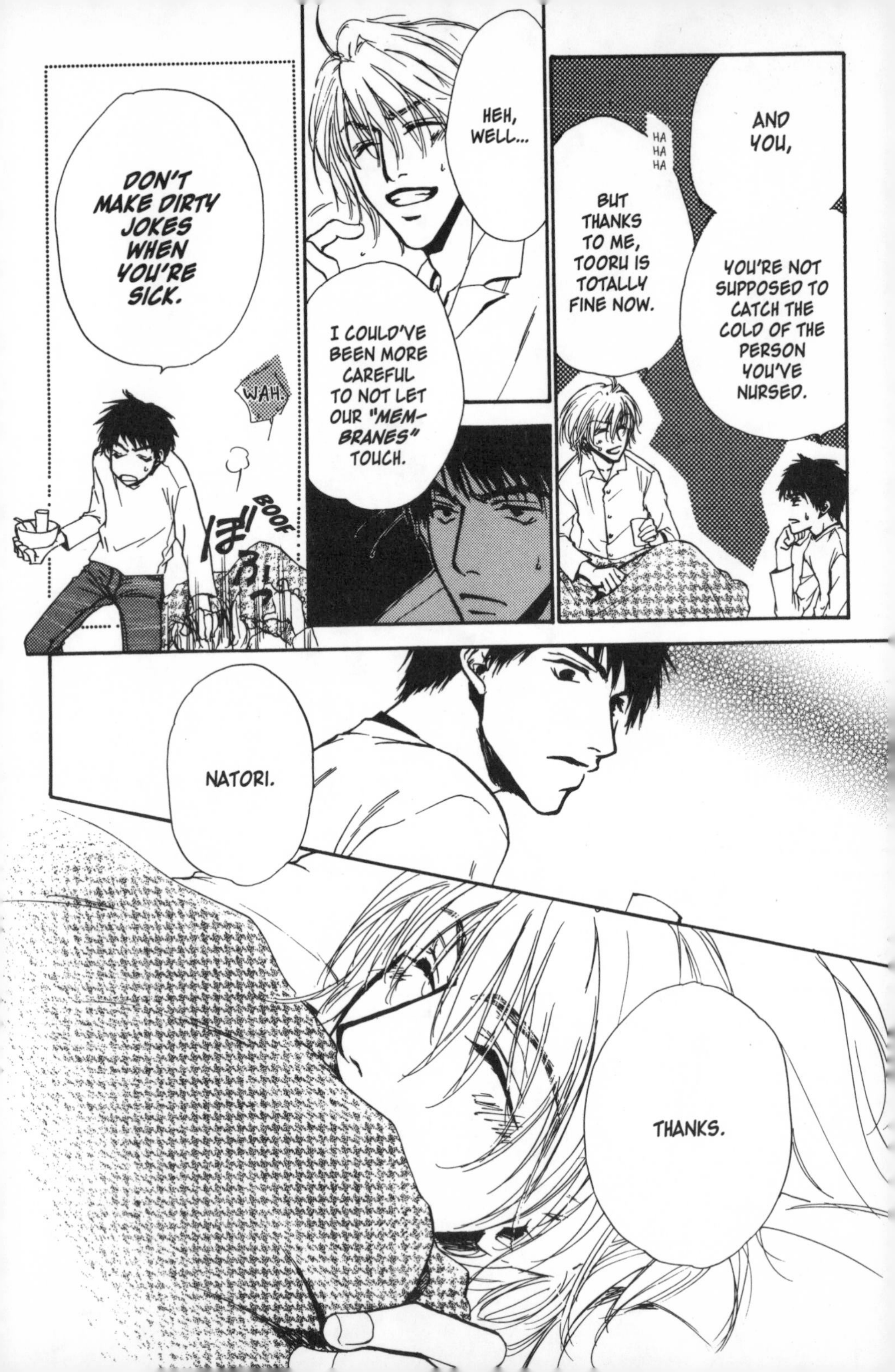
AND YOU,
YOU'RE NOT SUPPOSED TO CATCH THE COLD OF THE PERSON YOU'VE NURSED.
HA HA HA
BUT THANKS TO ME, TOORU IS TOTALLY FINE NOW.
HEH, WELL...
I COULD'VE BEEN MORE CAREFUL TO NOT LET OUR "MEM-BRANES" TOUCH.
DON'T MAKE DIRTY JOKES WHEN YOU'RE SICK.
WAH.
BOOF
ぼふっ
NATORI.
THANKS.

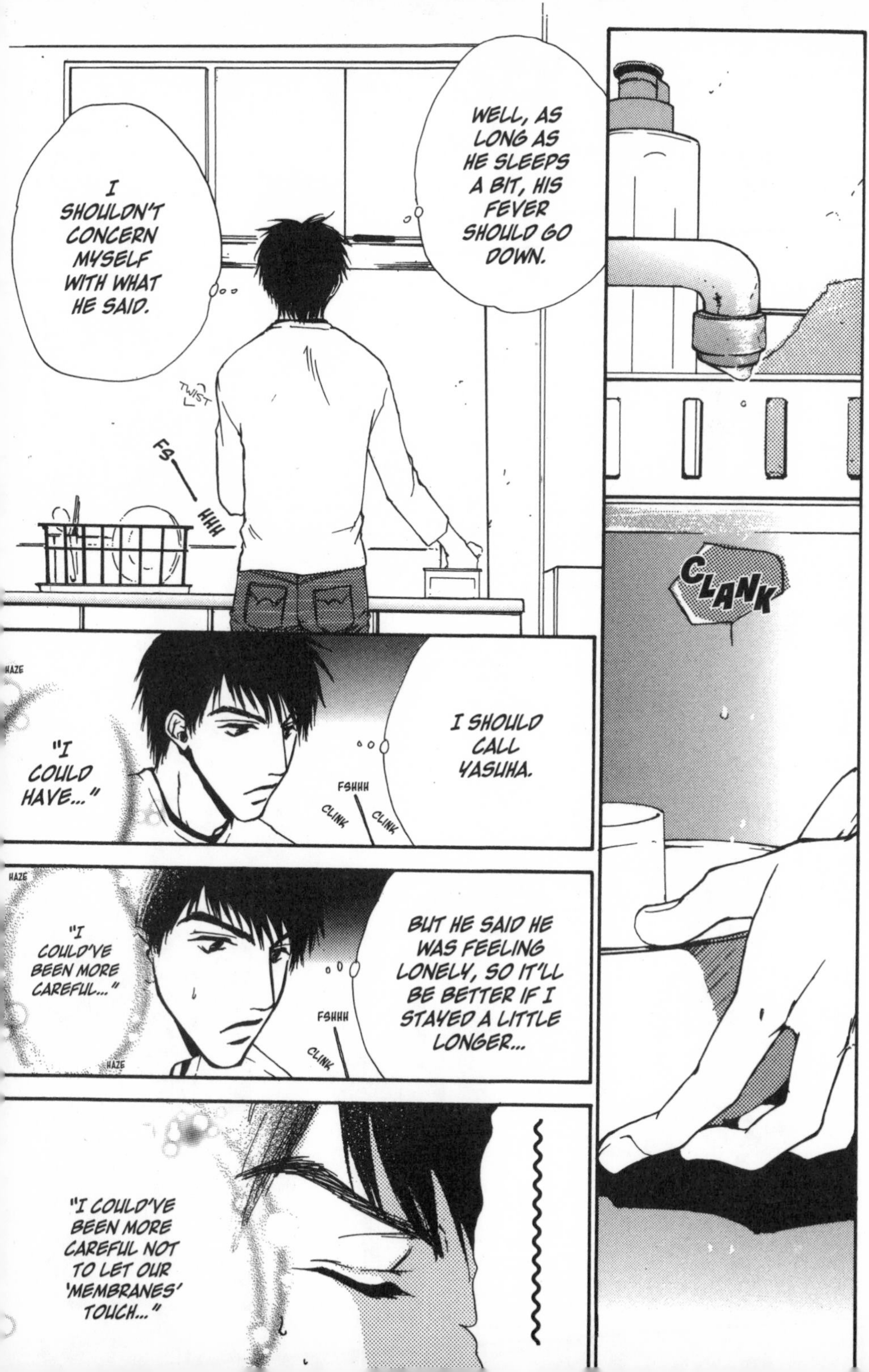
CLANK
WELL, AS LONG AS HE SLEEPS A BIT, HIS FEVER SHOULD GO DOWN.
I SHOULDN'T CONCERN MYSELF WITH WHAT HE SAID.
TWIST
FSHHH
I SHOULD CALL YASUHA.
FSHHH
CLINK
CLINK
"I COULD HAVE..."
HAZE
BUT HE SAID HE WAS FEELING LONELY, SO IT'LL BE BETTER IF I STAYED A LITTLE LONGER...
FSHHH
CLINK
"I COULD'VE BEEN MORE CAREFUL..."
HAZE
HAZE
"I COULD'VE BEEN MORE CAREFUL NOT TO LET OUR 'MEMBRANES' TOUCH..."

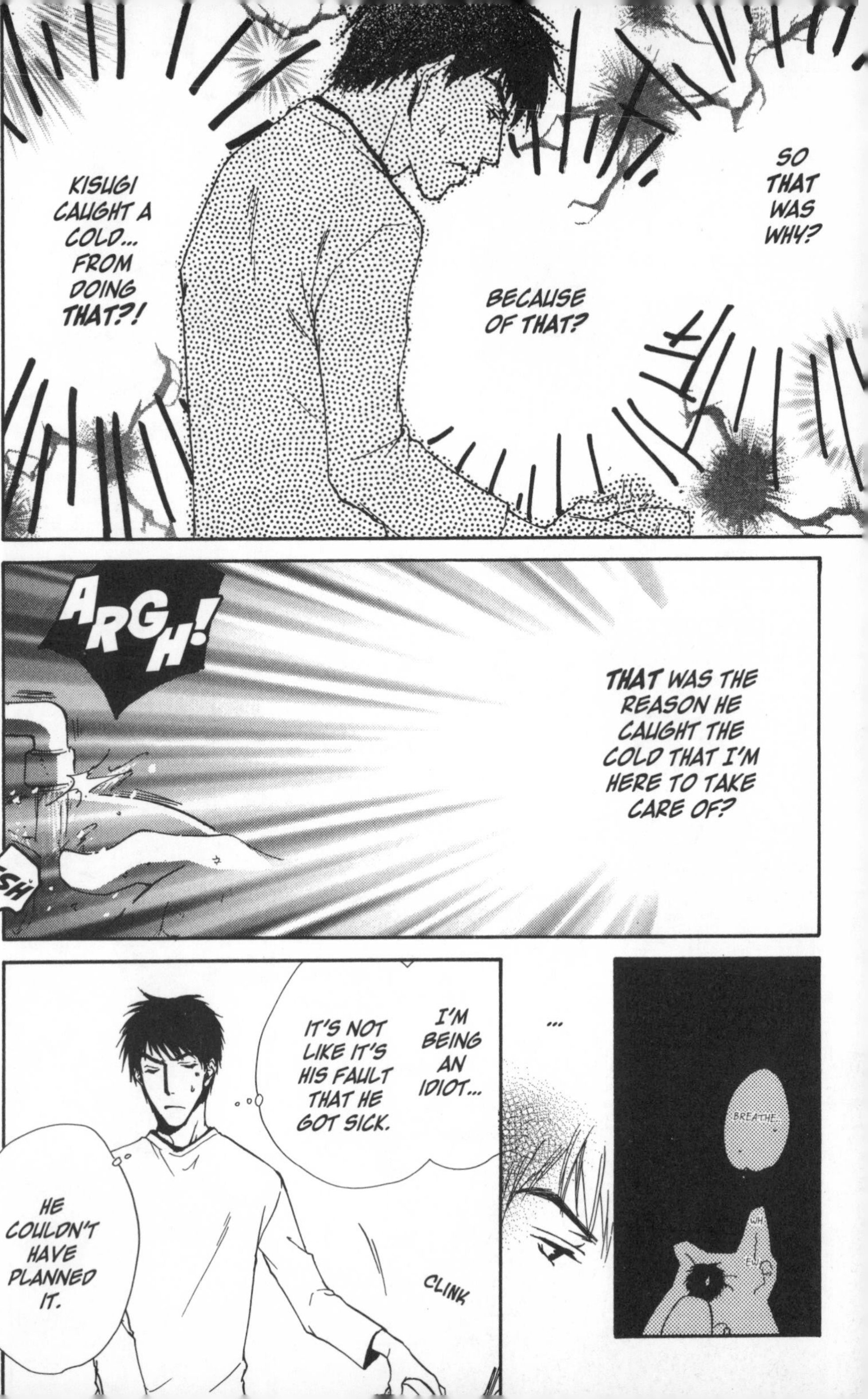
SO THAT WAS WHY?
BECAUSE OF THAT?
KISUGI CAUGHT A COLD... FROM DOING THAT?!
THAT WAS THE REASON HE CAUGHT THE COLD THAT I'M HERE TO TAKE CARE OF?
ARGH!
FSH
BREATHE...
...
I'M BEING AN IDIOT...
IT'S NOT LIKE IT'S HIS FAULT THAT HE GOT SICK.
HE COULDN'T HAVE PLANNED IT.
CLINK

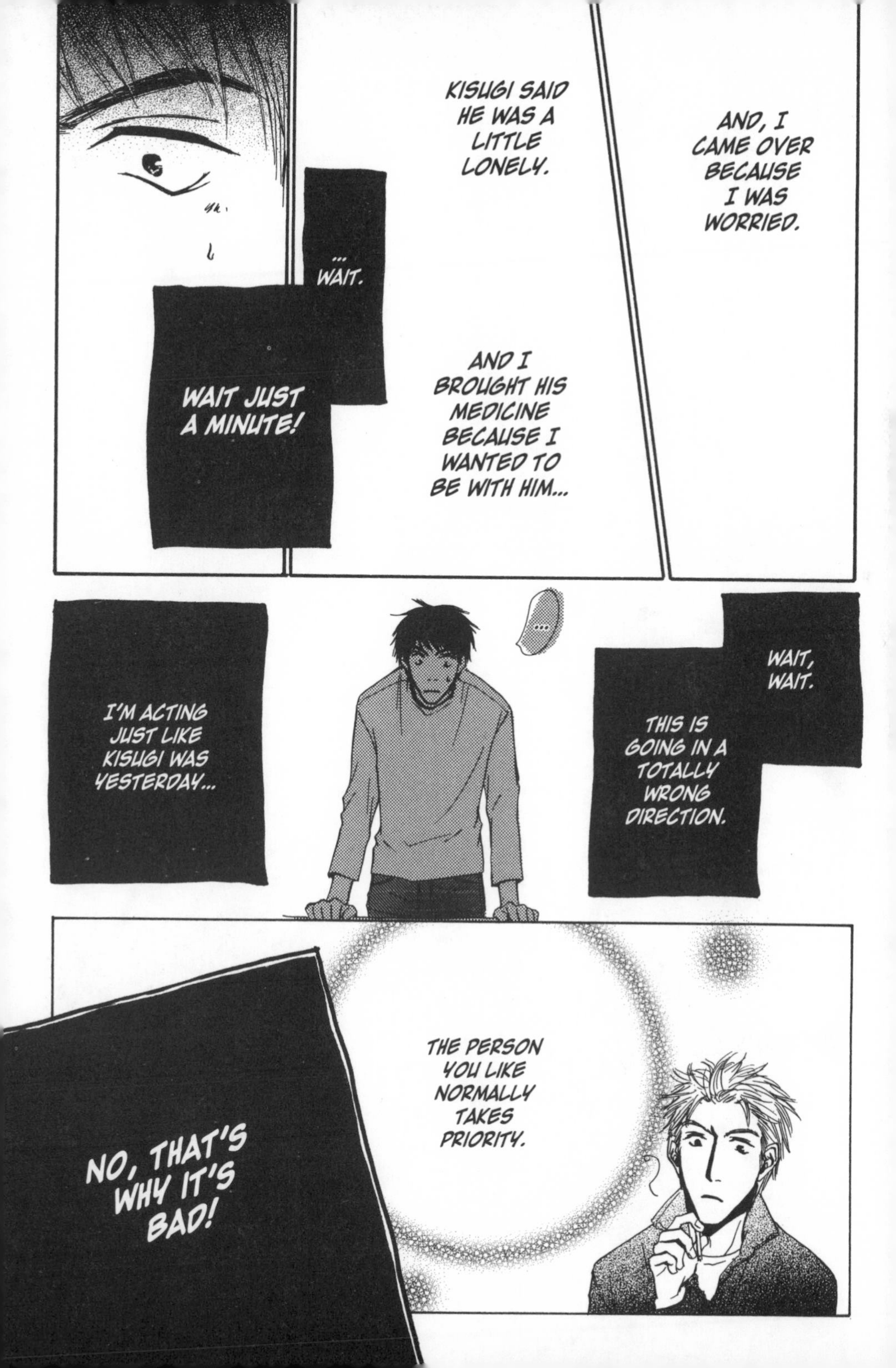
AND, I CAME OVER BECAUSE I WAS WORRIED.
KISUGI SAID HE WAS A LITTLE LONELY.
AND I BROUGHT HIS MEDICINE BECAUSE I WANTED TO BE WITH HIM...
...WAIT.
WAIT JUST A MINUTE!
WAIT, WAIT.
THIS IS GOING IN A TOTALLY WRONG DIRECTION.
...
I'M ACTING JUST LIKE KISUGI WAS YESTERDAY...
THE PERSON YOU LIKE NORMALLY TAKES PRIORITY.
NO, THAT'S WHY IT'S BAD!

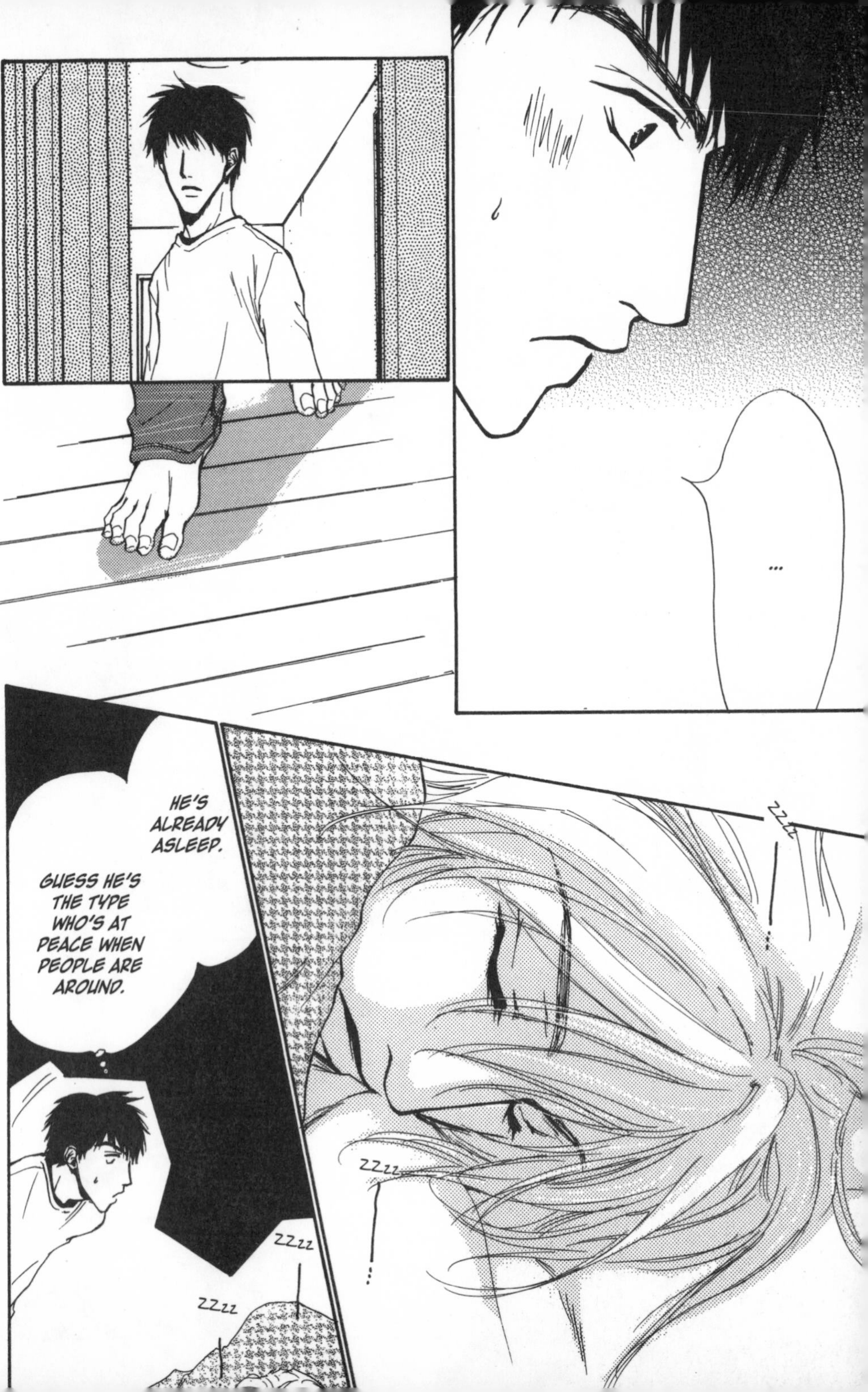
...
ZZZZ
...
ZZzz
...
HE'S ALREADY ASLEEP.
GUESS HE'S THE TYPE WHO'S AT PEACE WHEN PEOPLE ARE AROUND.
ZZzz
ZZzz

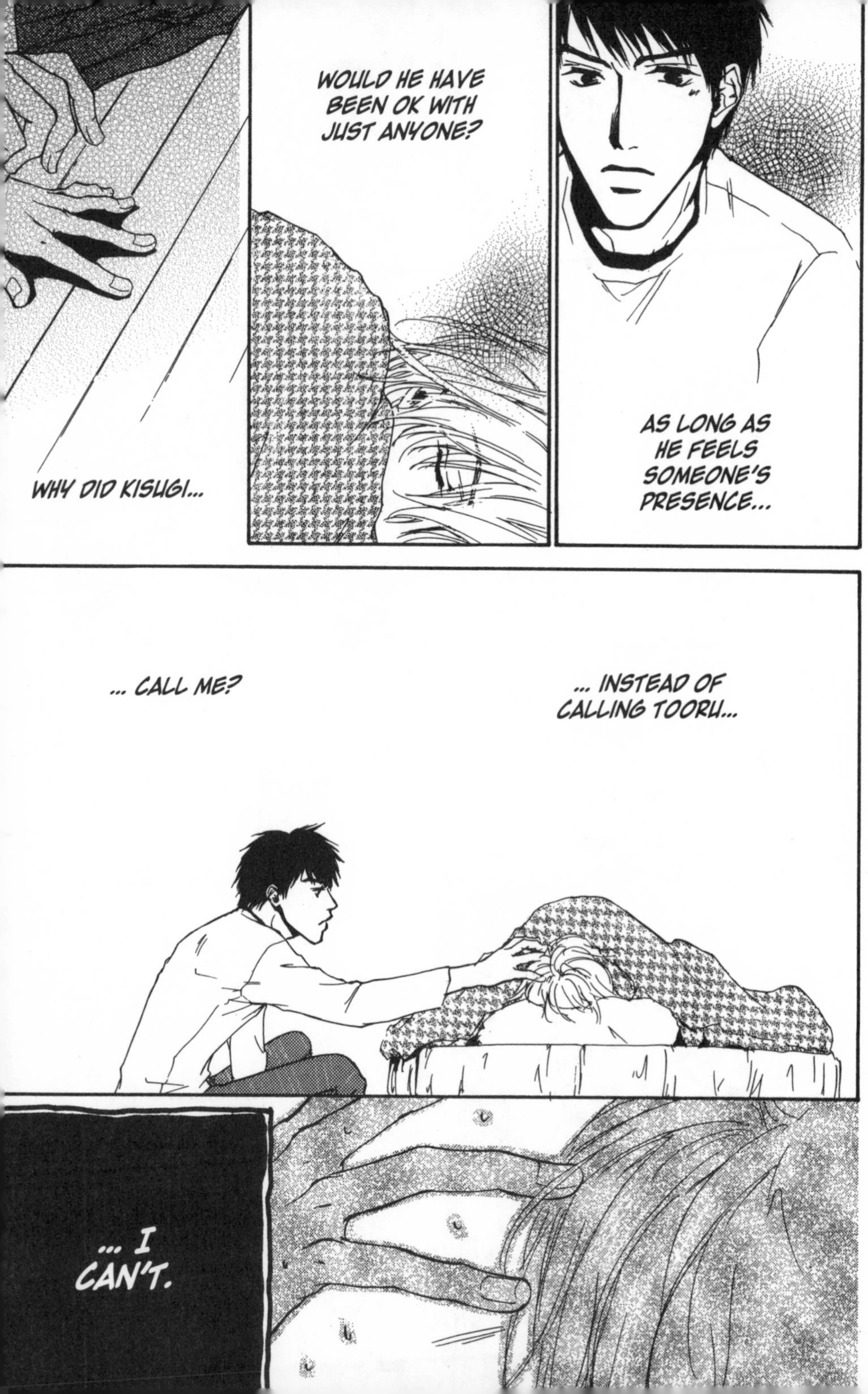
AS LONG AS HE FEELS SOMEONE'S PRESENCE...
WOULD HE HAVE BEEN OK WITH JUST ANYONE?
WHY DID KISUGI...
... INSTEAD OF CALLING TOORU...
... CALL ME?
... I CAN'T.

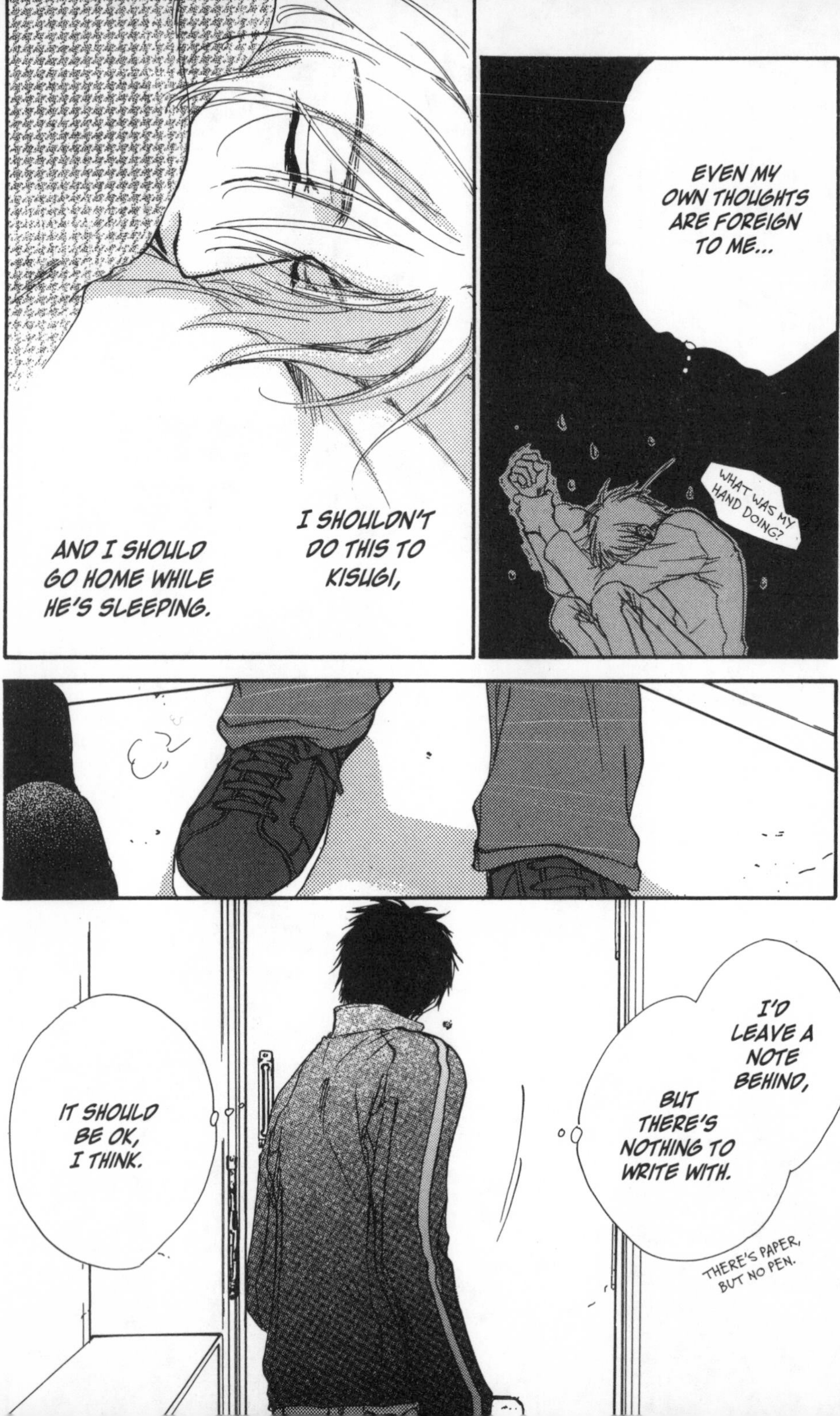
EVEN MY OWN THOUGHTS ARE FOREIGN TO ME...
WHAT WAS MY HAND DOING?
I SHOULDN'T DO THIS TO KISUGI,
AND I SHOULD GO HOME WHILE HE'S SLEEPING.
I'D LEAVE A NOTE BEHIND,
BUT THERE'S NOTHING TO WRITE WITH.
THERE'S PAPER, BUT NO PEN.
IT SHOULD BE OK, I THINK.

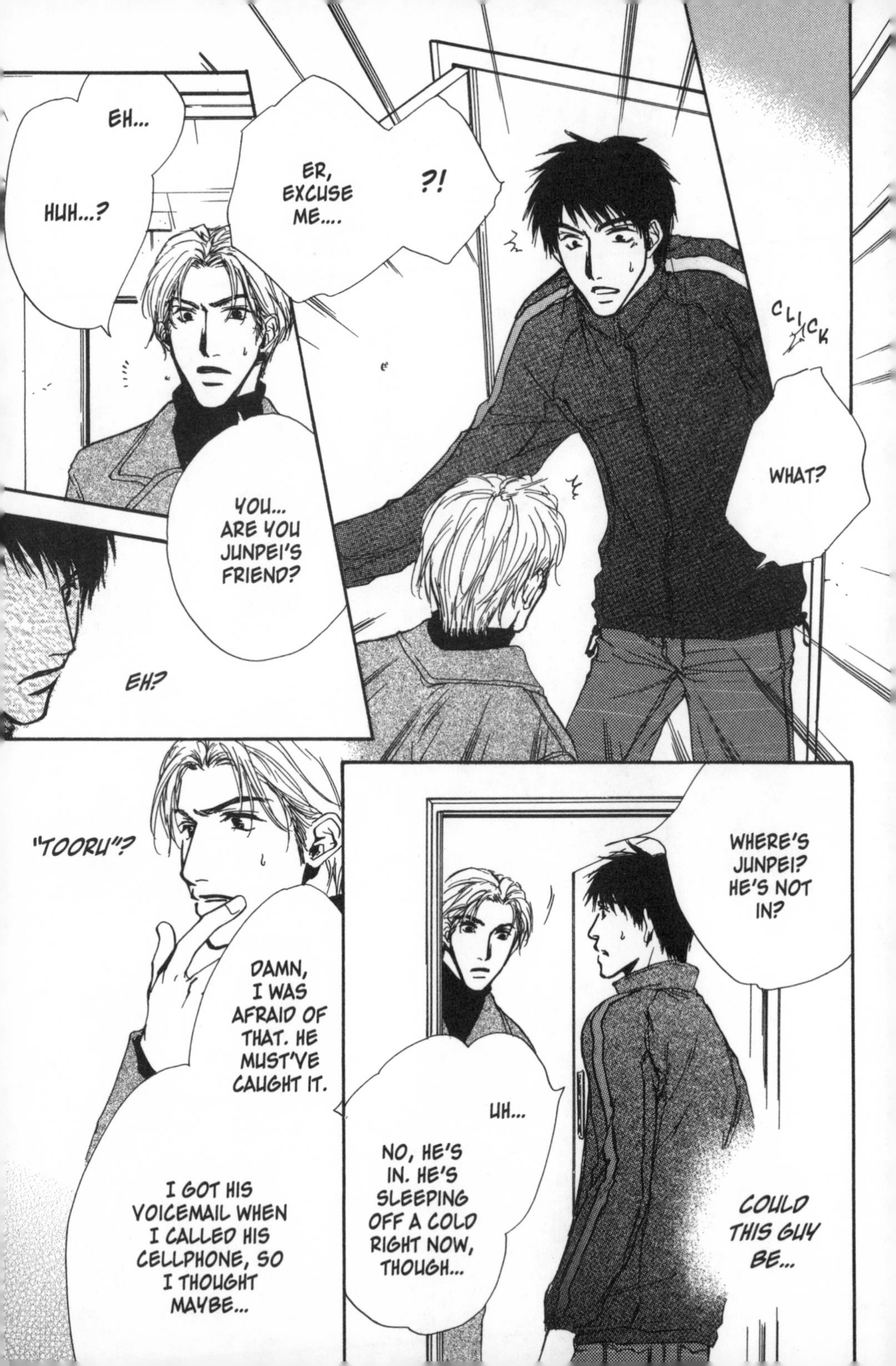
?!
ER, EXCUSE ME....
CLICK
WHAT?
EH...
HUH...?
YOU... ARE YOU JUNPEI'S FRIEND?
EH?
WHERE'S JUNPEI? HE'S NOT IN?
UH...
NO, HE'S IN. HE'S SLEEPING OFF A COLD RIGHT NOW, THOUGH...
COULD THIS GUY BE...
"TOORU"?
DAMN, I WAS AFRAID OF THAT. HE MUST'VE CAUGHT IT.
I GOT HIS VOICEMAIL WHEN I CALLED HIS CELLPHONE, SO I THOUGHT MAYBE...

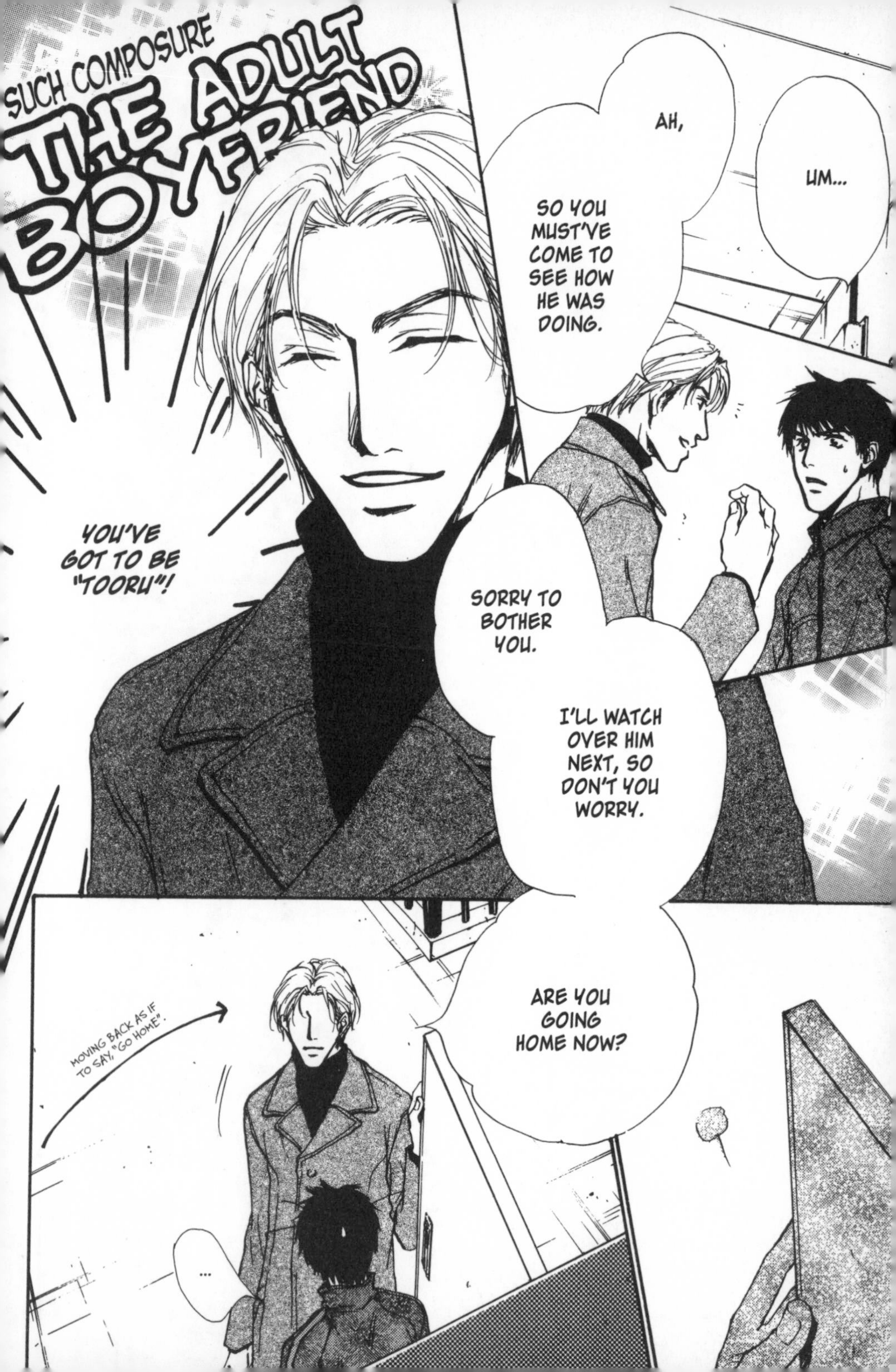
UM...
AH,
SO YOU MUST'VE COME TO SEE HOW HE WAS DOING.
SUCH COMPOSURE
THE ADULT BOYFRIEND
YOU'VE GOT TO BE "TOORU"!
SORRY TO BOTHER YOU.
I'LL WATCH OVER HIM NEXT, SO DON'T YOU WORRY.
ARE YOU GOING HOME NOW?
MOVING BACK AS IF TO SAY, "GO HOME".
...

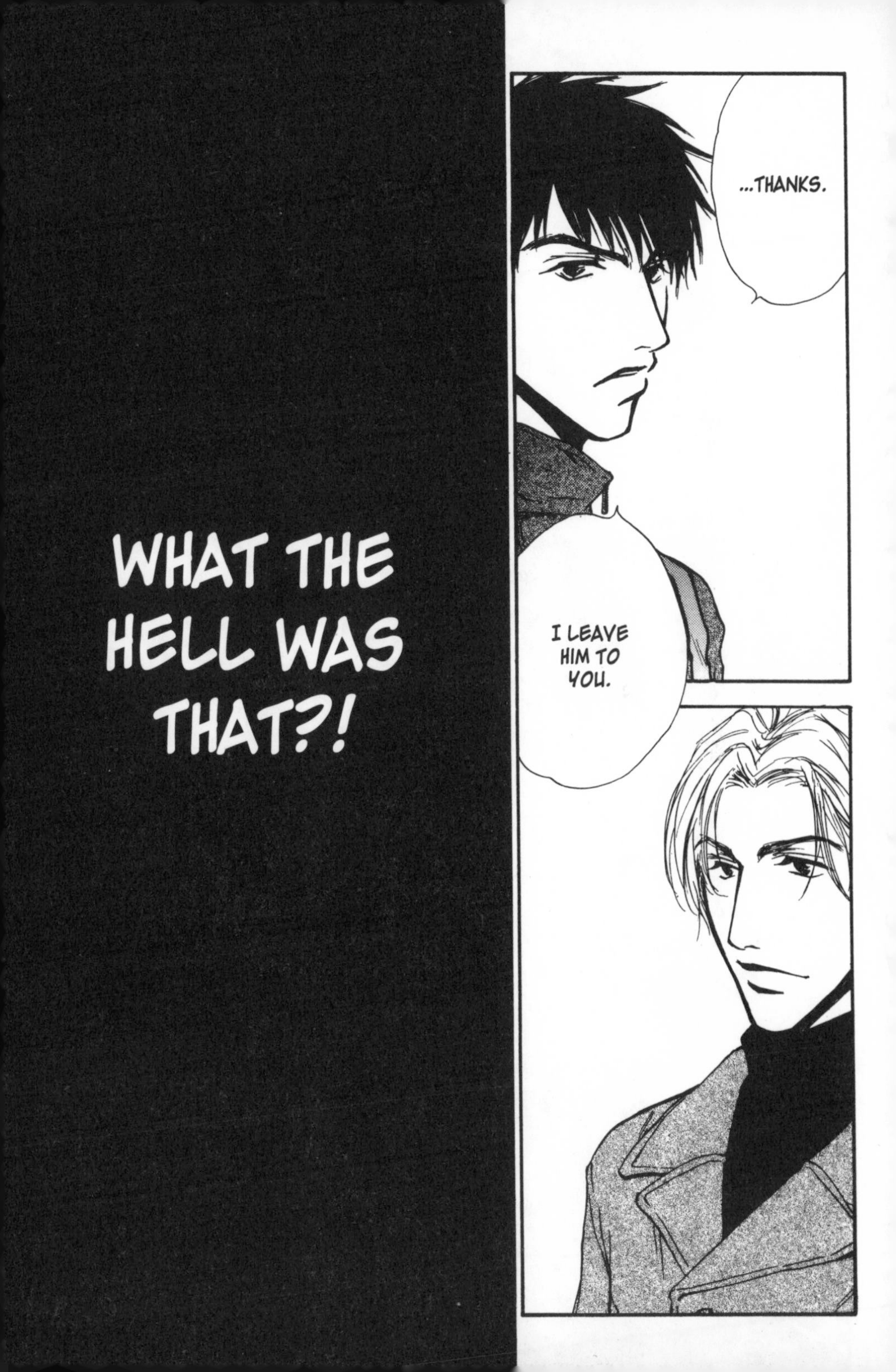
...THANKS.
I LEAVE HIM TO YOU.
WHAT THE HELL WAS THAT?!

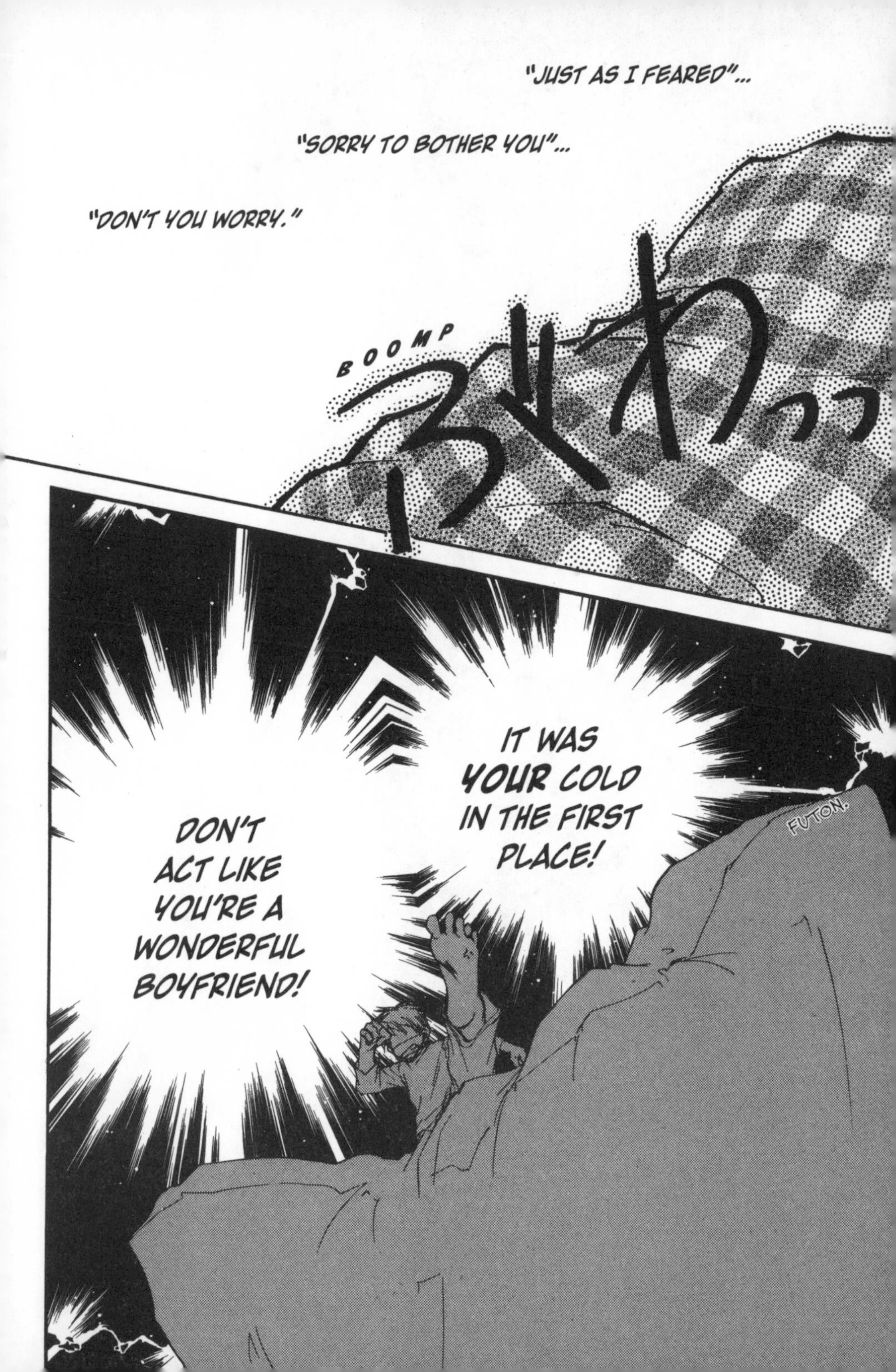
"JUST AS I FEARED"...
"SORRY TO BOTHER YOU"...
"DON'T YOU WORRY."
BOOMP
ろさわっっ
FUTON.
IT WAS **YOUR** COLD IN THE FIRST PLACE!
DON'T ACT LIKE YOU'RE A WONDERFUL BOYFRIEND!

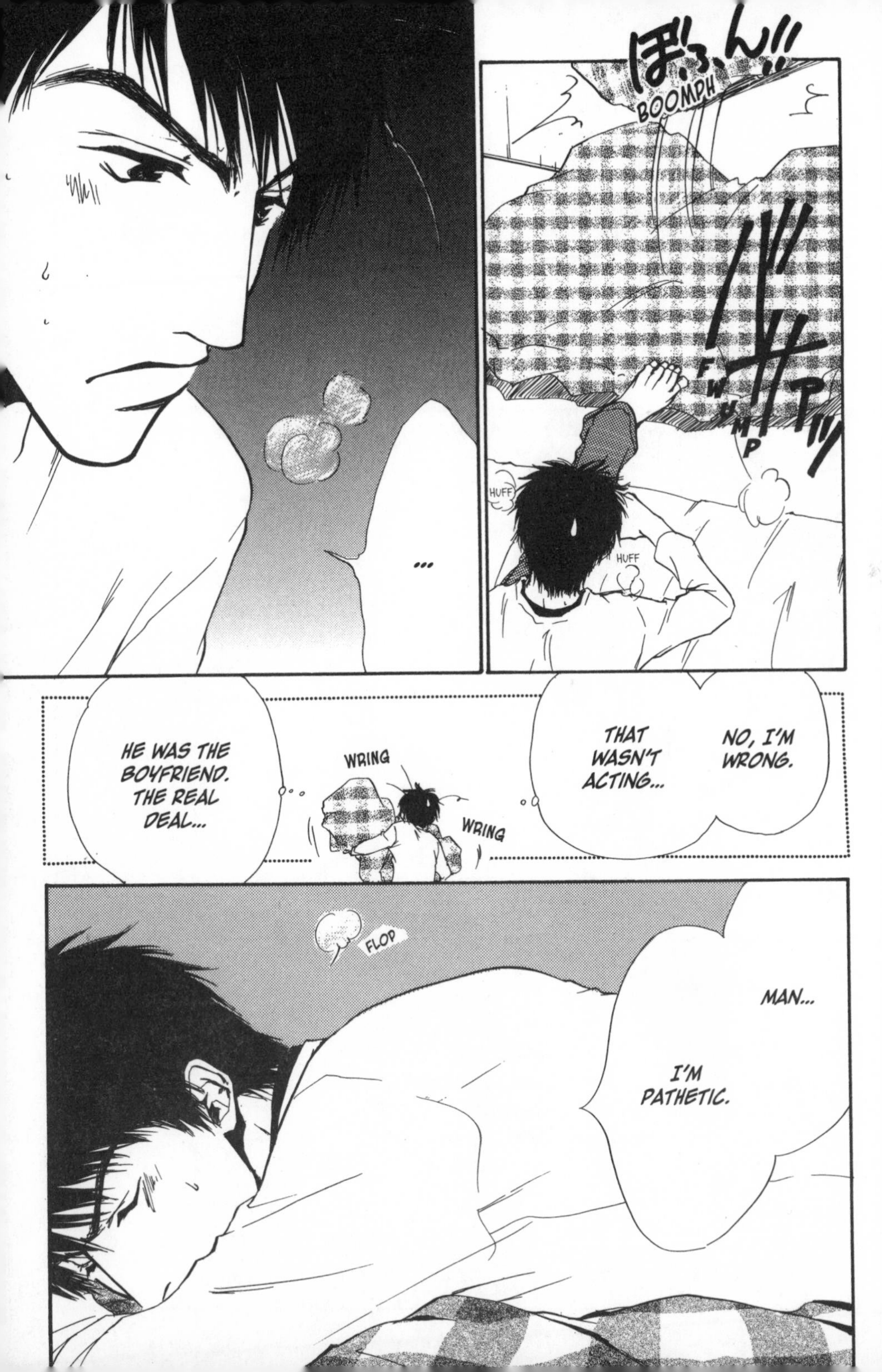
ぼふん!!
BOOMPH
FWUMP
HUFF
HUFF
...
NO, I'M WRONG.
THAT WASN'T ACTING...
WRING
WRING
HE WAS THE BOYFRIEND. THE REAL DEAL...
FLOP
MAN...
I'M PATHETIC.

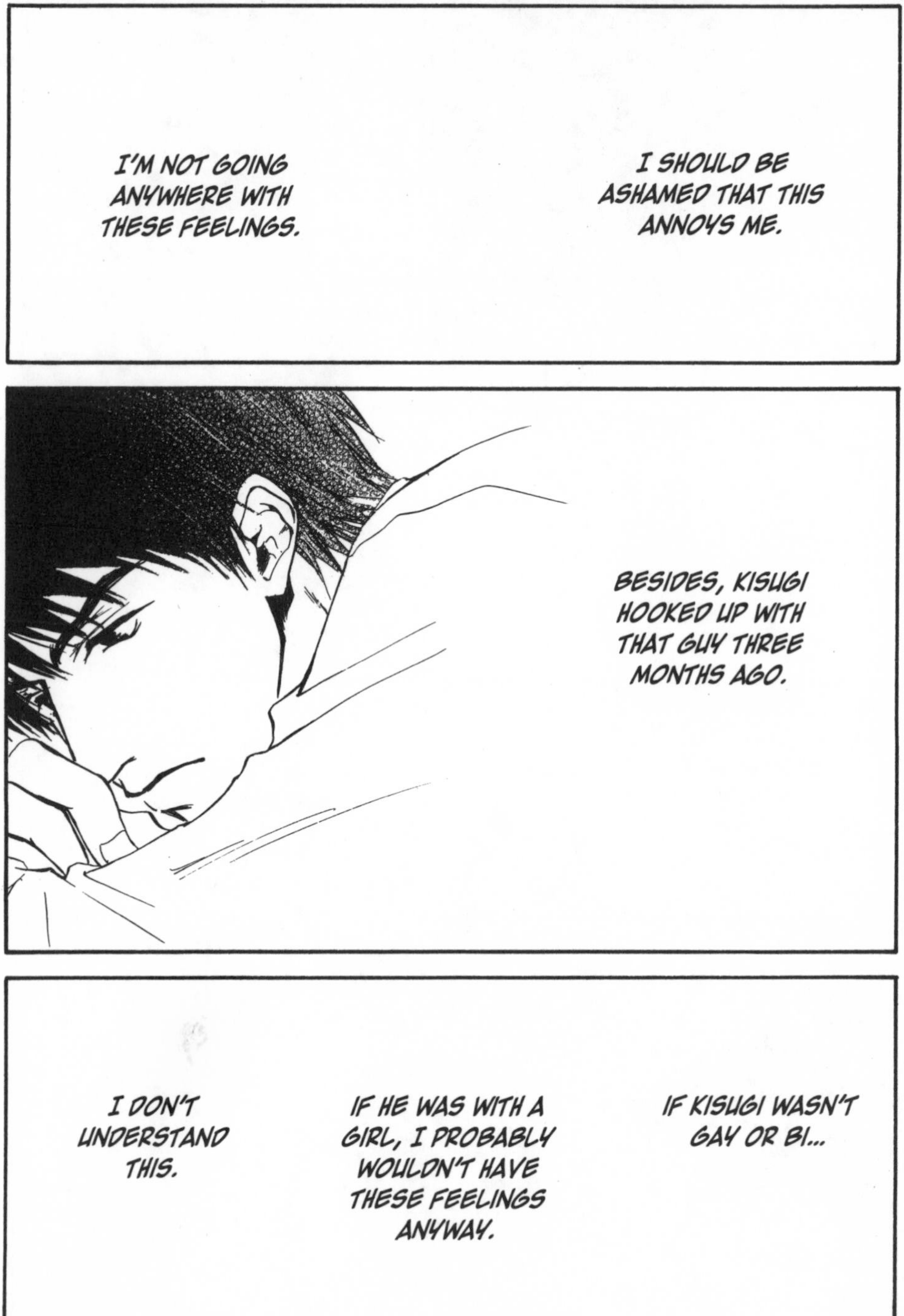
I SHOULD BE ASHAMED THAT THIS ANNOYS ME.
I'M NOT GOING ANYWHERE WITH THESE FEELINGS.
BESIDES, KISUGI HOOKED UP WITH THAT GUY THREE MONTHS AGO.
IF KISUGI WASN'T GAY OR BI...
IF HE WAS WITH A GIRL, I PROBABLY WOULDN'T HAVE THESE FEELINGS ANYWAY.
I DON'T UNDERSTAND THIS.

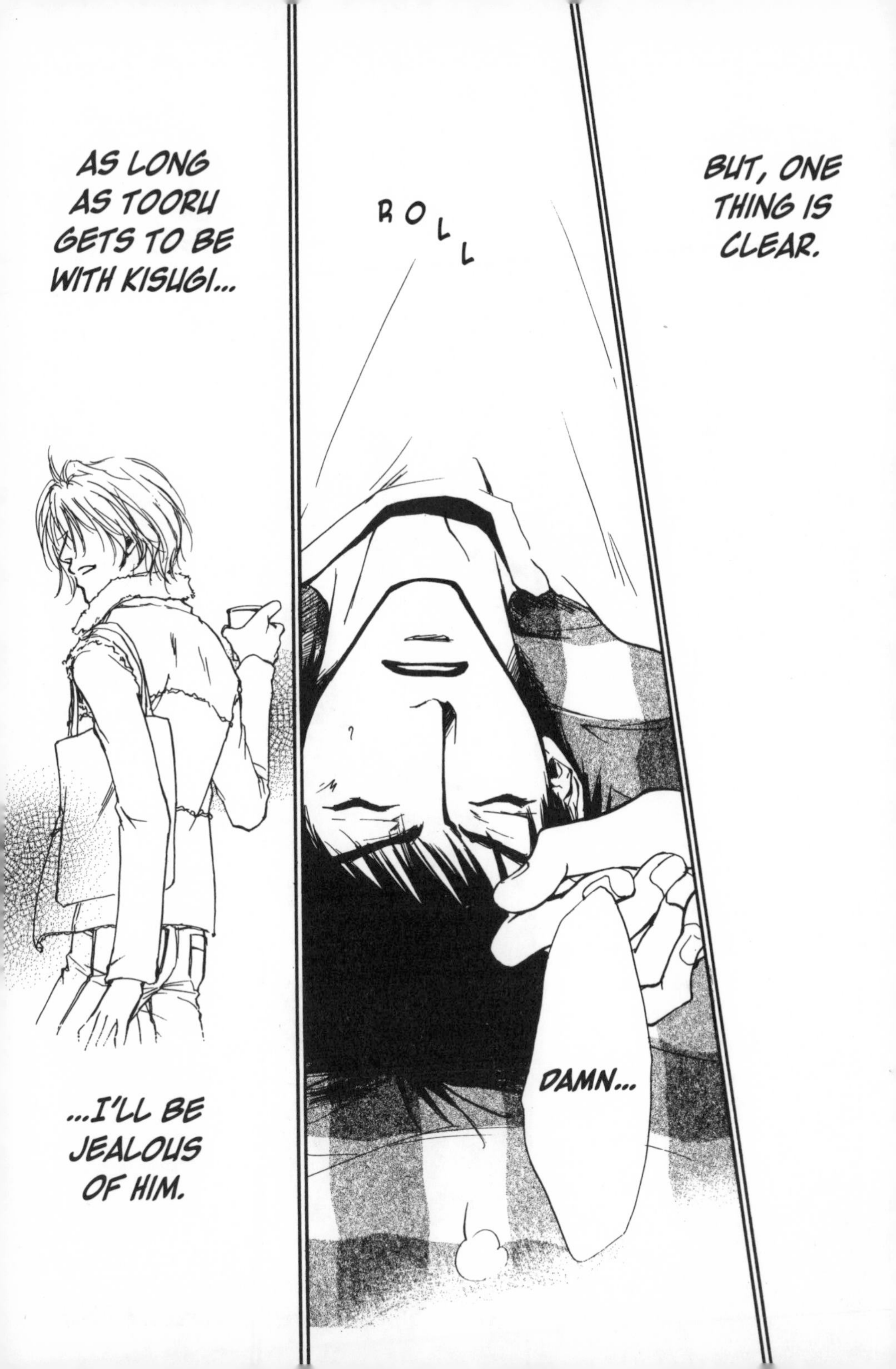
BUT, ONE THING IS CLEAR.
ROLL
DAMN...
AS LONG AS TOORU GETS TO BE WITH KISUGI...
...I'LL BE JEALOUS OF HIM.

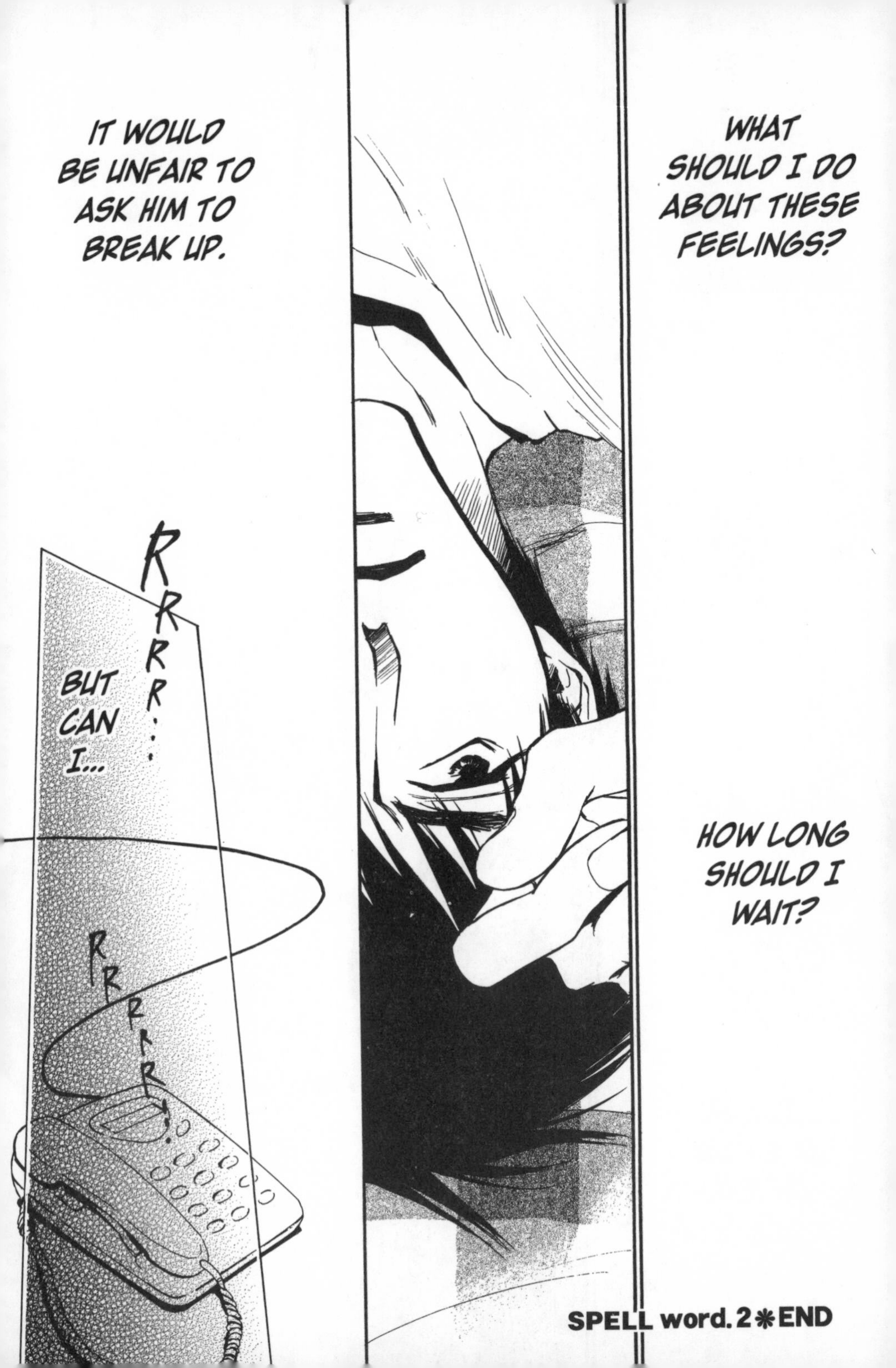
WHAT SHOULD I DO ABOUT THESE FEELINGS?
HOW LONG SHOULD I WAIT?
SPELL word. 2 * END
IT WOULD BE UNFAIR TO ASK HIM TO BREAK UP.
RRRR...
BUT CAN I...
RRRRRR...

スペル word.3 Spell

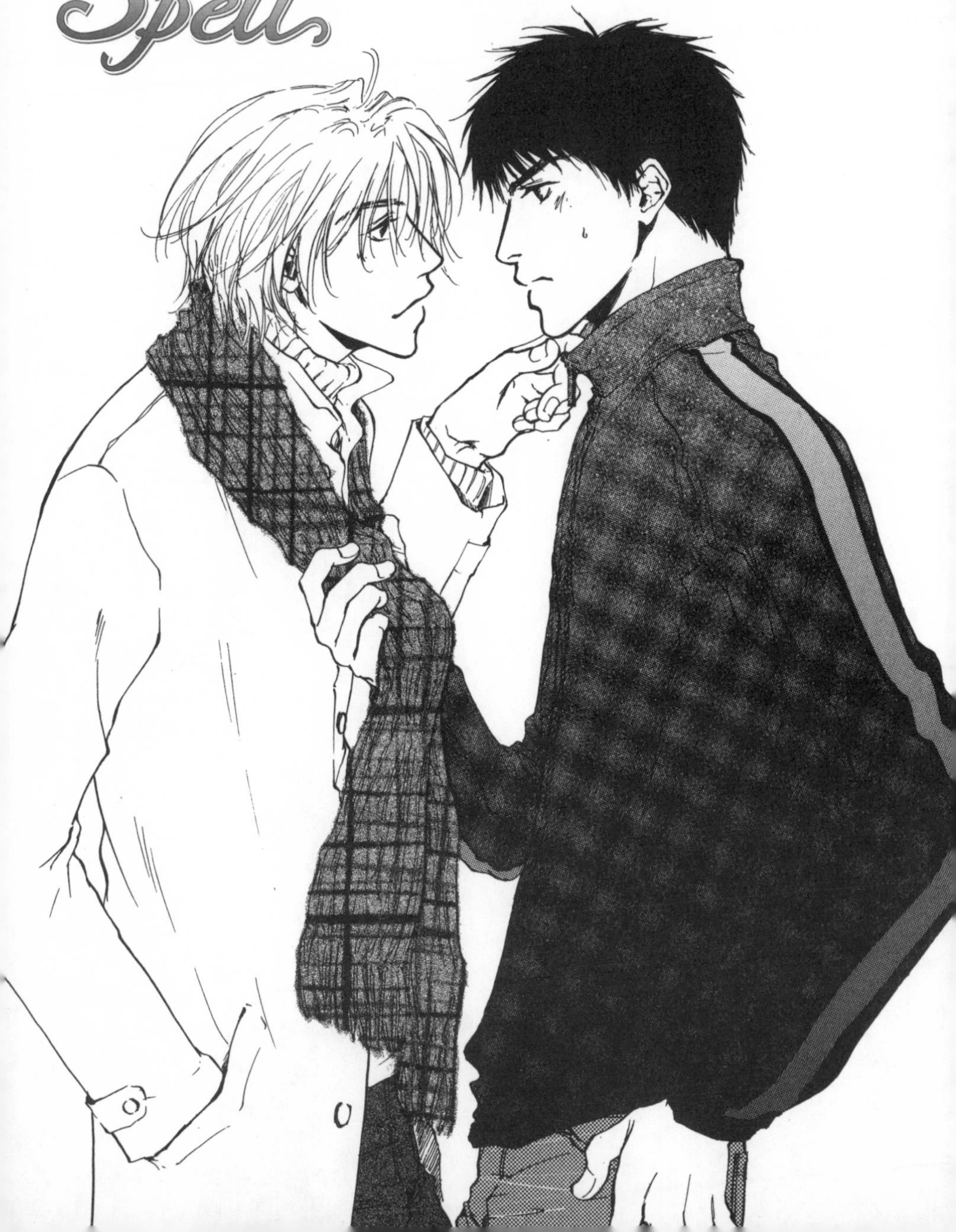

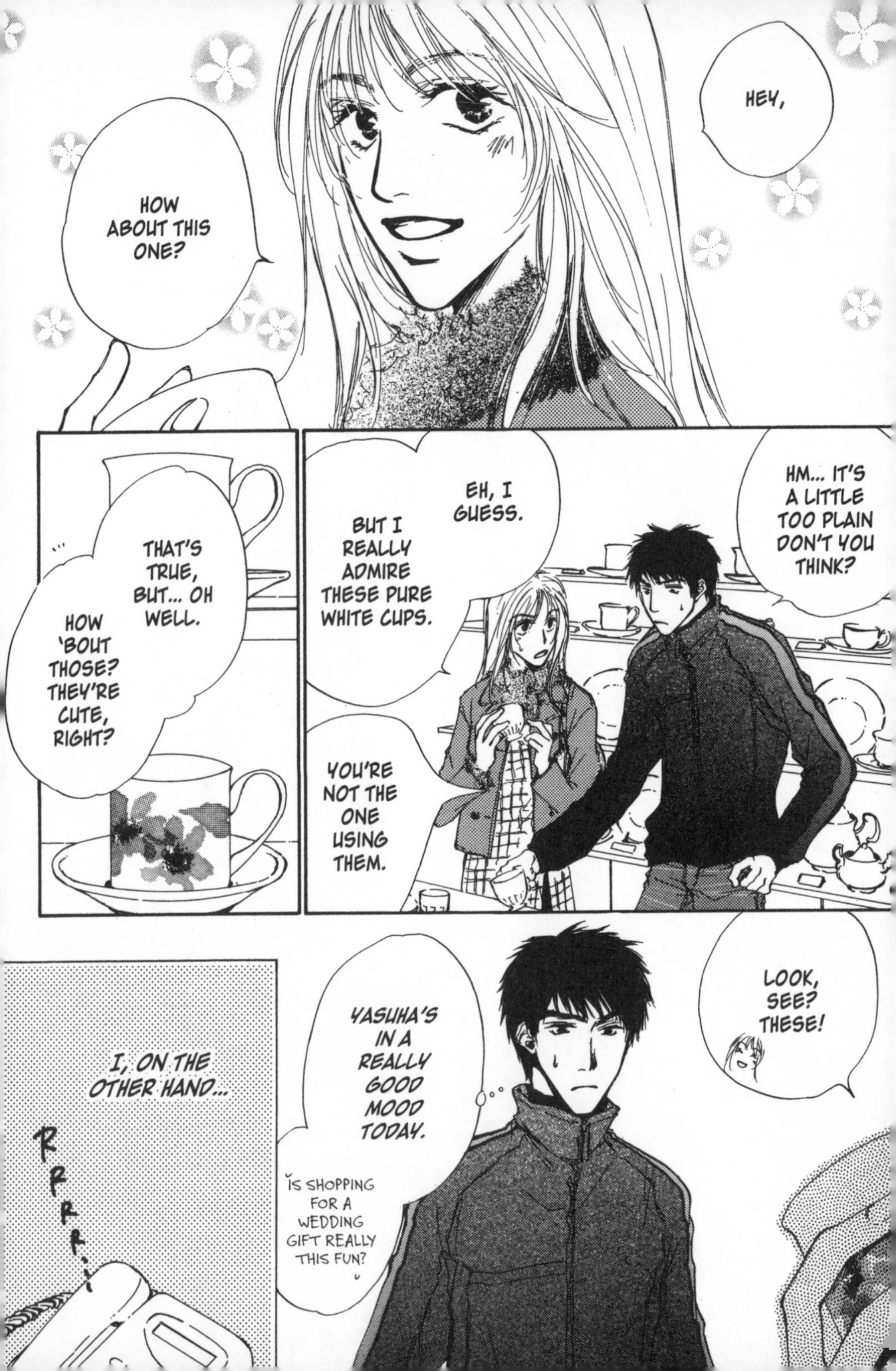
HEY,
HOW ABOUT THIS ONE?
HM... IT'S A LITTLE TOO PLAIN DON'T YOU THINK?
EH, I GUESS.
BUT I REALLY ADMIRE THESE PURE WHITE CUPS.
YOU'RE NOT THE ONE USING THEM.
THAT'S TRUE, BUT... OH WELL.
HOW 'BOUT THOSE? THEY'RE CUTE, RIGHT?
...
LOOK, SEE? THESE!
YASUHA'S IN A REALLY GOOD MOOD TODAY.
IS SHOPPING FOR A WEDDING GIFT REALLY THIS FUN?
I, ON THE OTHER HAND...
RRRR...

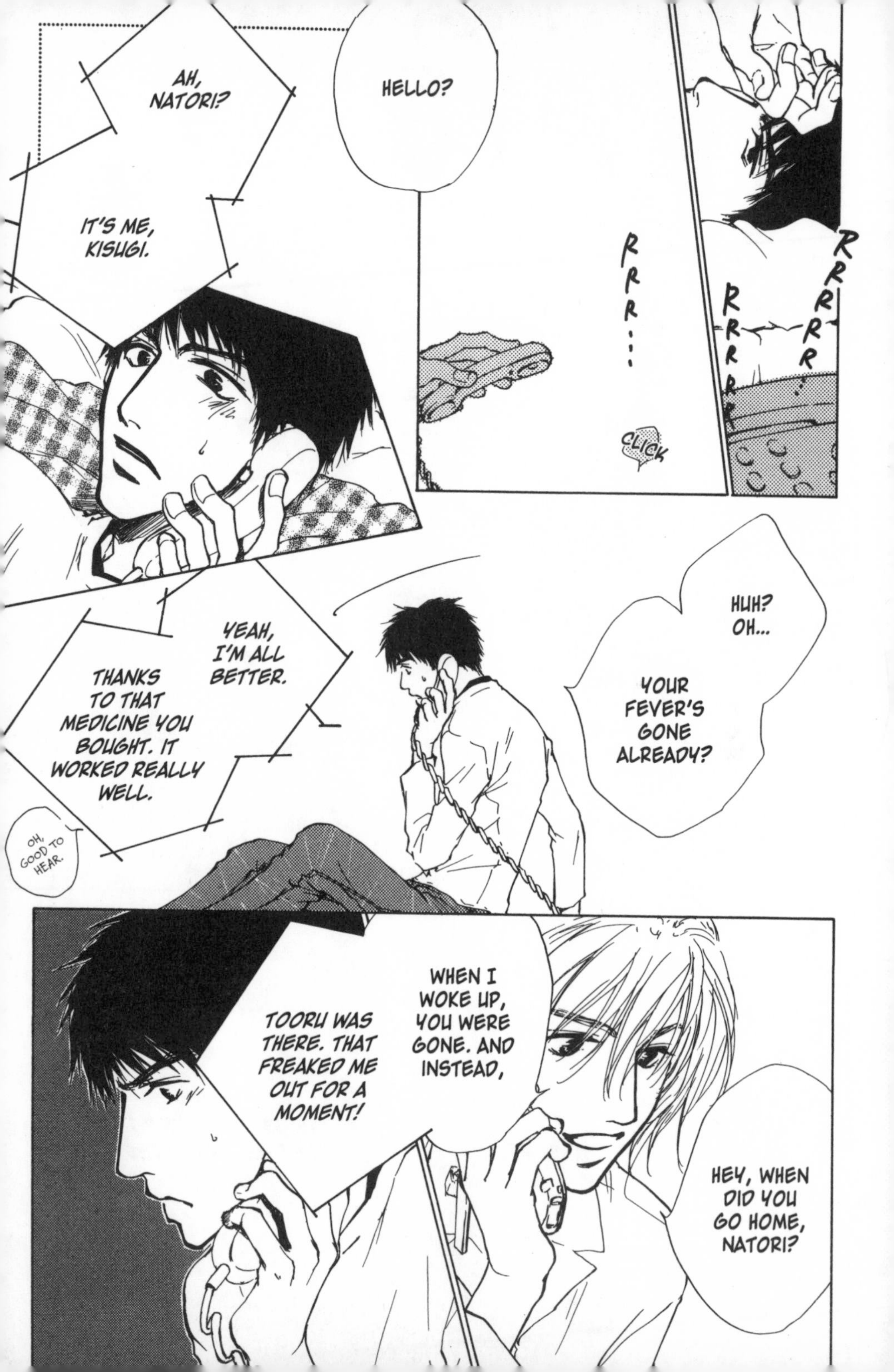
RRRRRR...
RRRRR
RRR...
CLICK
HELLO?
AH, NATORI?
IT'S ME, KISUGI.
HUH? OH...
YOUR FEVER'S GONE ALREADY?
YEAH, I'M ALL BETTER.
THANKS TO THAT MEDICINE YOU BOUGHT. IT WORKED REALLY WELL.
OH, GOOD TO HEAR.
HEY, WHEN DID YOU GO HOME, NATORI?
WHEN I WOKE UP, YOU WERE GONE. AND INSTEAD,
TOORU WAS THERE. THAT FREAKED ME OUT FOR A MOMENT!

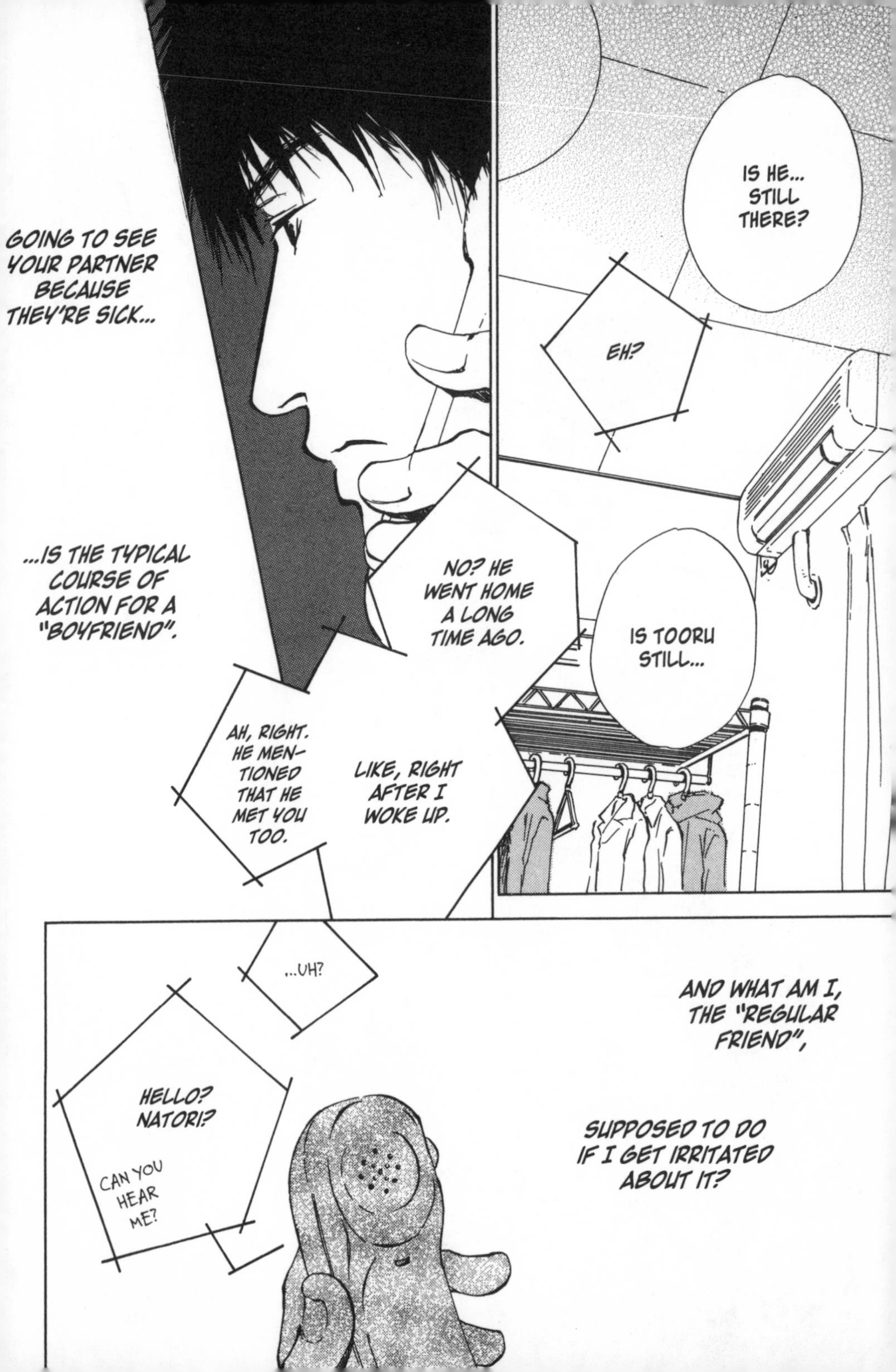

IS HE... STILL THERE?
EH?
IS TOORU STILL...
NO? HE WENT HOME A LONG TIME AGO.
LIKE, RIGHT AFTER I WOKE UP.
AH, RIGHT. HE MENTIONED THAT HE MET YOU TOO.
GOING TO SEE YOUR PARTNER BECAUSE THEY'RE SICK...
...IS THE TYPICAL COURSE OF ACTION FOR A "BOYFRIEND".
AND WHAT AM I, THE "REGULAR FRIEND",
SUPPOSED TO DO IF I GET IRRITATED ABOUT IT?
...UH?
HELLO? NATORI?
CAN YOU HEAR ME?

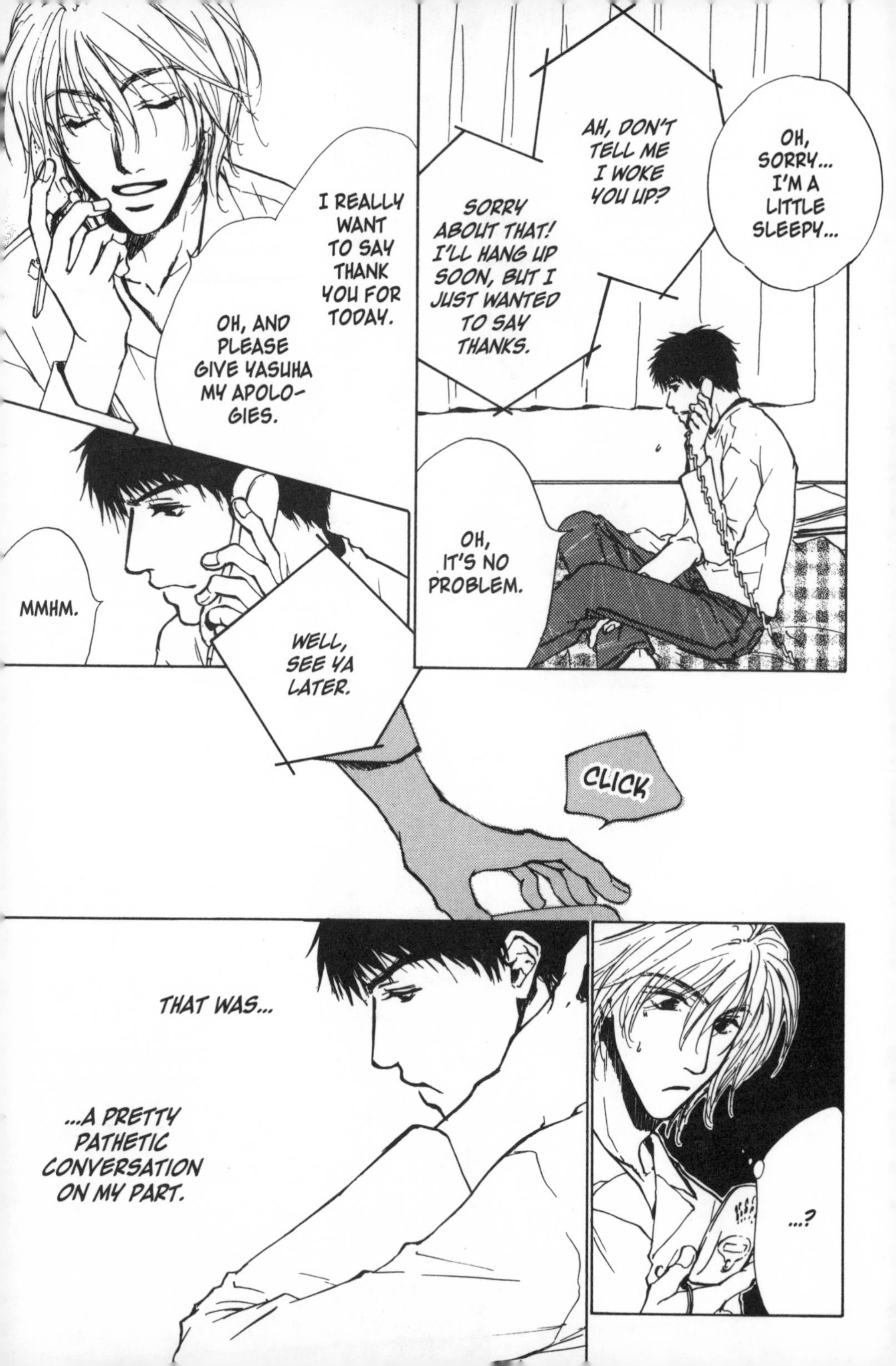
OH, SORRY... I'M A LITTLE SLEEPY...
AH, DON'T TELL ME I WOKE YOU UP?
SORRY ABOUT THAT! I'LL HANG UP SOON, BUT I JUST WANTED TO SAY THANKS.
OH, IT'S NO PROBLEM.
I REALLY WANT TO SAY THANK YOU FOR TODAY.
OH, AND PLEASE GIVE YASUHA MY APOLOGIES.
WELL, SEE YA LATER.
MMHM.
CLICK
...?
THAT WAS...
...A PRETTY PATHETIC CONVERSATION ON MY PART.

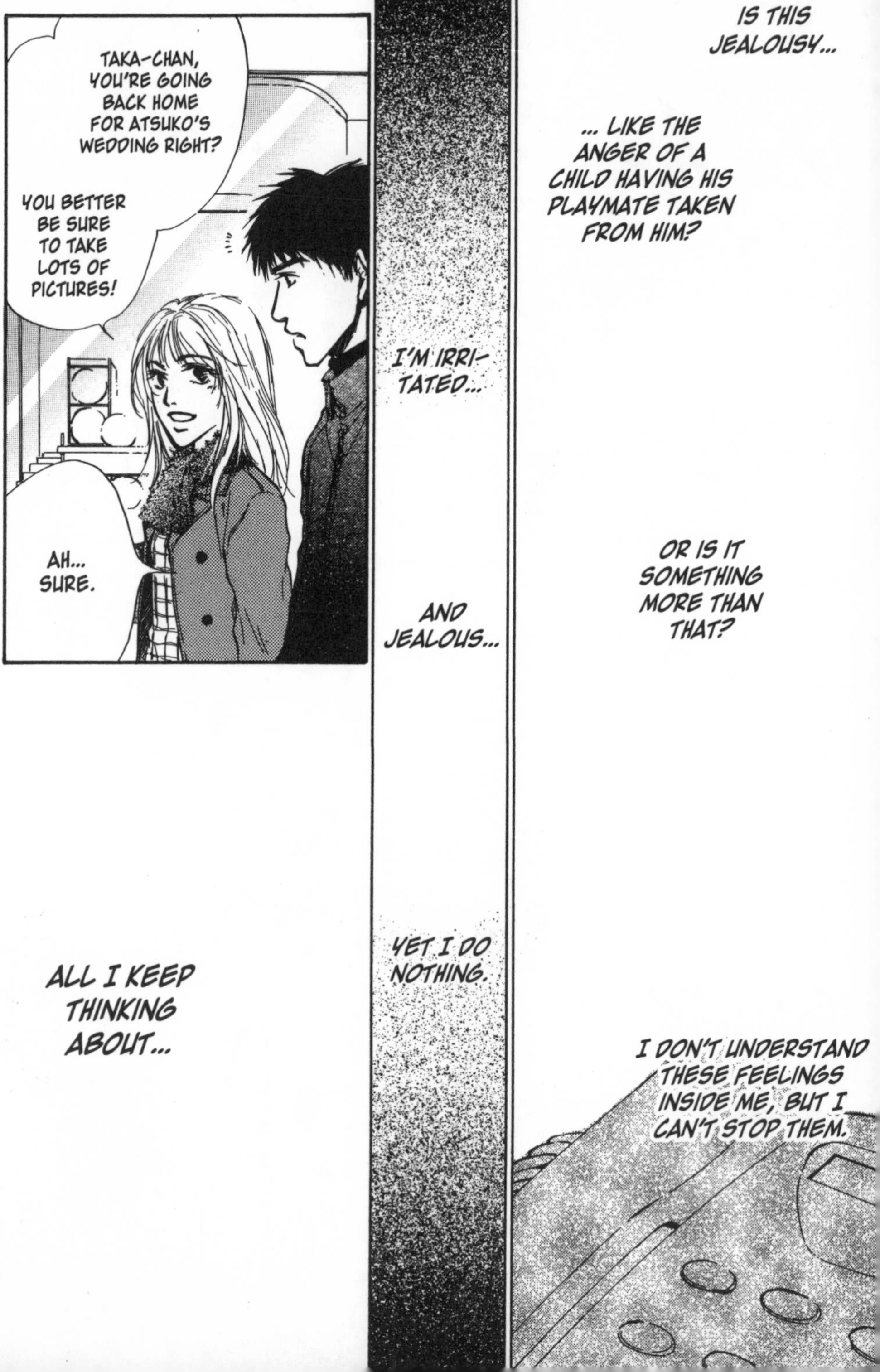
IS THIS JEALOUSY...
... LIKE THE ANGER OF A CHILD HAVING HIS PLAYMATE TAKEN FROM HIM?
OR IS IT SOMETHING MORE THAN THAT?
I DON'T UNDERSTAND THESE FEELINGS INSIDE ME, BUT I CAN'T STOP THEM.
I'M IRRI-TATED...
AND JEALOUS...
YET I DO NOTHING.
TAKA-CHAN, YOU'RE GOING BACK HOME FOR ATSUKO'S WEDDING RIGHT?
YOU BETTER BE SURE TO TAKE LOTS OF PICTURES!
AH... SURE.
ALL I KEEP THINKING ABOUT...

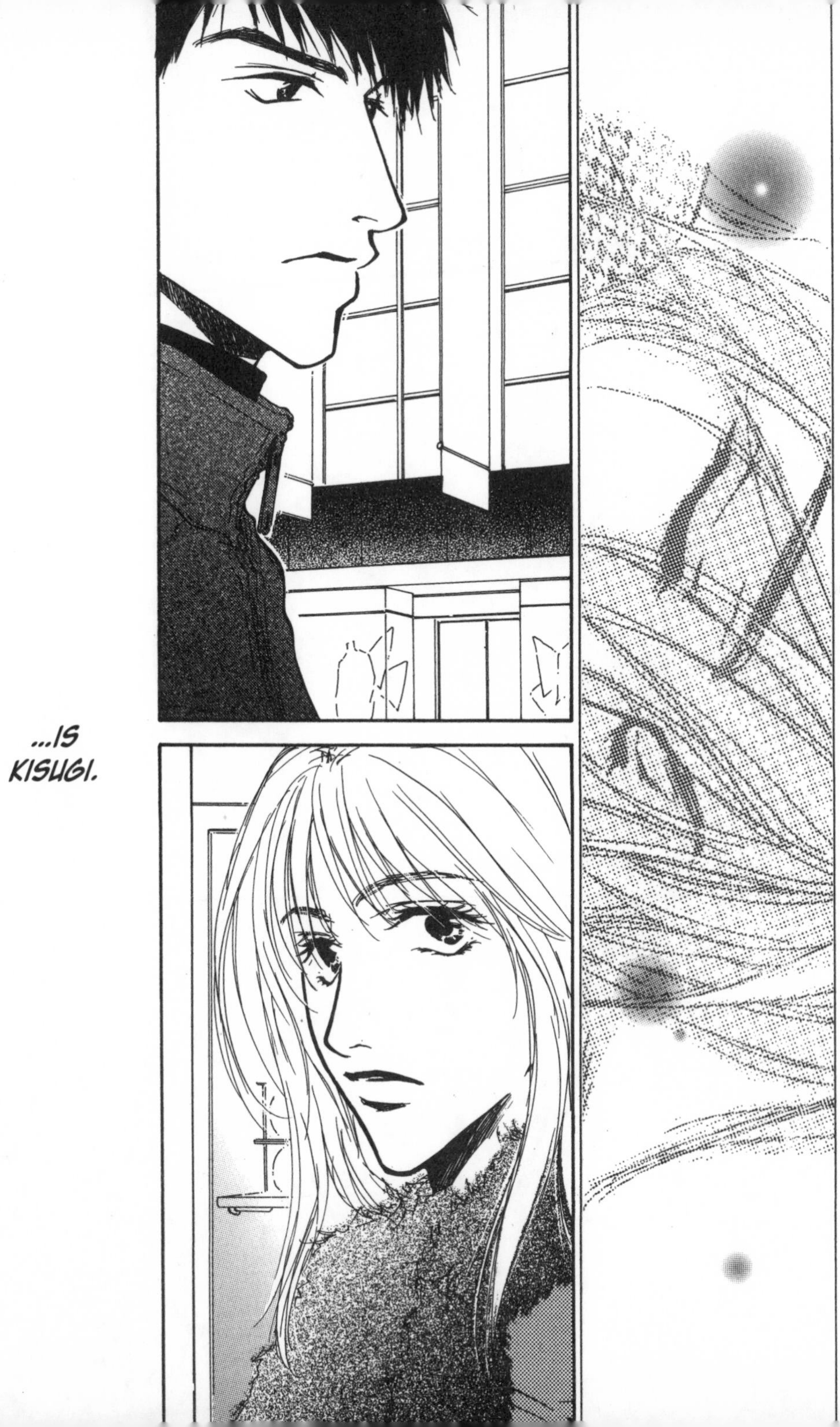
...IS
KISUGI.

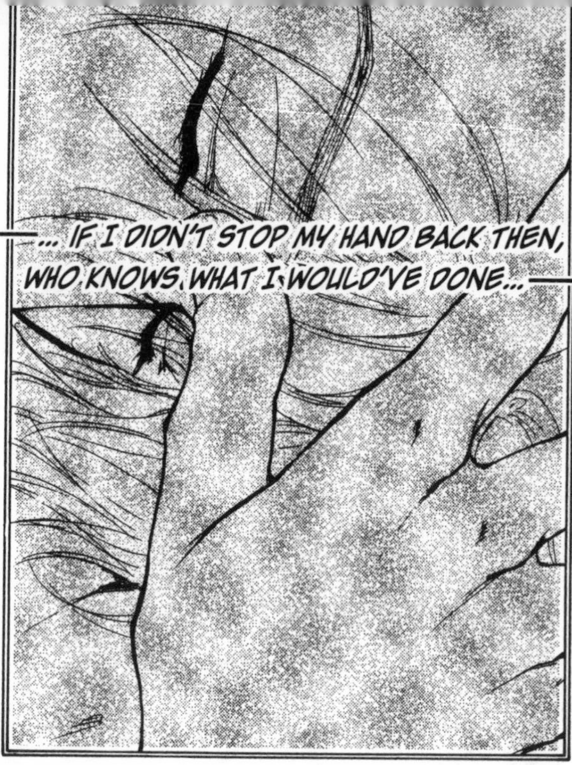
——... IF I DIDN'T STOP MY HAND BACK THEN, WHO KNOWS WHAT I WOULD'VE DONE...——

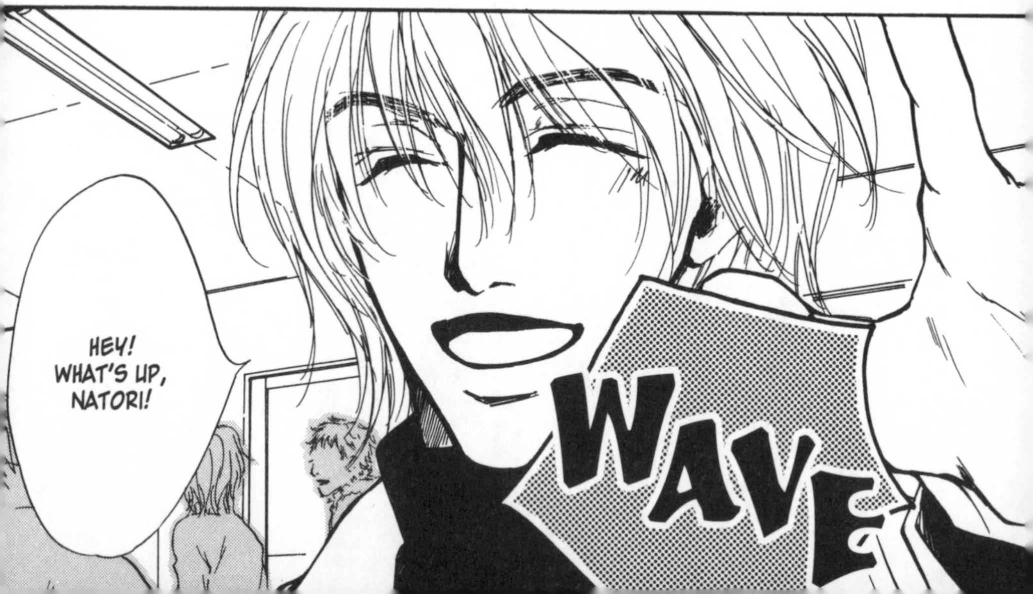
HEY! WHAT'S UP, NATORI!
WAVE

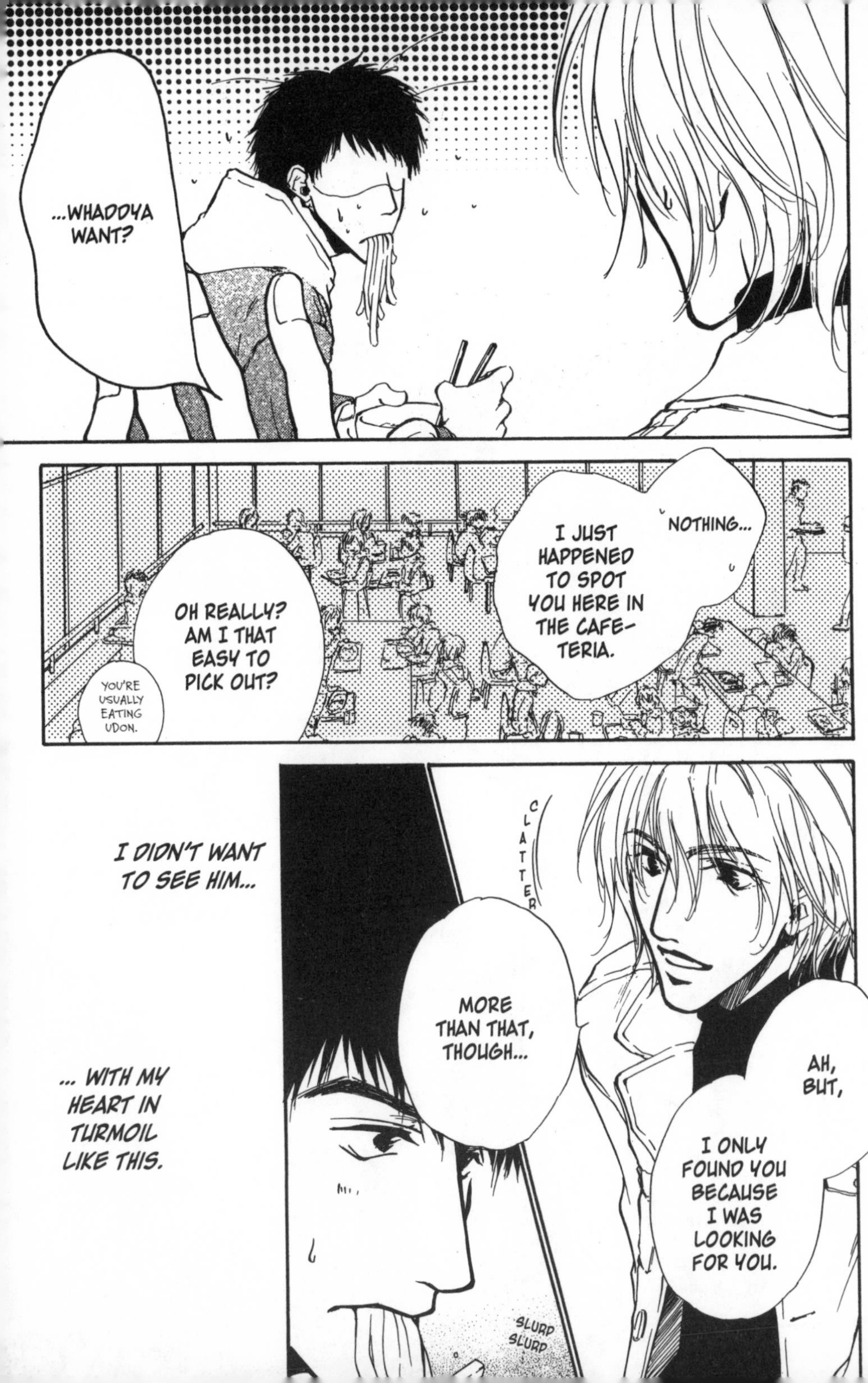
...WHADDYA WANT?
NOTHING...
I JUST HAPPENED TO SPOT YOU HERE IN THE CAFE-TERIA.
OH REALLY? AM I THAT EASY TO PICK OUT?
YOU'RE USUALLY EATING UDON.
CLATTER
AH, BUT,
I ONLY FOUND YOU BECAUSE I WAS LOOKING FOR YOU.
MORE THAN THAT, THOUGH...
I DIDN'T WANT TO SEE HIM...
... WITH MY HEART IN TURMOIL LIKE THIS.
SLURP SLURP

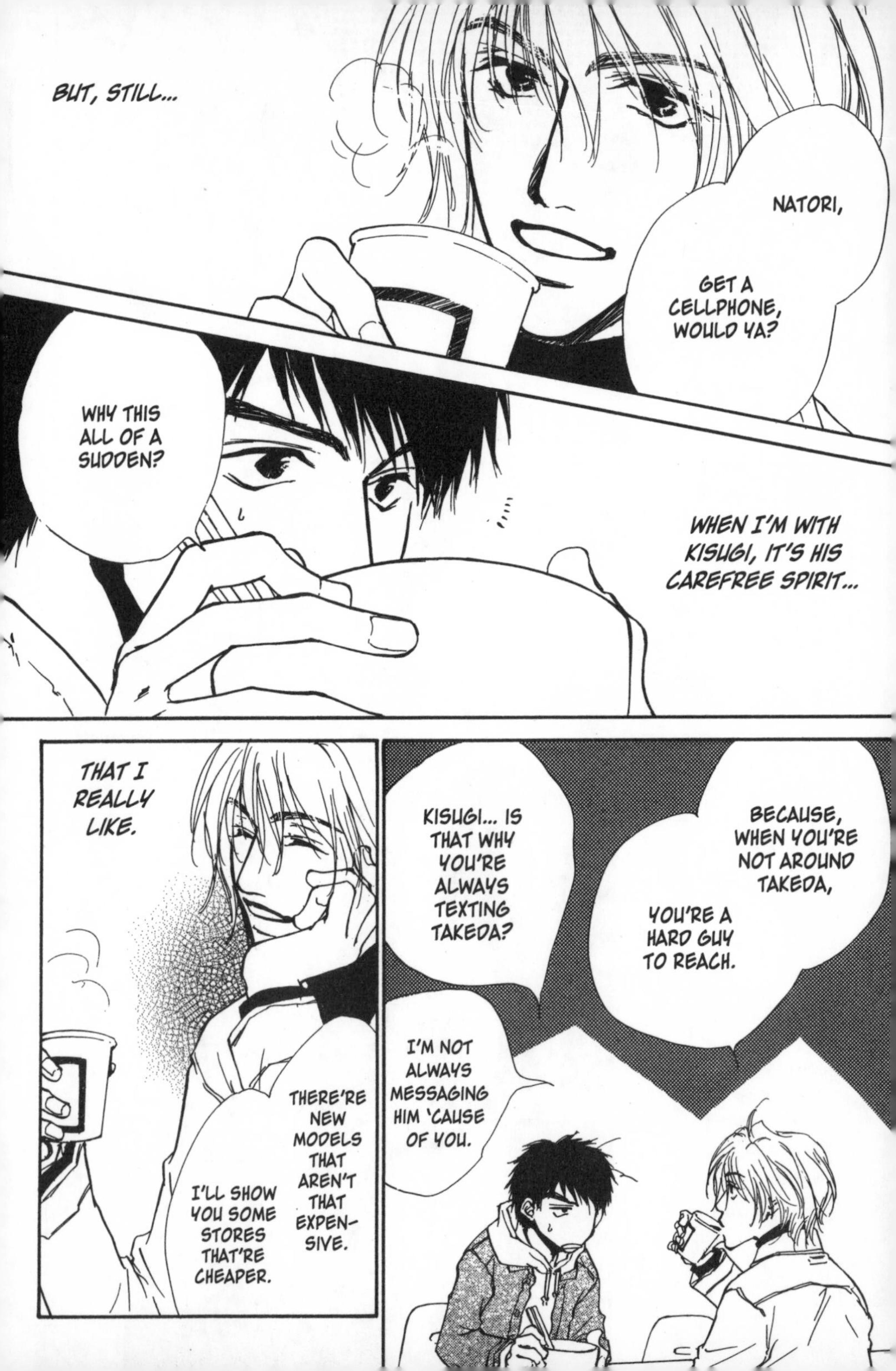
BUT, STILL...
NATORI,
GET A CELLPHONE, WOULD YA?
WHY THIS ALL OF A SUDDEN?
WHEN I'M WITH KISUGI, IT'S HIS CAREFREE SPIRIT...
BECAUSE, WHEN YOU'RE NOT AROUND TAKEDA,
YOU'RE A HARD GUY TO REACH.
KISUGI... IS THAT WHY YOU'RE ALWAYS TEXTING TAKEDA?
I'M NOT ALWAYS MESSAGING HIM 'CAUSE OF YOU.
THAT I REALLY LIKE.
THERE'RE NEW MODELS THAT AREN'T THAT EXPENSIVE.
I'LL SHOW YOU SOME STORES THAT'RE CHEAPER.

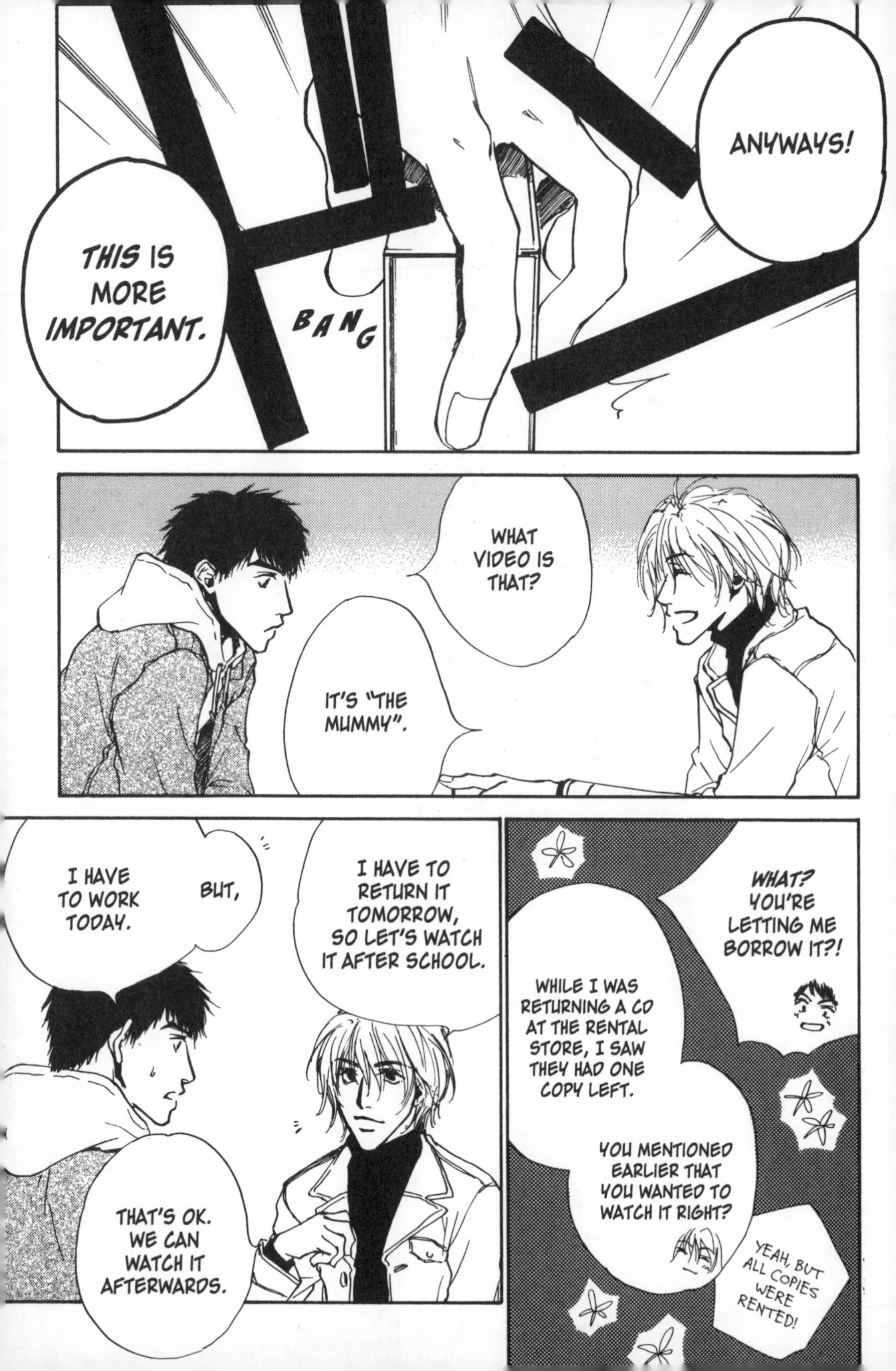
ANYWAYS!
BANG
THIS IS MORE IMPORTANT.
WHAT VIDEO IS THAT?
IT'S "THE MUMMY".
WHAT? YOU'RE LETTING ME BORROW IT?!
WHILE I WAS RETURNING A CD AT THE RENTAL STORE, I SAW THEY HAD ONE COPY LEFT.
YOU MENTIONED EARLIER THAT YOU WANTED TO WATCH IT RIGHT?
YEAH, BUT ALL COPIES WERE RENTED!
I HAVE TO RETURN IT TOMORROW, SO LET'S WATCH IT AFTER SCHOOL.
BUT,
I HAVE TO WORK TODAY.
THAT'S OK. WE CAN WATCH IT AFTERWARDS.

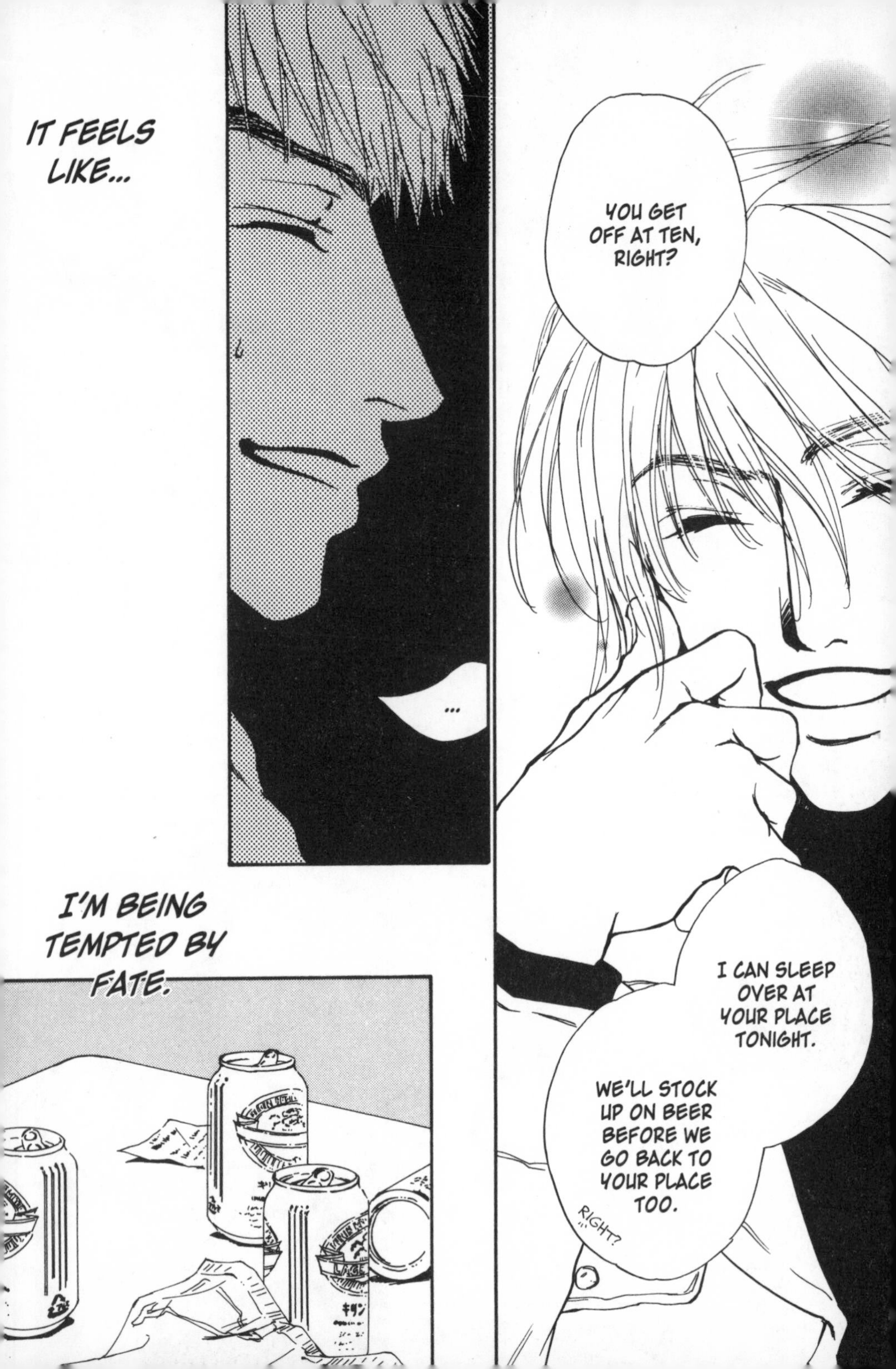
YOU GET OFF AT TEN, RIGHT?
I CAN SLEEP OVER AT YOUR PLACE TONIGHT.
WE'LL STOCK UP ON BEER BEFORE WE GO BACK TO YOUR PLACE TOO.
RIGHT?
IT FEELS LIKE...
...
I'M BEING TEMPTED BY FATE.

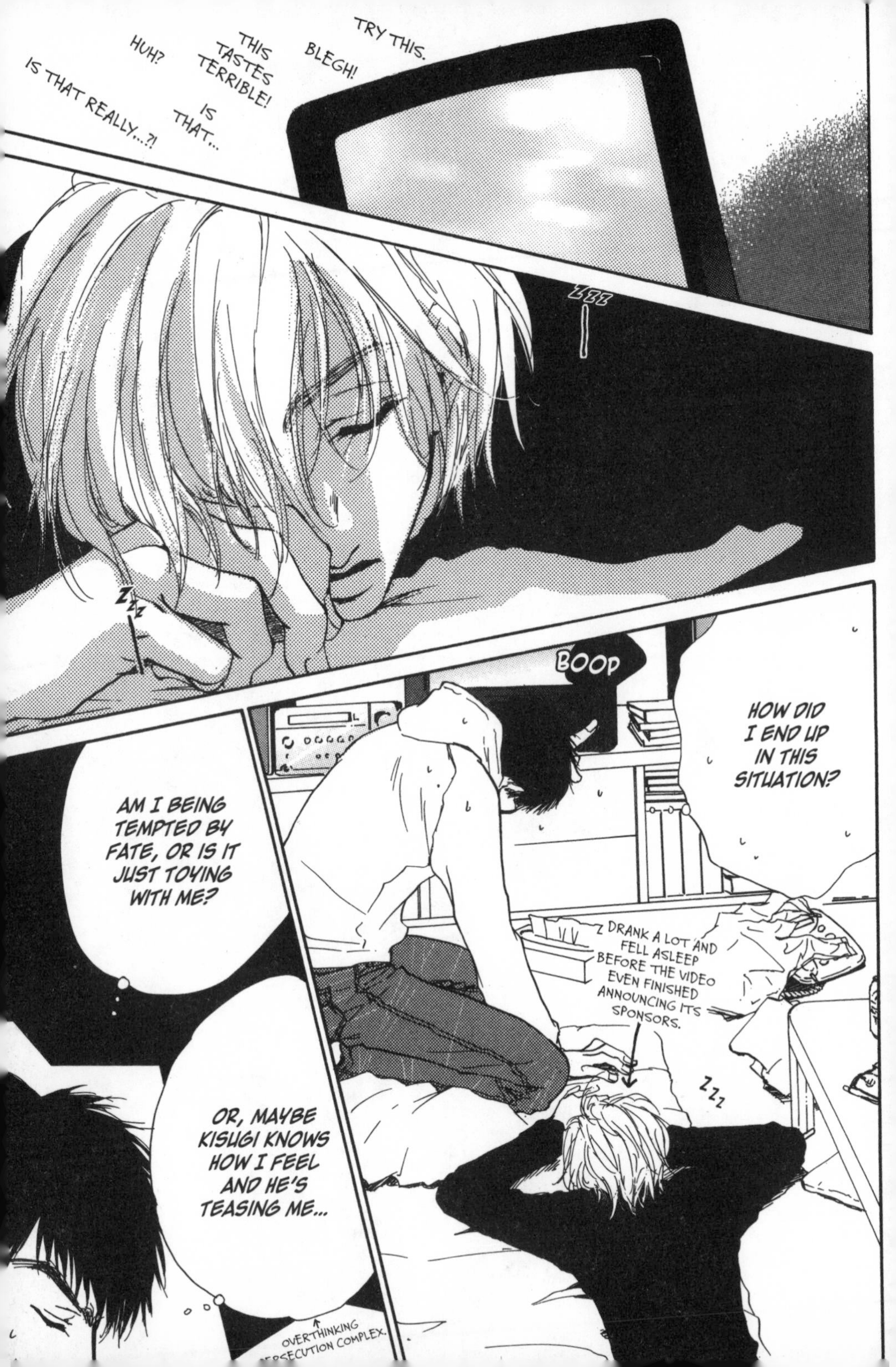
TRY THIS.
BLEGH!
THIS TASTES TERRIBLE!
HUH?
IS THAT...
IS THAT REALLY...?!
ZZZ
ZZZ
BOOP
HOW DID I END UP IN THIS SITUATION?
DRANK A LOT AND FELL ASLEEP BEFORE THE VIDEO EVEN FINISHED ANNOUNCING ITS SPONSORS.
ZZZ
AM I BEING TEMPTED BY FATE, OR IS IT JUST TOYING WITH ME?
OR, MAYBE KISUGI KNOWS HOW I FEEL AND HE'S TEASING ME...
OVERTHINKING PERSECUTION COMPLEX.

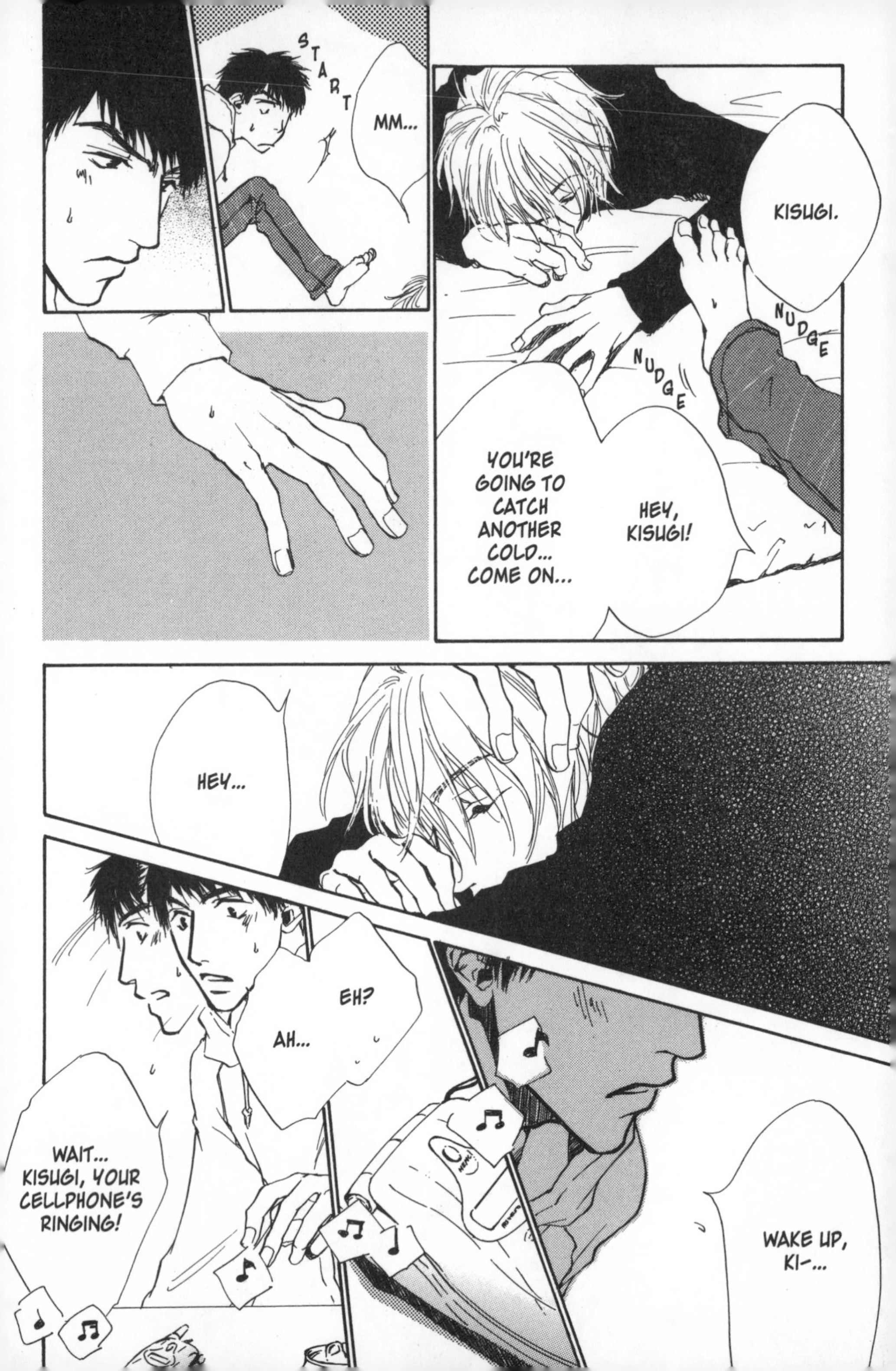
KISUGI.
NUDGE
NUDGE
HEY, KISUGI!
YOU'RE GOING TO CATCH ANOTHER COLD... COME ON...
START
MM...
HEY...
WAKE UP, KI-...
EH?
AH...
WAIT... KISUGI, YOUR CELLPHONE'S RINGING!

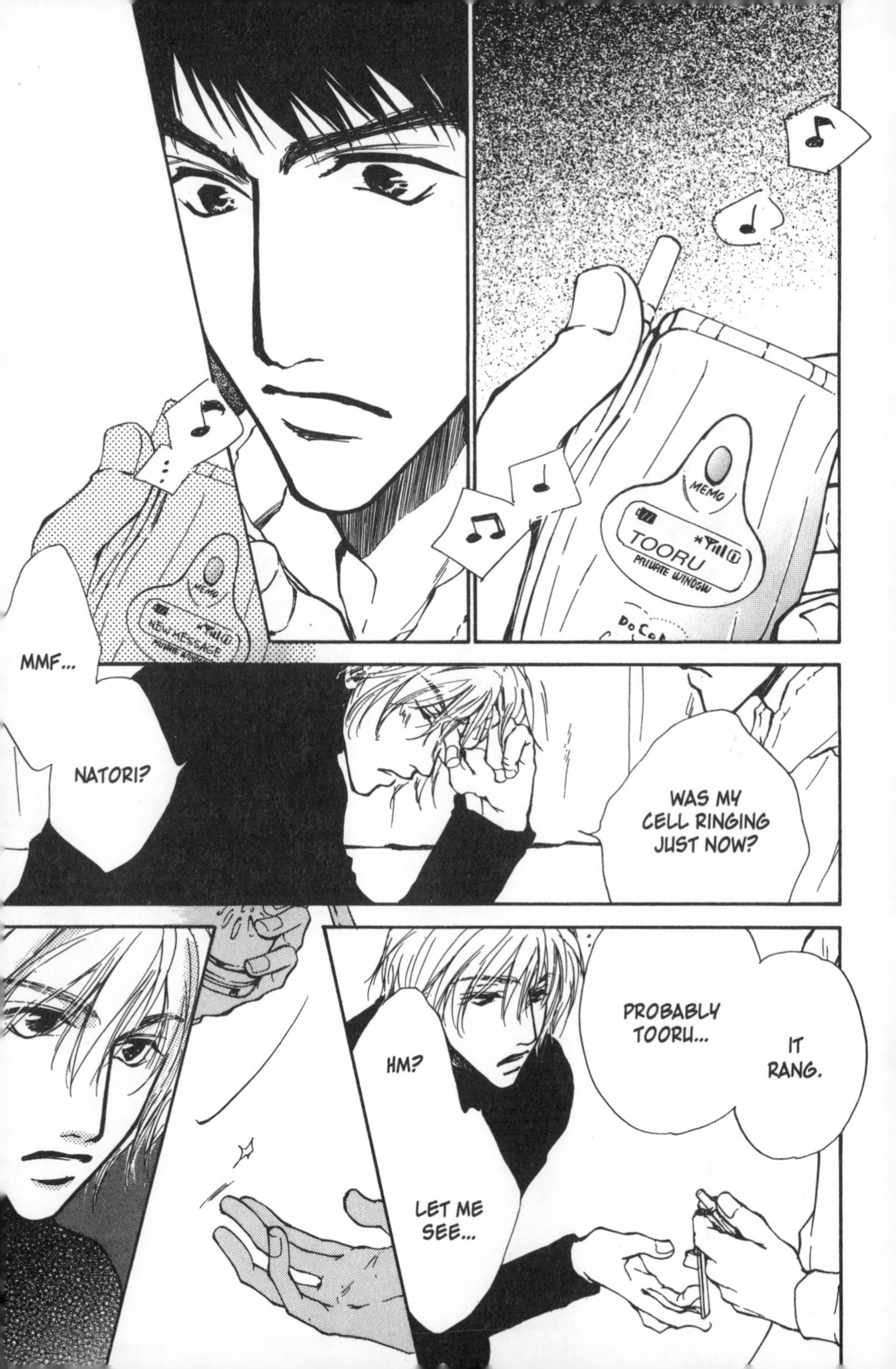
MEMO
TOORU
PRIVATE WINDOW
DoCoMo
MEMO
NEW MESSAGE
WAS MY CELL RINGING JUST NOW?
MMF...
NATORI?
IT RANG.
PROBABLY TOORU...
HM?
LET ME SEE...

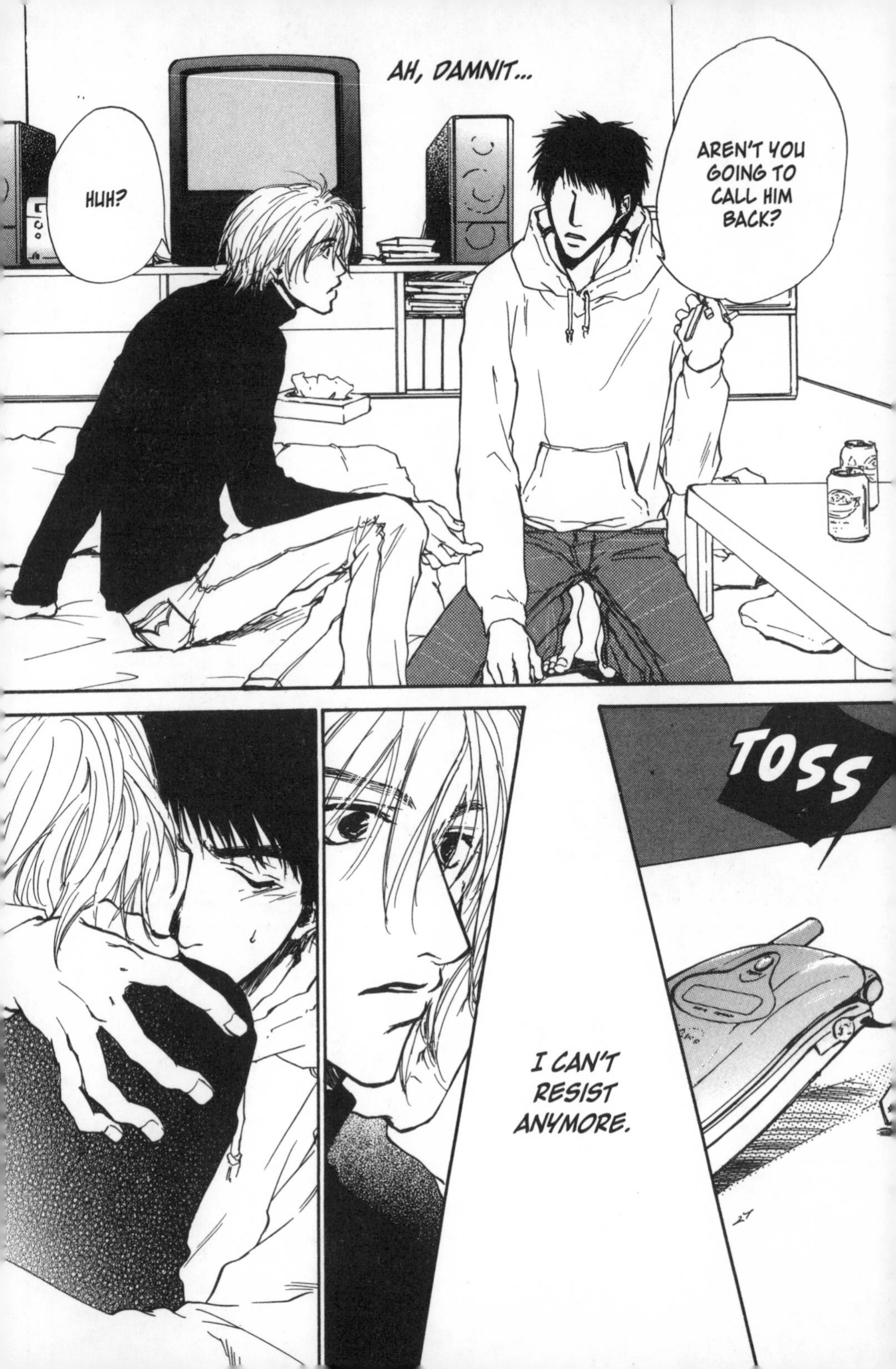
AREN'T YOU GOING TO CALL HIM BACK?
AH, DAMNIT...
HUH?
TOSS
I CAN'T RESIST ANYMORE.

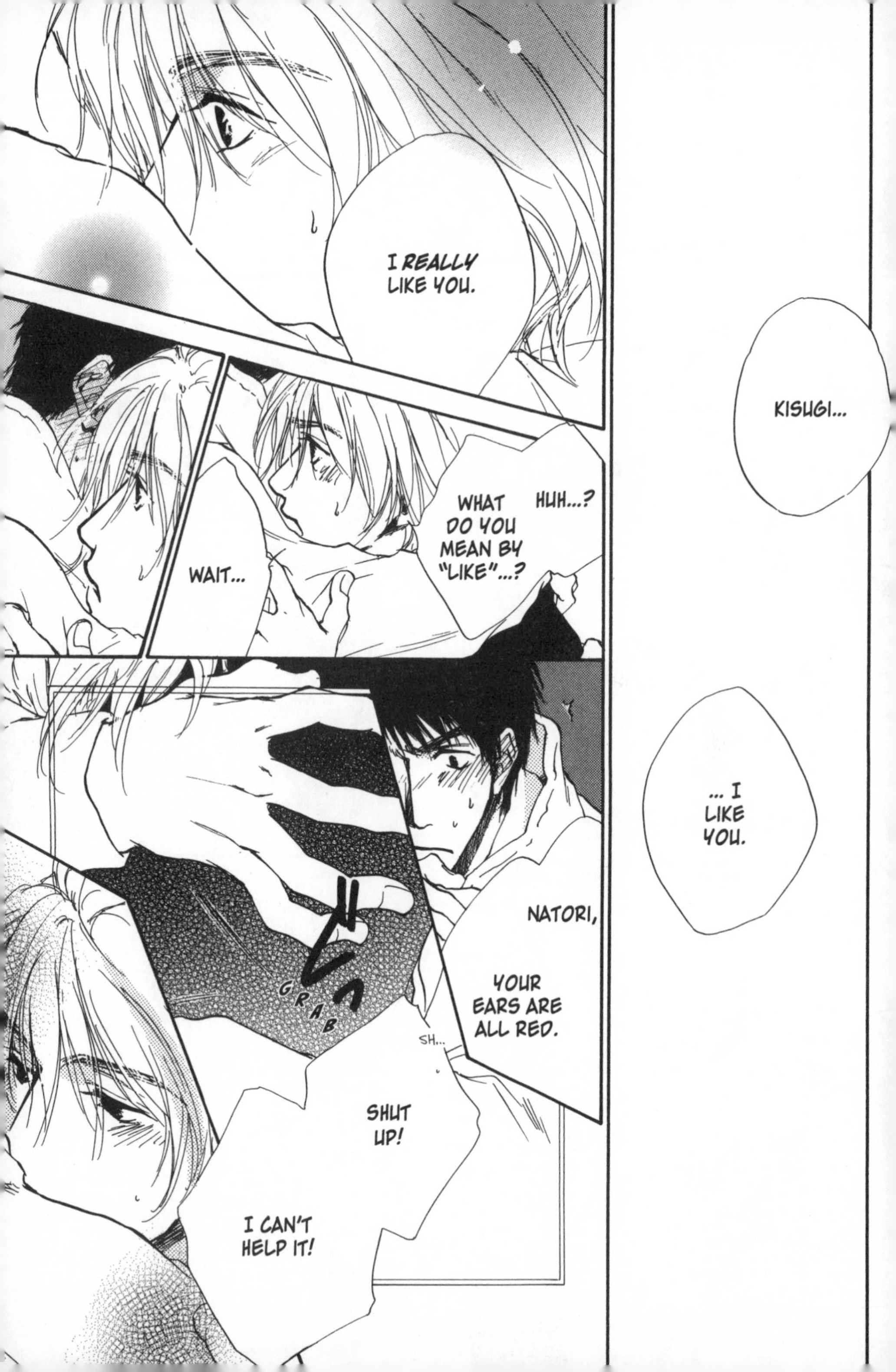
KISUGI...
... I LIKE YOU.
I REALLY LIKE YOU.
HUH...?
WHAT DO YOU MEAN BY "LIKE"...?
WAIT...
NATORI,
YOUR EARS ARE ALL RED.
GRAB
SH...
SHUT UP!
I CAN'T HELP IT!

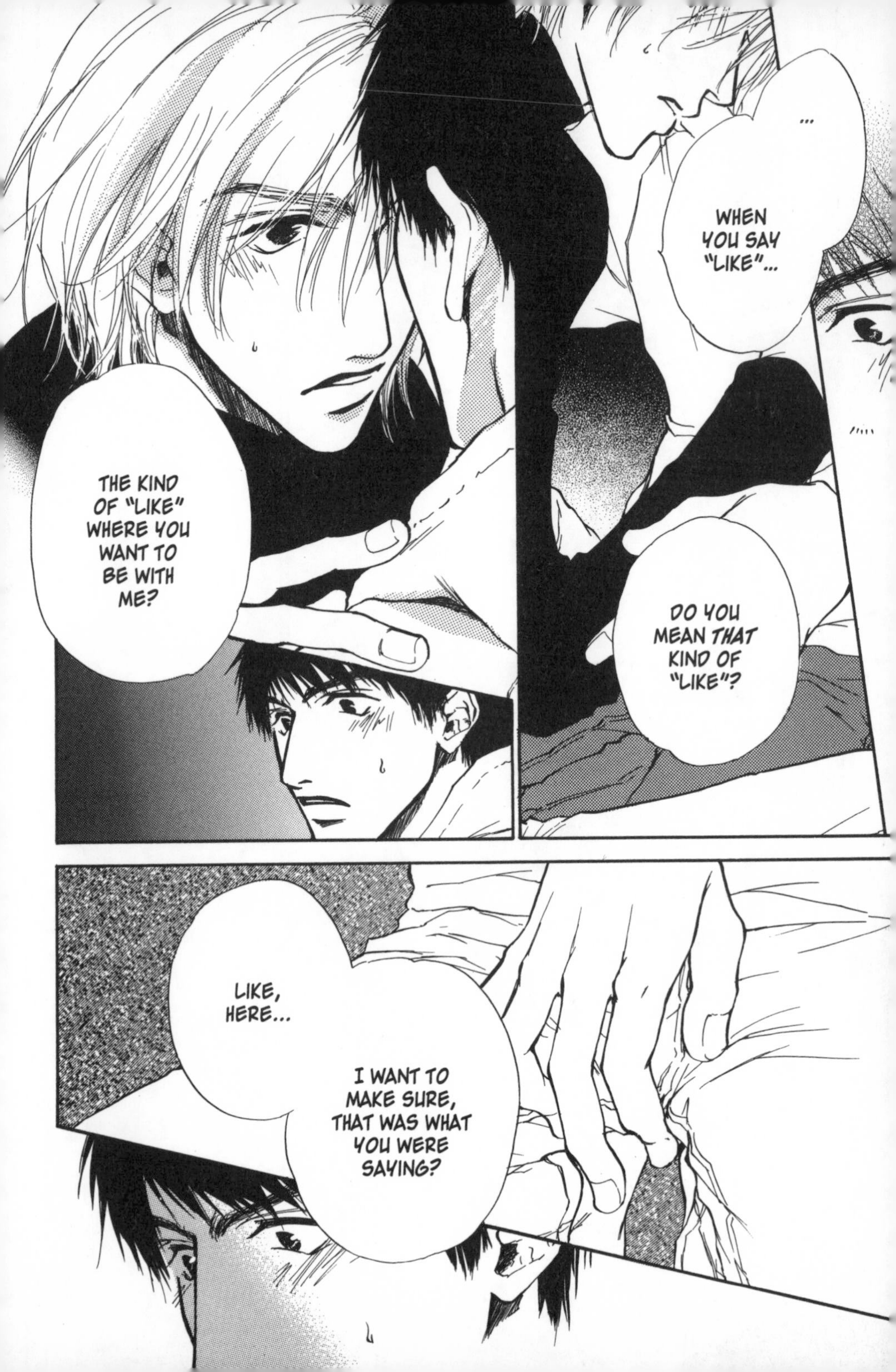
...
WHEN YOU SAY "LIKE"...
...
DO YOU MEAN *THAT* KIND OF "LIKE"?
THE KIND OF "LIKE" WHERE YOU WANT TO BE WITH ME?
LIKE, HERE...
I WANT TO MAKE SURE, THAT WAS WHAT YOU WERE SAYING?

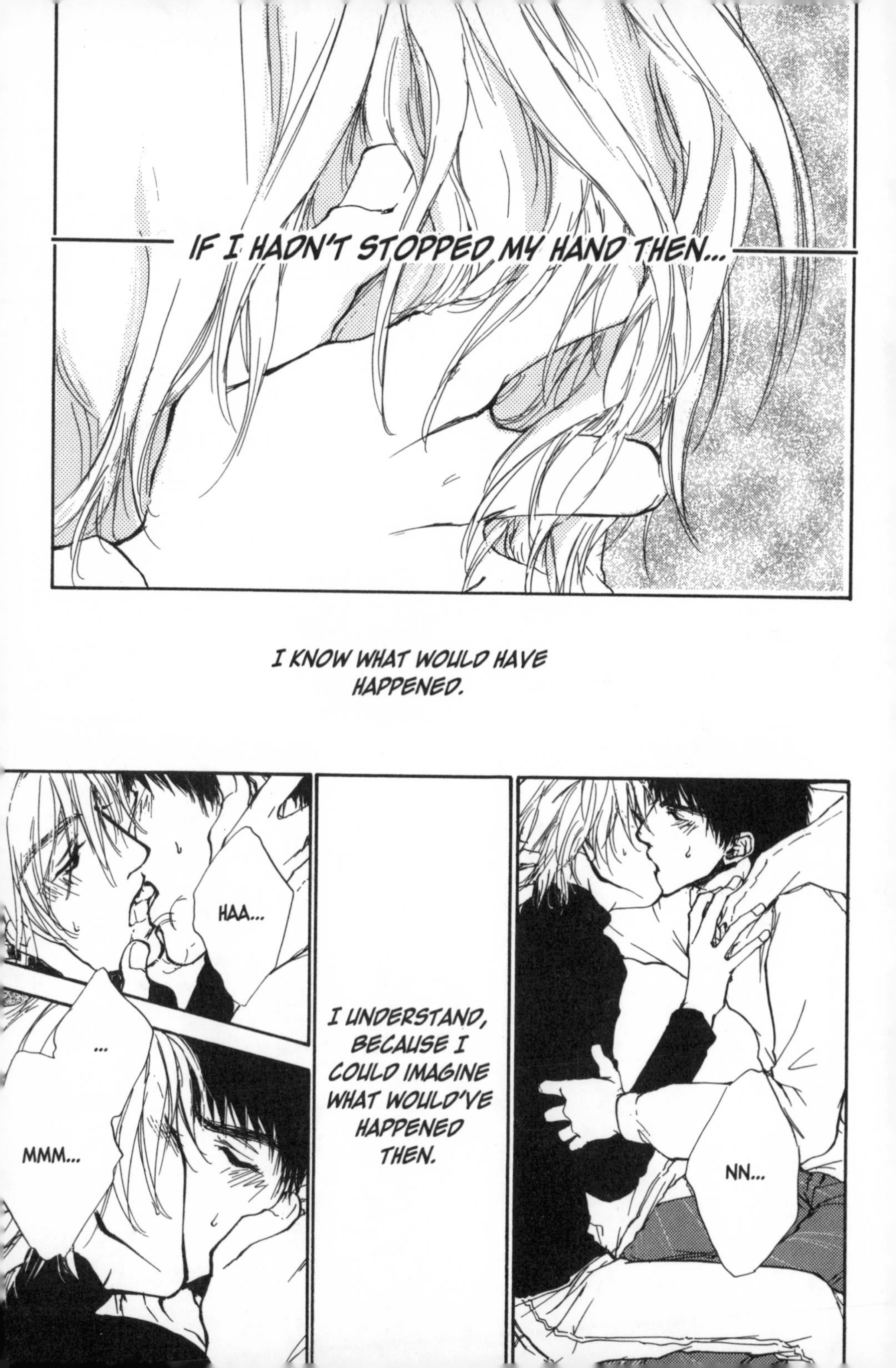
IF I HADN'T STOPPED MY HAND THEN...
I KNOW WHAT WOULD HAVE HAPPENED.
NN...
I UNDERSTAND, BECAUSE I COULD IMAGINE WHAT WOULD'VE HAPPENED THEN.
HAA...
...
MMM...

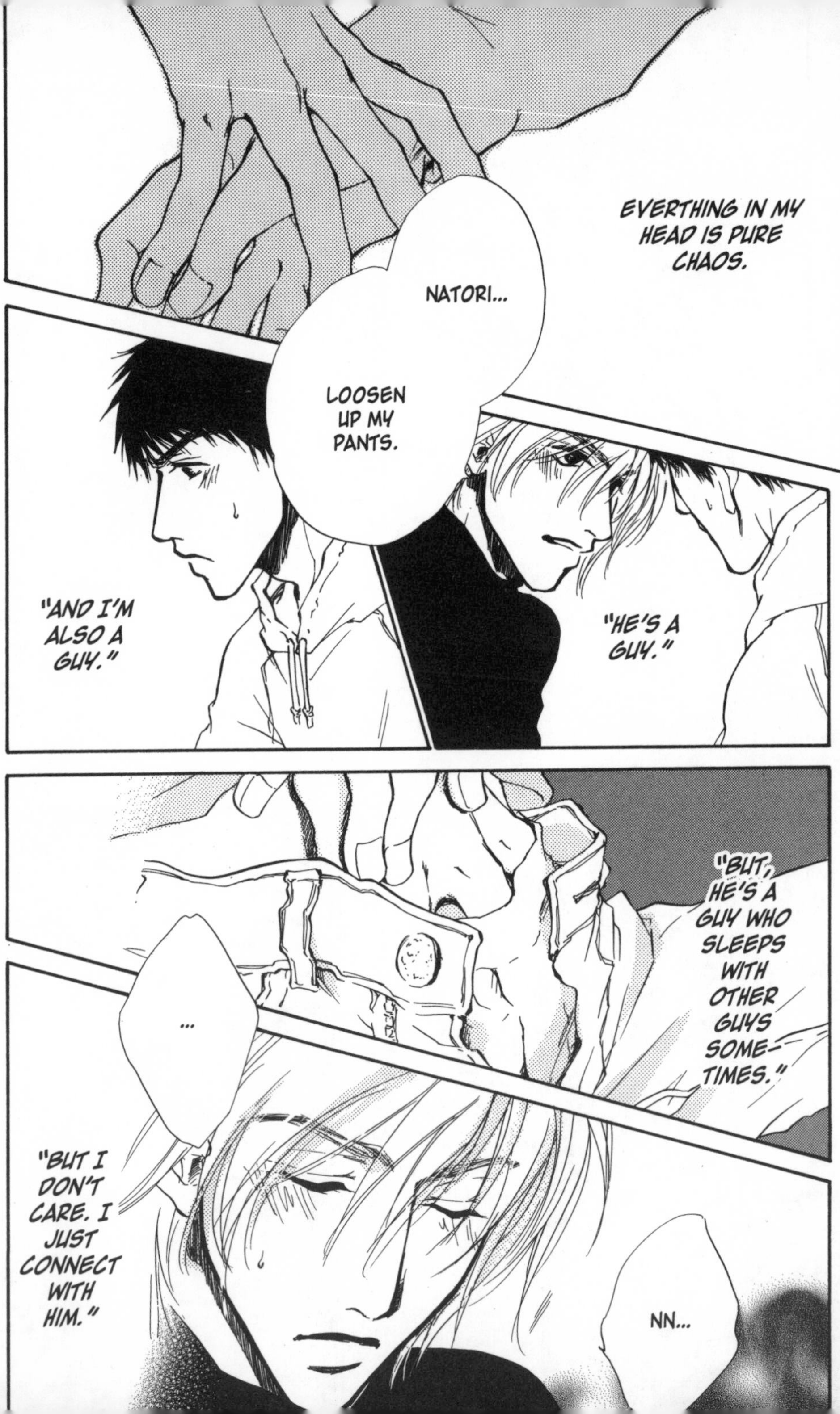
EVERTHING IN MY HEAD IS PURE CHAOS.
NATORI...
LOOSEN UP MY PANTS.
"HE'S A GUY."
"AND I'M ALSO A GUY."
"BUT, HE'S A GUY WHO SLEEPS WITH OTHER GUYS SOME-TIMES."
...
NN...
"BUT I DON'T CARE. I JUST CONNECT WITH HIM."

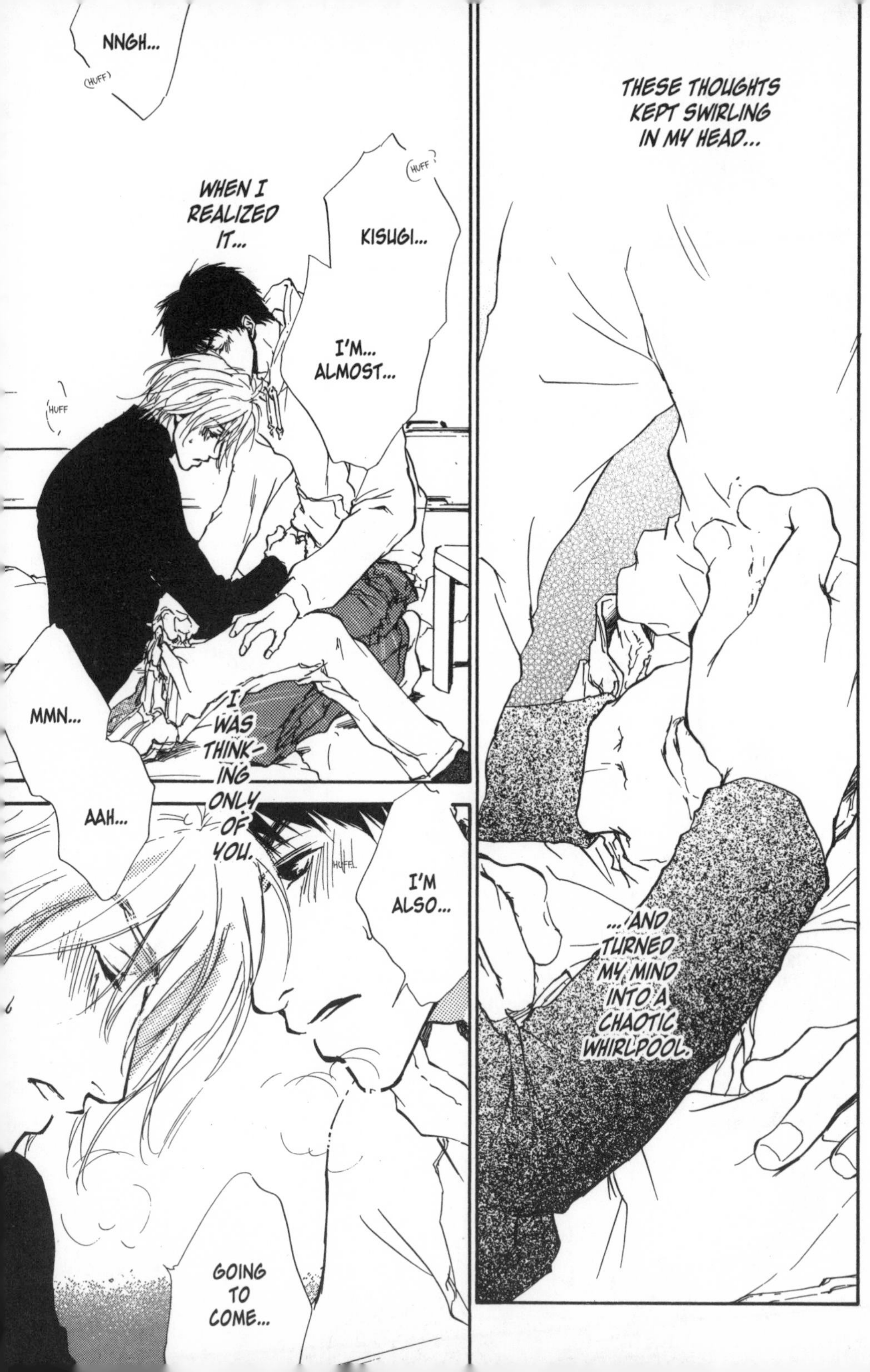
THESE THOUGHTS KEPT SWIRLING IN MY HEAD...
...AND TURNED MY MIND INTO A CHAOTIC WHIRLPOOL.
HUFF
KISUGI...
WHEN I REALIZED IT...
NNGH...
(HUFF)
I'M... ALMOST...
HUFF
I WAS THINKING ONLY OF YOU.
MMN...
I'M ALSO...
HUFF...
AAH...
GOING TO COME...

I WAS THINKING ONLY OF KISUGI.

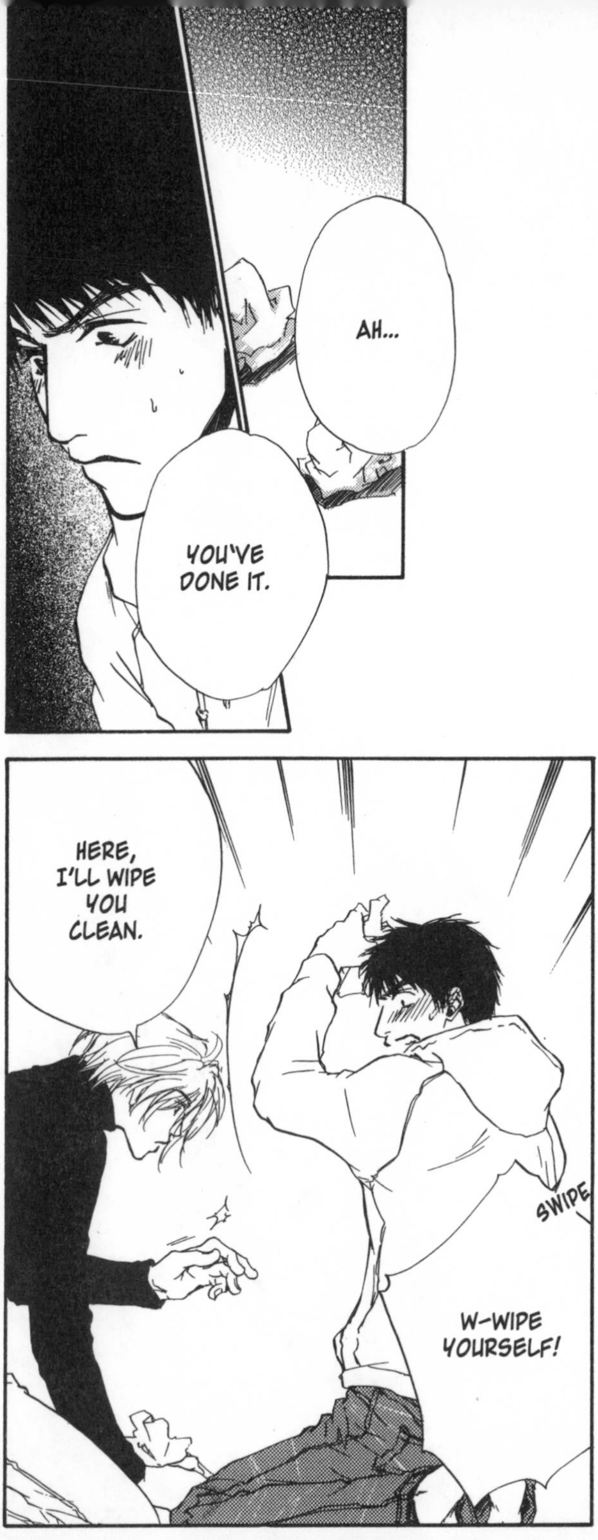
AH...
YOU'VE DONE IT.
HERE, I'LL WIPE YOU CLEAN.
SWIPE
W-WIPE YOURSELF!

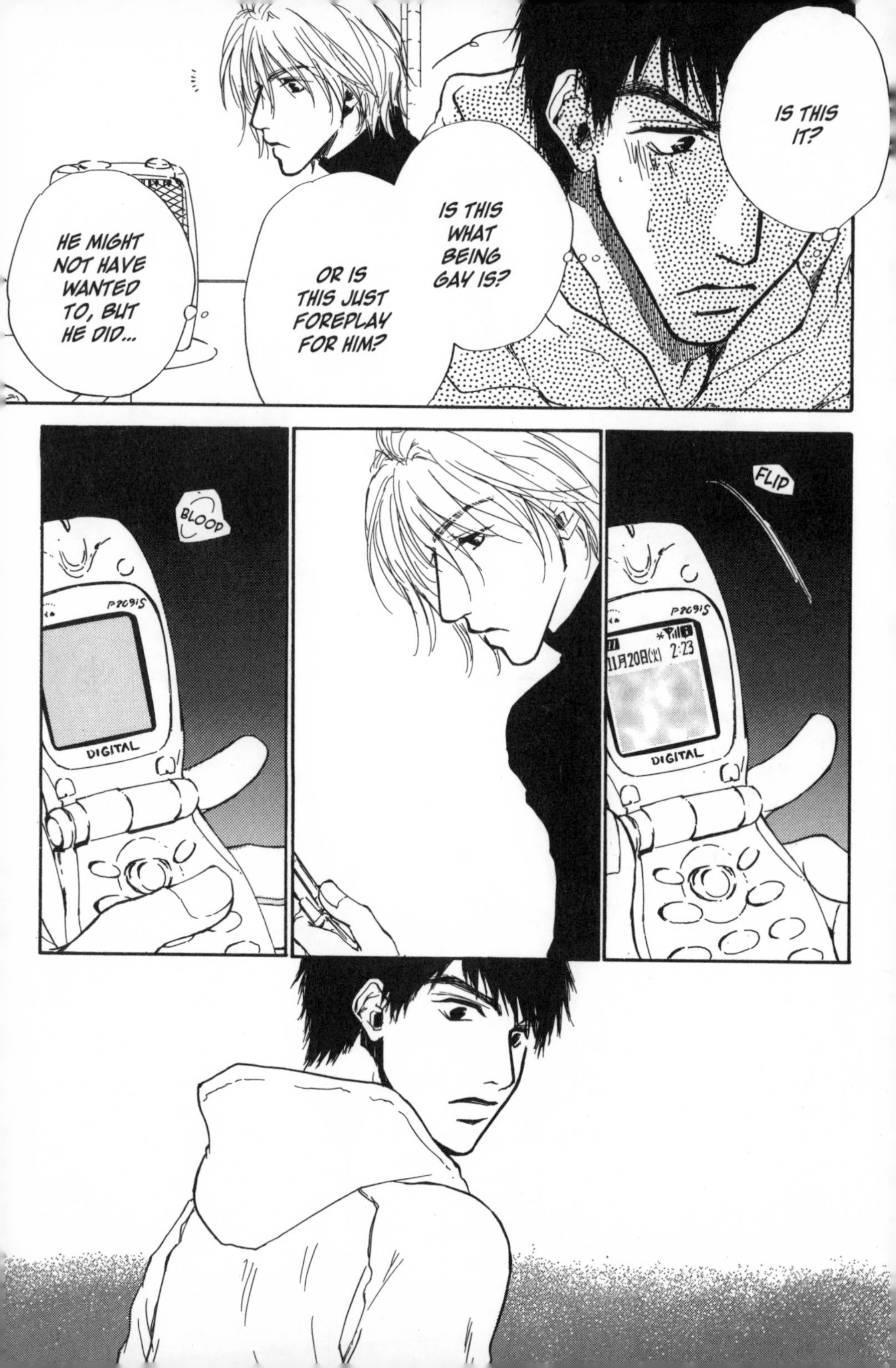
IS THIS IT?
IS THIS WHAT BEING GAY IS?
OR IS THIS JUST FOREPLAY FOR HIM?
HE MIGHT NOT HAVE WANTED TO, BUT HE DID...
FLIP
DIGITAL
DIGITAL
BLOOP

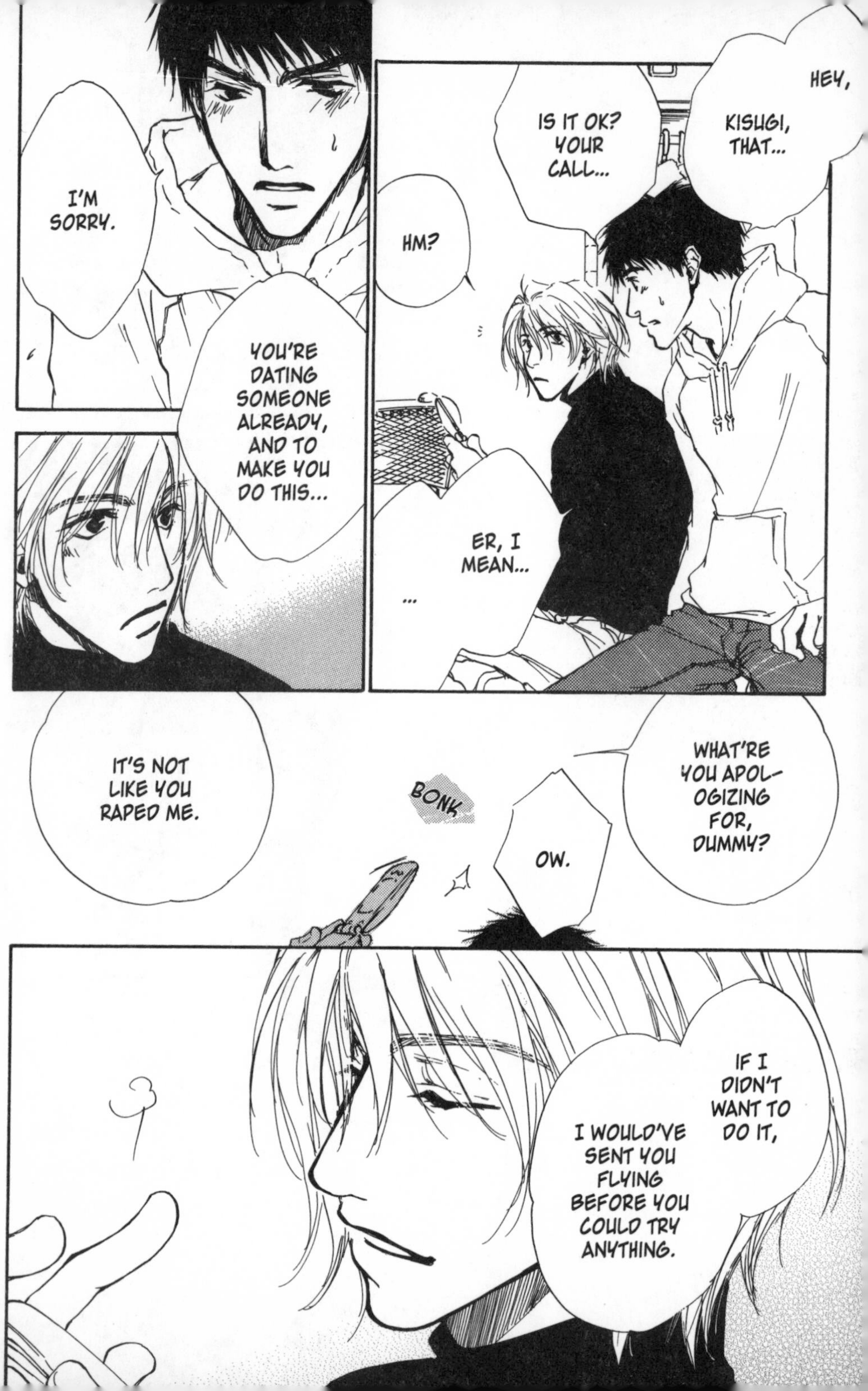
HEY, KISUGI, THAT...
IS IT OK? YOUR CALL...
HM?
ER, I MEAN...
...
I'M SORRY.
YOU'RE DATING SOMEONE ALREADY, AND TO MAKE YOU DO THIS...
WHAT'RE YOU APOLOGIZING FOR, DUMMY?
BONK
OW.
IT'S NOT LIKE YOU RAPED ME.
IF I DIDN'T WANT TO DO IT,
I WOULD'VE SENT YOU FLYING BEFORE YOU COULD TRY ANYTHING.

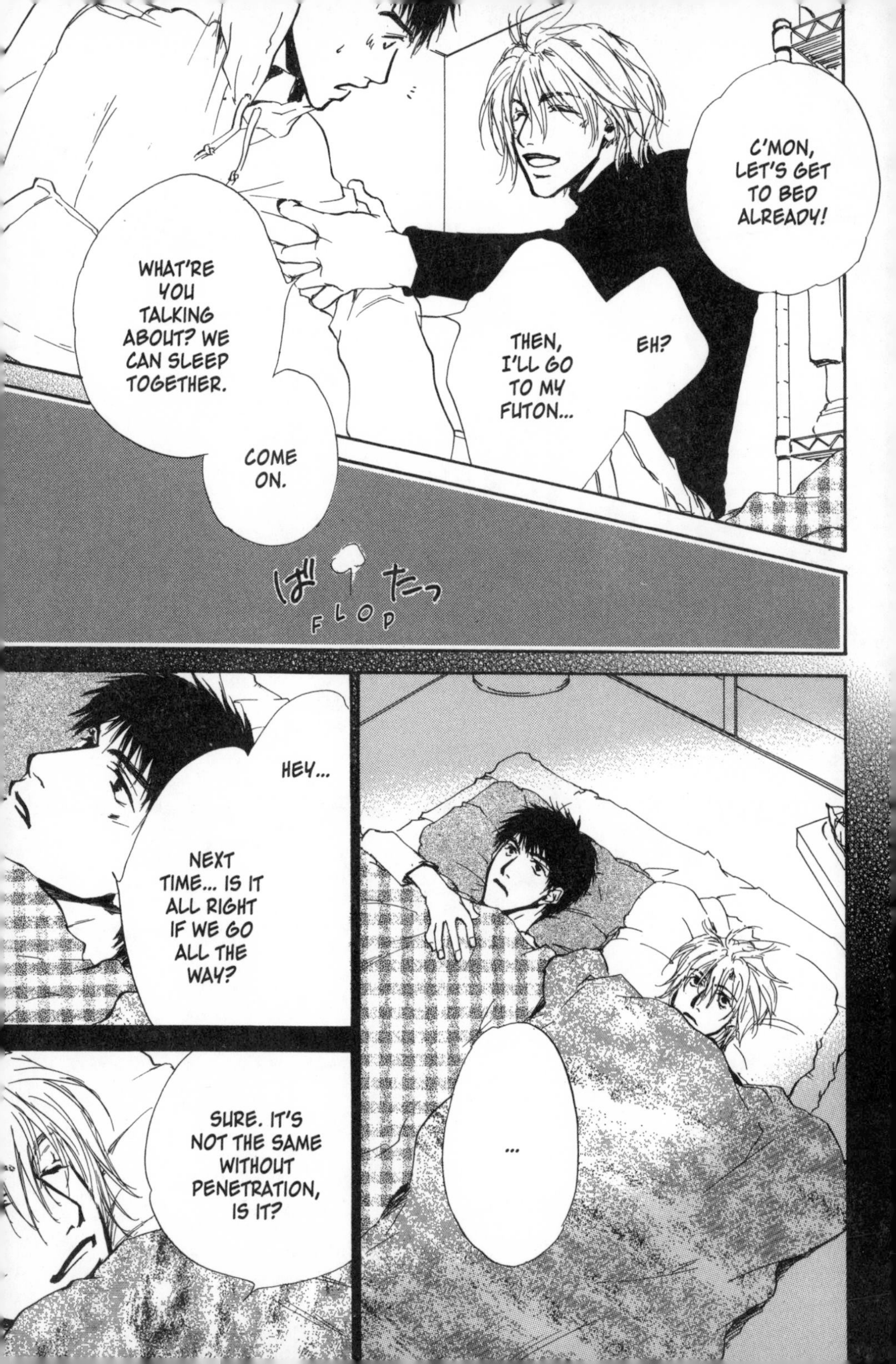
C'MON, LET'S GET TO BED ALREADY!
EH?
THEN, I'LL GO TO MY FUTON...
WHAT'RE YOU TALKING ABOUT? WE CAN SLEEP TOGETHER.
COME ON.
ばたっ
FLOP
...
HEY...
NEXT TIME... IS IT ALL RIGHT IF WE GO ALL THE WAY?
SURE. IT'S NOT THE SAME WITHOUT PENETRATION, IS IT?

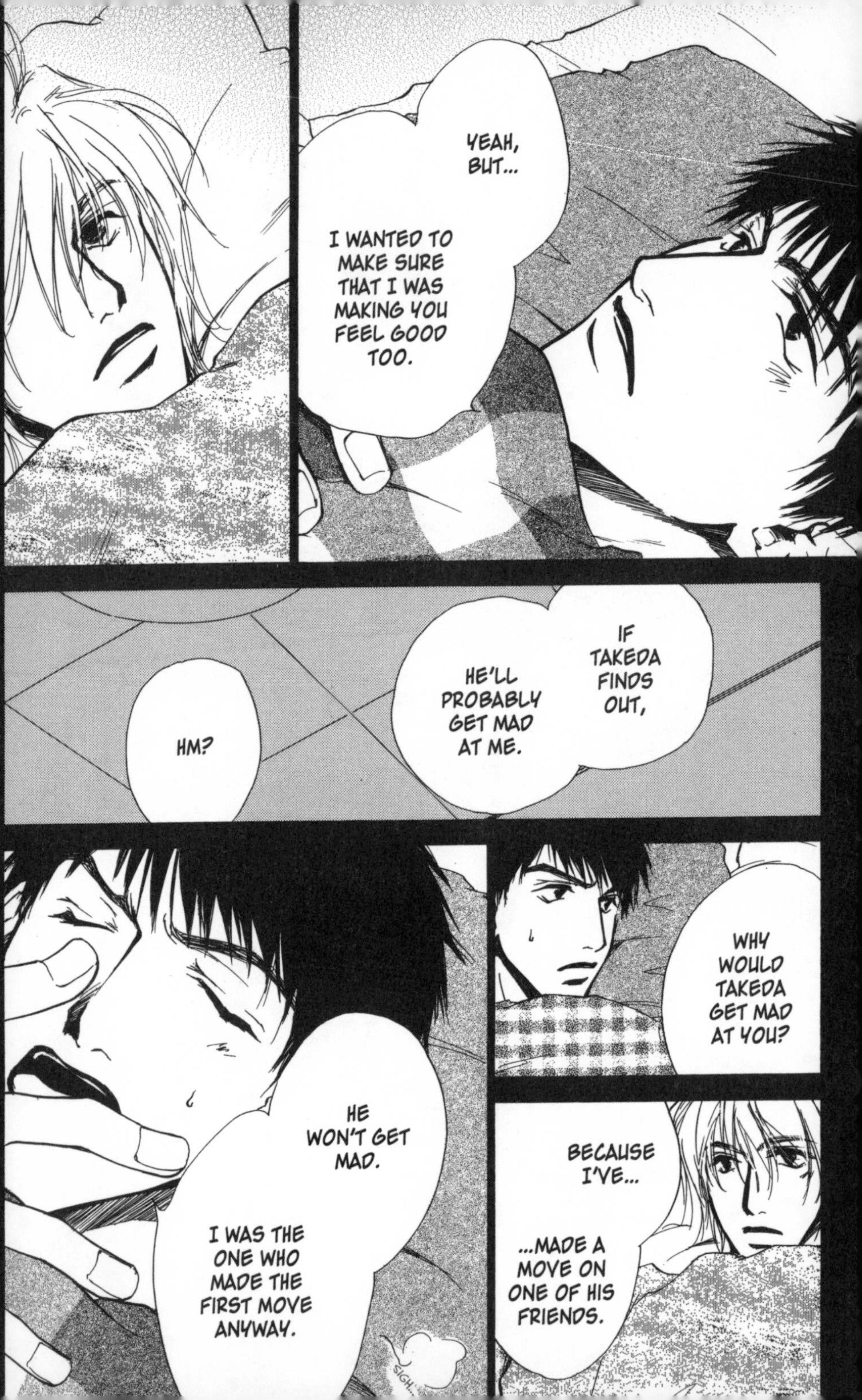
YEAH, BUT...
I WANTED TO MAKE SURE THAT I WAS MAKING YOU FEEL GOOD TOO.
IF TAKEDA FINDS OUT,
HE'LL PROBABLY GET MAD AT ME.
HM?
WHY WOULD TAKEDA GET MAD AT YOU?
BECAUSE I'VE...
...MADE A MOVE ON ONE OF HIS FRIENDS.
HE WON'T GET MAD.
I WAS THE ONE WHO MADE THE FIRST MOVE ANYWAY.
SIGH...

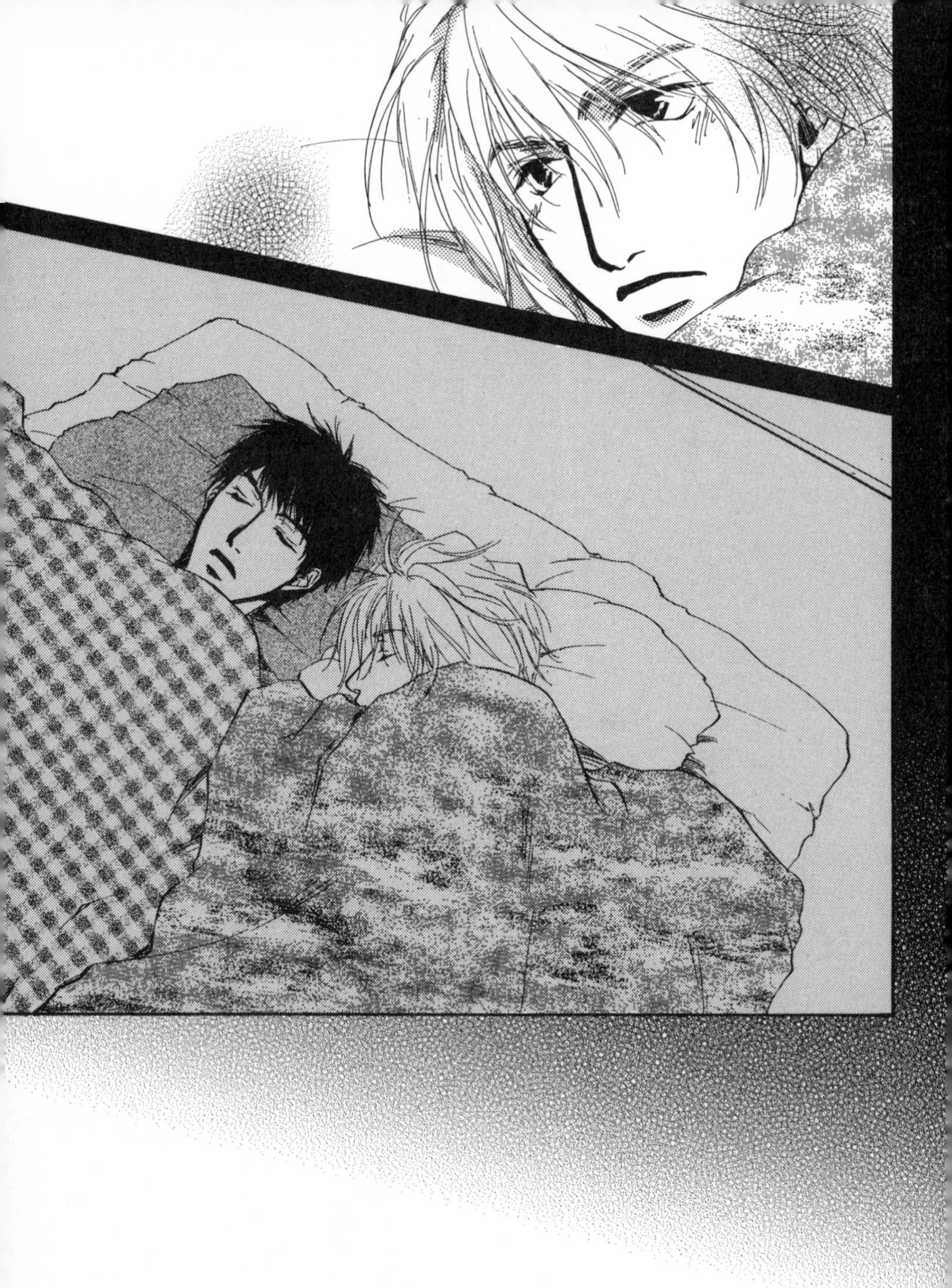

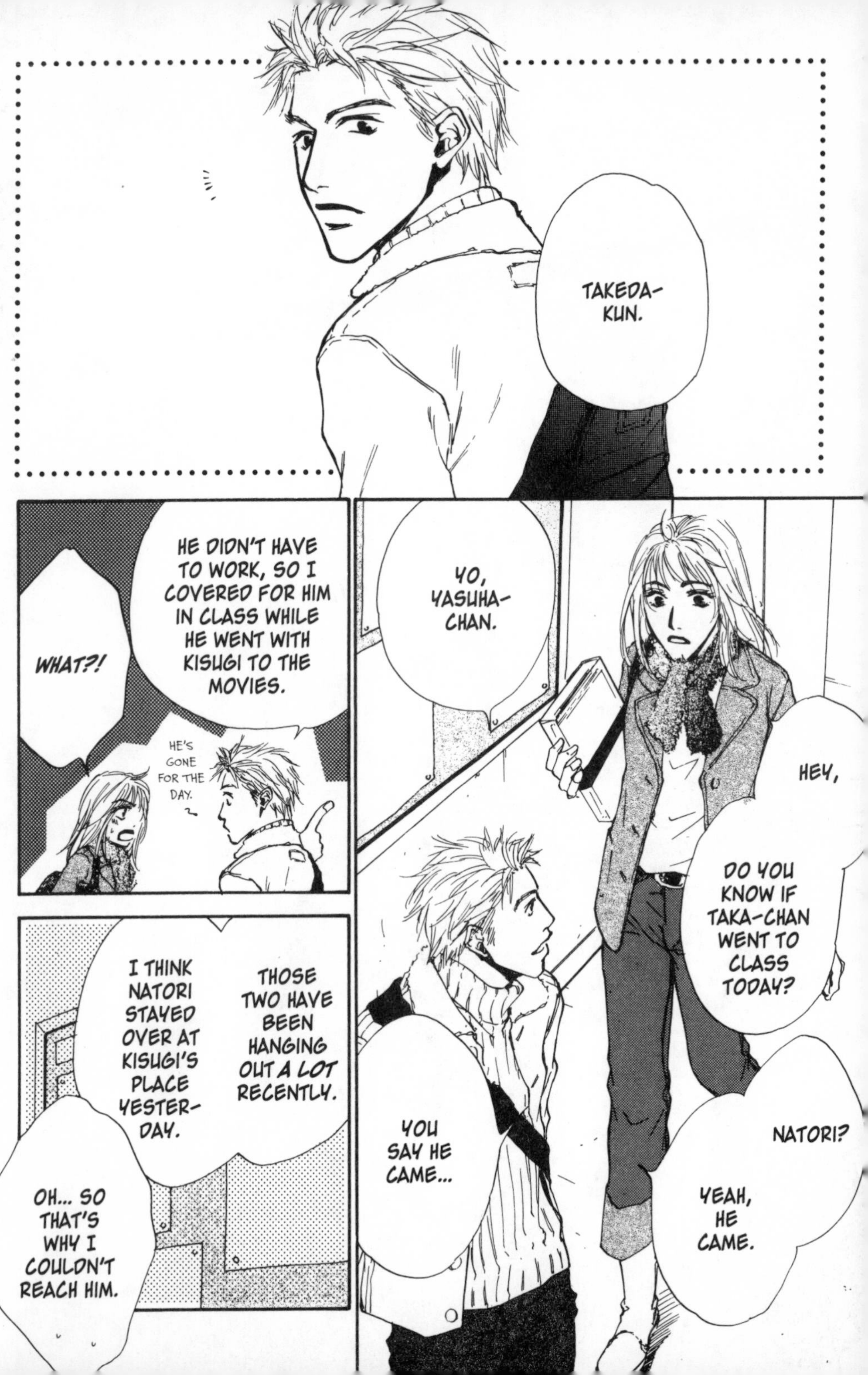
TAKEDA-KUN.
YO, YASUHA-CHAN.
HEY,
DO YOU KNOW IF TAKA-CHAN WENT TO CLASS TODAY?
NATORI?
YEAH, HE CAME.
YOU SAY HE CAME...
HE DIDN'T HAVE TO WORK, SO I COVERED FOR HIM IN CLASS WHILE HE WENT WITH KISUGI TO THE MOVIES.
WHAT?!
HE'S GONE FOR THE DAY.
THOSE TWO HAVE BEEN HANGING OUT A *LOT* RECENTLY.
I THINK NATORI STAYED OVER AT KISUGI'S PLACE YESTER-DAY.
OH... SO THAT'S WHY I COULDN'T REACH HIM.

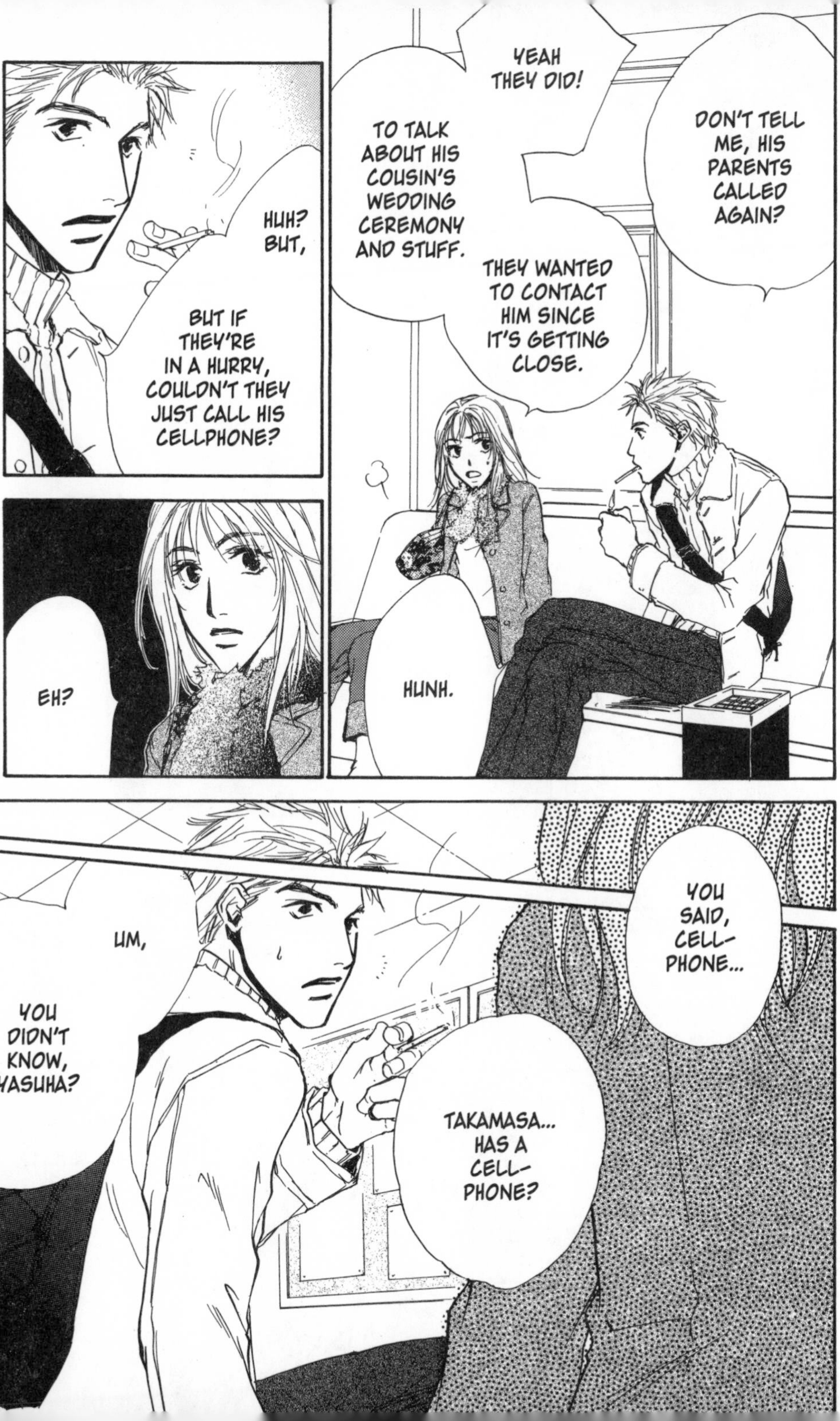
DON'T TELL ME, HIS PARENTS CALLED AGAIN?
YEAH THEY DID!
TO TALK ABOUT HIS COUSIN'S WEDDING CEREMONY AND STUFF.
THEY WANTED TO CONTACT HIM SINCE IT'S GETTING CLOSE.
HUNH.
HUH? BUT,
BUT IF THEY'RE IN A HURRY, COULDN'T THEY JUST CALL HIS CELLPHONE?
EH?
YOU SAID, CELL-PHONE...
TAKAMASA... HAS A CELL-PHONE?
UM,
YOU DIDN'T KNOW, YASUHA?

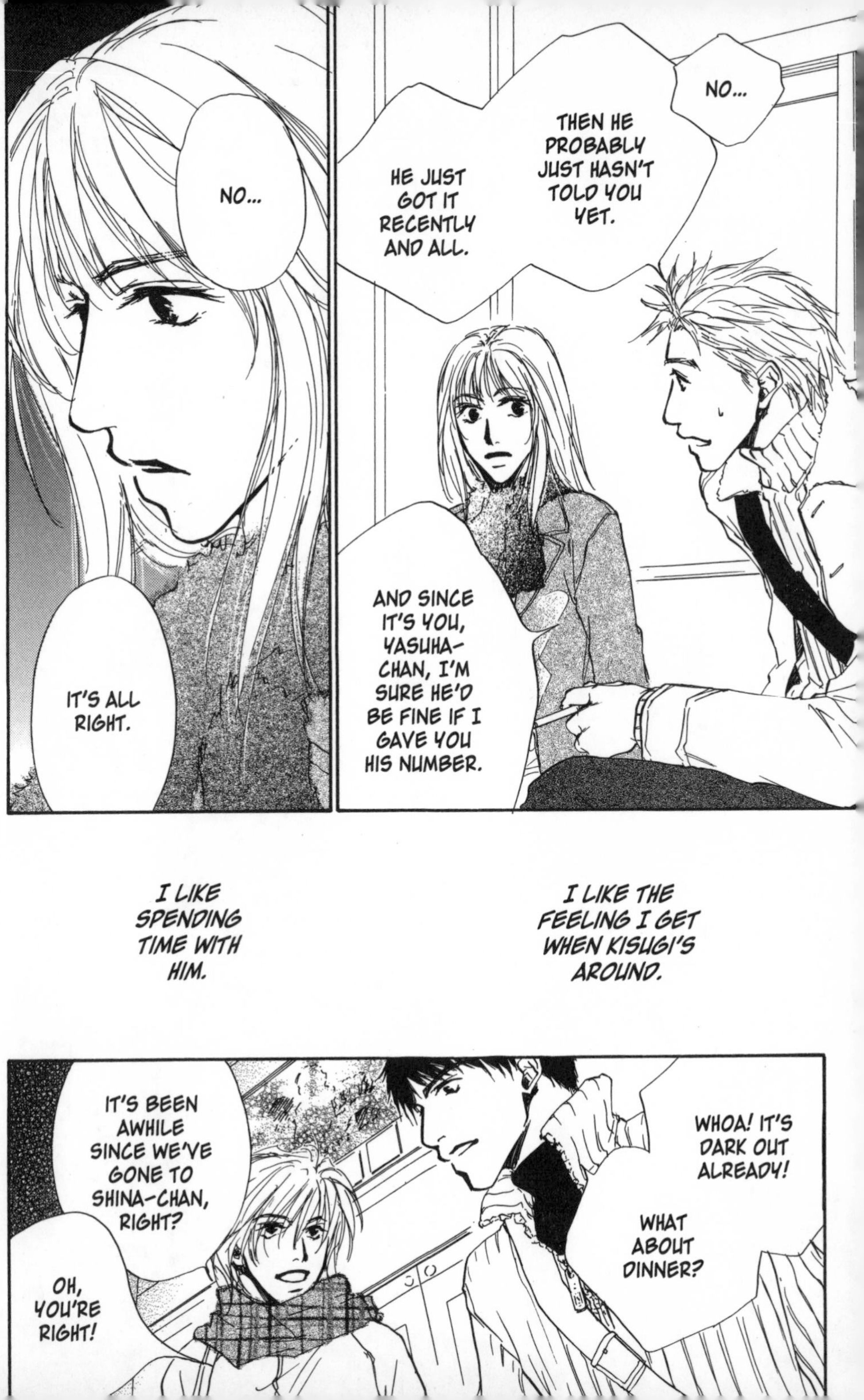
NO...
THEN HE PROBABLY JUST HASN'T TOLD YOU YET.
HE JUST GOT IT RECENTLY AND ALL.
AND SINCE IT'S YOU, YASUHA-CHAN, I'M SURE HE'D BE FINE IF I GAVE YOU HIS NUMBER.
NO...
IT'S ALL RIGHT.
I LIKE THE FEELING I GET WHEN KISUGI'S AROUND.
I LIKE SPENDING TIME WITH HIM.
WHOA! IT'S DARK OUT ALREADY!
WHAT ABOUT DINNER?
IT'S BEEN AWHILE SINCE WE'VE GONE TO SHINA-CHAN, RIGHT?
OH, YOU'RE RIGHT!

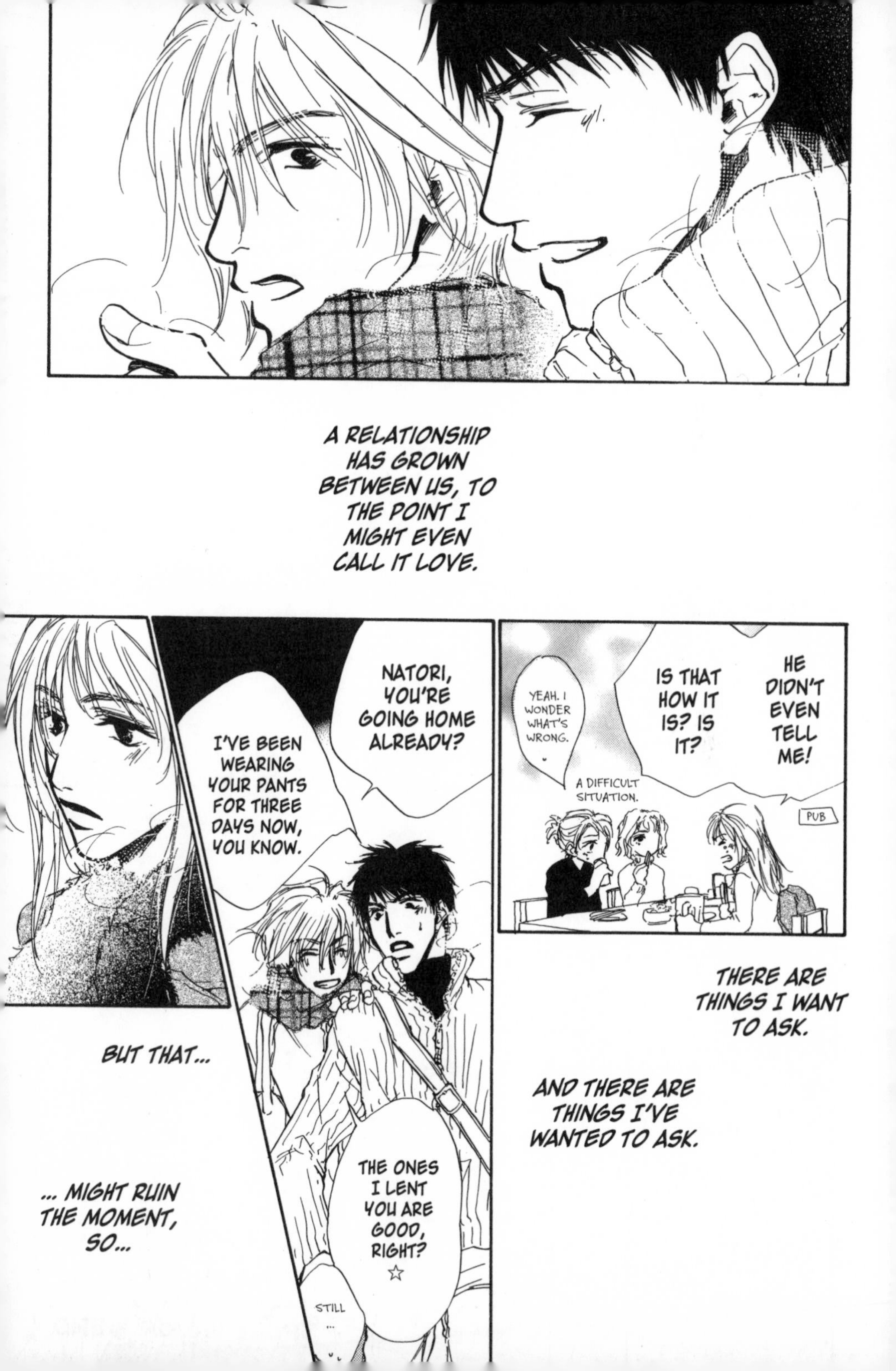
A RELATIONSHIP HAS GROWN BETWEEN US, TO THE POINT I MIGHT EVEN CALL IT LOVE.
HE DIDN'T EVEN TELL ME!
IS THAT HOW IT IS? IS IT?
YEAH. I WONDER WHAT'S WRONG.
A DIFFICULT SITUATION.
PUB
THERE ARE THINGS I WANT TO ASK.
AND THERE ARE THINGS I'VE WANTED TO ASK.
NATORI, YOU'RE GOING HOME ALREADY?
I'VE BEEN WEARING YOUR PANTS FOR THREE DAYS NOW, YOU KNOW.
THE ONES I LENT YOU ARE GOOD, RIGHT? ☆
STILL ...
BUT THAT...
... MIGHT RUIN THE MOMENT, SO...

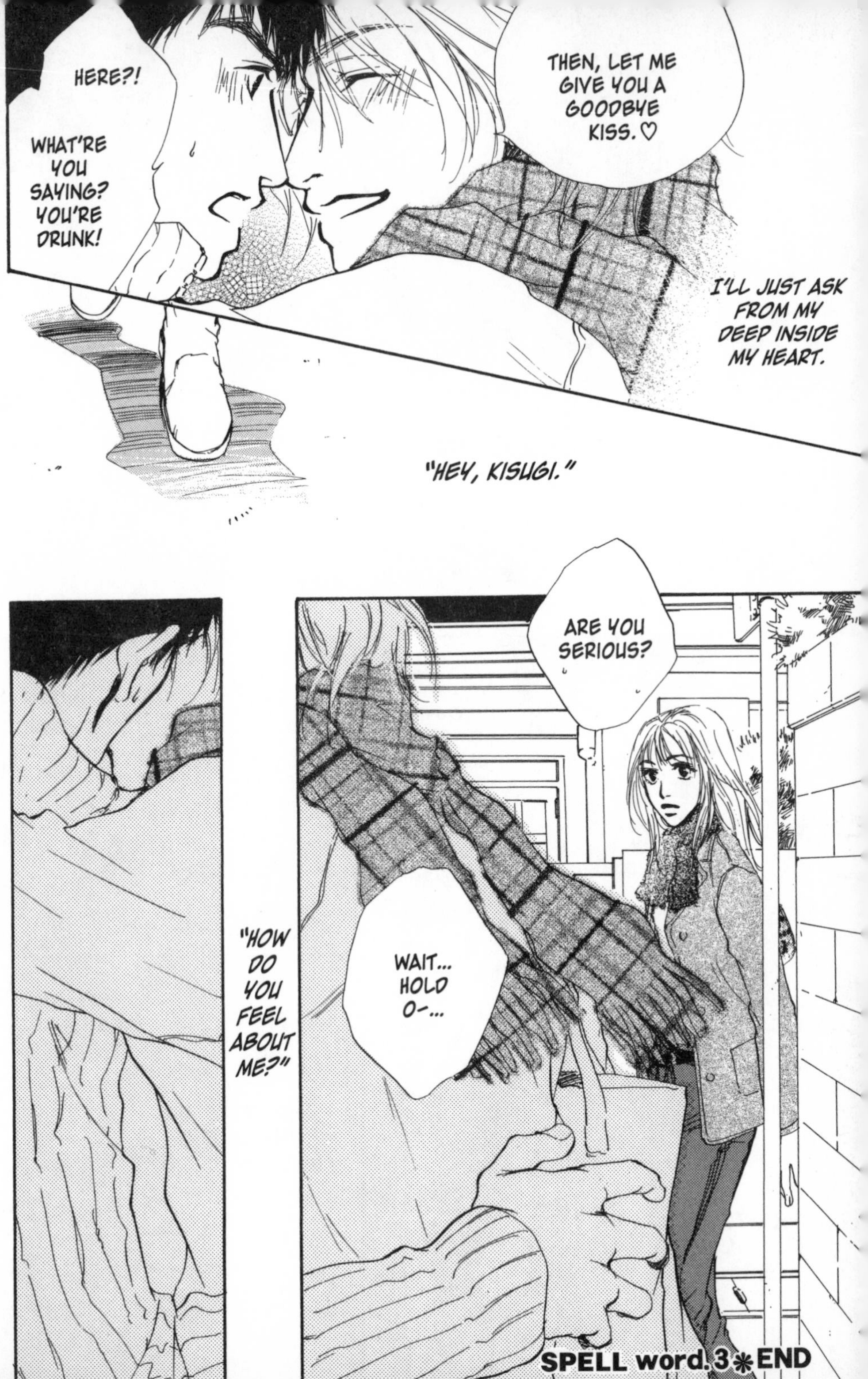
THEN, LET ME GIVE YOU A GOODBYE KISS. ♡
HERE?!
WHAT'RE YOU SAYING? YOU'RE DRUNK!
I'LL JUST ASK FROM MY DEEP INSIDE MY HEART.
"HEY, KISUGI."
ARE YOU SERIOUS?
WAIT... HOLD O-...
"HOW DO YOU FEEL ABOUT ME?"
SPELL word. 3 * END

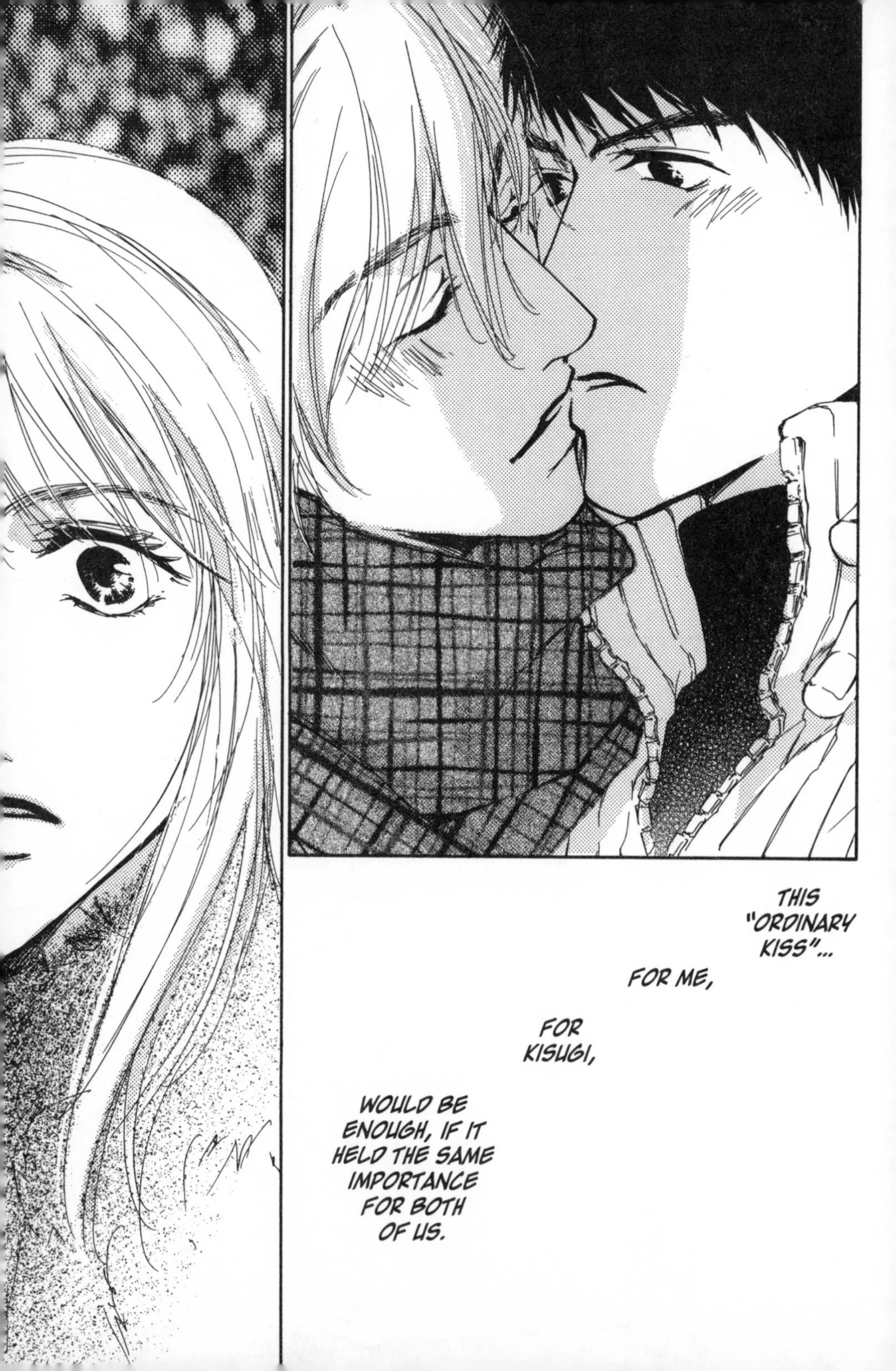
THIS "ORDINARY KISS"...
FOR ME,
FOR KISUGI,
WOULD BE ENOUGH, IF IT HELD THE SAME IMPORTANCE FOR BOTH OF US.

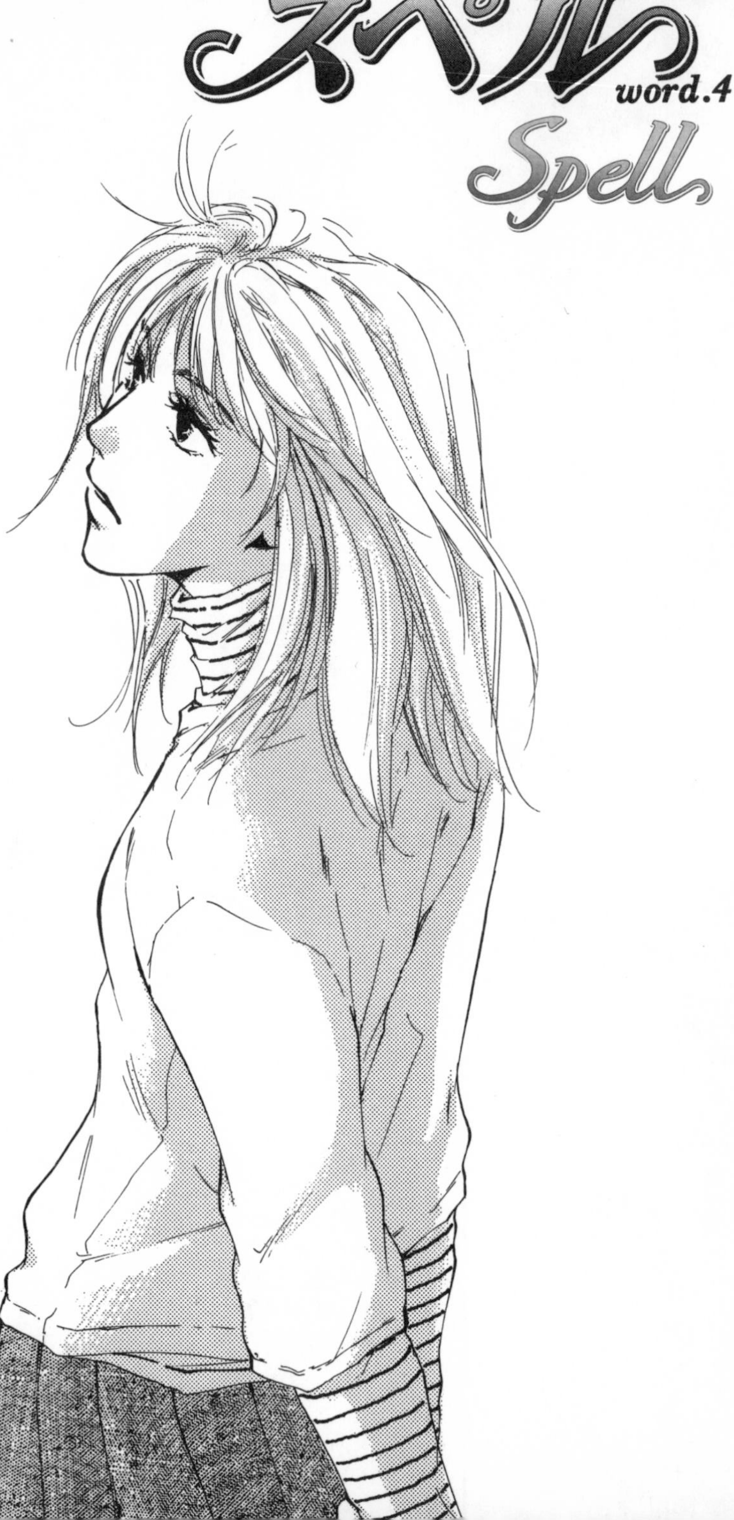
スペル
word.4
Spell

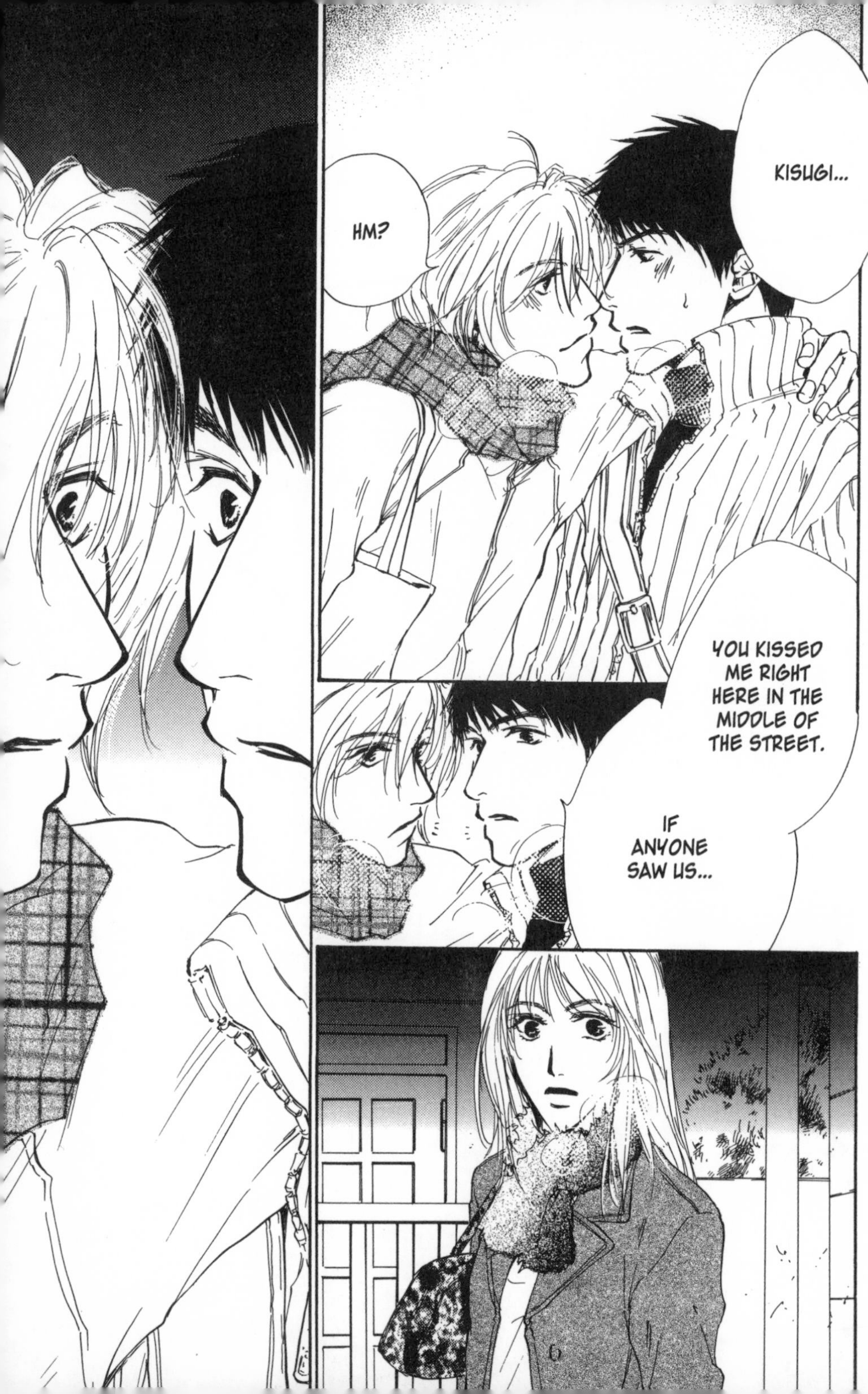
KISUGI...
HM?
YOU KISSED ME RIGHT HERE IN THE MIDDLE OF THE STREET.
IF ANYONE SAW US...

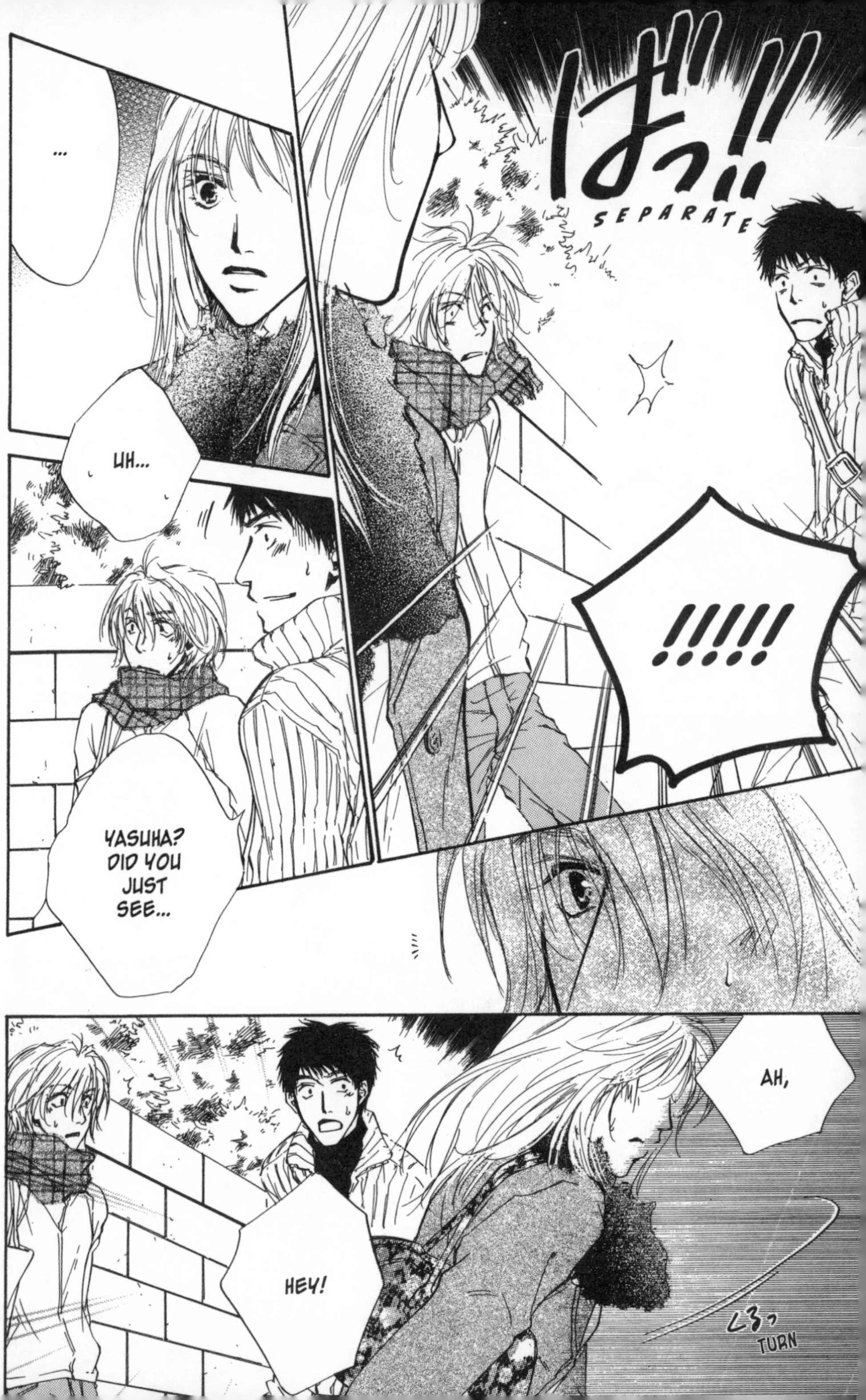
ばっ!!
SEPARATE
!!!!!!
...
UH...
YASUHA? DID YOU JUST SEE...
AH,
くるっ
TURN
HEY!

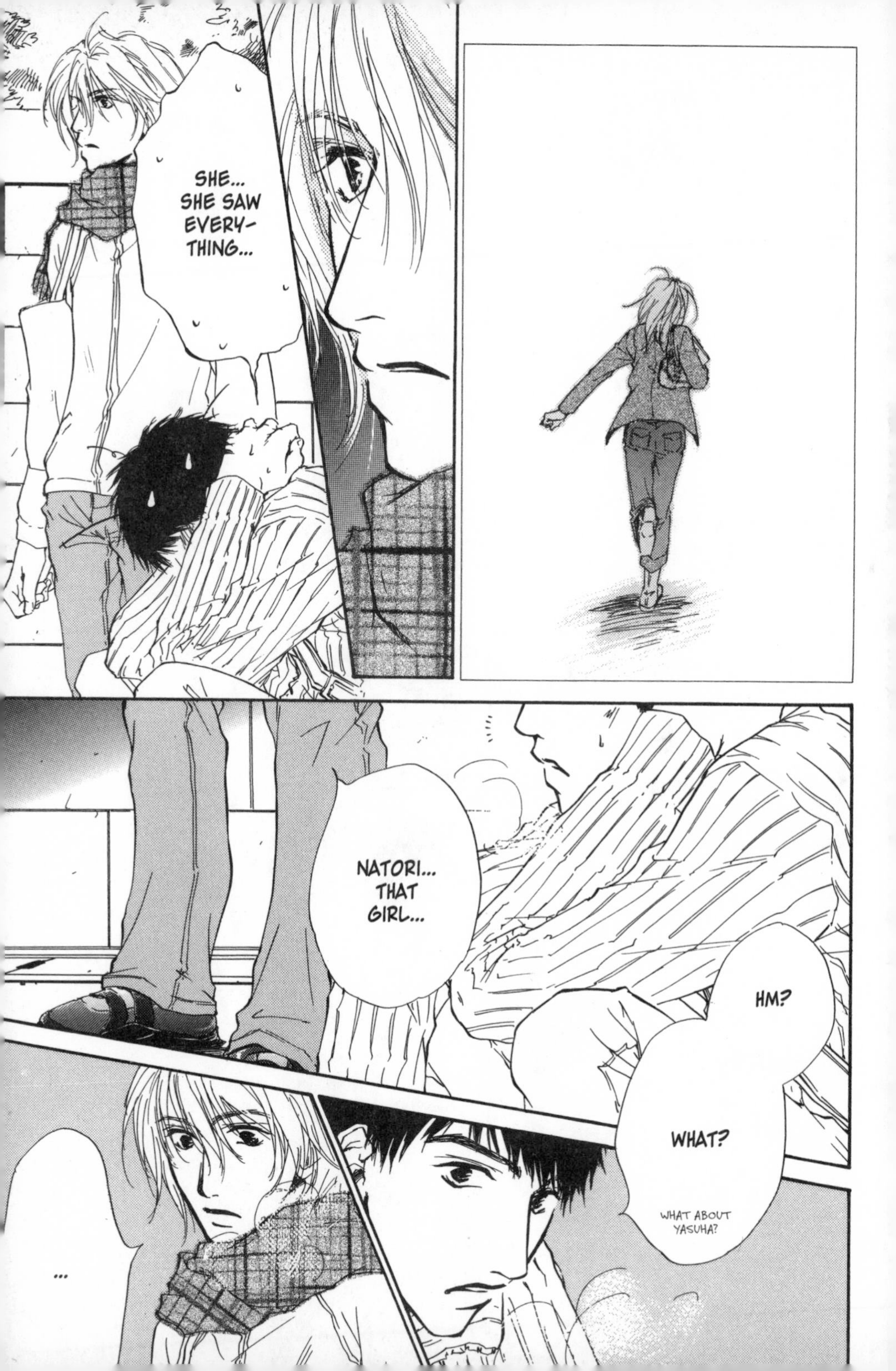
SHE... SHE SAW EVERY-THING...
NATORI... THAT GIRL...
HM?
WHAT?
WHAT ABOUT YASUHA?
...

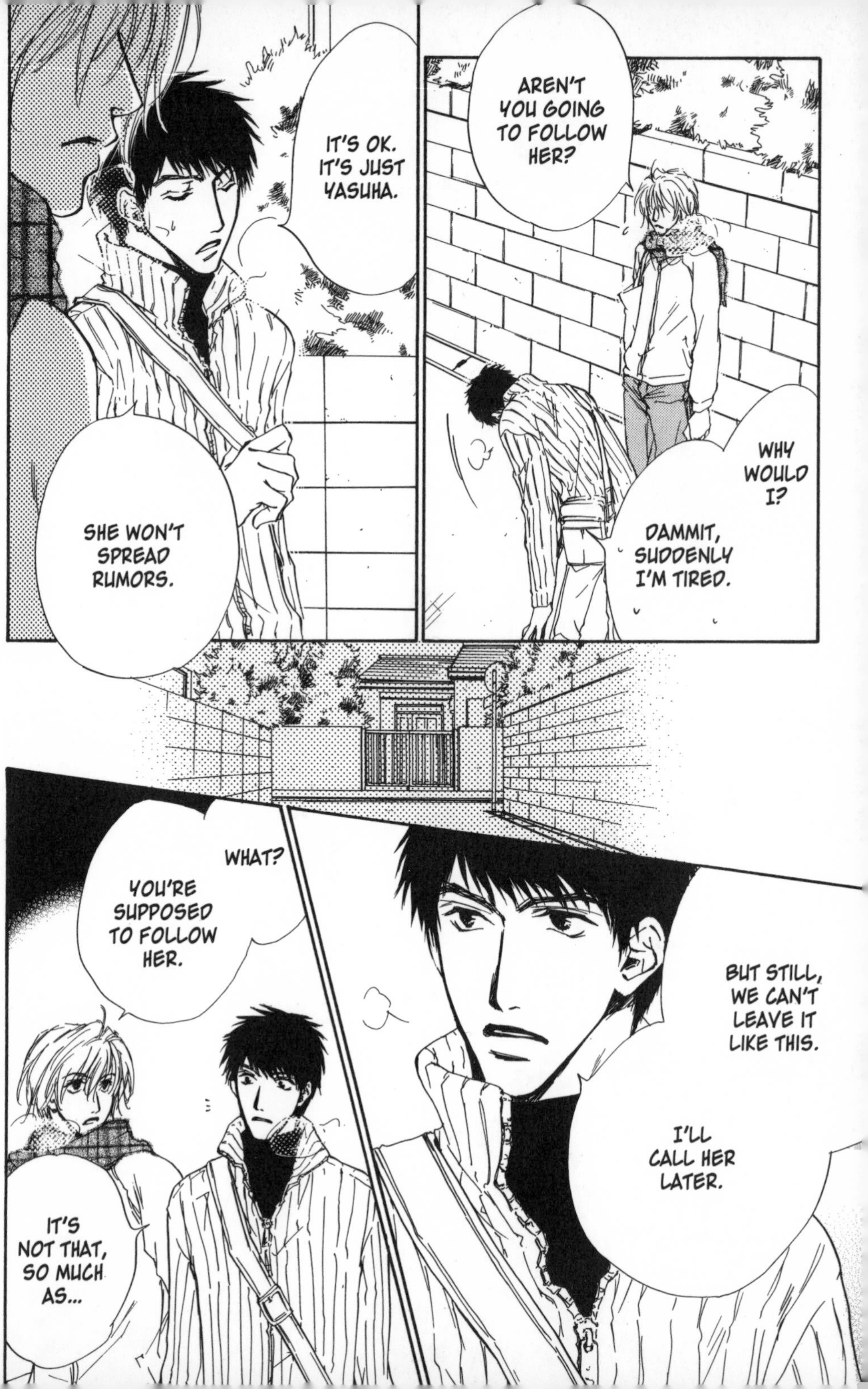
AREN'T YOU GOING TO FOLLOW HER?
WHY WOULD I?
DAMMIT, SUDDENLY I'M TIRED.
IT'S OK. IT'S JUST YASUHA.
SHE WON'T SPREAD RUMORS.
BUT STILL, WE CAN'T LEAVE IT LIKE THIS.
I'LL CALL HER LATER.
WHAT?
YOU'RE SUPPOSED TO FOLLOW HER.
IT'S NOT THAT, SO MUCH AS...

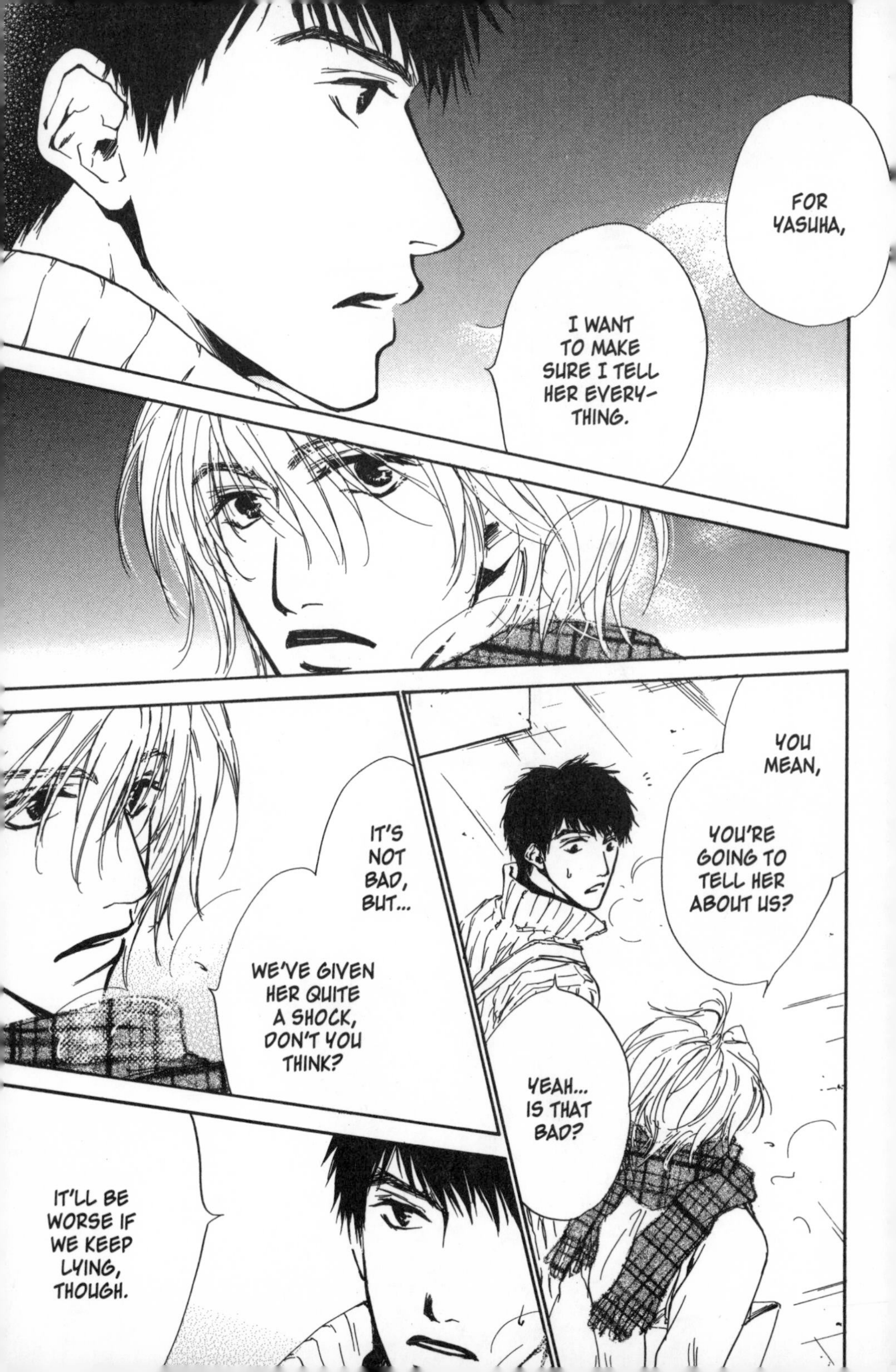
FOR YASUHA,
I WANT TO MAKE SURE I TELL HER EVERY-THING.
YOU MEAN,
YOU'RE GOING TO TELL HER ABOUT US?
YEAH... IS THAT BAD?
IT'S NOT BAD, BUT...
WE'VE GIVEN HER QUITE A SHOCK, DON'T YOU THINK?
IT'LL BE WORSE IF WE KEEP LYING, THOUGH.

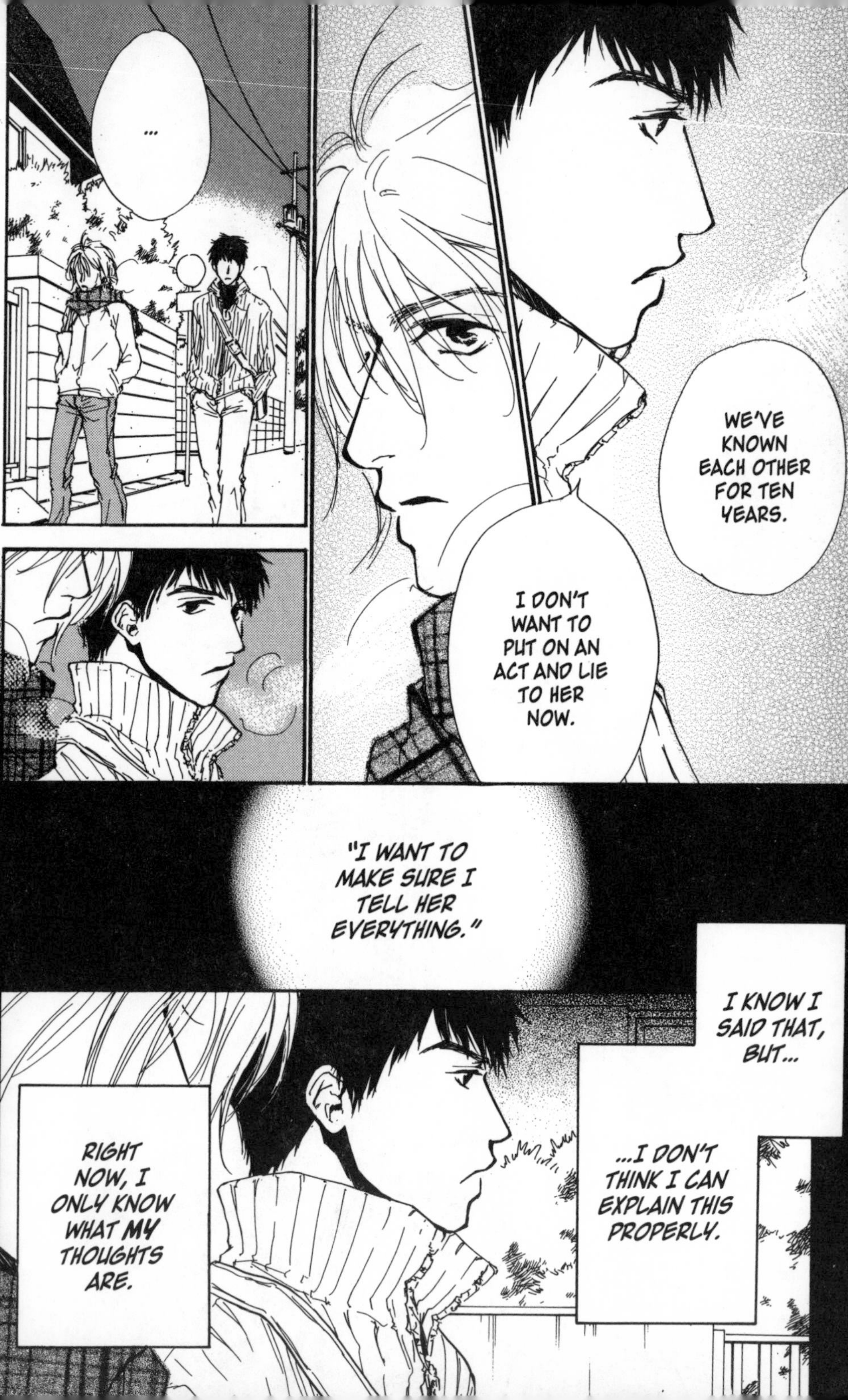
WE'VE KNOWN EACH OTHER FOR TEN YEARS.
I DON'T WANT TO PUT ON AN ACT AND LIE TO HER NOW.
...
"I WANT TO MAKE SURE I TELL HER EVERYTHING."
I KNOW I SAID THAT, BUT...
...I DON'T THINK I CAN EXPLAIN THIS PROPERLY.
RIGHT NOW, I ONLY KNOW WHAT MY THOUGHTS ARE.

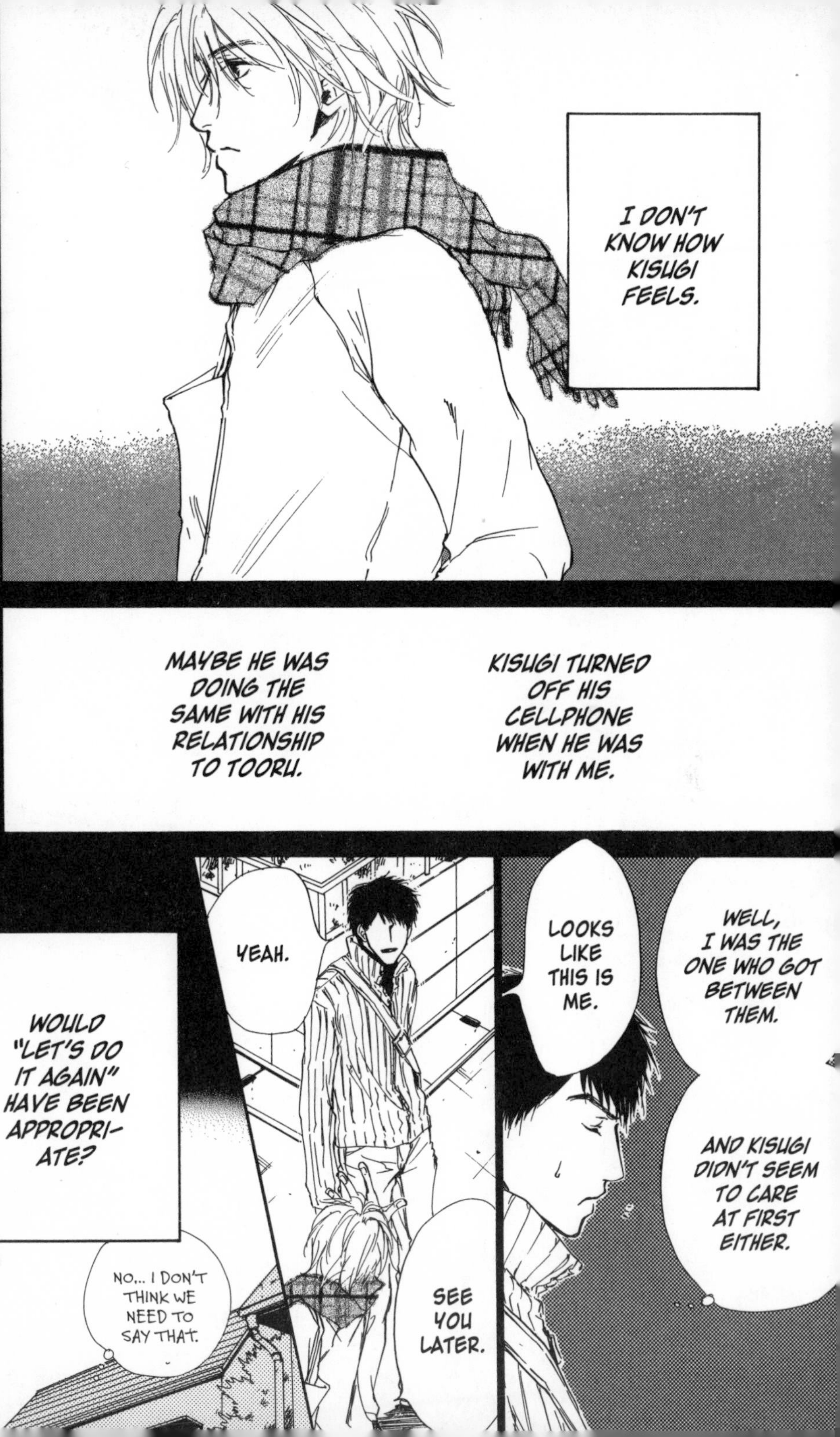
I DON'T KNOW HOW KISUGI FEELS.
KISUGI TURNED OFF HIS CELLPHONE WHEN HE WAS WITH ME.
MAYBE HE WAS DOING THE SAME WITH HIS RELATIONSHIP TO TOORU.
WELL, I WAS THE ONE WHO GOT BETWEEN THEM.
LOOKS LIKE THIS IS ME.
AND KISUGI DIDN'T SEEM TO CARE AT FIRST EITHER.
YEAH.
SEE YOU LATER.
WOULD "LET'S DO IT AGAIN" HAVE BEEN APPROPRIATE?
NO... I DON'T THINK WE NEED TO SAY THAT.

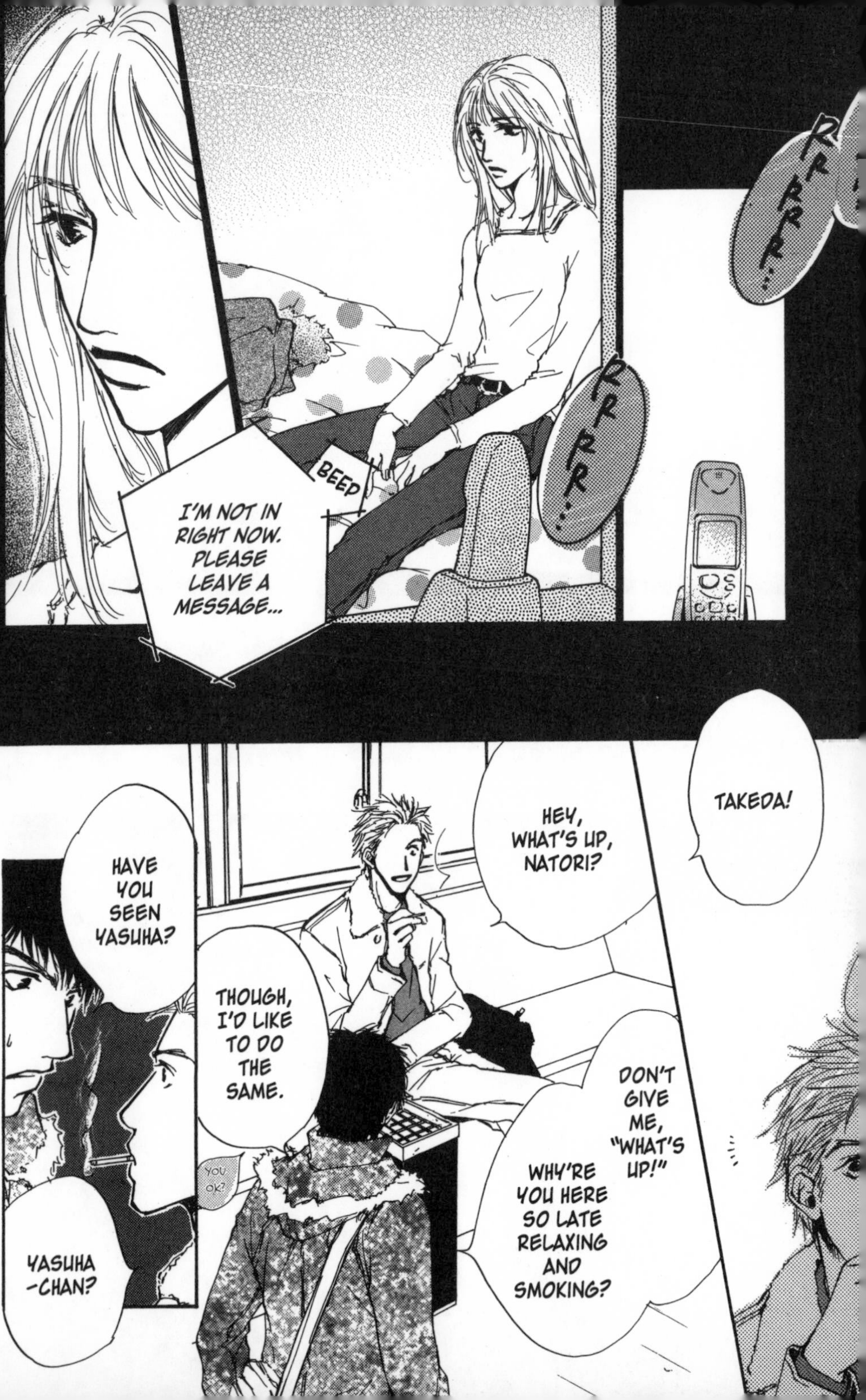
RRRR..
RRRR..
BEEP
I'M NOT IN RIGHT NOW. PLEASE LEAVE A MESSAGE...
TAKEDA!
HEY, WHAT'S UP, NATORI?
DON'T GIVE ME, "WHAT'S UP!"
WHY'RE YOU HERE SO LATE RELAXING AND SMOKING?
THOUGH, I'D LIKE TO DO THE SAME.
YOU OK?
HAVE YOU SEEN YASUHA?
YASUHA-CHAN?

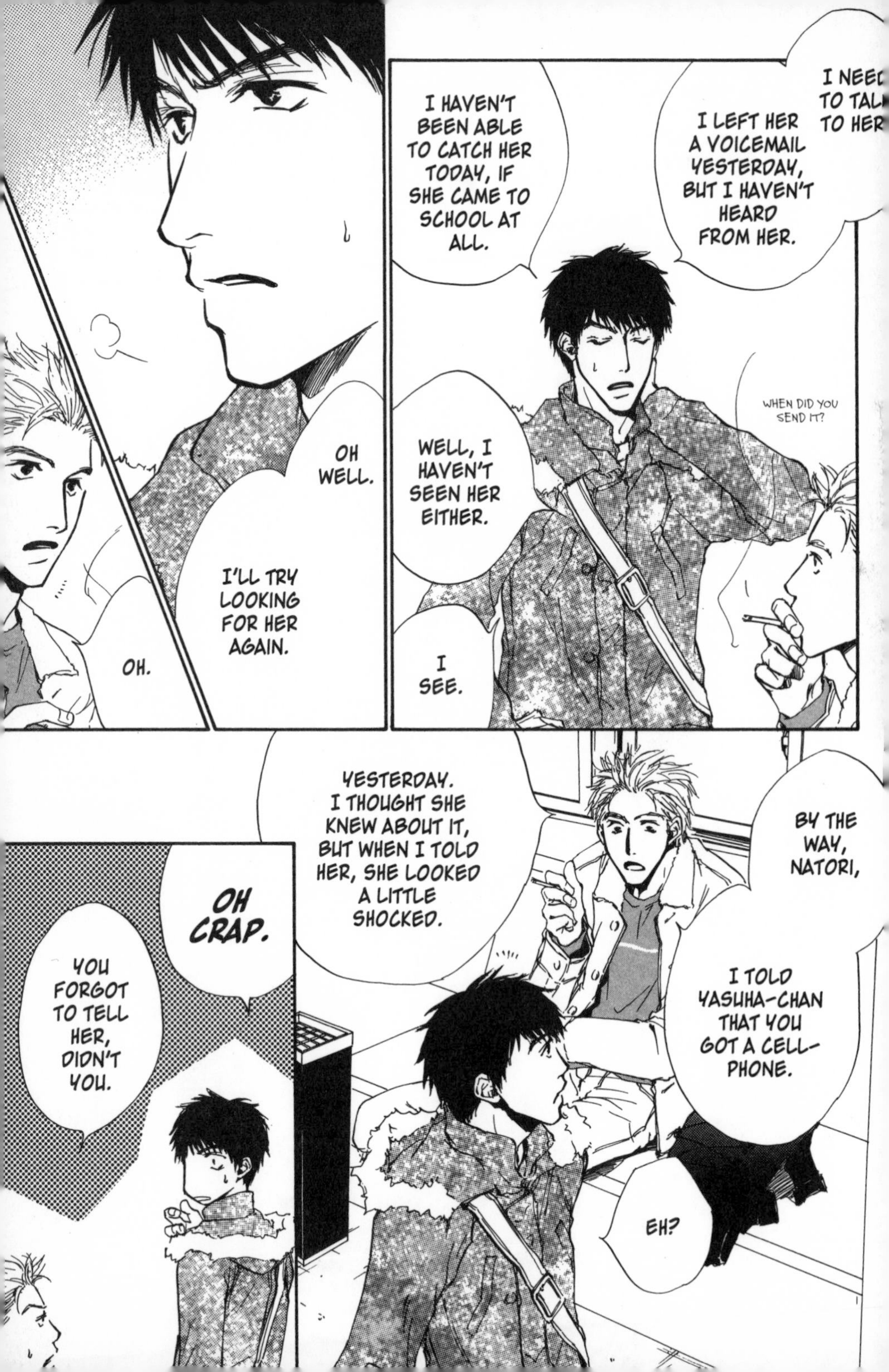
I NEED TO TAL TO HER
I LEFT HER A VOICEMAIL YESTERDAY, BUT I HAVEN'T HEARD FROM HER.
I HAVEN'T BEEN ABLE TO CATCH HER TODAY, IF SHE CAME TO SCHOOL AT ALL.
WHEN DID YOU SEND IT?
WELL, I HAVEN'T SEEN HER EITHER.
I SEE.
OH WELL.
I'LL TRY LOOKING FOR HER AGAIN.
OH.
BY THE WAY, NATORI,
I TOLD YASUHA-CHAN THAT YOU GOT A CELL-PHONE.
EH?
YESTERDAY. I THOUGHT SHE KNEW ABOUT IT, BUT WHEN I TOLD HER, SHE LOOKED A LITTLE SHOCKED.
OH CRAP.
YOU FORGOT TO TELL HER, DIDN'T YOU.

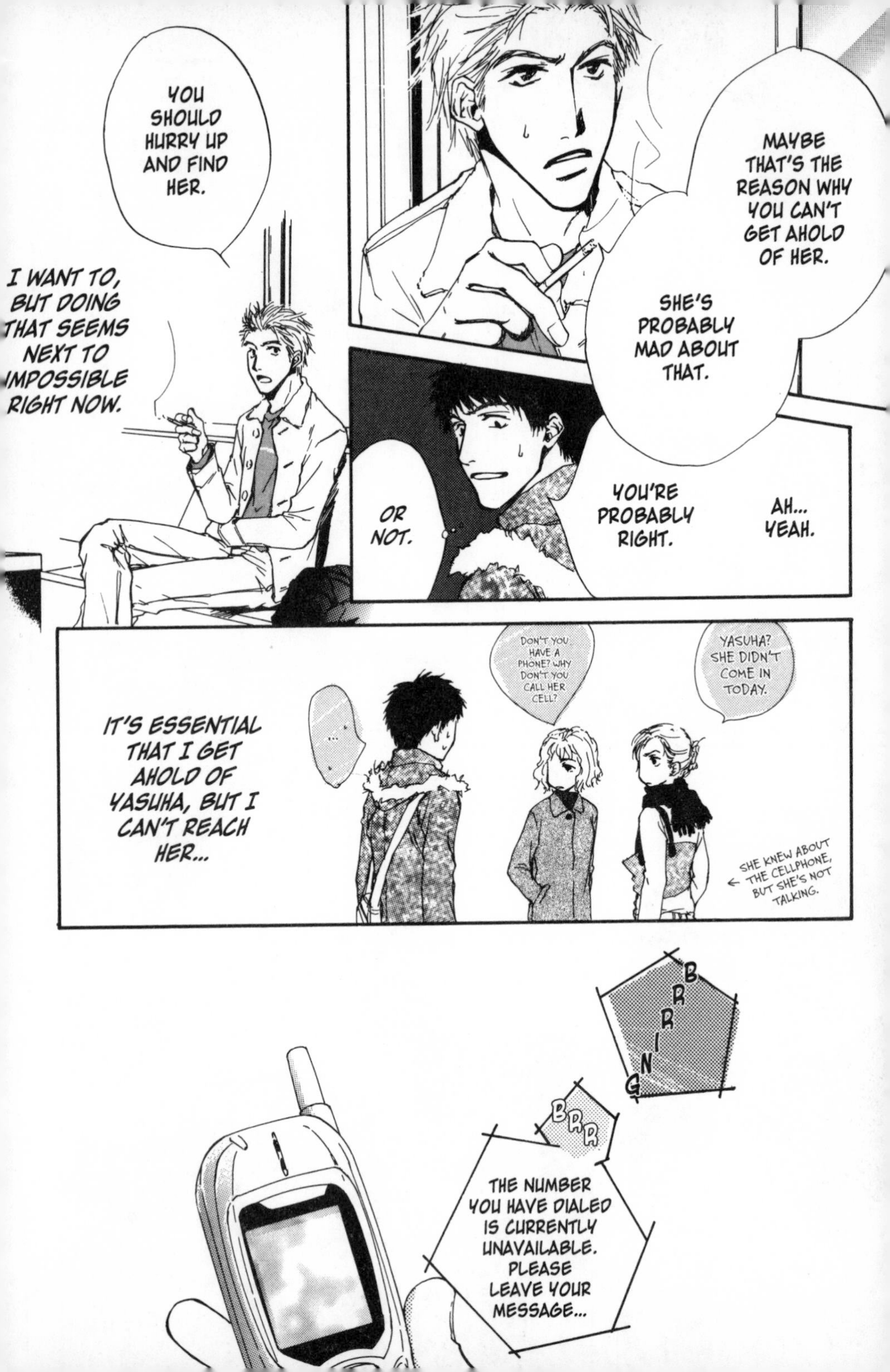

MAYBE THAT'S THE REASON WHY YOU CAN'T GET AHOLD OF HER.
SHE'S PROBABLY MAD ABOUT THAT.
AH... YEAH.
YOU'RE PROBABLY RIGHT.
OR NOT.
YOU SHOULD HURRY UP AND FIND HER.
I WANT TO, BUT DOING THAT SEEMS NEXT TO IMPOSSIBLE RIGHT NOW.
YASUHA? SHE DIDN'T COME IN TODAY.
SHE KNEW ABOUT THE CELLPHONE, BUT SHE'S NOT TALKING.
DON'T YOU HAVE A PHONE? WHY DON'T YOU CALL HER CELL?
...
IT'S ESSENTIAL THAT I GET AHOLD OF YASUHA, BUT I CAN'T REACH HER...
BRRING
BRR
THE NUMBER YOU HAVE DIALED IS CURRENTLY UNAVAILABLE. PLEASE LEAVE YOUR MESSAGE...

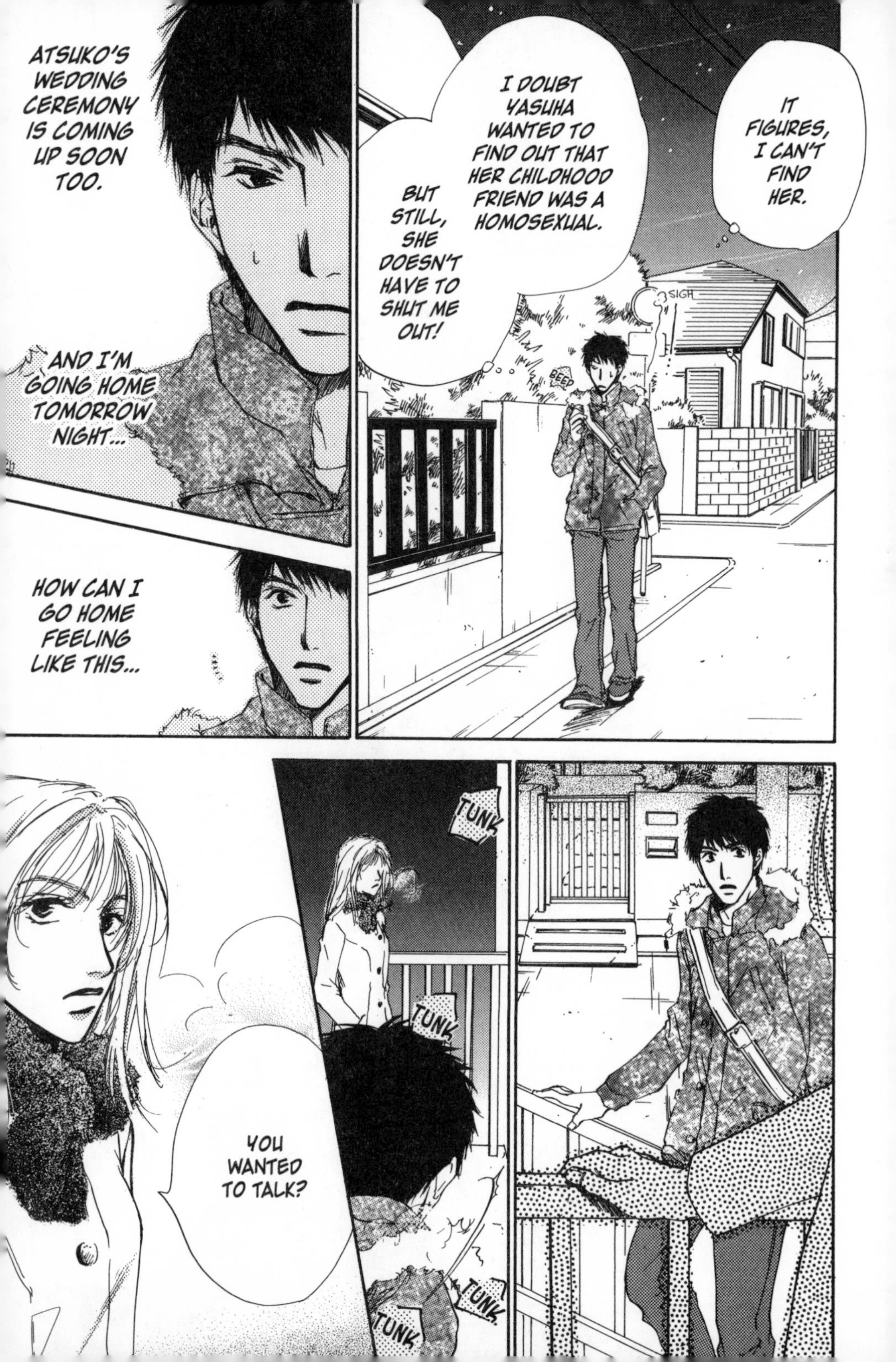
IT FIGURES, I CAN'T FIND HER.
I DOUBT YASUHA WANTED TO FIND OUT THAT HER CHILDHOOD FRIEND WAS A HOMOSEXUAL.
BUT STILL, SHE DOESN'T HAVE TO SHUT ME OUT!
SIGH
BEEP
ATSUKO'S WEDDING CEREMONY IS COMING UP SOON TOO.
AND I'M GOING HOME TOMORROW NIGHT...
HOW CAN I GO HOME FEELING LIKE THIS...
TUNK
TUNK
TUNK
TUNK
YOU WANTED TO TALK?

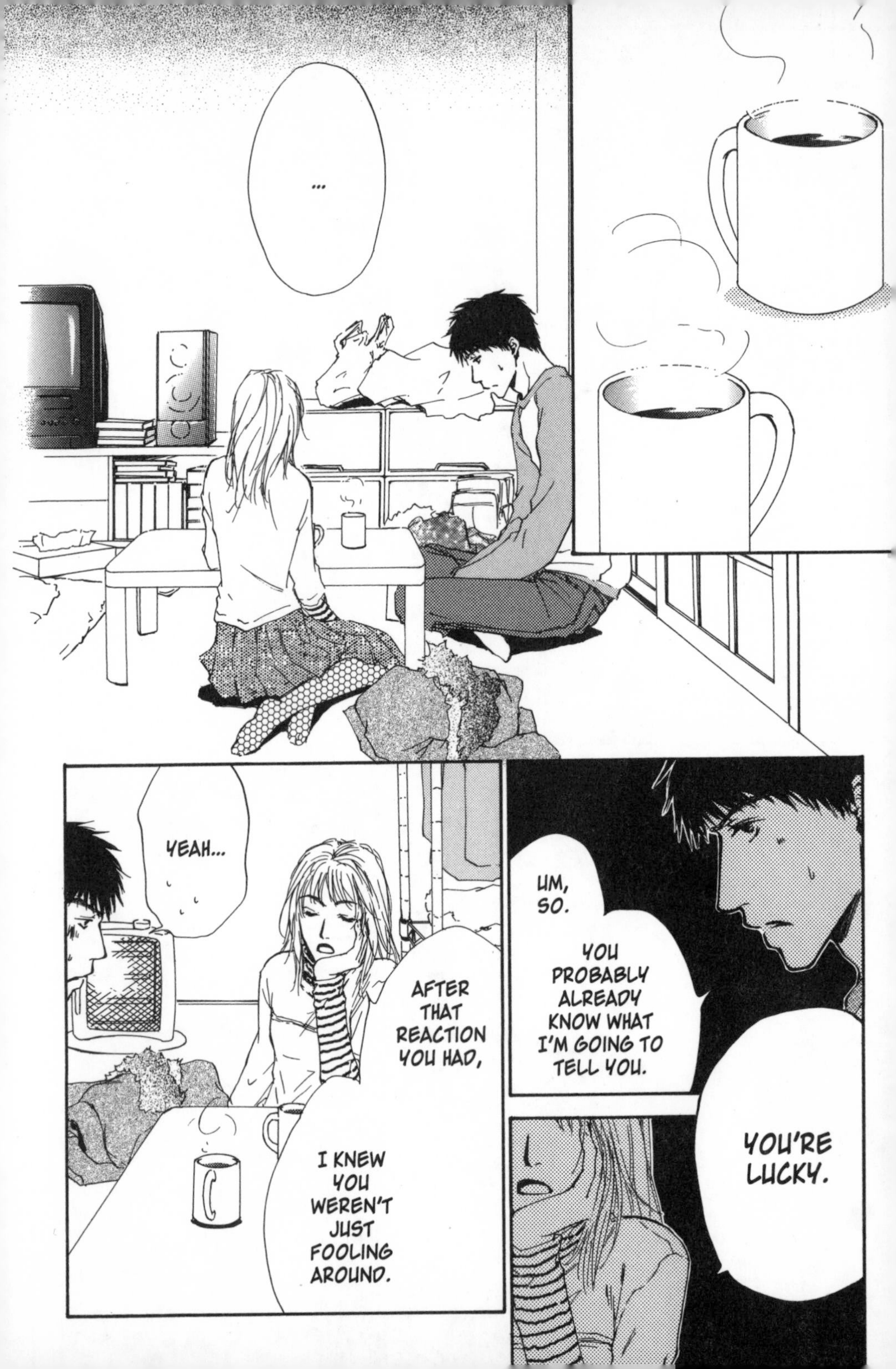
...
UM, SO.
YOU PROBABLY ALREADY KNOW WHAT I'M GOING TO TELL YOU.
YOU'RE LUCKY.
YEAH...
AFTER THAT REACTION YOU HAD,
I KNEW YOU WEREN'T JUST FOOLING AROUND.

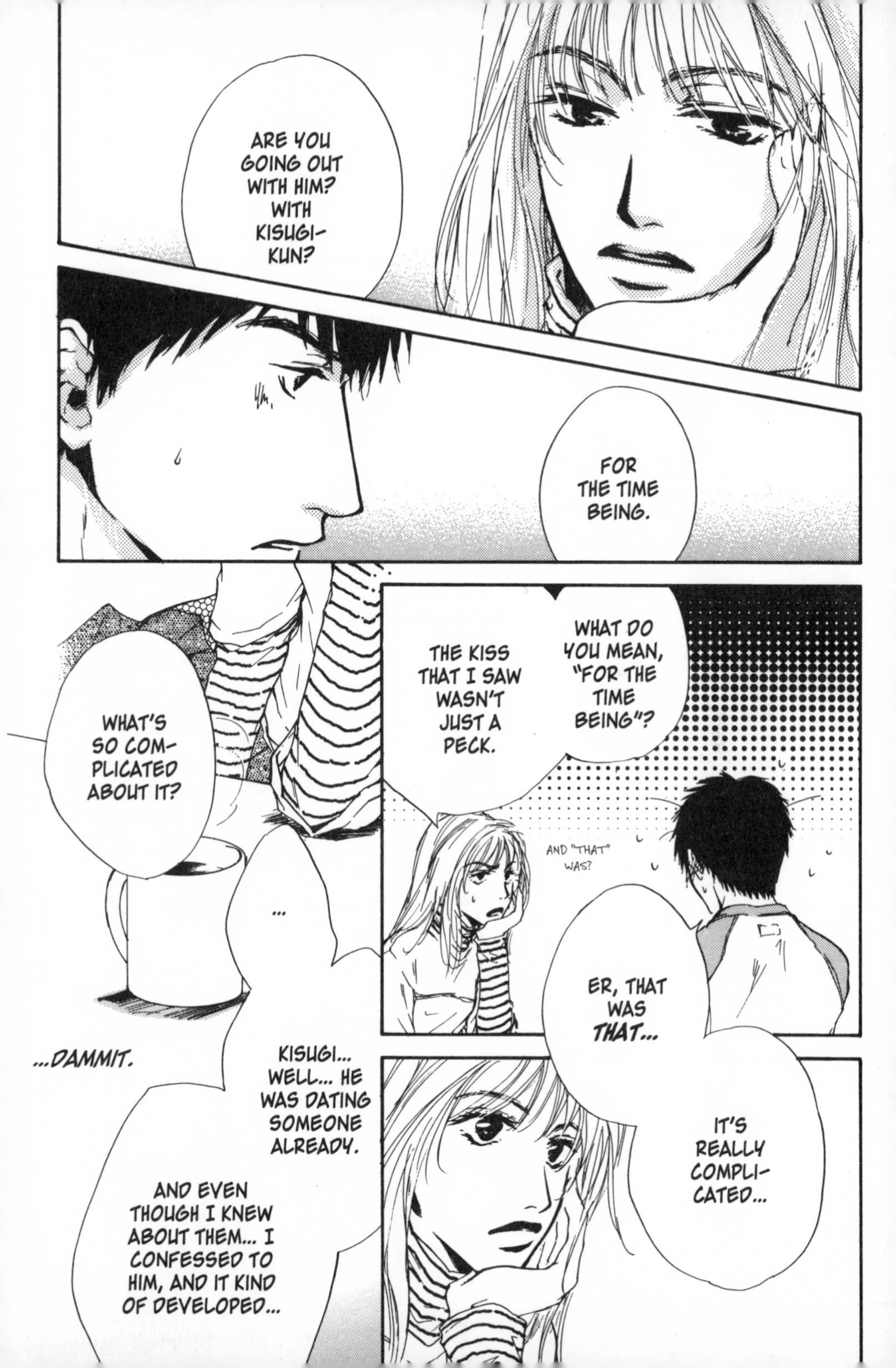
ARE YOU GOING OUT WITH HIM? WITH KISUGI-KUN?
FOR THE TIME BEING.
WHAT DO YOU MEAN, "FOR THE TIME BEING"?
THE KISS THAT I SAW WASN'T JUST A PECK.
AND "THAT" WAS?
ER, THAT WAS *THAT*...
IT'S REALLY COMPLICATED...
WHAT'S SO COMPLICATED ABOUT IT?
...
KISUGI... WELL... HE WAS DATING SOMEONE ALREADY.
AND EVEN THOUGH I KNEW ABOUT THEM... I CONFESSED TO HIM, AND IT KIND OF DEVELOPED...
...DAMMIT.

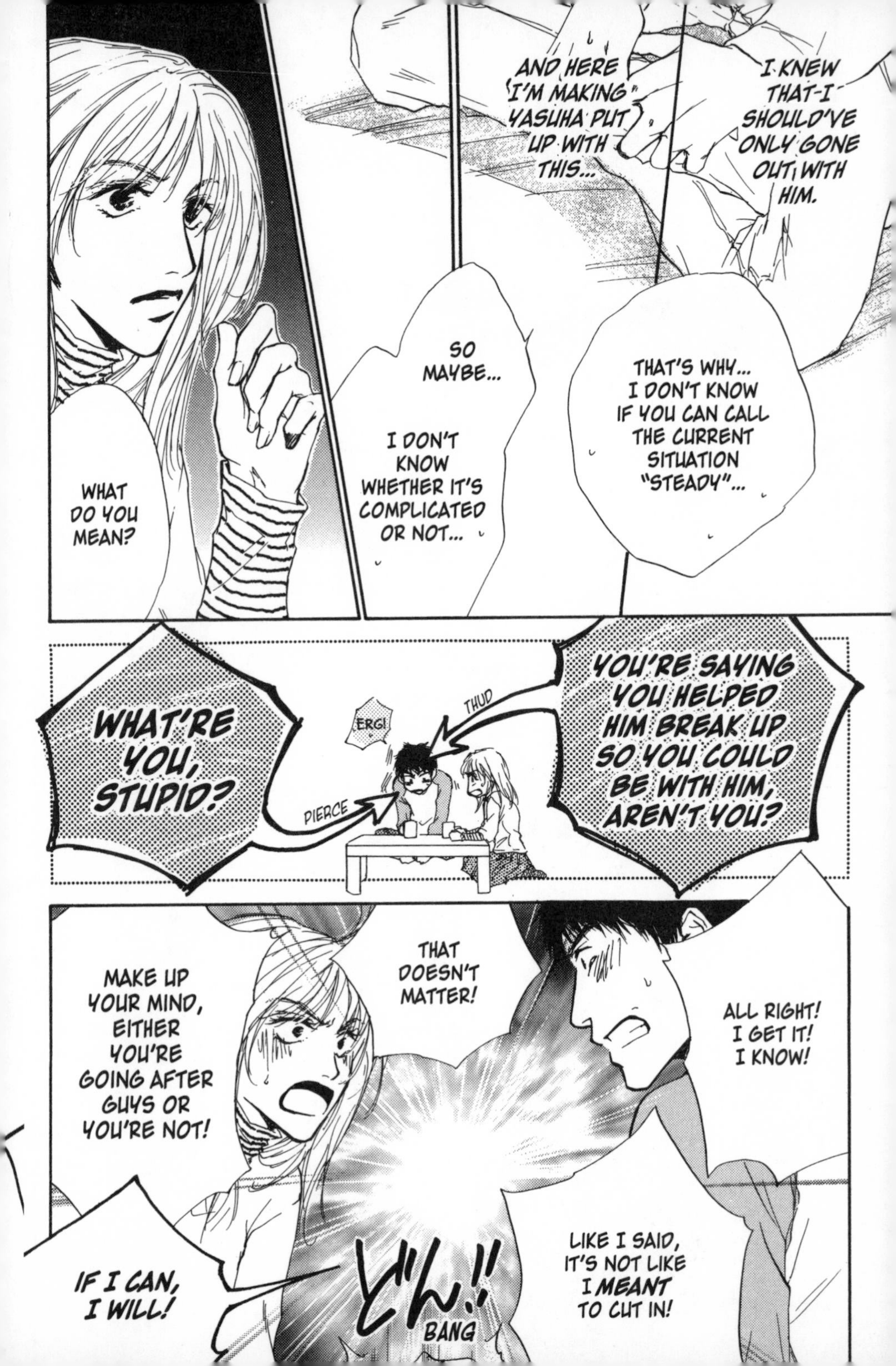
I KNEW THAT I SHOULD'VE ONLY GONE OUT WITH HIM.
THAT'S WHY... I DON'T KNOW IF YOU CAN CALL THE CURRENT SITUATION "STEADY"...
AND HERE I'M MAKING YASUHA PUT UP WITH THIS...
SO MAYBE...
I DON'T KNOW WHETHER IT'S COMPLICATED OR NOT...
WHAT DO YOU MEAN?
YOU'RE SAYING YOU HELPED HIM BREAK UP SO YOU COULD BE WITH HIM, AREN'T YOU?
THUD
ERG!
PIERCE
WHAT'RE YOU, STUPID?
ALL RIGHT! I GET IT! I KNOW!
THAT DOESN'T MATTER!
MAKE UP YOUR MIND, EITHER YOU'RE GOING AFTER GUYS OR YOU'RE NOT!
LIKE I SAID, IT'S NOT LIKE I *MEANT* TO CUT IN!
どん!!
BANG
IF I CAN, I WILL!

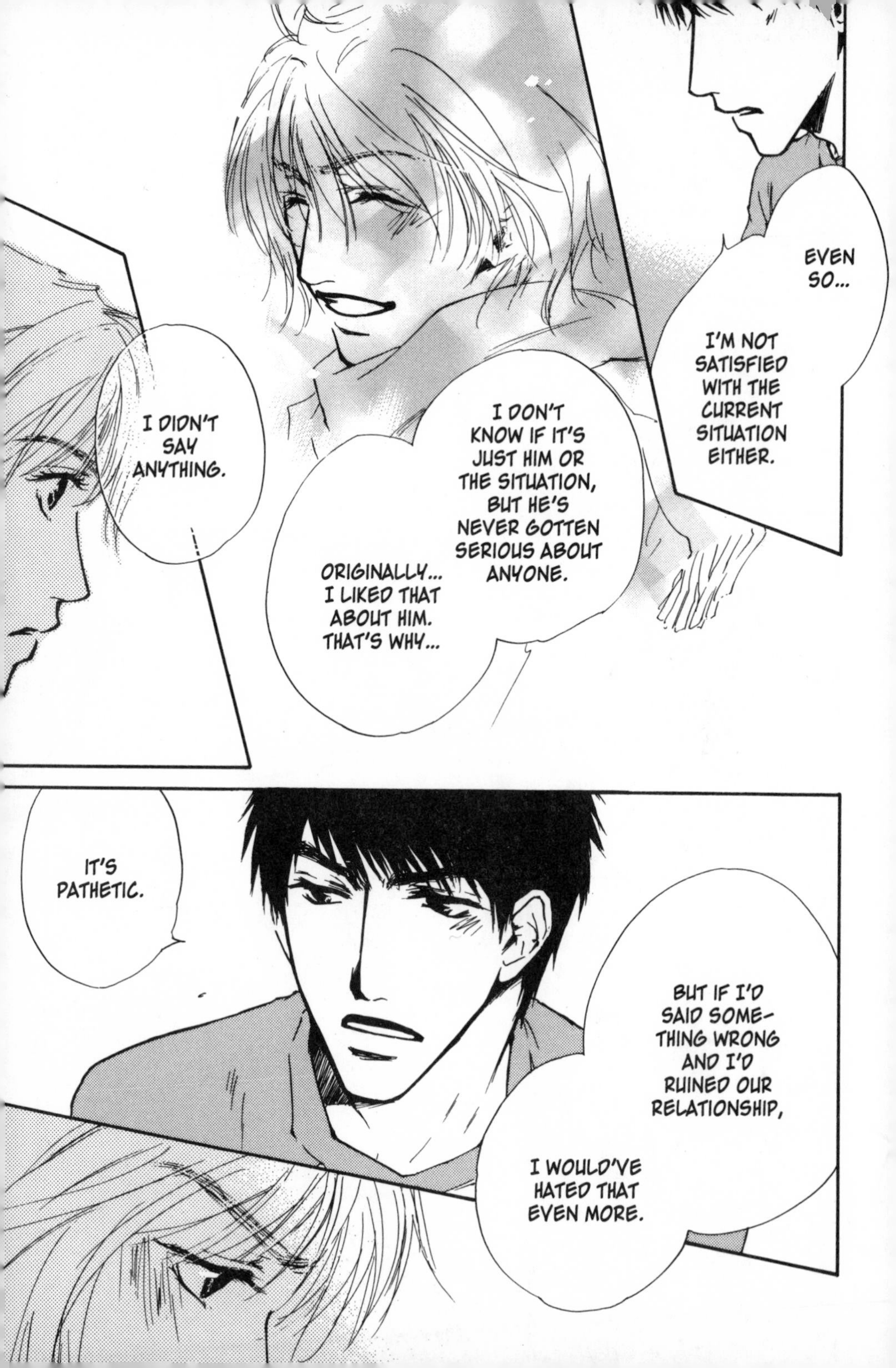
EVEN SO...
I'M NOT SATISFIED WITH THE CURRENT SITUATION EITHER.
I DON'T KNOW IF IT'S JUST HIM OR THE SITUATION, BUT HE'S NEVER GOTTEN SERIOUS ABOUT ANYONE.
ORIGINALLY... I LIKED THAT ABOUT HIM. THAT'S WHY...
I DIDN'T SAY ANYTHING.
BUT IF I'D SAID SOME-THING WRONG AND I'D RUINED OUR RELATIONSHIP,
I WOULD'VE HATED THAT EVEN MORE.
IT'S PATHETIC.

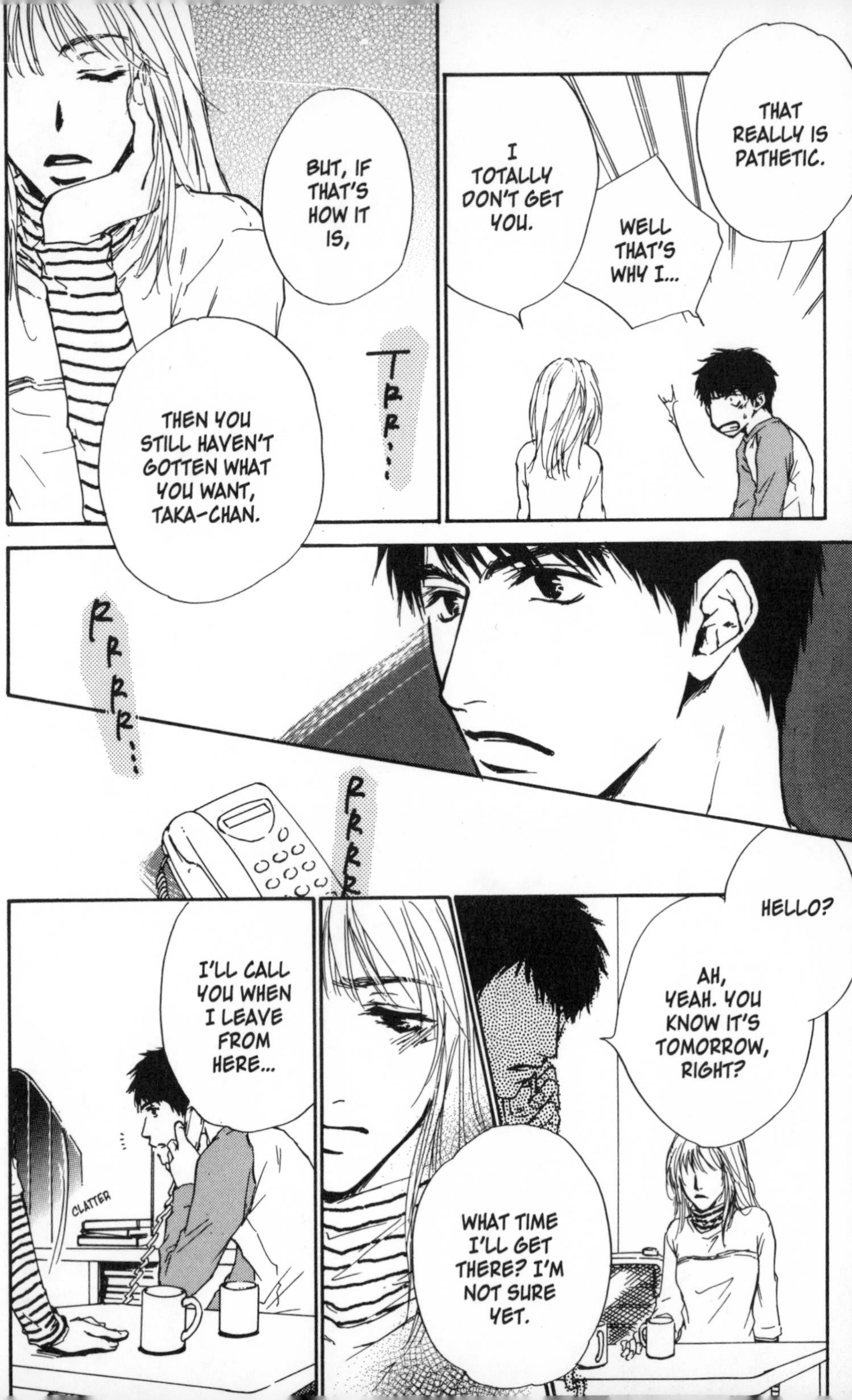
THAT REALLY IS PATHETIC.
I TOTALLY DON'T GET YOU.
WELL THAT'S WHY I...
BUT, IF THAT'S HOW IT IS,
THEN YOU STILL HAVEN'T GOTTEN WHAT YOU WANT, TAKA-CHAN.
TRR...
RRRR...
RRRRR
HELLO?
AH, YEAH. YOU KNOW IT'S TOMORROW, RIGHT?
WHAT TIME I'LL GET THERE? I'M NOT SURE YET.
I'LL CALL YOU WHEN I LEAVE FROM HERE...
CLATTER

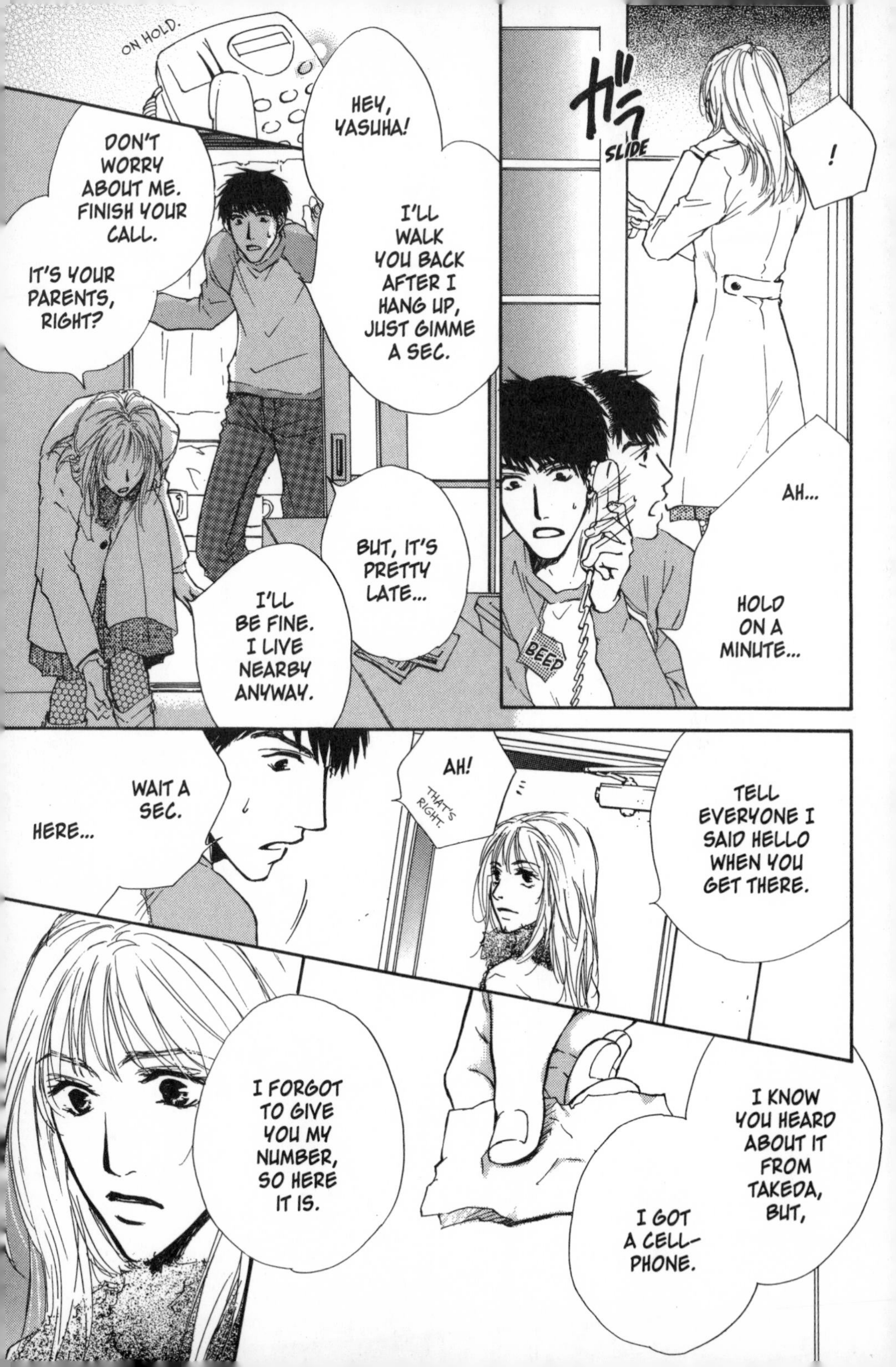
ガラ
SLIDE
!
AH...
HOLD ON A MINUTE...
BEEP
ON HOLD.
HEY, YASUHA!
I'LL WALK YOU BACK AFTER I HANG UP, JUST GIMME A SEC.
DON'T WORRY ABOUT ME. FINISH YOUR CALL.
IT'S YOUR PARENTS, RIGHT?
BUT, IT'S PRETTY LATE...
I'LL BE FINE. I LIVE NEARBY ANYWAY.
TELL EVERYONE I SAID HELLO WHEN YOU GET THERE.
AH!
THAT'S RIGHT.
...
WAIT A SEC.
HERE...
I KNOW YOU HEARD ABOUT IT FROM TAKEDA, BUT,
I GOT A CELL-PHONE.
I FORGOT TO GIVE YOU MY NUMBER, SO HERE IT IS.

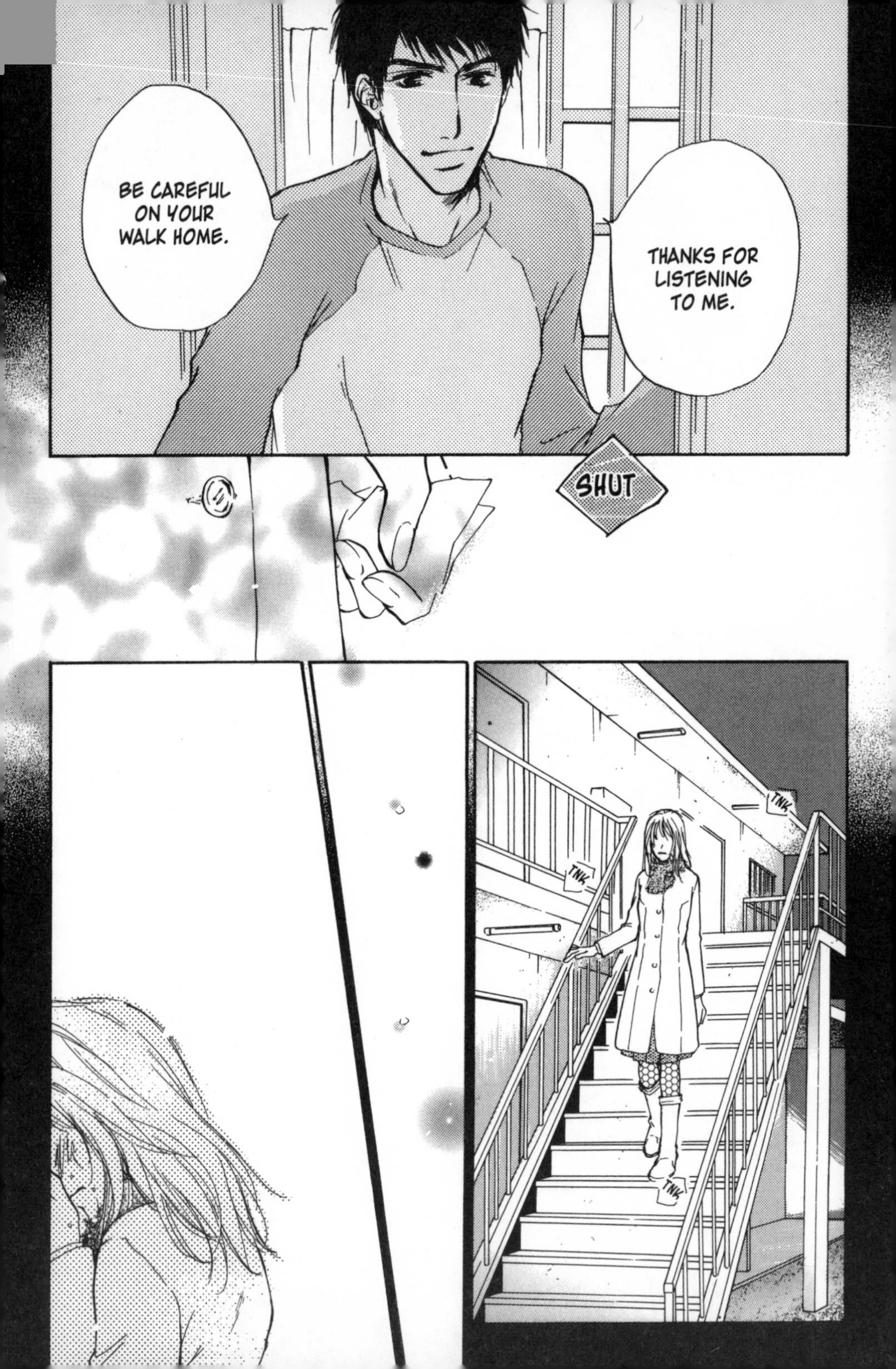
THANKS FOR LISTENING TO ME.
BE CAREFUL ON YOUR WALK HOME.
SHUT
TNK
TNK
TNK

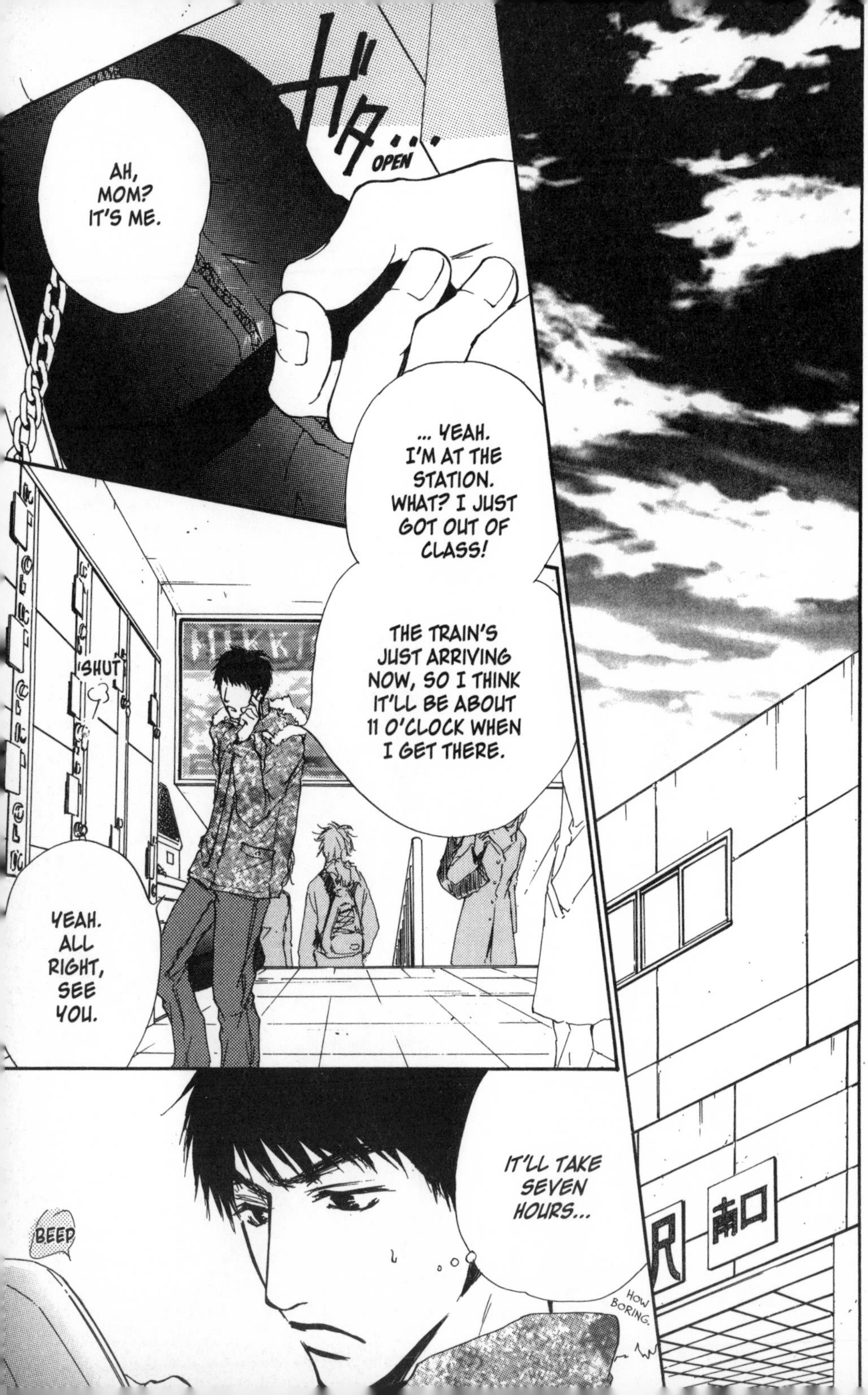
ガバ...
OPEN
AH, MOM? IT'S ME.
... YEAH. I'M AT THE STATION. WHAT? I JUST GOT OUT OF CLASS!
THE TRAIN'S JUST ARRIVING NOW, SO I THINK IT'LL BE ABOUT 11 O'CLOCK WHEN I GET THERE.
SHUT
YEAH. ALL RIGHT, SEE YOU.
BEEP
IT'LL TAKE SEVEN HOURS...
南口
HOW BORING.

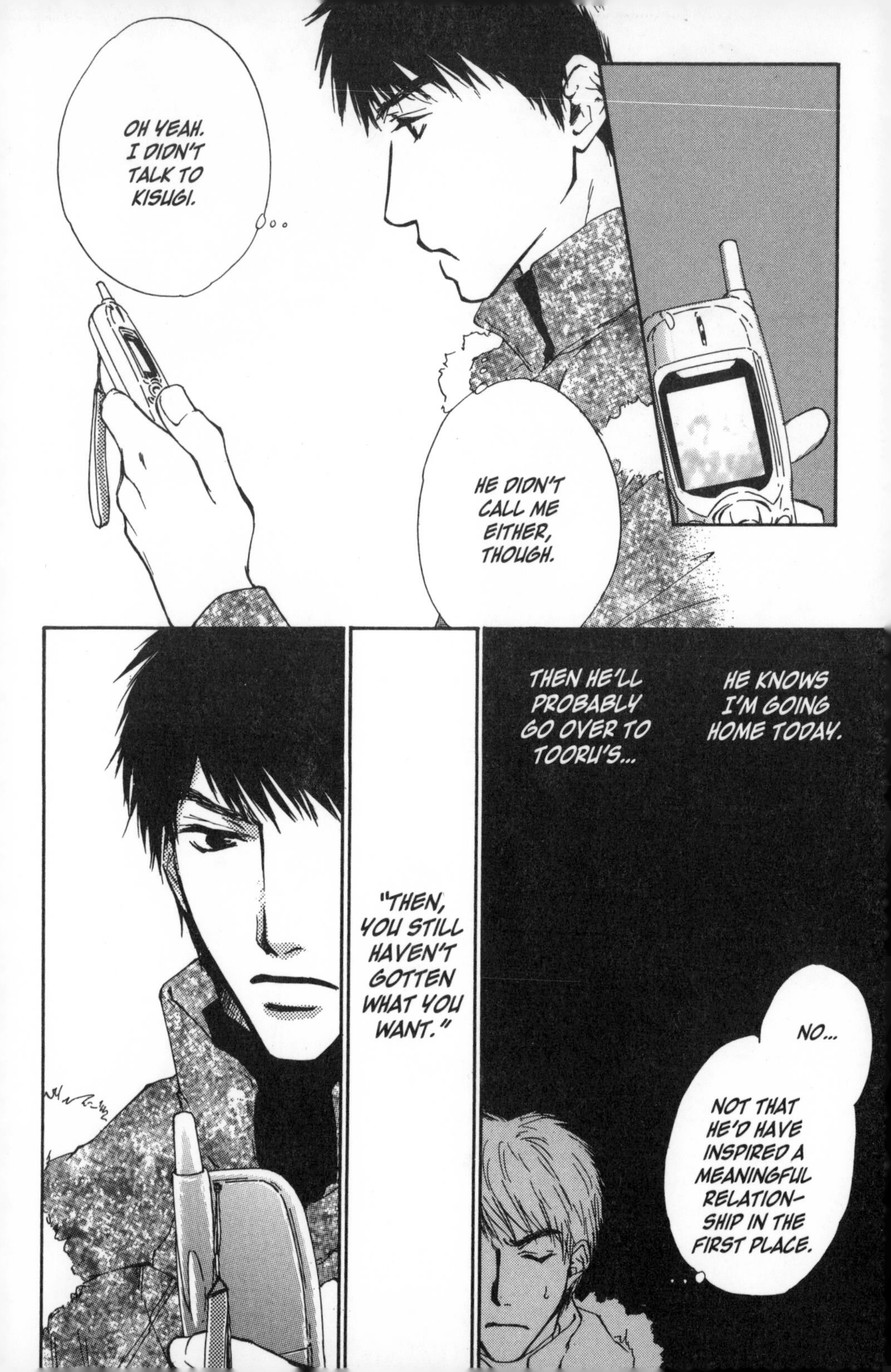
OH YEAH. I DIDN'T TALK TO KISUGI.
HE DIDN'T CALL ME EITHER, THOUGH.
HE KNOWS I'M GOING HOME TODAY.
THEN HE'LL PROBABLY GO OVER TO TOORU'S...
NO...
NOT THAT HE'D HAVE INSPIRED A MEANINGFUL RELATION-SHIP IN THE FIRST PLACE.
"THEN, YOU STILL HAVEN'T GOTTEN WHAT YOU WANT."

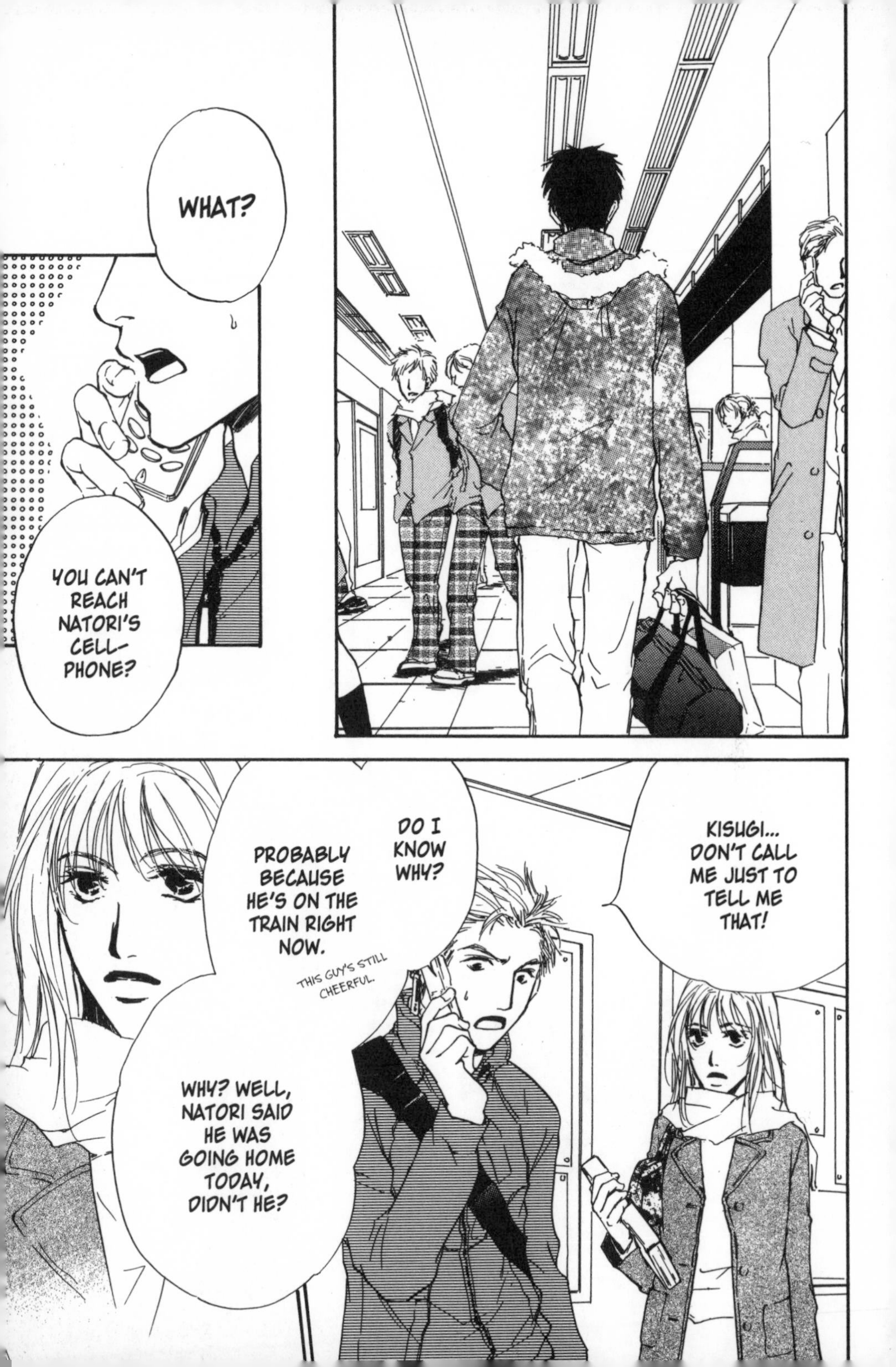
WHAT?
YOU CAN'T REACH NATORI'S CELL-PHONE?
KISUGI... DON'T CALL ME JUST TO TELL ME THAT!
DO I KNOW WHY?
PROBABLY BECAUSE HE'S ON THE TRAIN RIGHT NOW.
THIS GUY'S STILL CHEERFUL.
WHY? WELL, NATORI SAID HE WAS GOING HOME TODAY, DIDN'T HE?

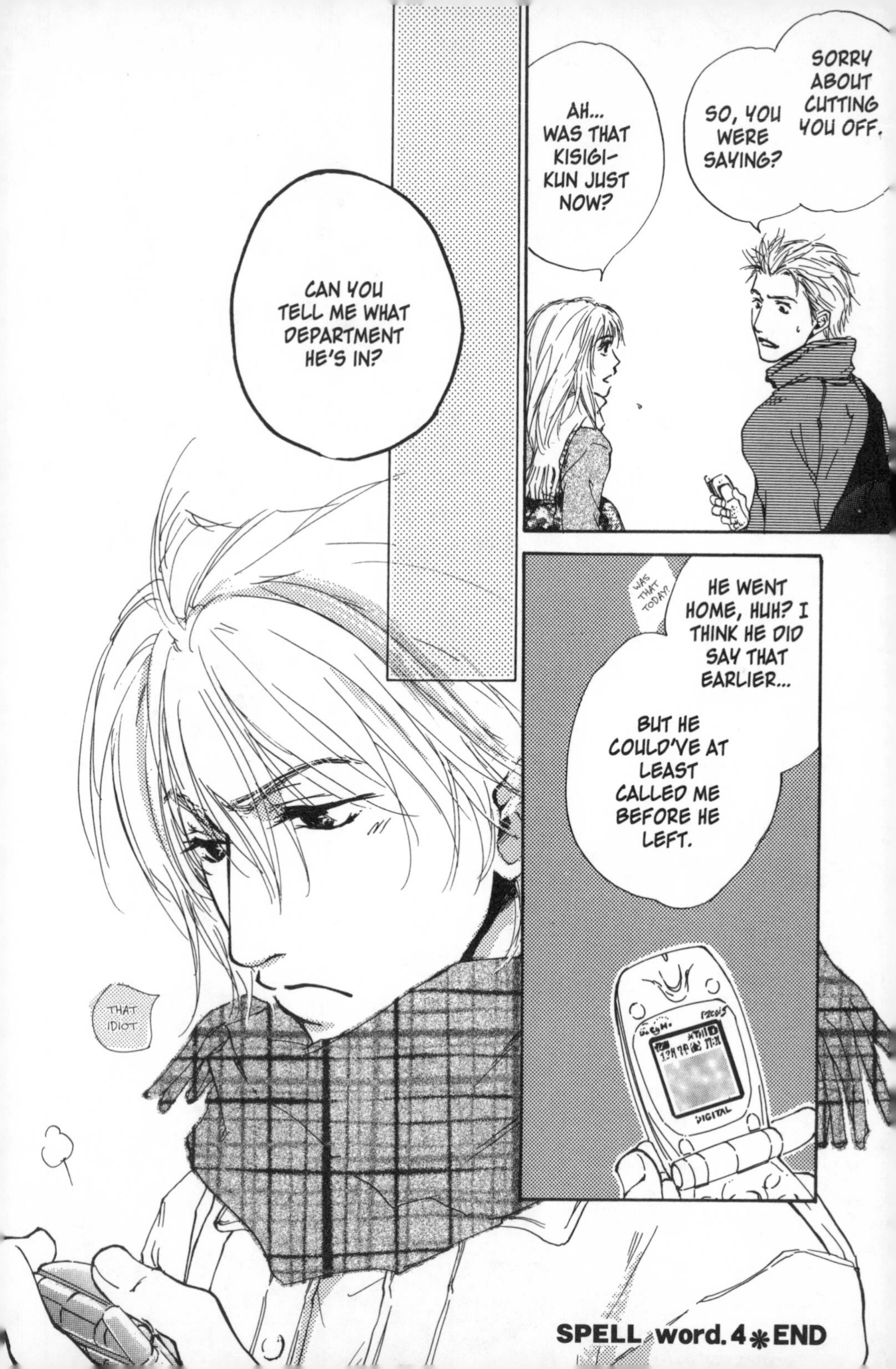
SORRY ABOUT CUTTING YOU OFF.
SO, YOU WERE SAYING?
AH... WAS THAT KISIGI-KUN JUST NOW?
WAS THAT TODAY?
HE WENT HOME, HUH? I THINK HE DID SAY THAT EARLIER...
BUT HE COULD'VE AT LEAST CALLED ME BEFORE HE LEFT.
DIGITAL
CAN YOU TELL ME WHAT DEPARTMENT HE'S IN?
THAT IDIOT
SPELL word.4 * END

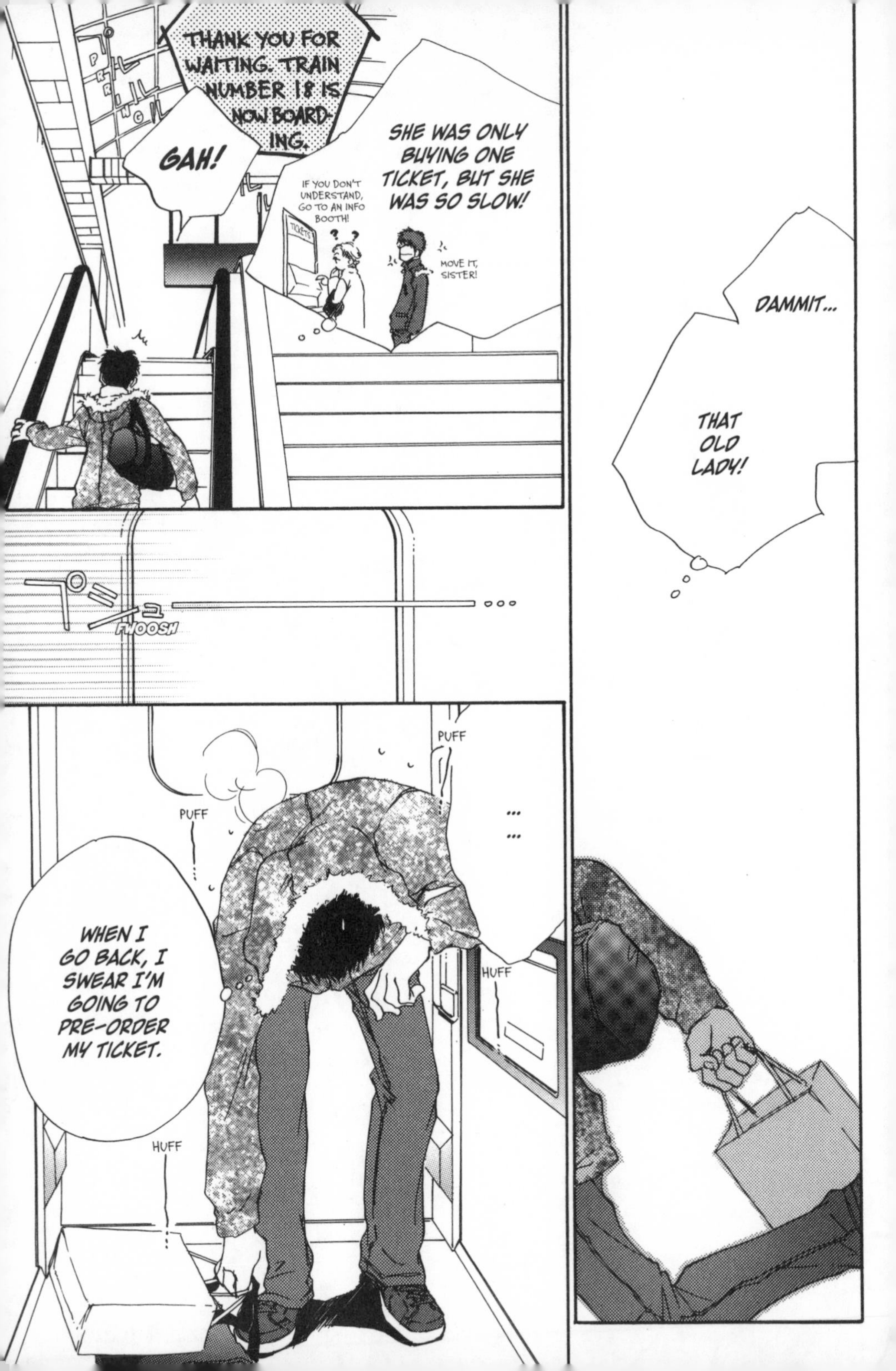
DAMMIT...
THAT OLD LADY!
THANK YOU FOR WAITING. TRAIN NUMBER 18 IS NOW BOARDING.
SHE WAS ONLY BUYING ONE TICKET, BUT SHE WAS SO SLOW!
MOVE IT, SISTER!
IF YOU DON'T UNDERSTAND, GO TO AN INFO BOOTH!
TICKETS
GAH!
FWOOSH
...
PUFF
...
...
PUFF
HUFF
WHEN I GO BACK, I SWEAR I'M GOING TO PRE-ORDER MY TICKET.
HUFF

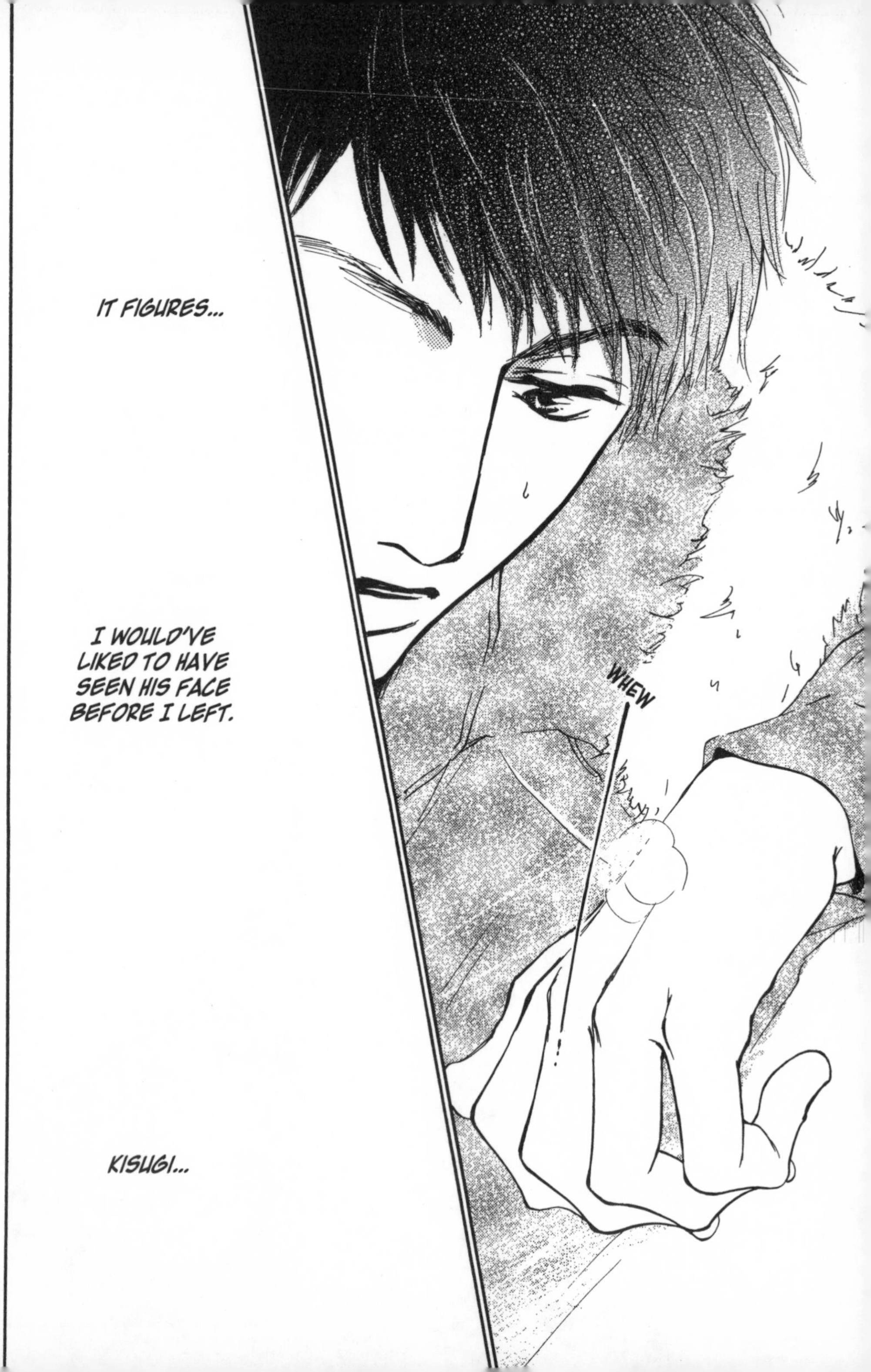
WHEW
IT FIGURES...
I WOULD'VE LIKED TO HAVE SEEN HIS FACE BEFORE I LEFT.
KISUGI...

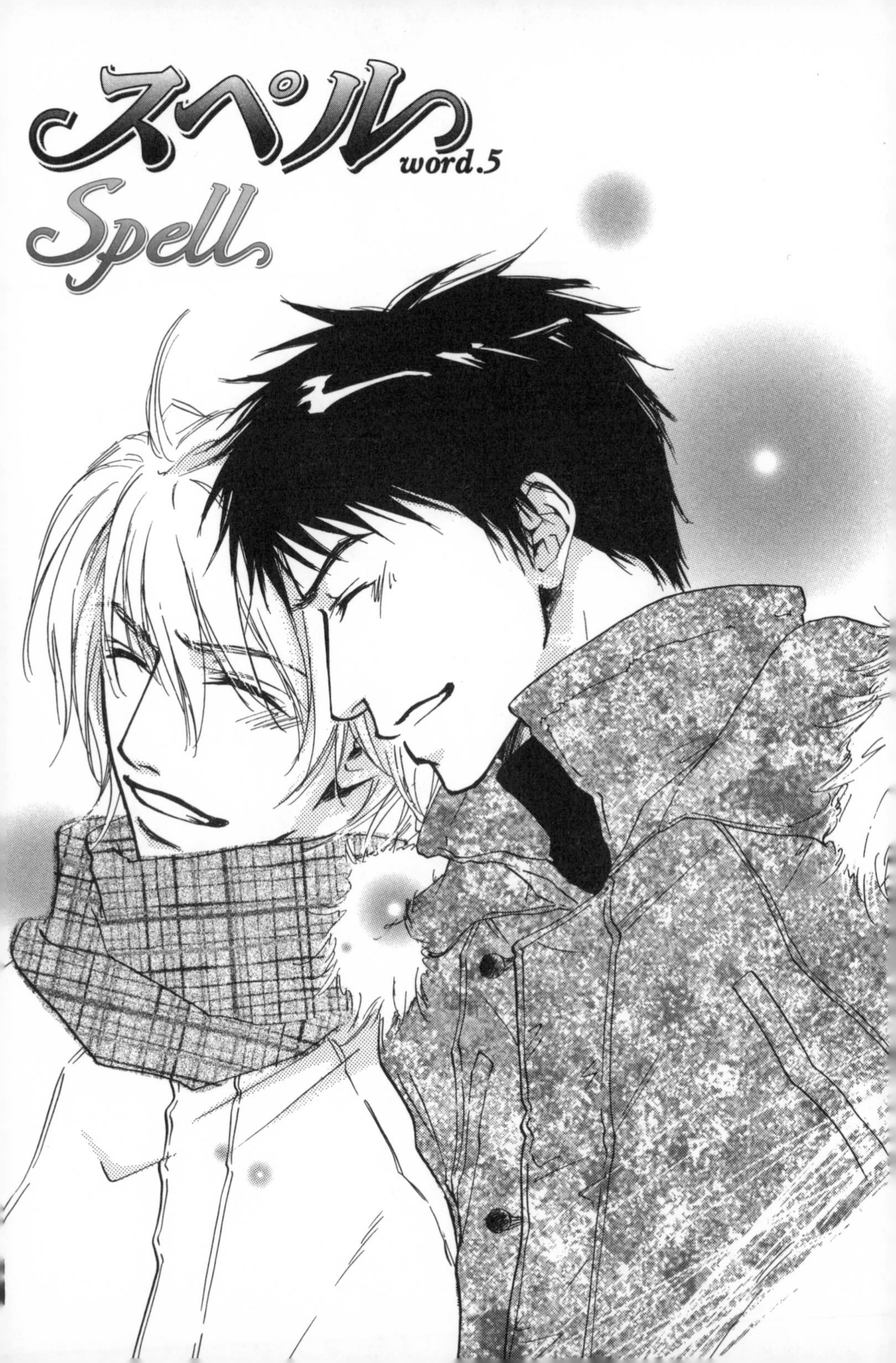
スペル
word.5
Spell

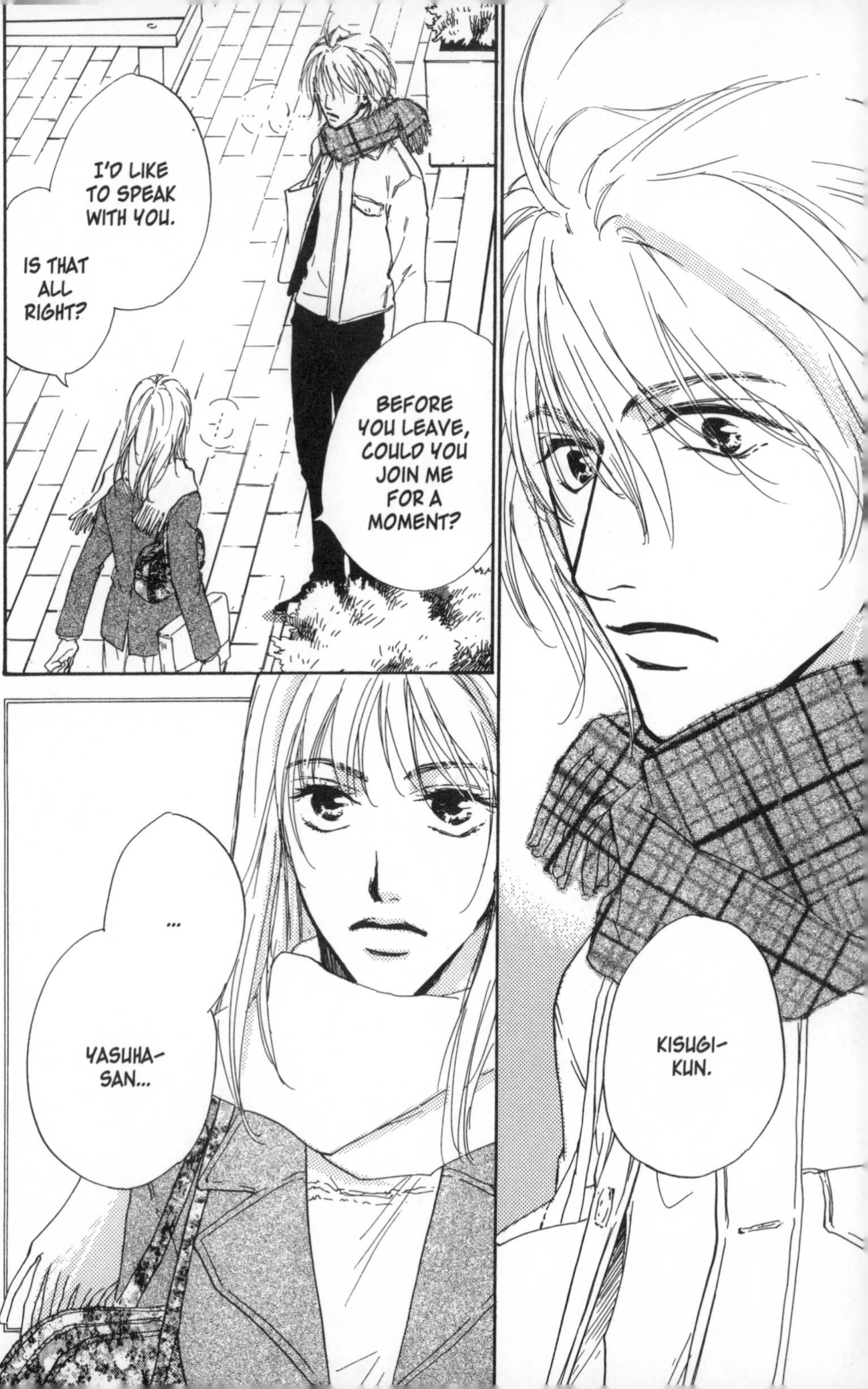
KISUGI-KUN.
BEFORE YOU LEAVE, COULD YOU JOIN ME FOR A MOMENT?
I'D LIKE TO SPEAK WITH YOU.
IS THAT ALL RIGHT?
...
YASUHA-SAN...

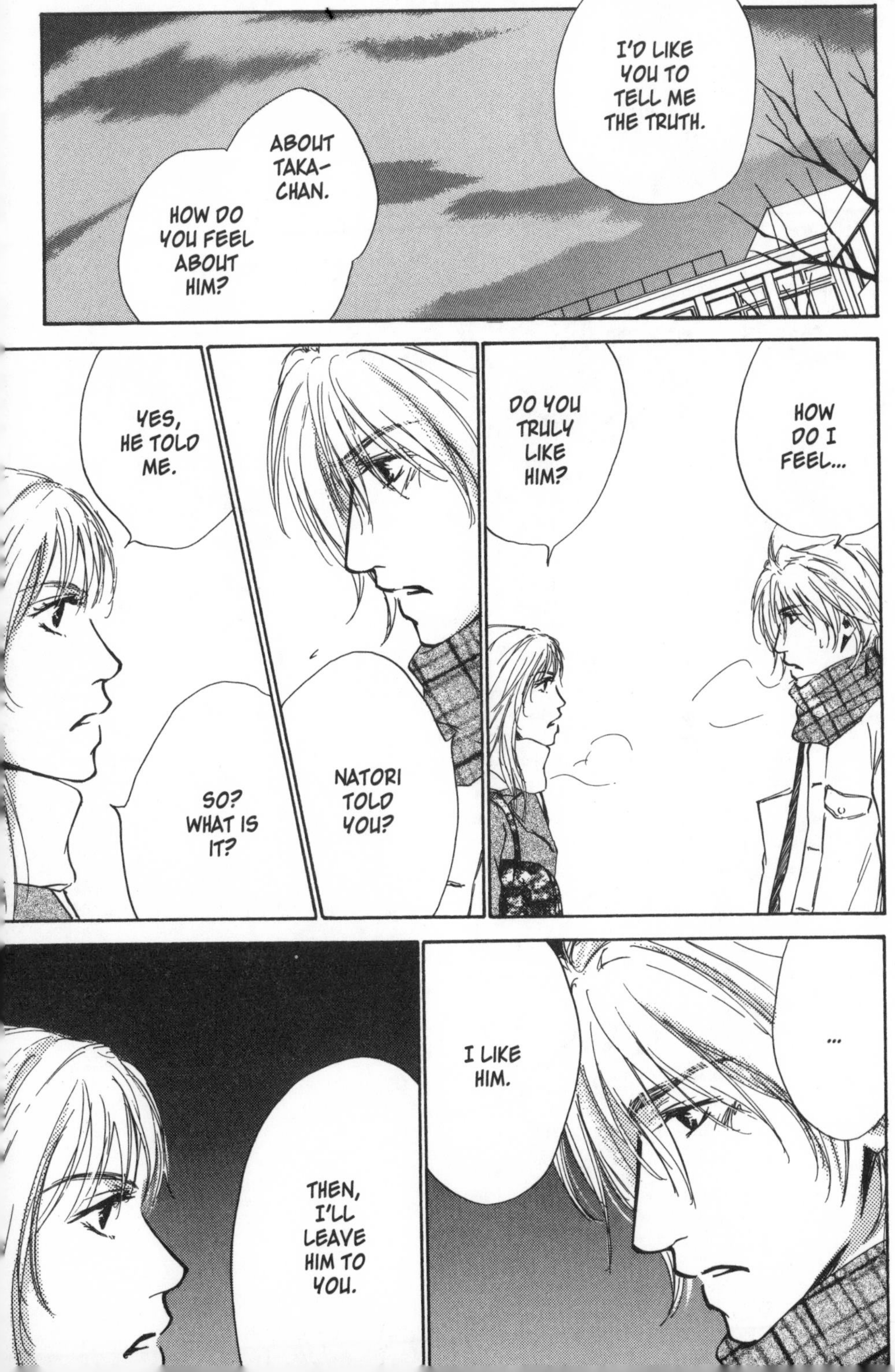
I'D LIKE YOU TO TELL ME THE TRUTH.
ABOUT TAKA-CHAN.
HOW DO YOU FEEL ABOUT HIM?
HOW DO I FEEL...
DO YOU TRULY LIKE HIM?
NATORI TOLD YOU?
YES, HE TOLD ME.
SO? WHAT IS IT?
...
I LIKE HIM.
THEN, I'LL LEAVE HIM TO YOU.

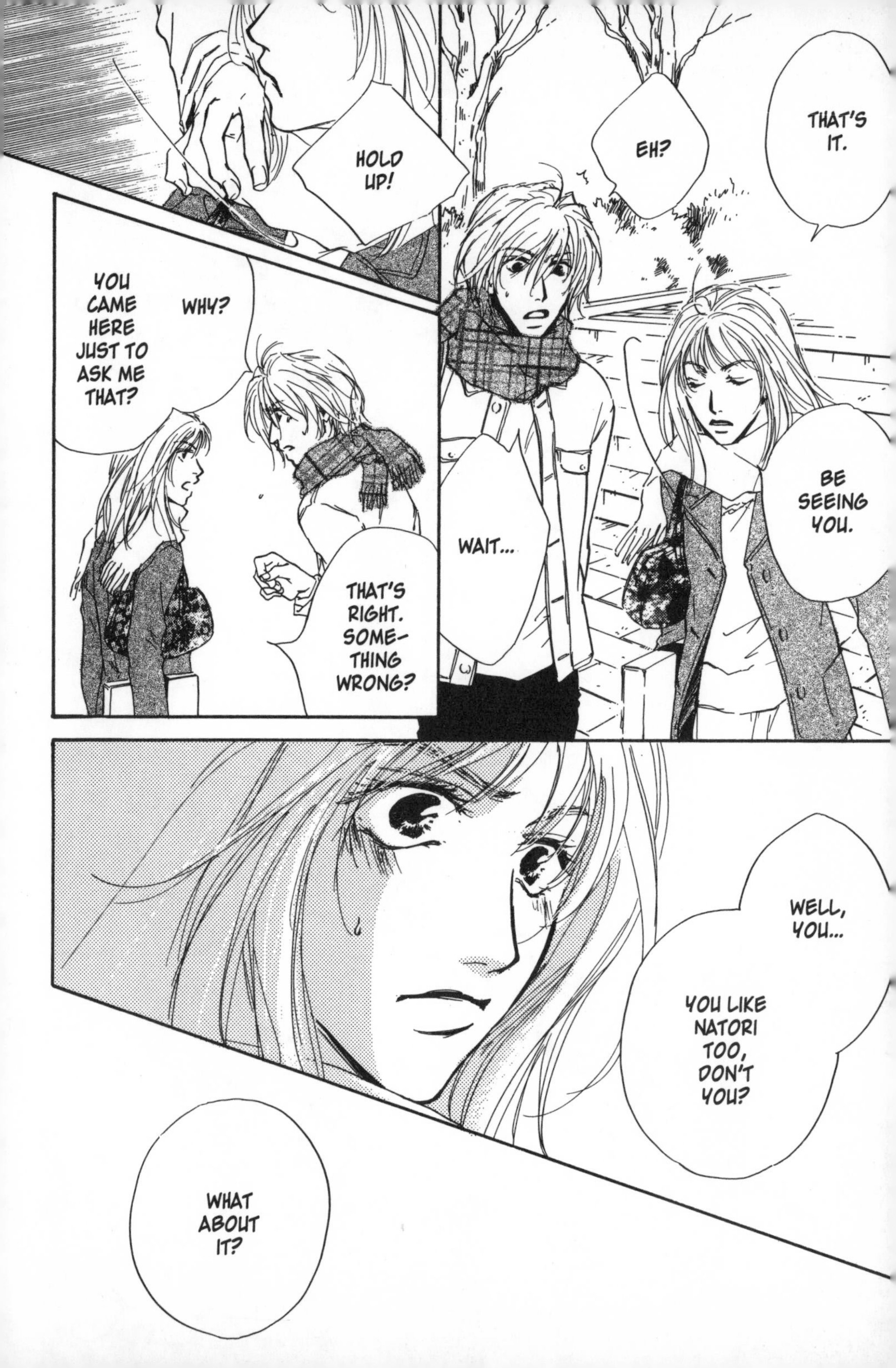
THAT'S IT.
EH?
BE SEEING YOU.
WAIT...
HOLD UP!
WHY?
YOU CAME HERE JUST TO ASK ME THAT?
THAT'S RIGHT. SOME-THING WRONG?
WELL, YOU...
YOU LIKE NATORI TOO, DON'T YOU?
WHAT ABOUT IT?

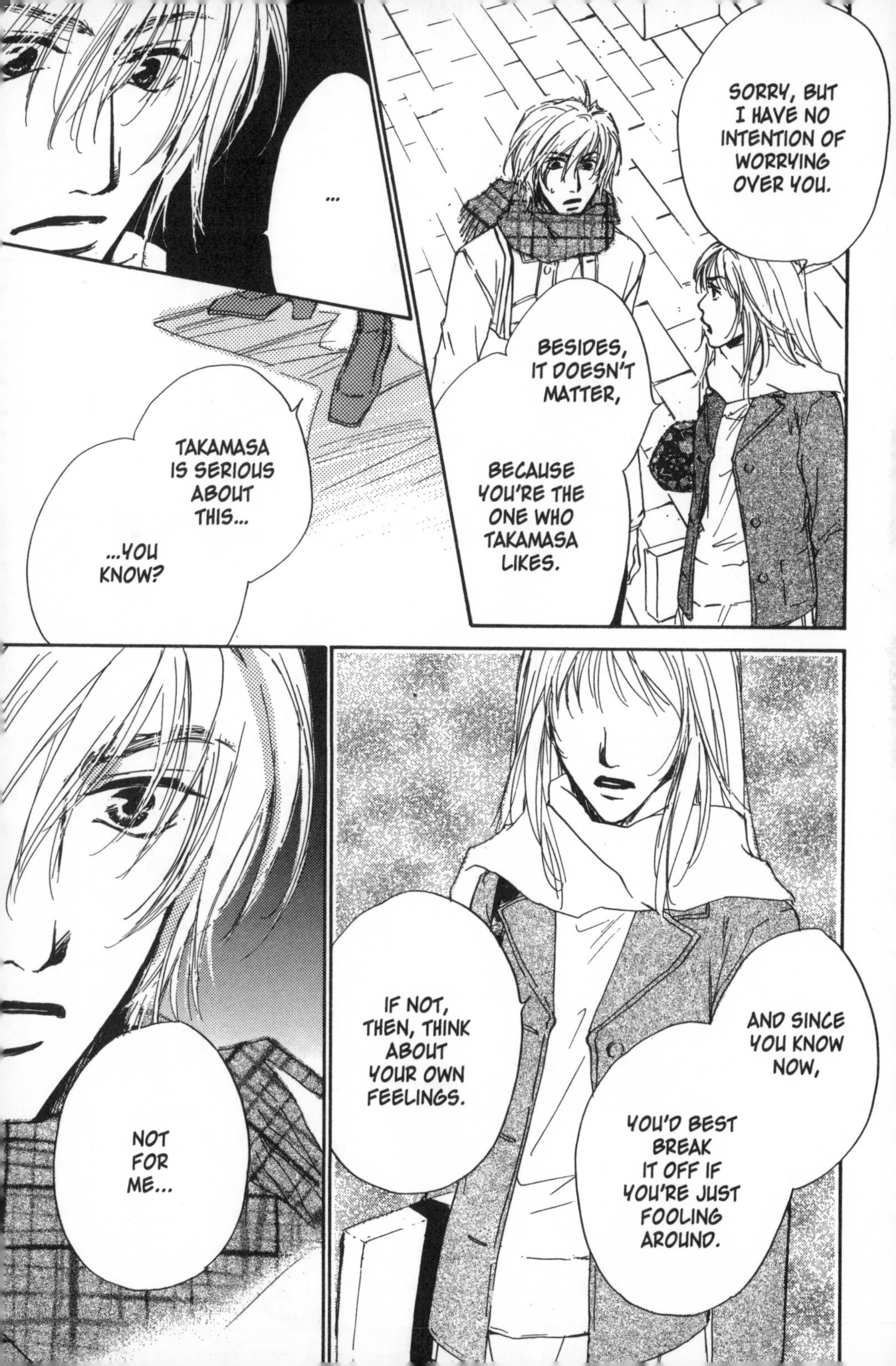
SORRY, BUT I HAVE NO INTENTION OF WORRYING OVER YOU.
BESIDES, IT DOESN'T MATTER,
BECAUSE YOU'RE THE ONE WHO TAKAMASA LIKES.
...
TAKAMASA IS SERIOUS ABOUT THIS...
...YOU KNOW?
AND SINCE YOU KNOW NOW,
YOU'D BEST BREAK IT OFF IF YOU'RE JUST FOOLING AROUND.
IF NOT, THEN, THINK ABOUT YOUR OWN FEELINGS.
NOT FOR ME...

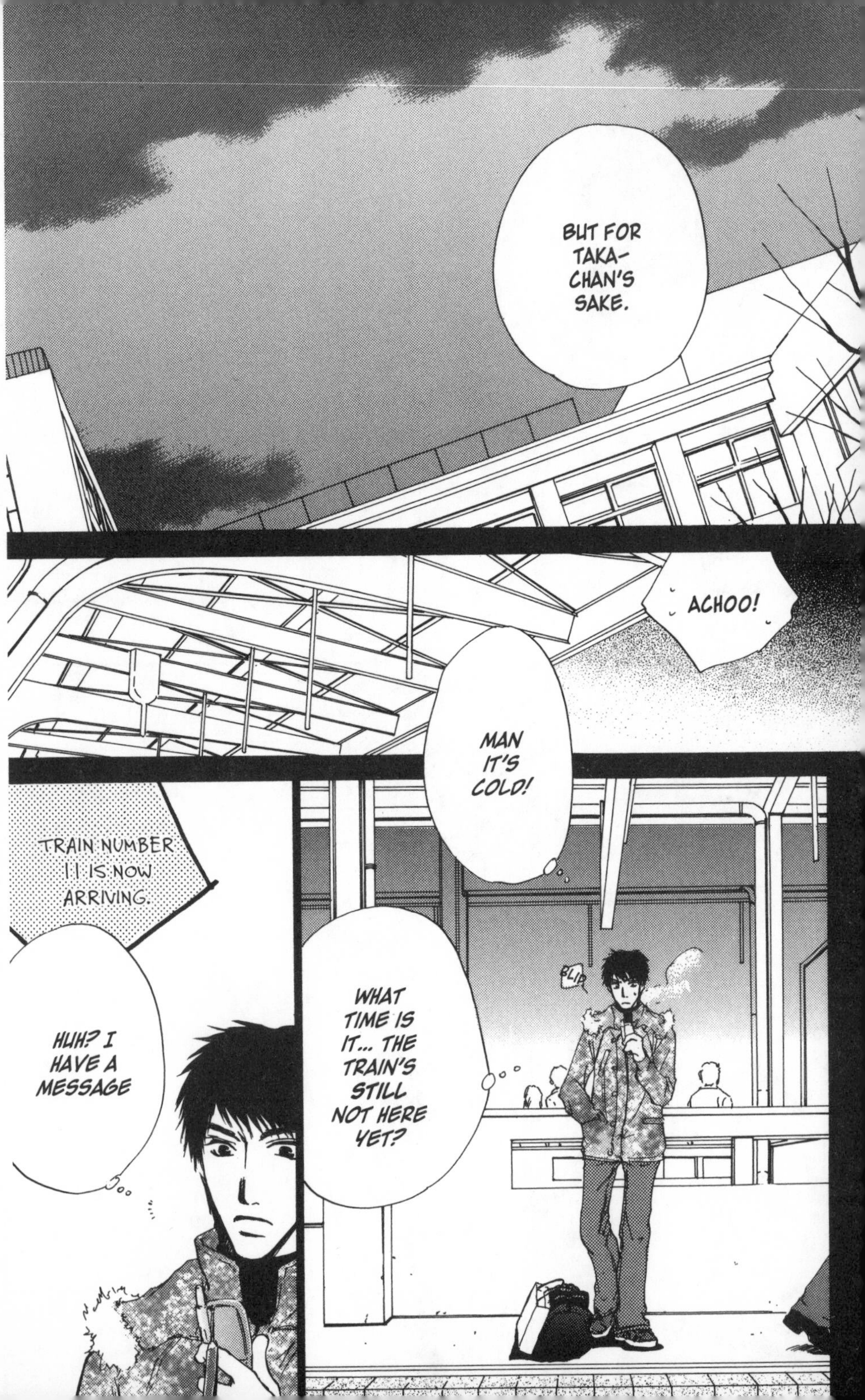
BUT FOR TAKA-CHAN'S SAKE.
ACHOO!
MAN IT'S COLD!
BLIP
WHAT TIME IS IT... THE TRAIN'S STILL NOT HERE YET?
TRAIN NUMBER 11 IS NOW ARRIVING.
HUH? I HAVE A MESSAGE

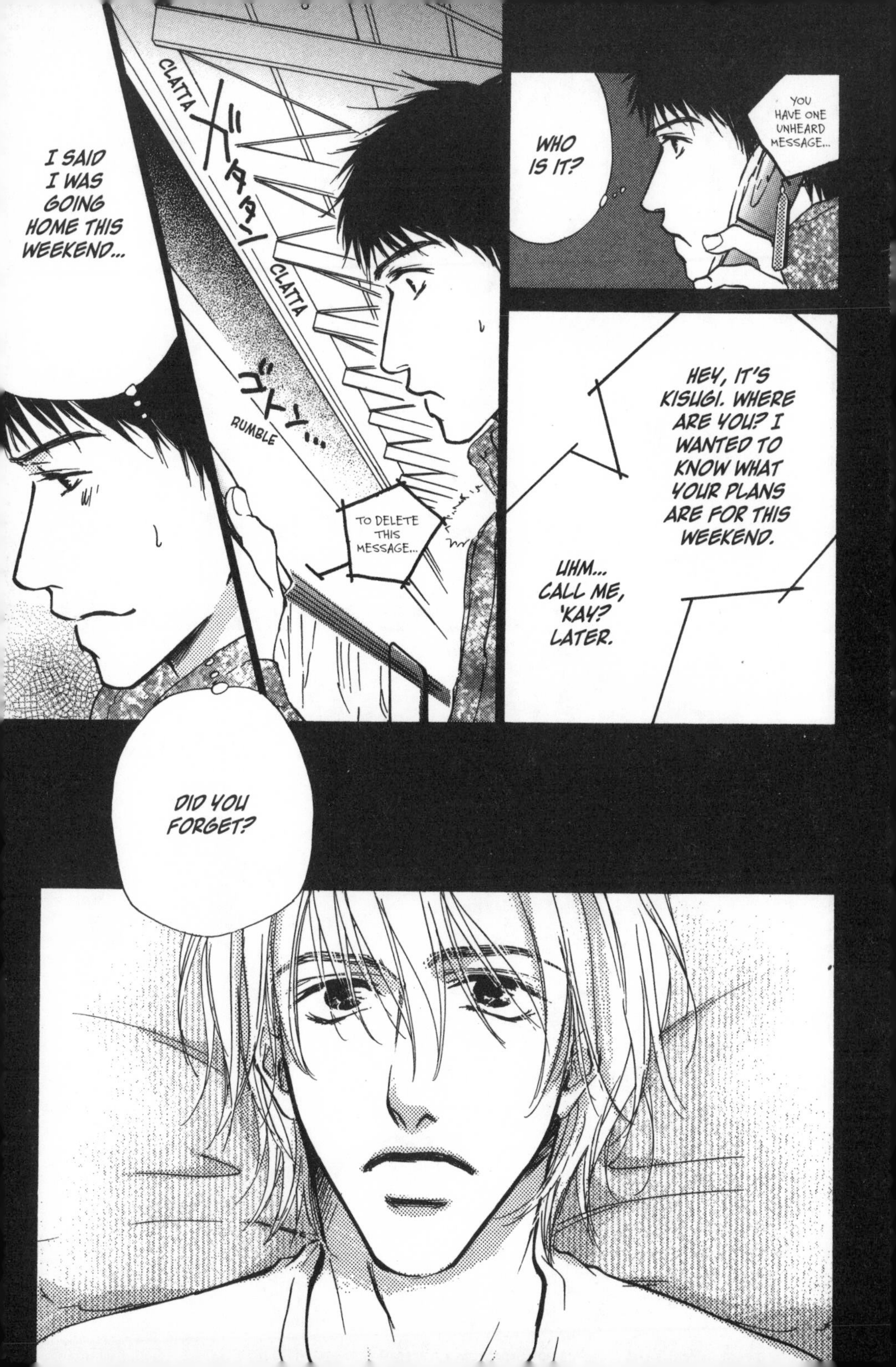
YOU HAVE ONE UNHEARD MESSAGE...
WHO IS IT?
HEY, IT'S KISUGI. WHERE ARE YOU? I WANTED TO KNOW WHAT YOUR PLANS ARE FOR THIS WEEKEND.
UHM... CALL ME, 'KAY? LATER.
CLATTA
ガタタン
CLATTA
TO DELETE THIS MESSAGE...
ゴトン…
RUMBLE
I SAID I WAS GOING HOME THIS WEEKEND...
DID YOU FORGET?

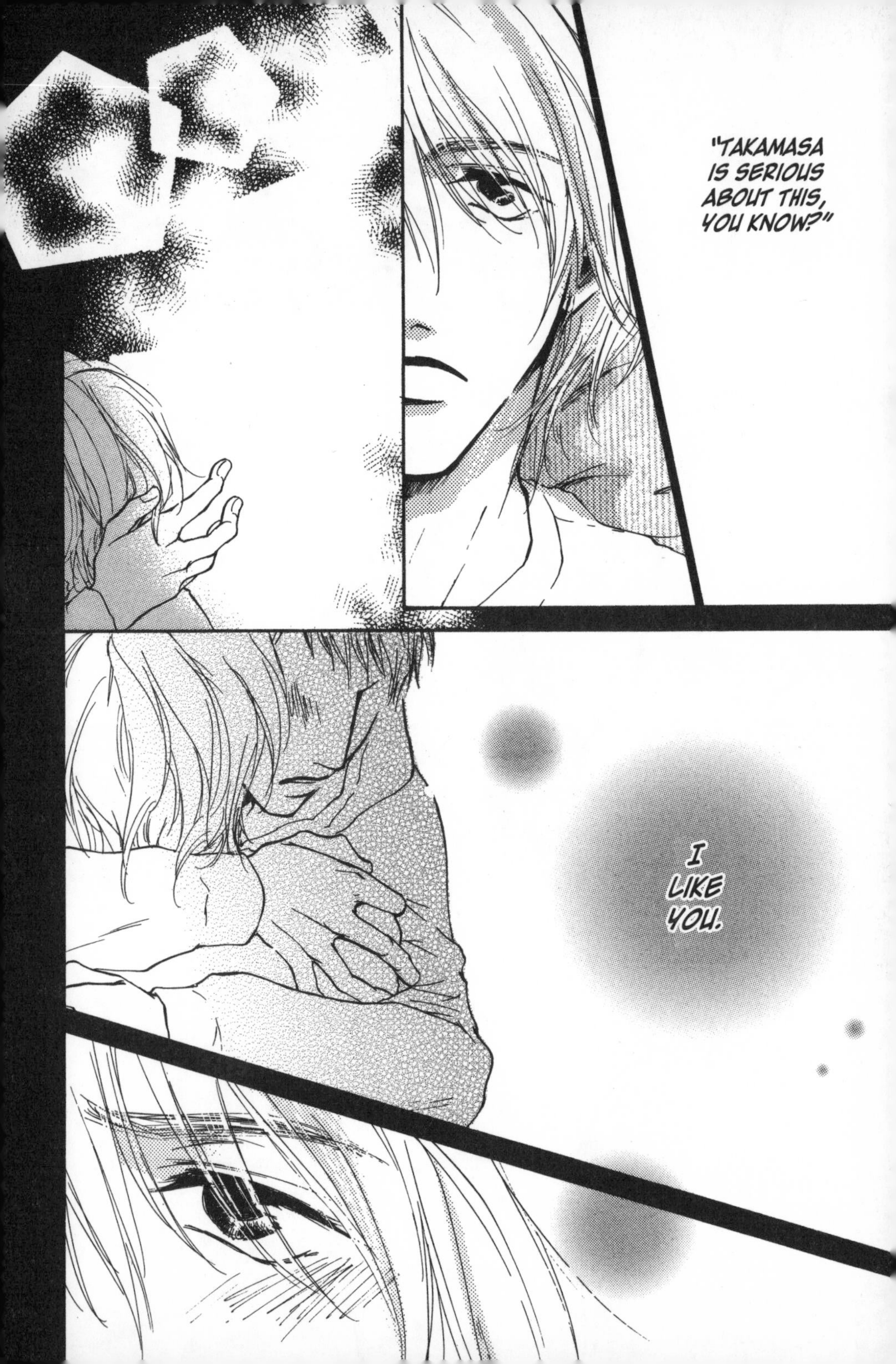
"TAKAMASA IS SERIOUS ABOUT THIS, YOU KNOW?"
I LIKE YOU.

...

KISUGI...

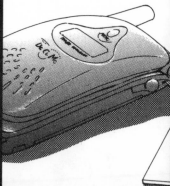

POOF

FIGURES THAT I'D JUST GET HIS VOICEMAIL.

THAT'S TOO SELFISH OF ME.

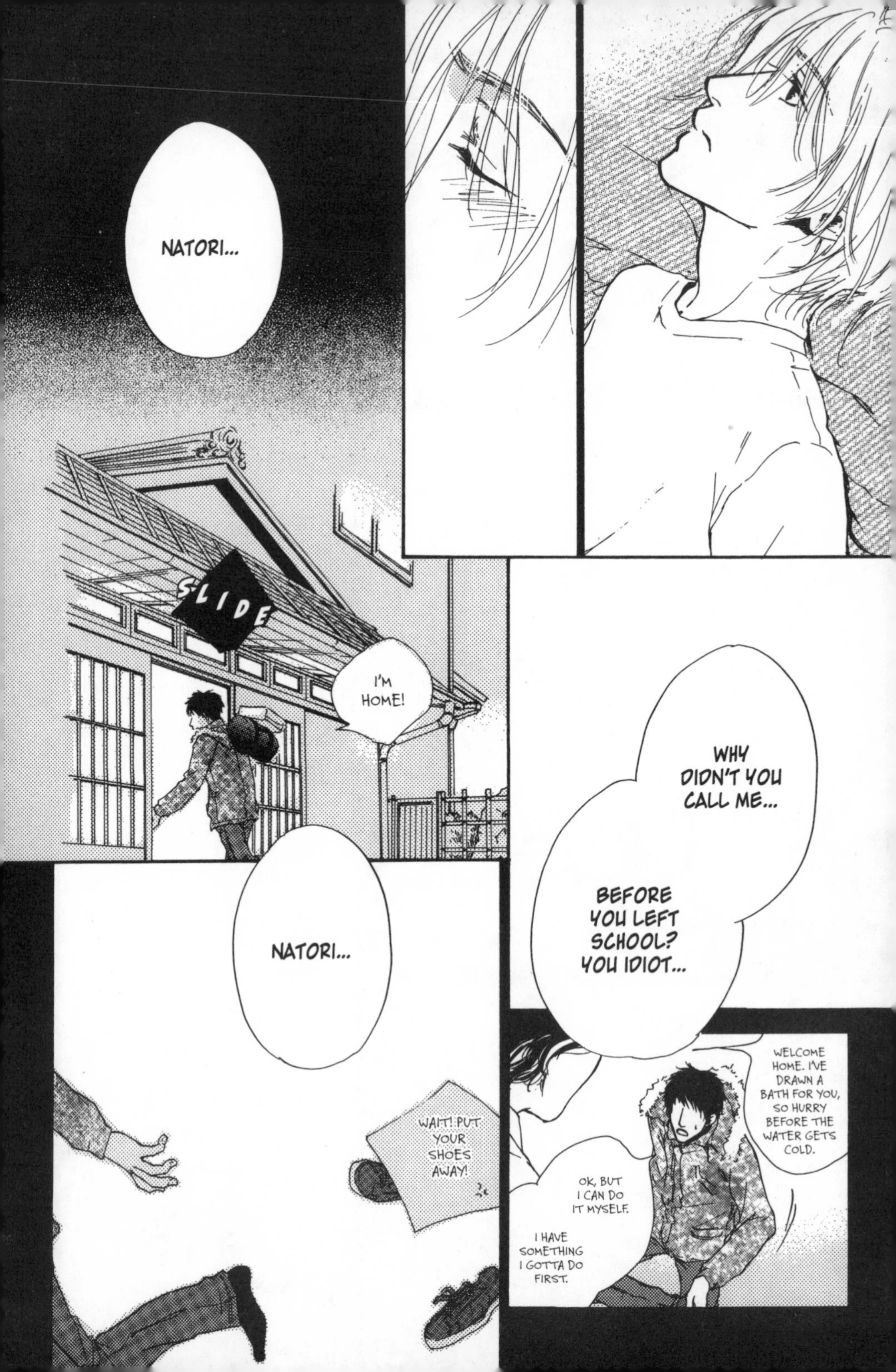
NATORI...
SLIDE
I'M HOME!
WHY DIDN'T YOU CALL ME...
BEFORE YOU LEFT SCHOOL? YOU IDIOT...
WELCOME HOME. I'VE DRAWN A BATH FOR YOU, SO HURRY BEFORE THE WATER GETS COLD.
OK, BUT I CAN DO IT MYSELF.
I HAVE SOMETHING I GOTTA DO FIRST.
NATORI...
WAIT! PUT YOUR SHOES AWAY!

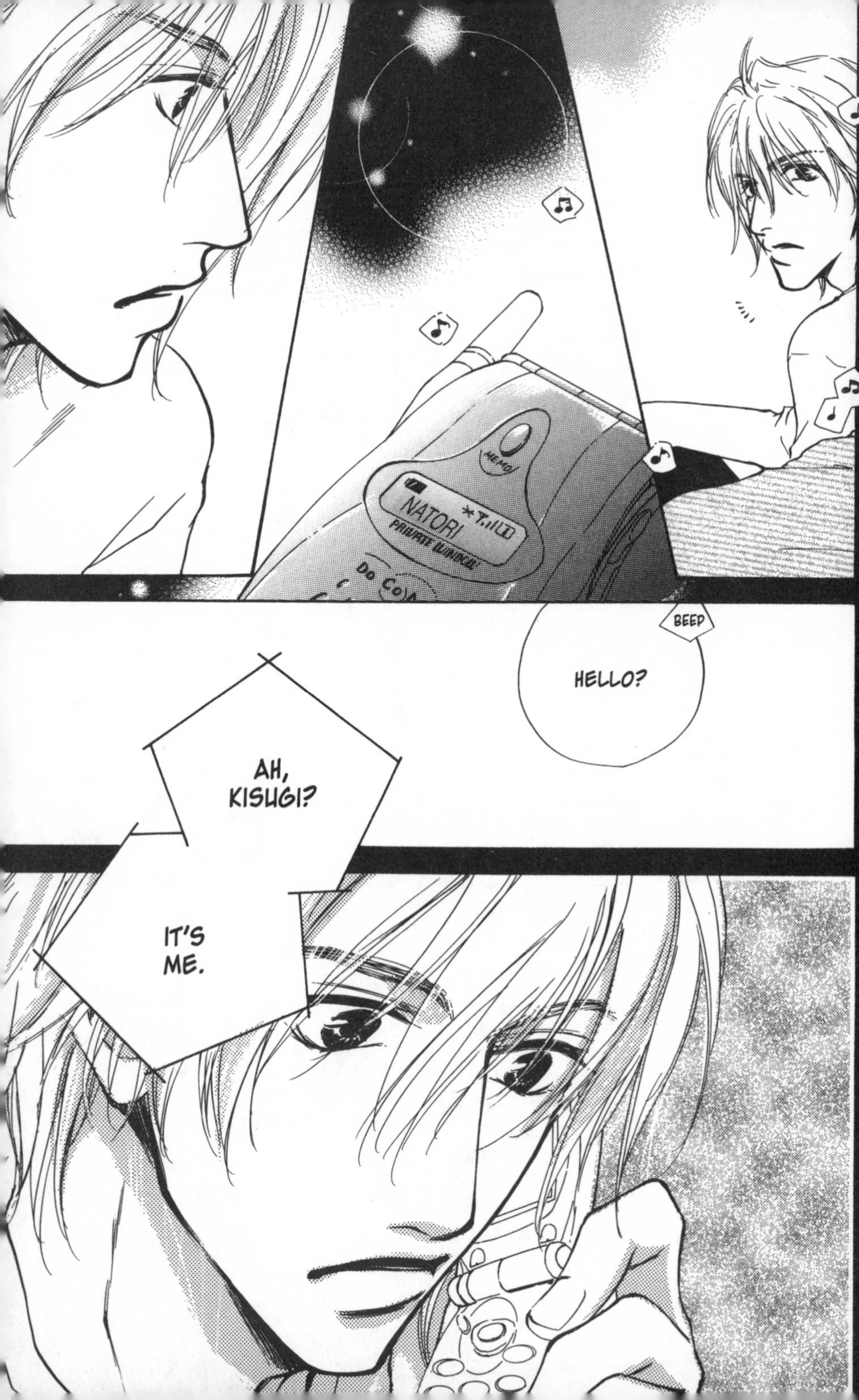
NATORI
BEEP
HELLO?
AH, KISUGI?
IT'S ME.

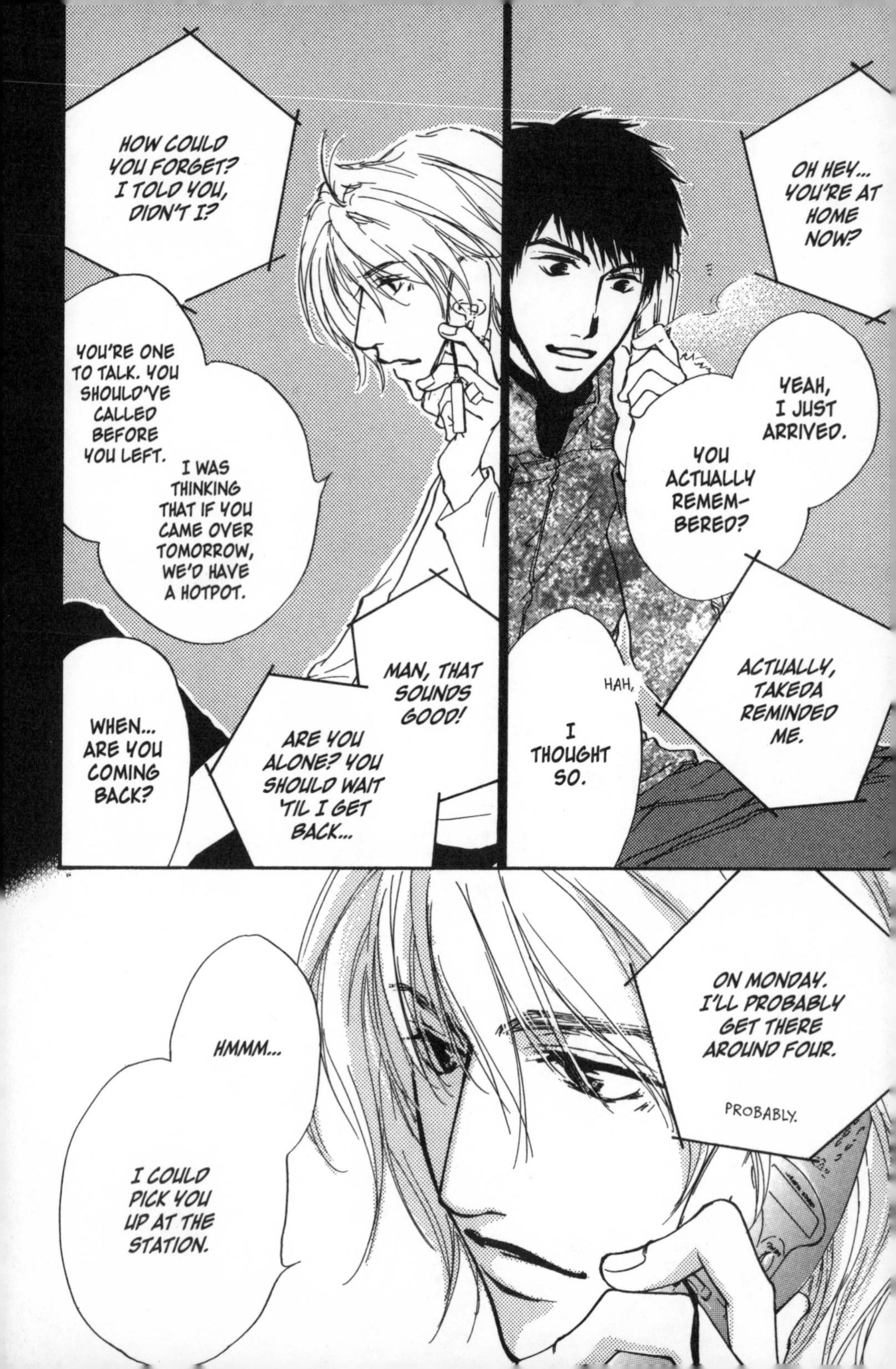
OH HEY... YOU'RE AT HOME NOW?
YEAH, I JUST ARRIVED.
YOU ACTUALLY REMEMBERED?
ACTUALLY, TAKEDA REMINDED ME.
HAH, I THOUGHT SO.
HOW COULD YOU FORGET? I TOLD YOU, DIDN'T I?
YOU'RE ONE TO TALK. YOU SHOULD'VE CALLED BEFORE YOU LEFT.
I WAS THINKING THAT IF YOU CAME OVER TOMORROW, WE'D HAVE A HOTPOT.
MAN, THAT SOUNDS GOOD!
ARE YOU ALONE? YOU SHOULD WAIT 'TIL I GET BACK...
WHEN... ARE YOU COMING BACK?
ON MONDAY. I'LL PROBABLY GET THERE AROUND FOUR.
PROBABLY.
HMMM...
I COULD PICK YOU UP AT THE STATION.

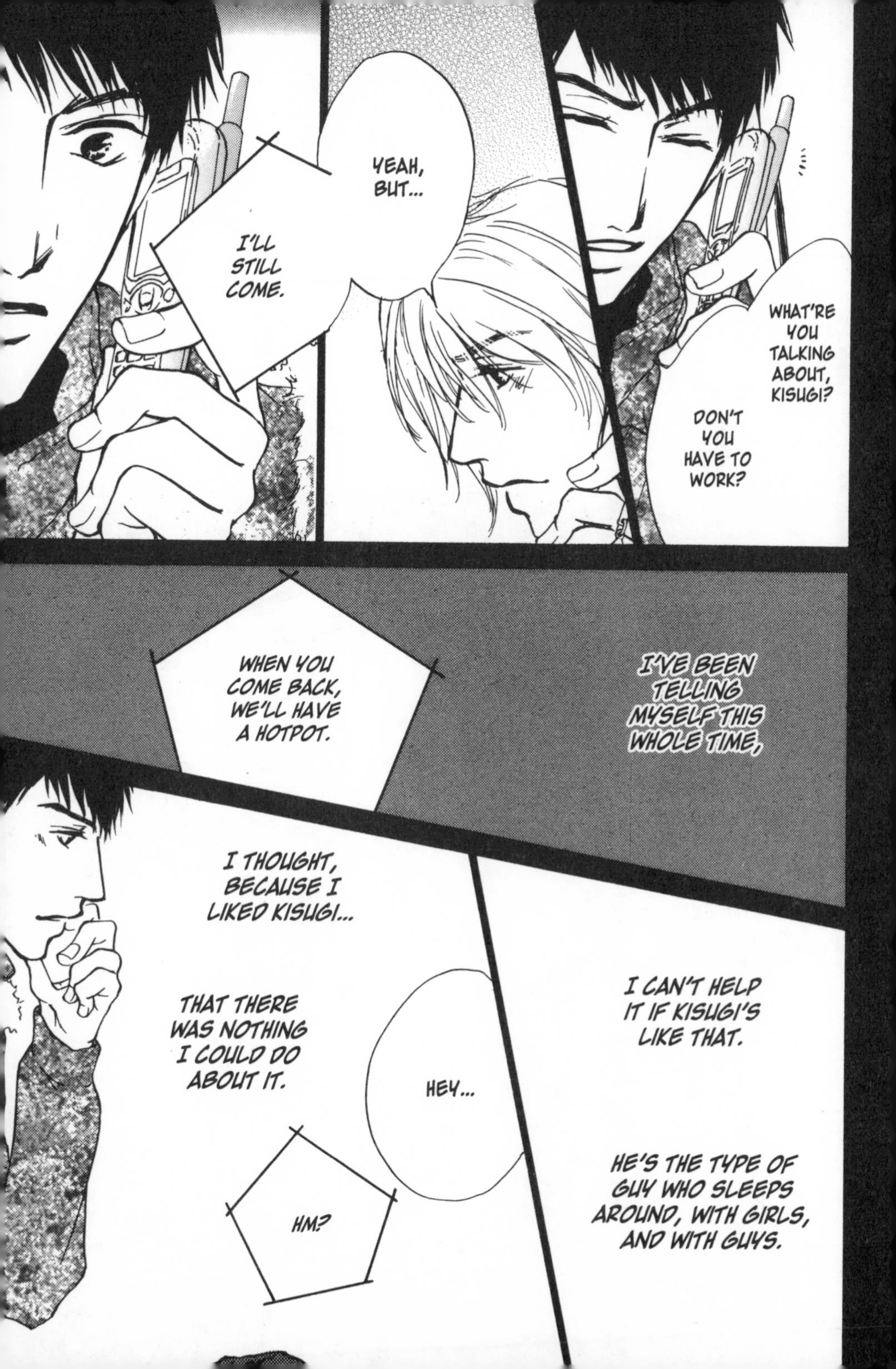
WHAT'RE YOU TALKING ABOUT, KISUGI?
DON'T YOU HAVE TO WORK?
YEAH, BUT...
I'LL STILL COME.
I'VE BEEN TELLING MYSELF THIS WHOLE TIME,
WHEN YOU COME BACK, WE'LL HAVE A HOTPOT.
I CAN'T HELP IT IF KISUGI'S LIKE THAT.
HE'S THE TYPE OF GUY WHO SLEEPS AROUND, WITH GIRLS, AND WITH GUYS.
I THOUGHT, BECAUSE I LIKED KISUGI...
THAT THERE WAS NOTHING I COULD DO ABOUT IT.
HEY...
HM?

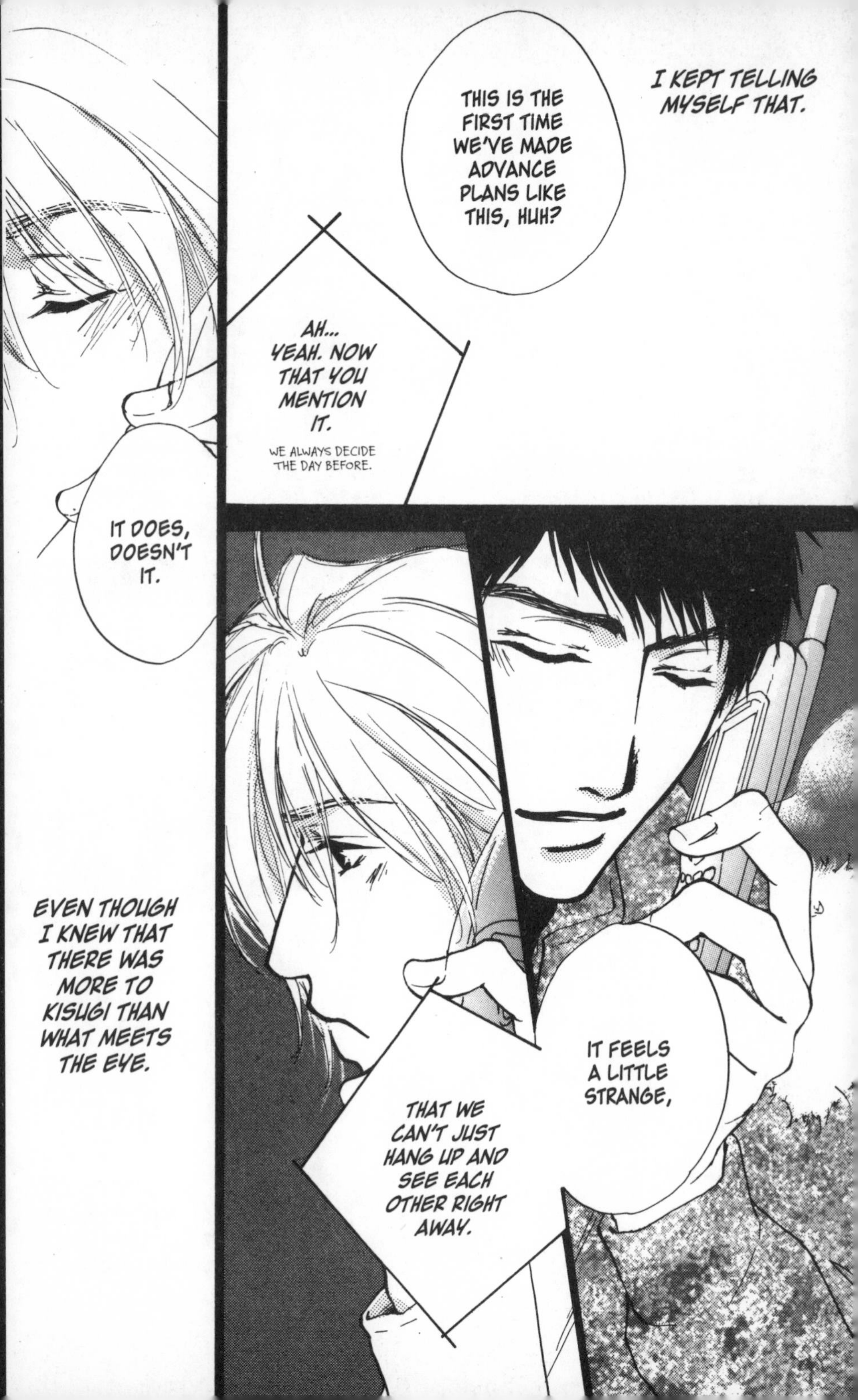
I KEPT TELLING MYSELF THAT.
THIS IS THE FIRST TIME WE'VE MADE ADVANCE PLANS LIKE THIS, HUH?
AH... YEAH. NOW THAT YOU MENTION IT.
WE ALWAYS DECIDE THE DAY BEFORE.
IT FEELS A LITTLE STRANGE,
THAT WE CAN'T JUST HANG UP AND SEE EACH OTHER RIGHT AWAY.
IT DOES, DOESN'T IT.
EVEN THOUGH I KNEW THAT THERE WAS MORE TO KISUGI THAN WHAT MEETS THE EYE.

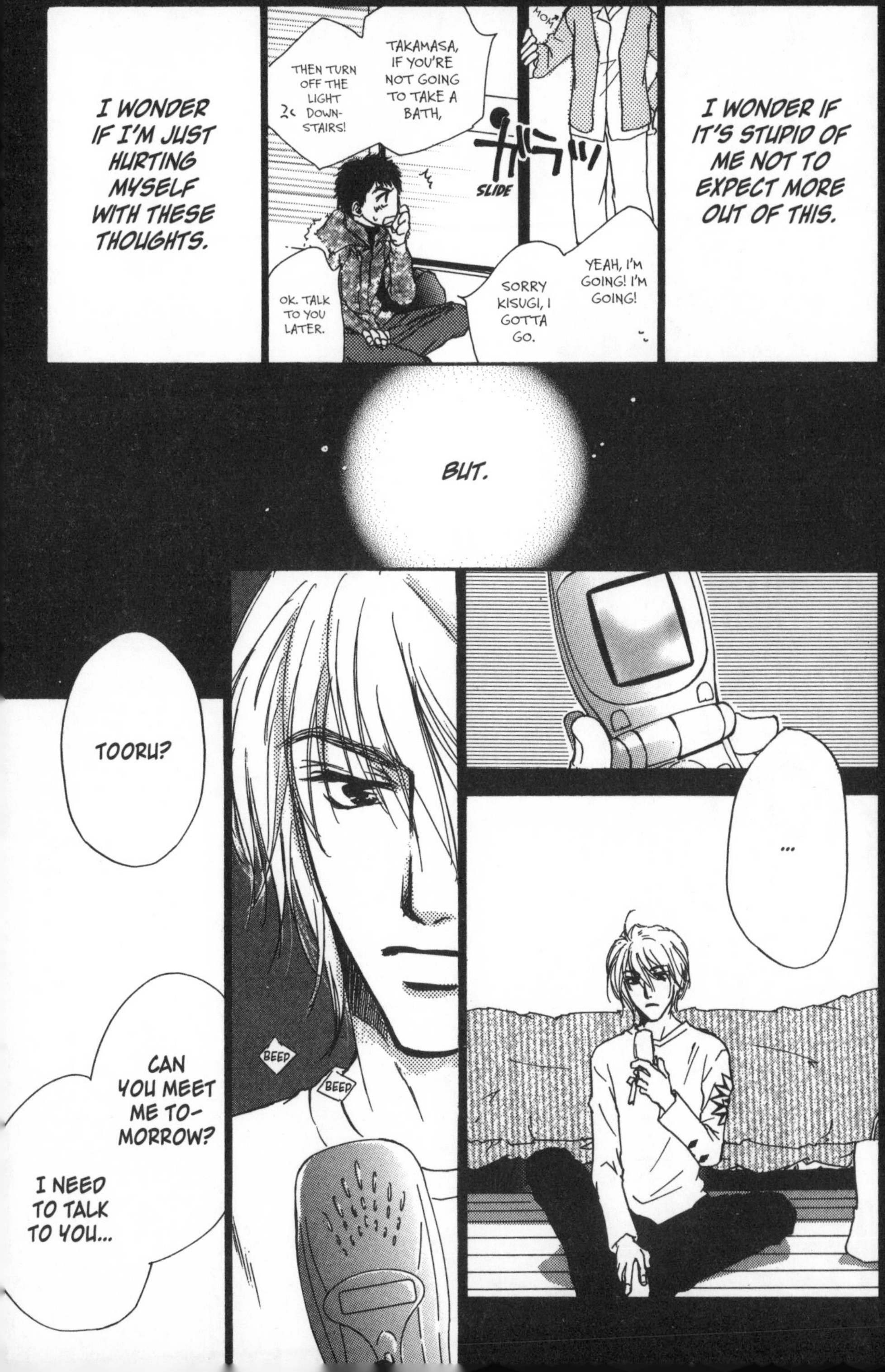
I WONDER IF IT'S STUPID OF ME NOT TO EXPECT MORE OUT OF THIS.
MOM
TAKAMASA, IF YOU'RE NOT GOING TO TAKE A BATH,
THEN TURN OFF THE LIGHT DOWN-STAIRS!
ガラッ
SLIDE
YEAH, I'M GOING! I'M GOING!
SORRY KISUGI, I GOTTA GO.
OK. TALK TO YOU LATER.
I WONDER IF I'M JUST HURTING MYSELF WITH THESE THOUGHTS.
BUT.
...
TOORU?
BEEP
BEEP
CAN YOU MEET ME TO-MORROW?
I NEED TO TALK TO YOU...

IN THE END, THE ONE I TRULY WANT...

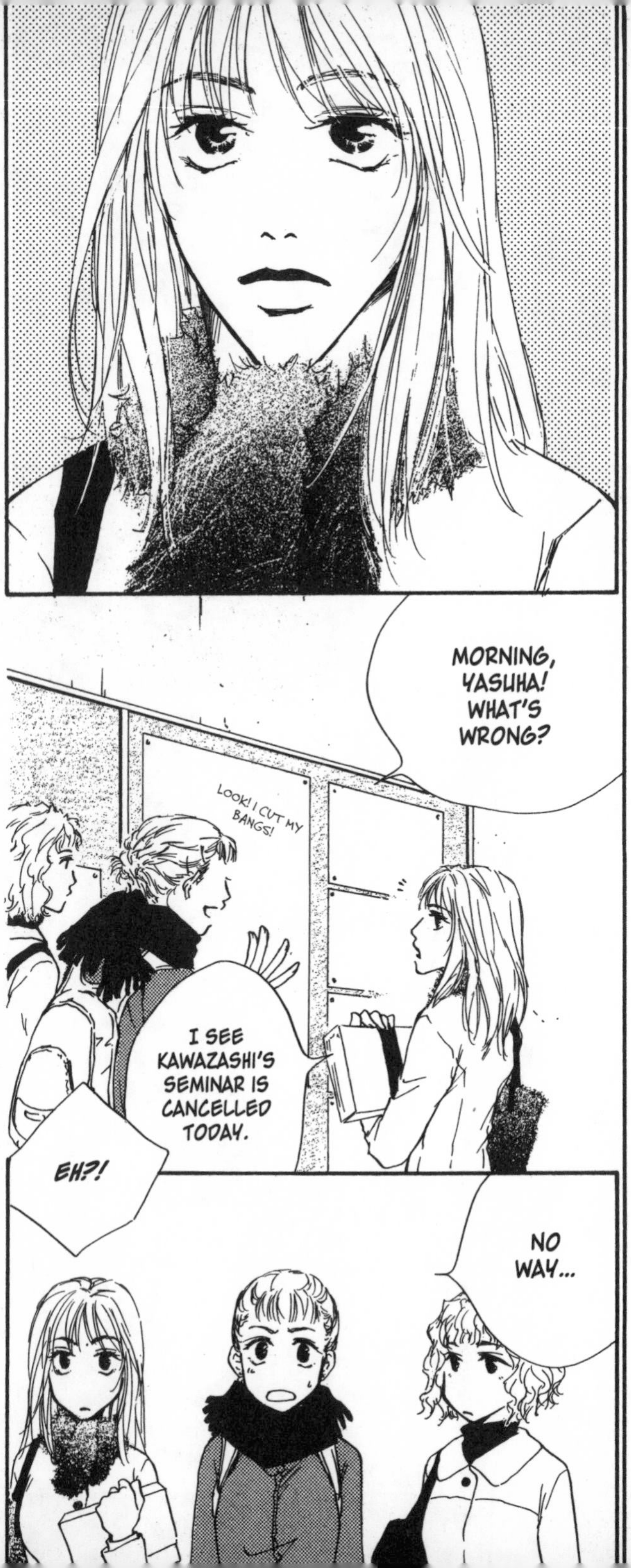
MORNING, YASUHA! WHAT'S WRONG?
LOOK! I CUT MY BANGS!
I SEE KAWAZASHI'S SEMINAR IS CANCELLED TODAY.
EH?!
NO WAY...

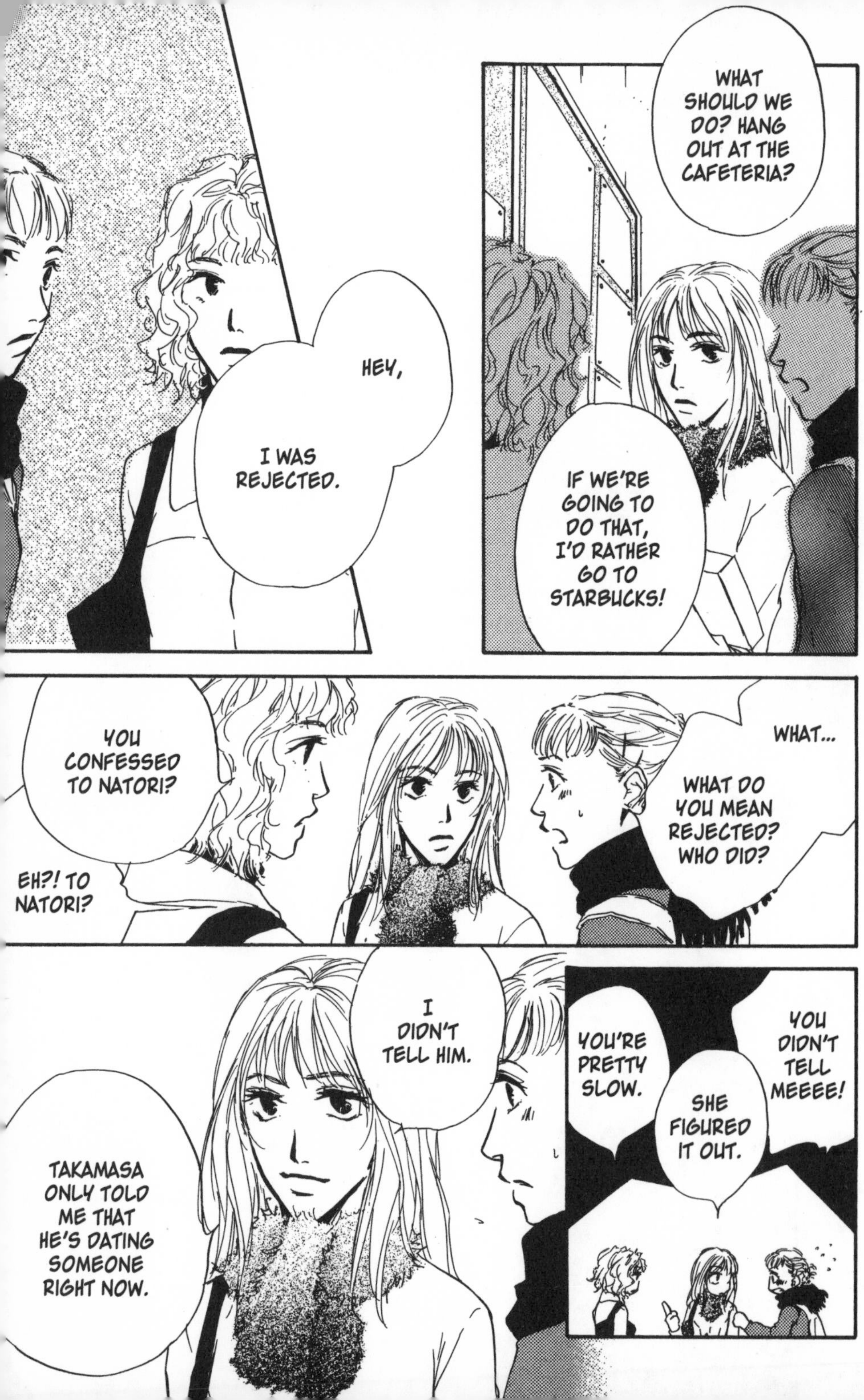
WHAT SHOULD WE DO? HANG OUT AT THE CAFETERIA?
IF WE'RE GOING TO DO THAT, I'D RATHER GO TO STARBUCKS!
HEY,
I WAS REJECTED.
WHAT...
WHAT DO YOU MEAN REJECTED? WHO DID?
YOU CONFESSED TO NATORI?
EH?! TO NATORI?
YOU DIDN'T TELL MEEEE!
SHE FIGURED IT OUT.
YOU'RE PRETTY SLOW.
I DIDN'T TELL HIM.
TAKAMASA ONLY TOLD ME THAT HE'S DATING SOMEONE RIGHT NOW.

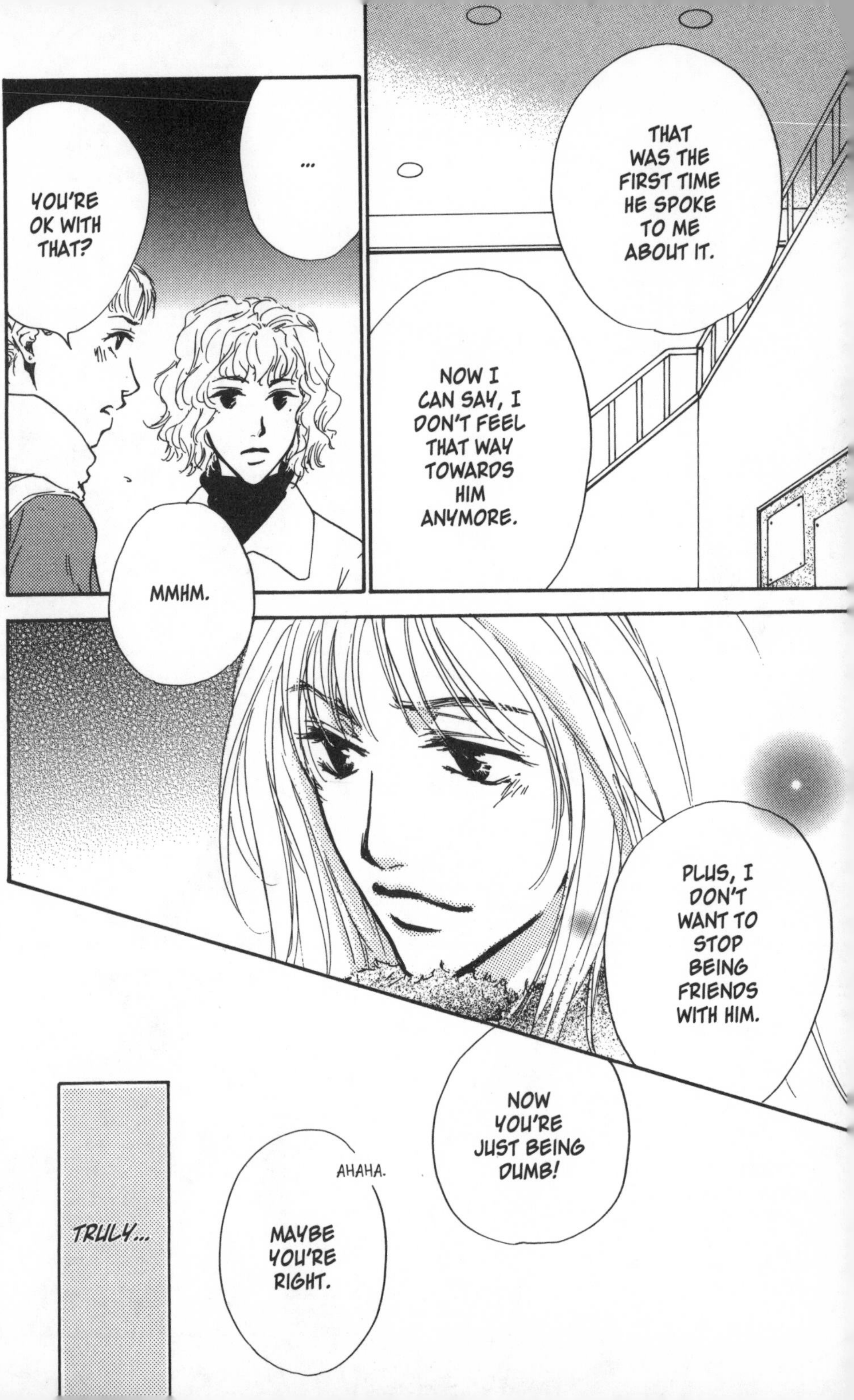
THAT WAS THE FIRST TIME HE SPOKE TO ME ABOUT IT.
NOW I CAN SAY, I DON'T FEEL THAT WAY TOWARDS HIM ANYMORE.
...
YOU'RE OK WITH THAT?
MMHM.
PLUS, I DON'T WANT TO STOP BEING FRIENDS WITH HIM.
NOW YOU'RE JUST BEING DUMB!
AHAHA.
MAYBE YOU'RE RIGHT.
TRULY...

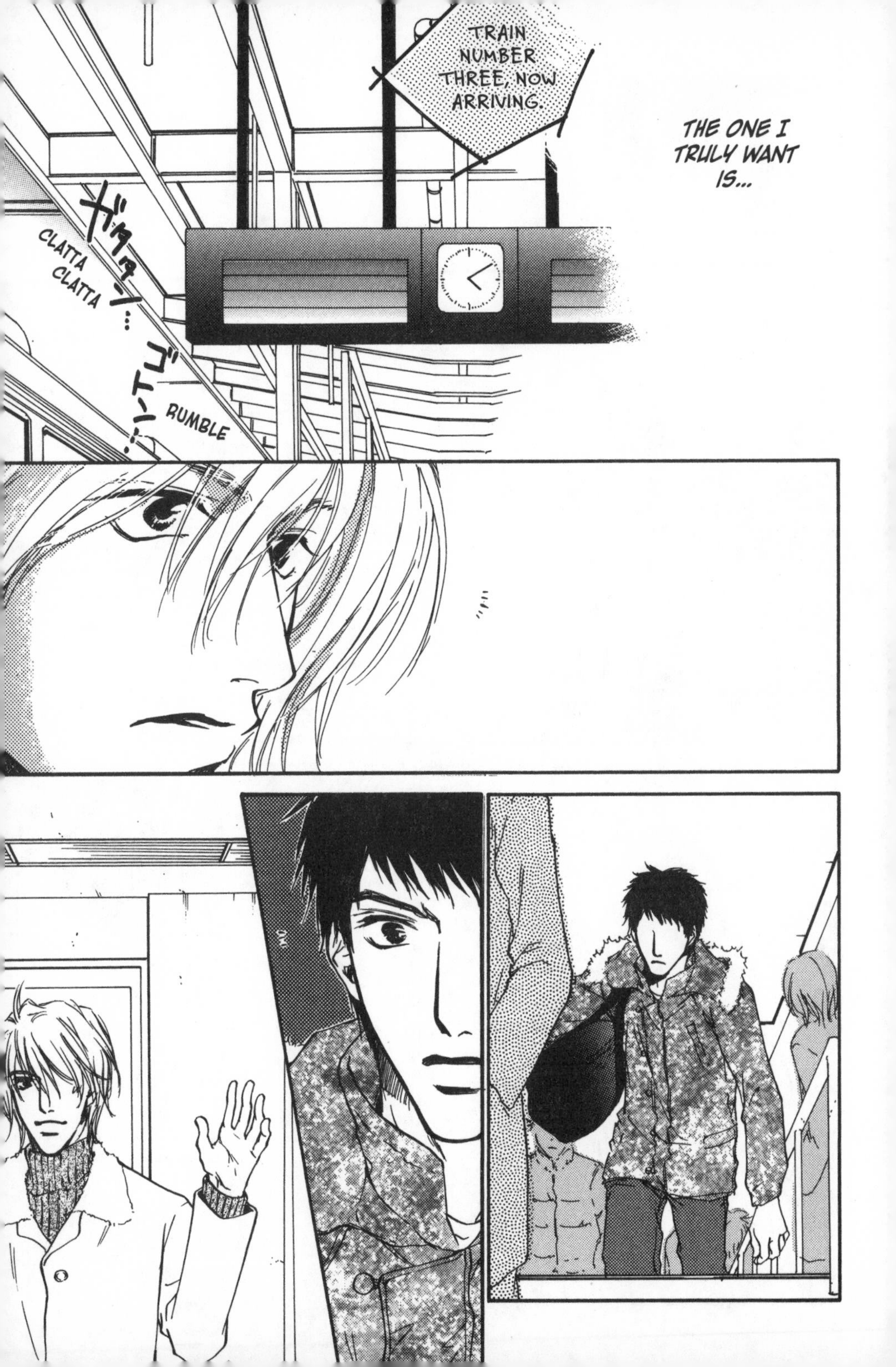
THE ONE I TRULY WANT IS...
TRAIN NUMBER THREE, NOW ARRIVING.
ガタン…
CLATTA CLATTA
ゴトン…
RUMBLE
…

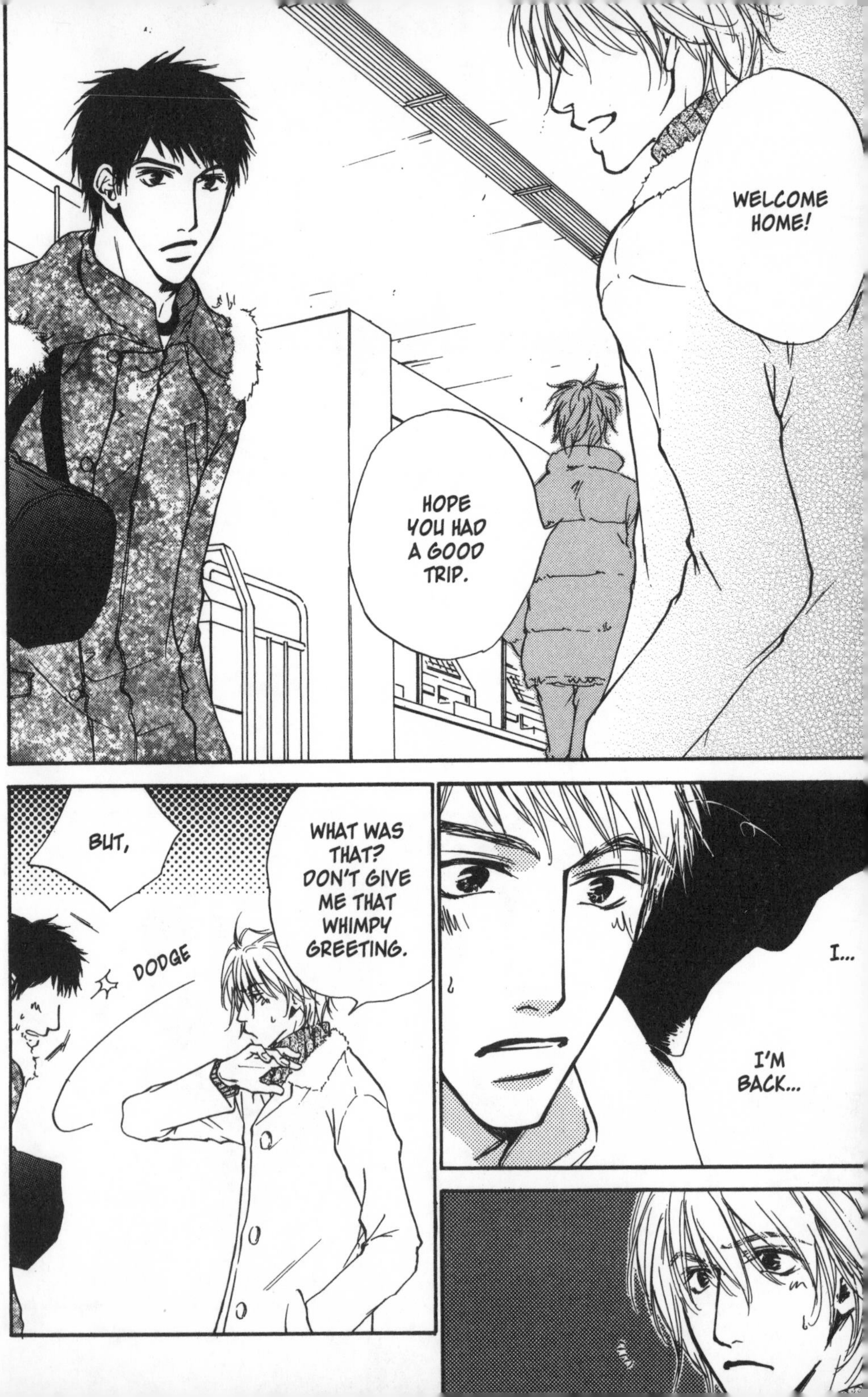
WELCOME HOME!
HOPE YOU HAD A GOOD TRIP.
I...
I'M BACK...
WHAT WAS THAT? DON'T GIVE ME THAT WHIMPY GREETING.
BUT,
DODGE

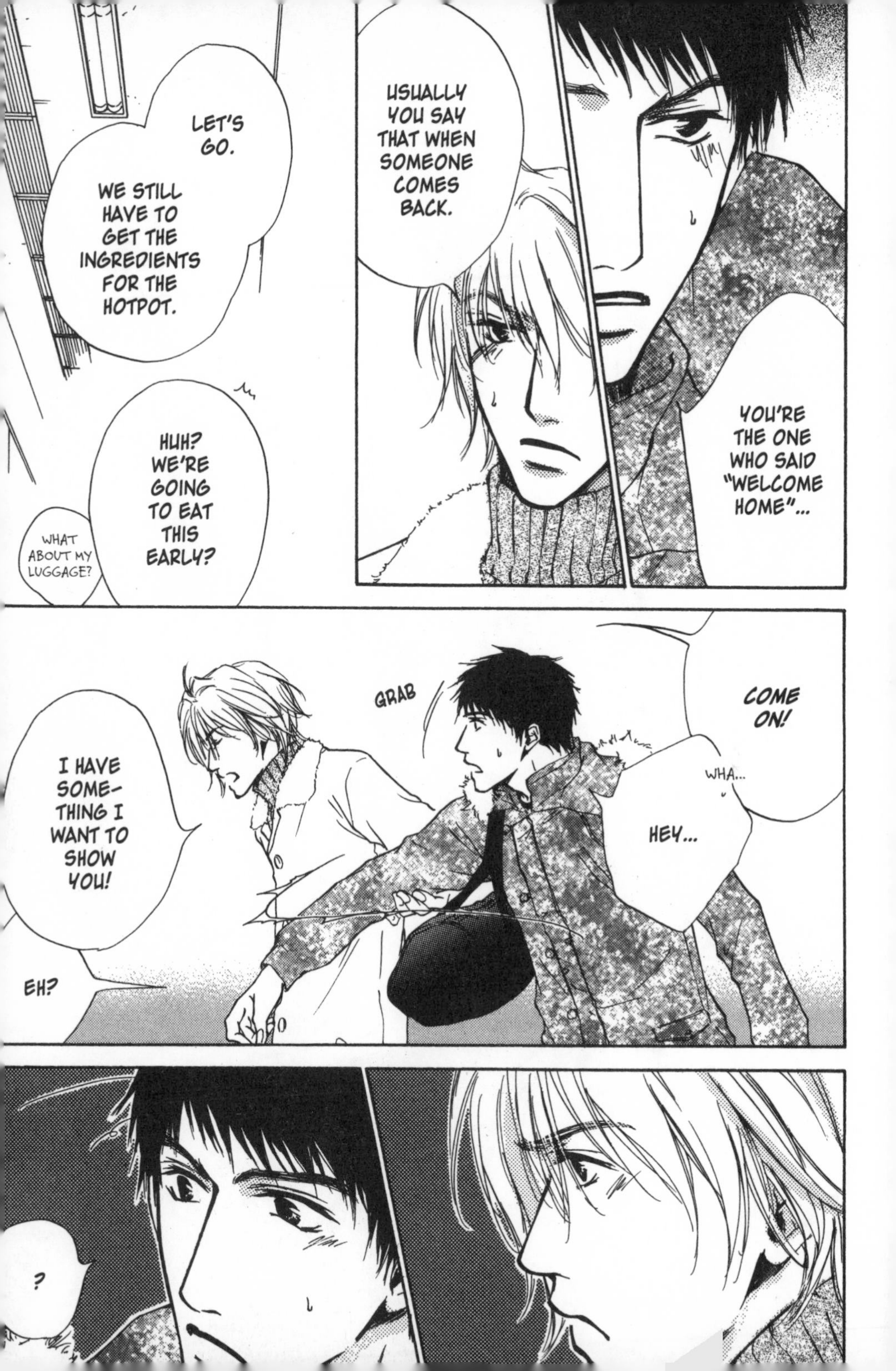

USUALLY YOU SAY THAT WHEN SOMEONE COMES BACK.
YOU'RE THE ONE WHO SAID "WELCOME HOME"...
LET'S GO.
WE STILL HAVE TO GET THE INGREDIENTS FOR THE HOTPOT.
HUH? WE'RE GOING TO EAT THIS EARLY?
WHAT ABOUT MY LUGGAGE?
COME ON!
GRAB
WHA...
HEY...
I HAVE SOME-THING I WANT TO SHOW YOU!
EH?
?

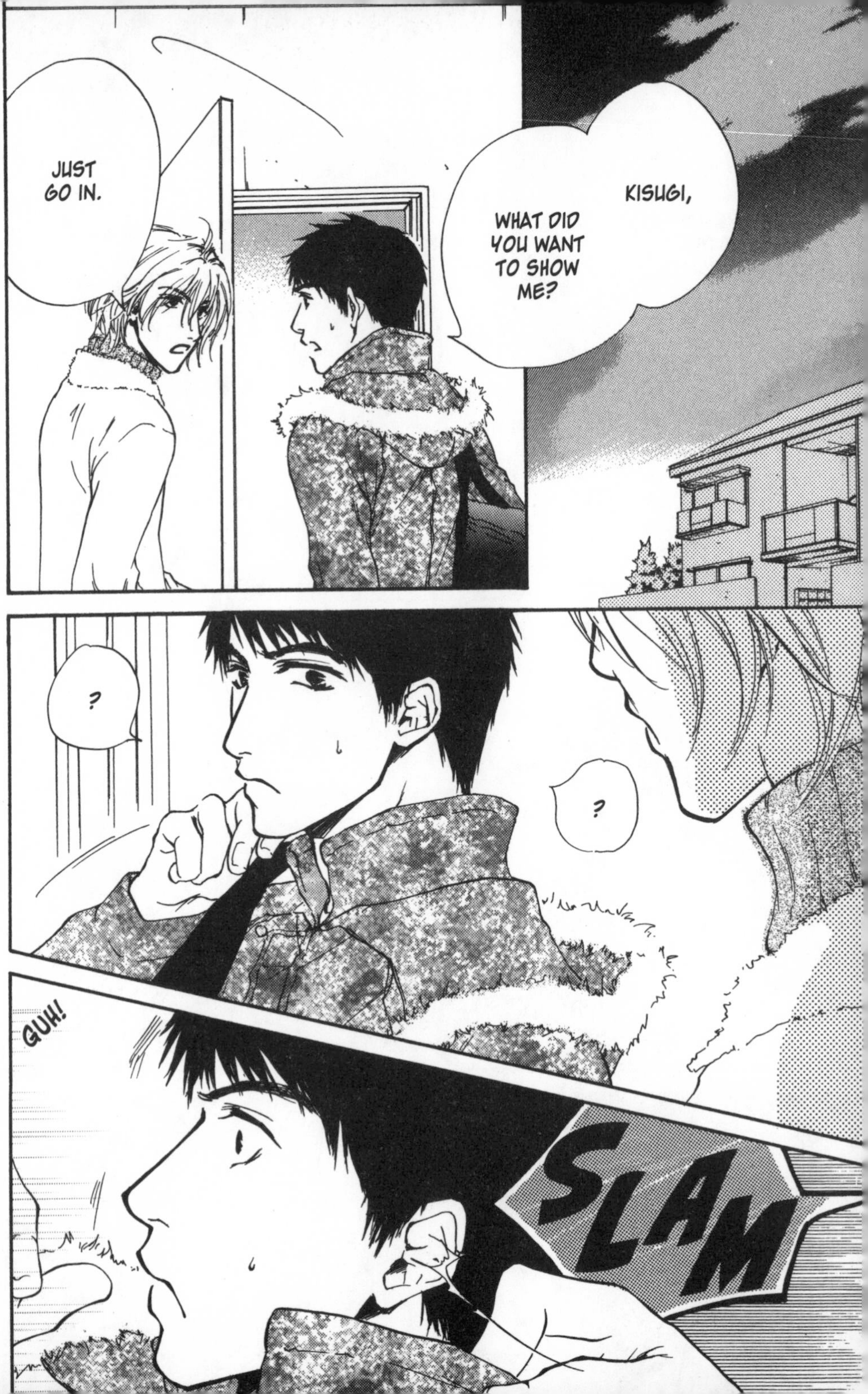
KISUGI, WHAT DID YOU WANT TO SHOW ME?
JUST GO IN.
?
?
SLAM
GUH!

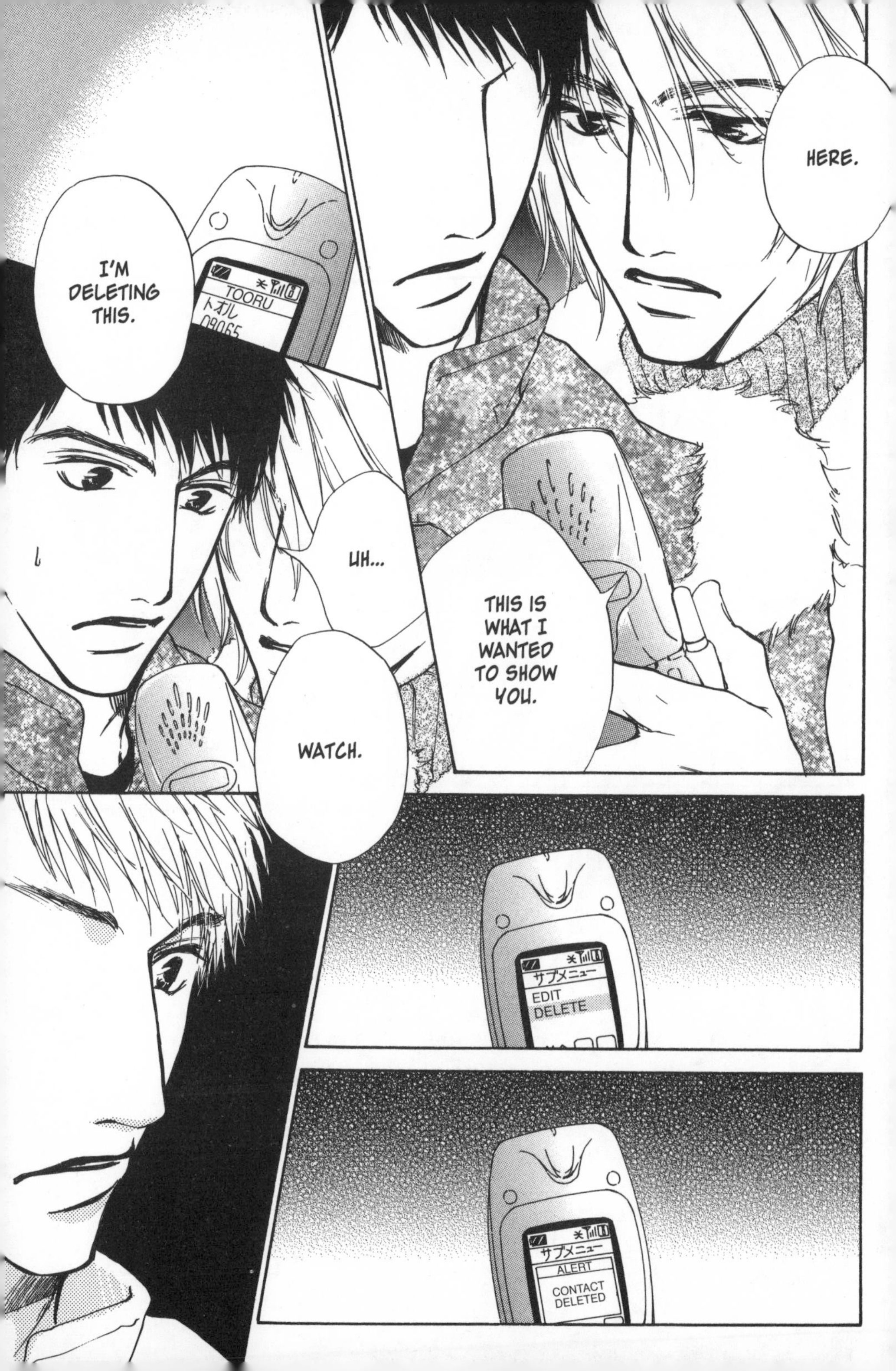
HERE.
THIS IS WHAT I WANTED TO SHOW YOU.
TOORU
トオル
09065
I'M DELETING THIS.
UH...
WATCH.
サブメニュー
EDIT
DELETE
サブメニュー
ALERT
CONTACT DELETED

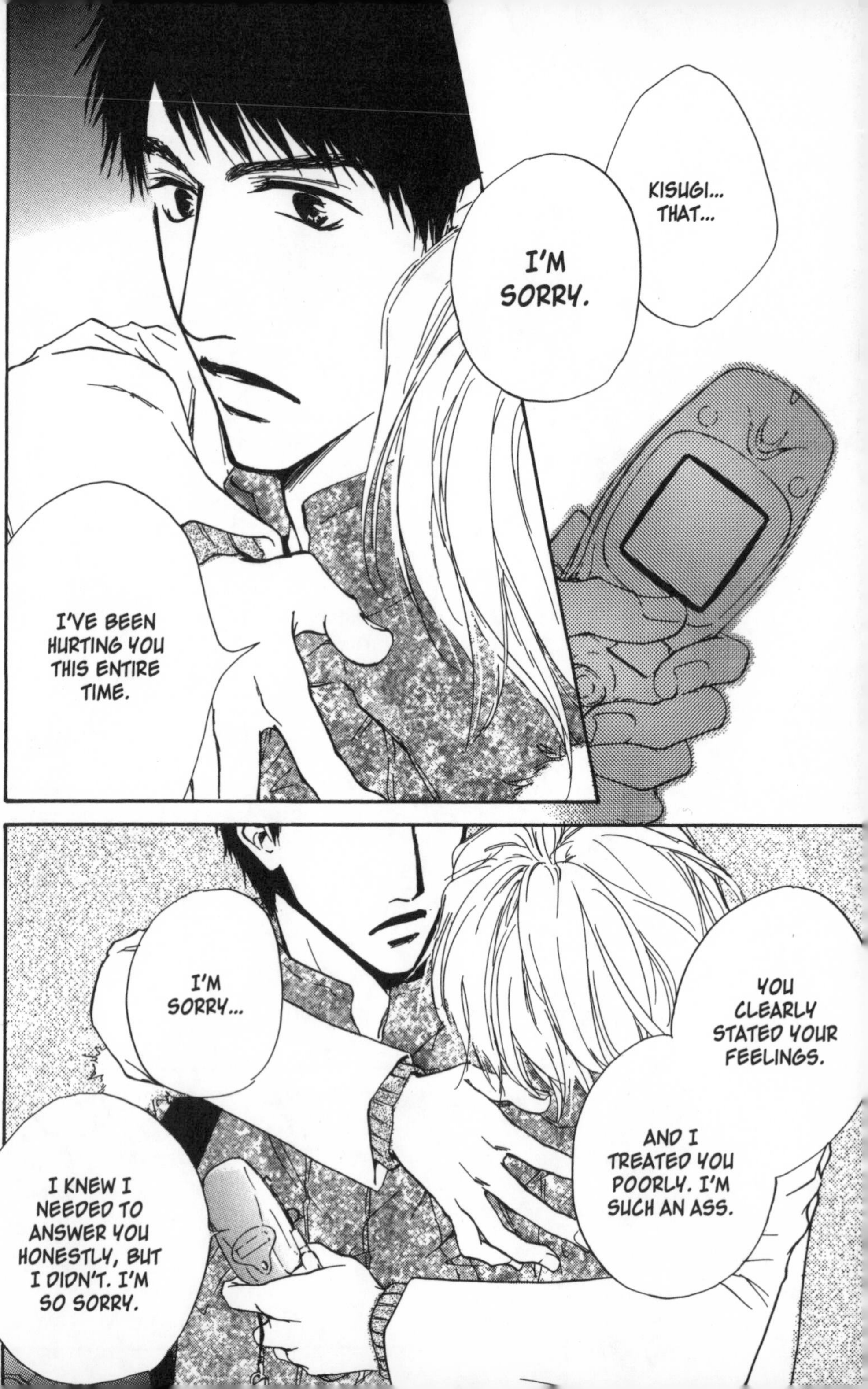
KISUGI... THAT...
I'M SORRY.
I'VE BEEN HURTING YOU THIS ENTIRE TIME.
YOU CLEARLY STATED YOUR FEELINGS.
AND I TREATED YOU POORLY. I'M SUCH AN ASS.
I'M SORRY...
I KNEW I NEEDED TO ANSWER YOU HONESTLY, BUT I DIDN'T. I'M SO SORRY.

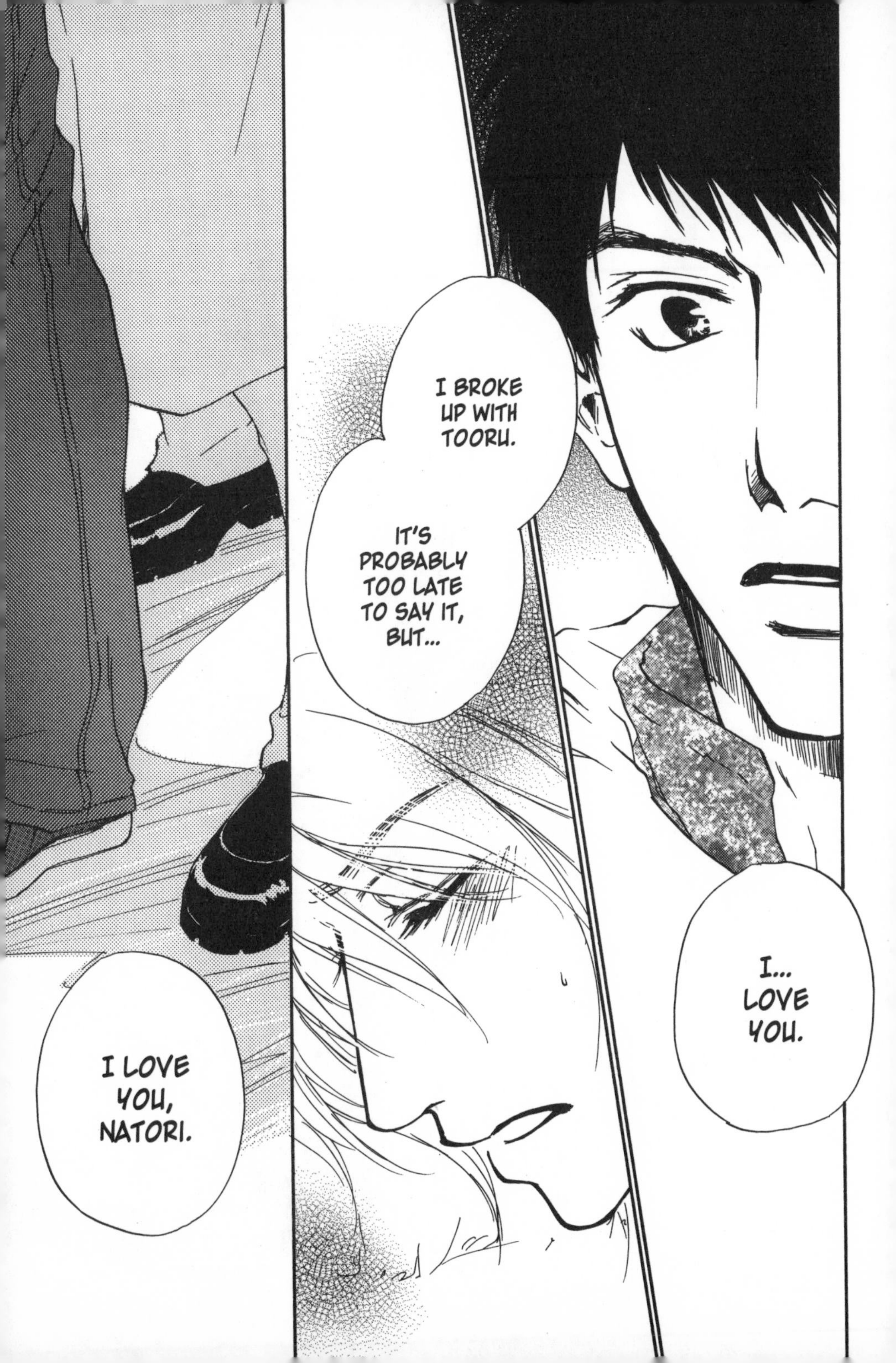
I BROKE UP WITH TOORU.
IT'S PROBABLY TOO LATE TO SAY IT, BUT...
I... LOVE YOU.
I LOVE YOU, NATORI.

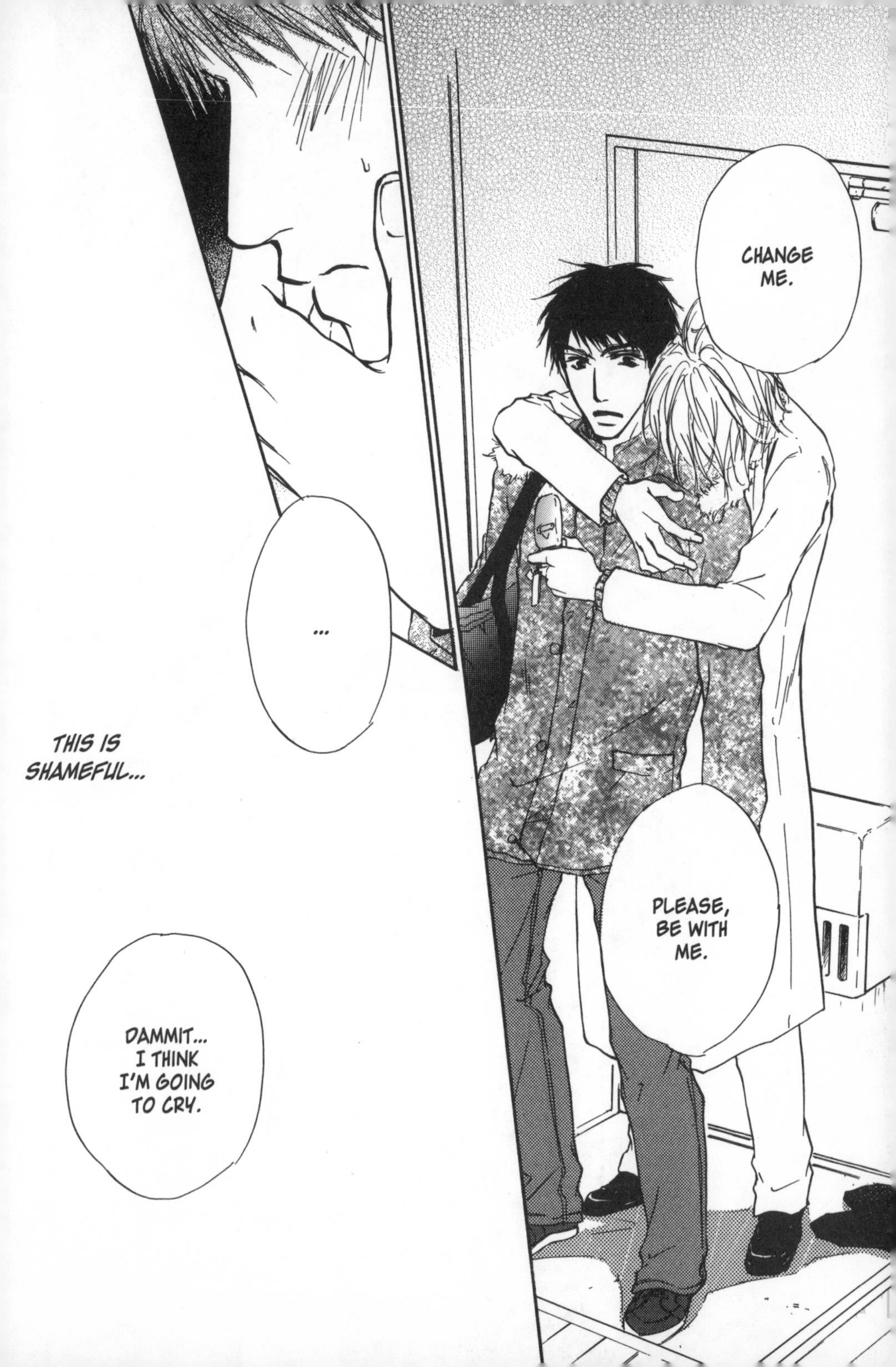
CHANGE ME.
PLEASE, BE WITH ME.
...
THIS IS SHAMEFUL...
DAMMIT... I THINK I'M GOING TO CRY.

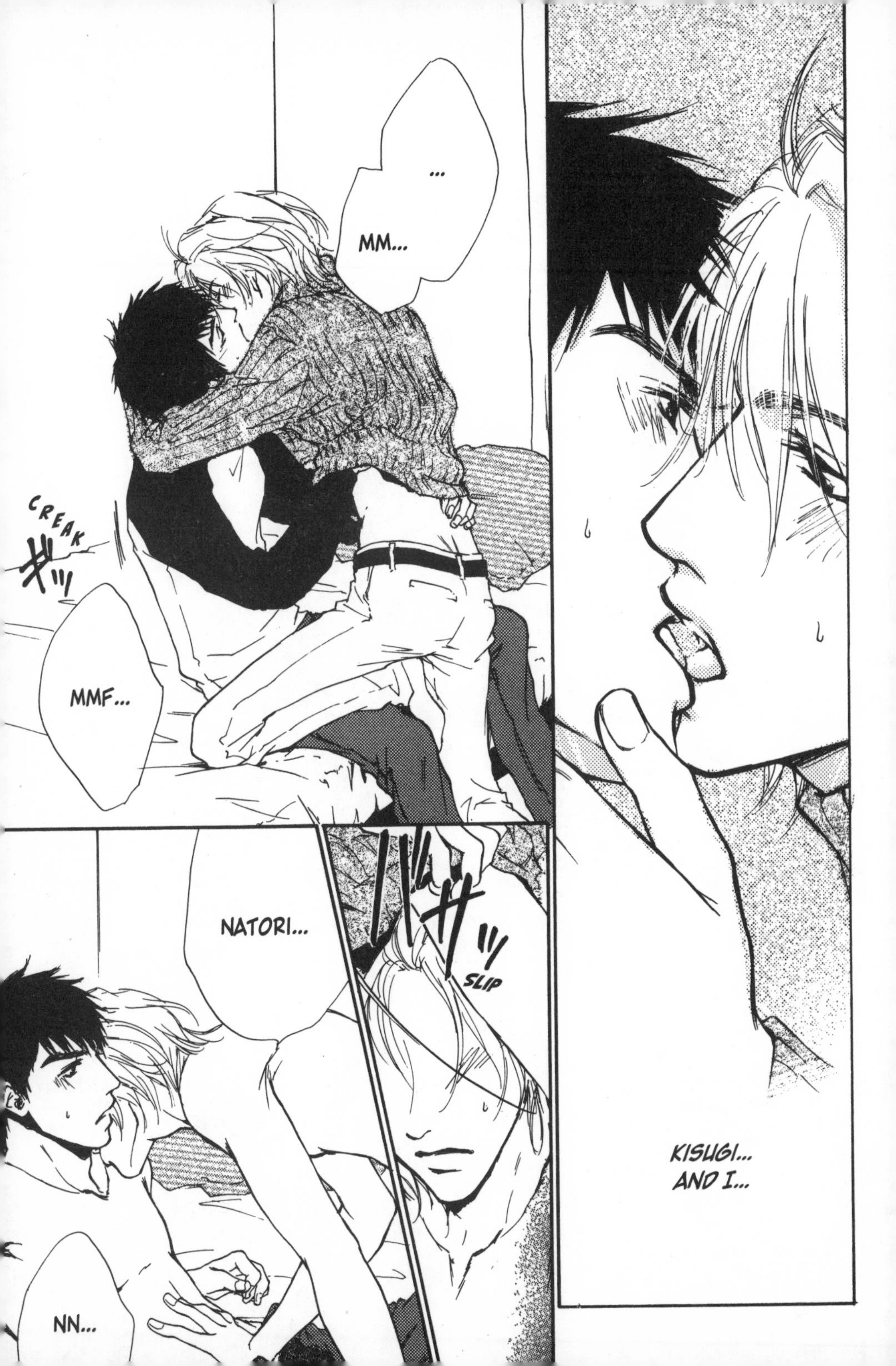
KISUGI... AND I...
...
MM...
CREAK
MMF...
SLIP
NATORI...
NN...

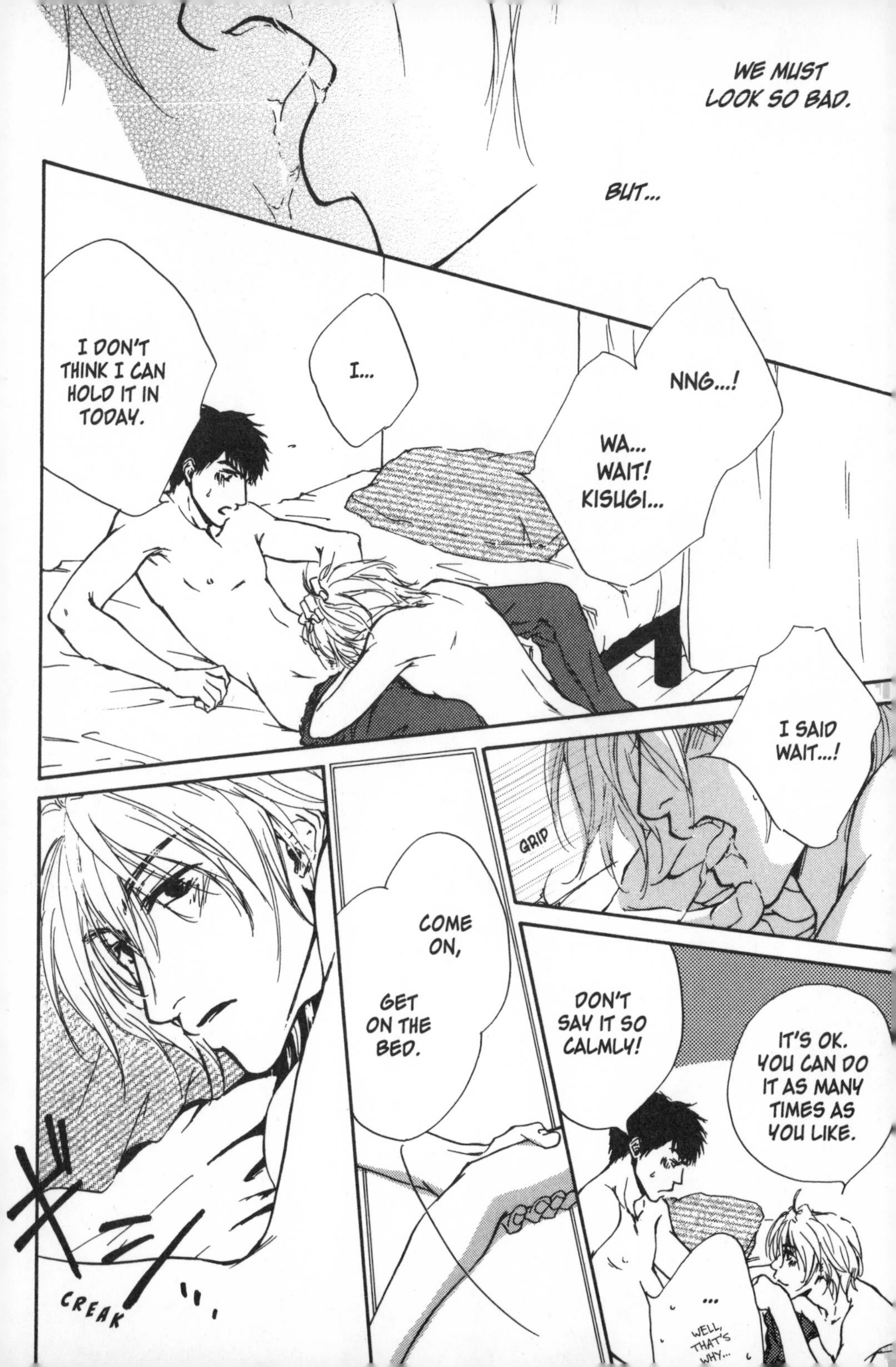

WE MUST LOOK SO BAD.
BUT...
NNG...!
WA... WAIT! KISUGI...
I...
I DON'T THINK I CAN HOLD IT IN TODAY.
I SAID WAIT...!
GRIP
IT'S OK. YOU CAN DO IT AS MANY TIMES AS YOU LIKE.
DON'T SAY IT SO CALMLY!
...
WELL, THAT'S WHY...
COME ON,
GET ON THE BED.
CREAK

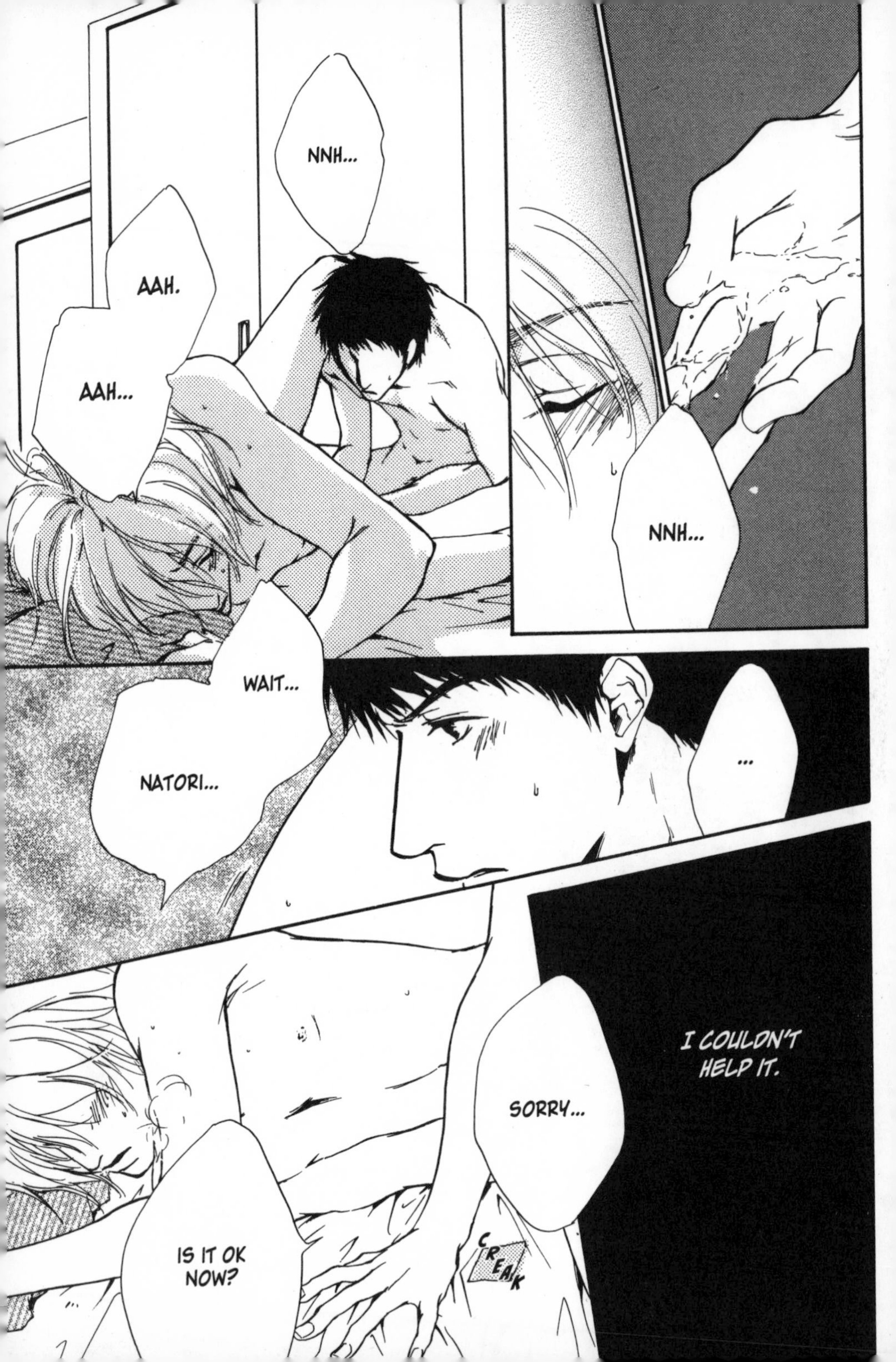
NNH...
NNH...
AAH.
AAH...
WAIT... NATORI...
...
I COULDN'T HELP IT.
SORRY...
CREAK
IS IT OK NOW?
...

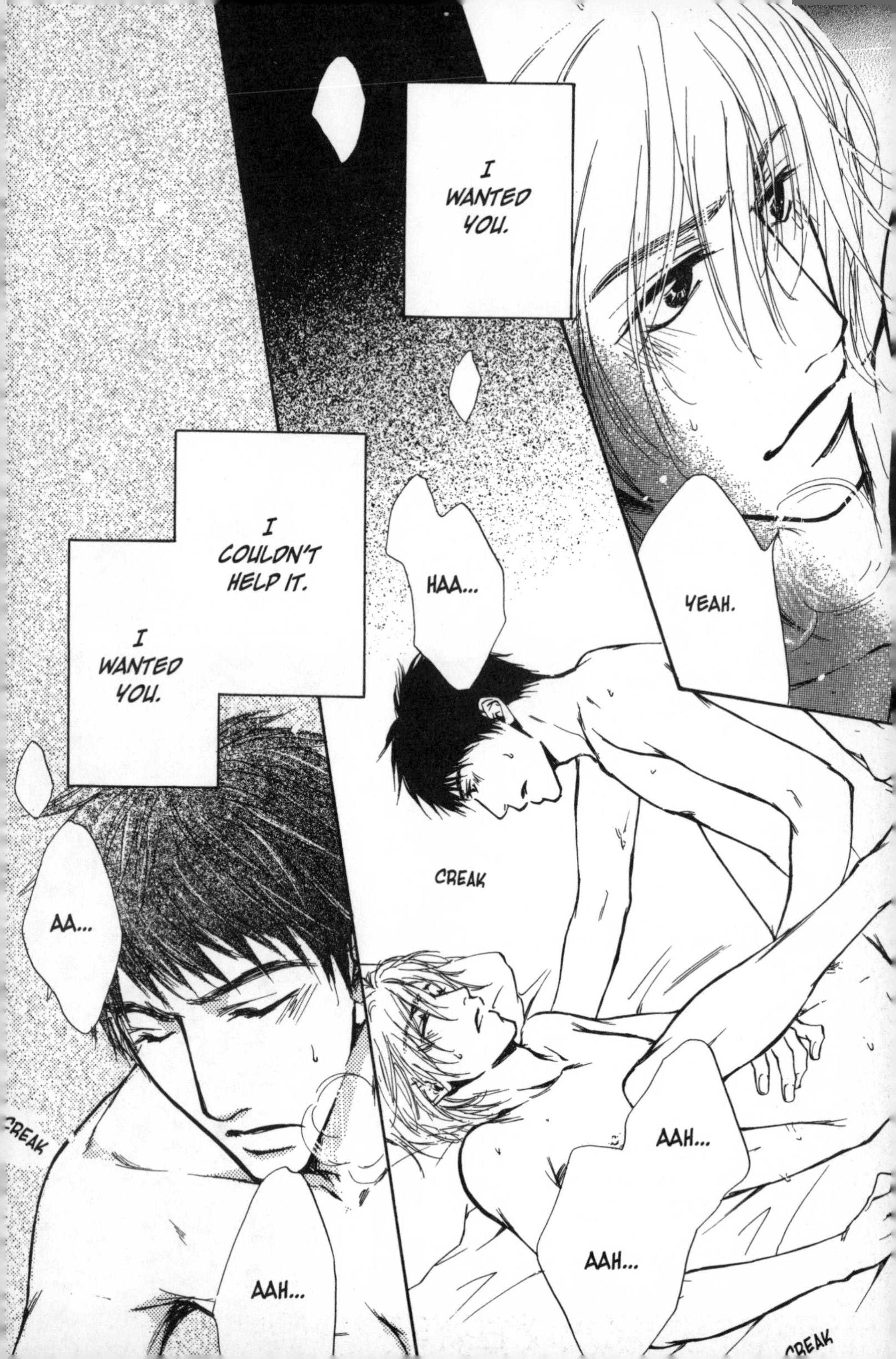
I WANTED YOU.
YEAH.
HAA...
CREAK
AAH...
AAH...
CREAK
I COULDN'T HELP IT.
I WANTED YOU.
AA...
CREAK
AAH...

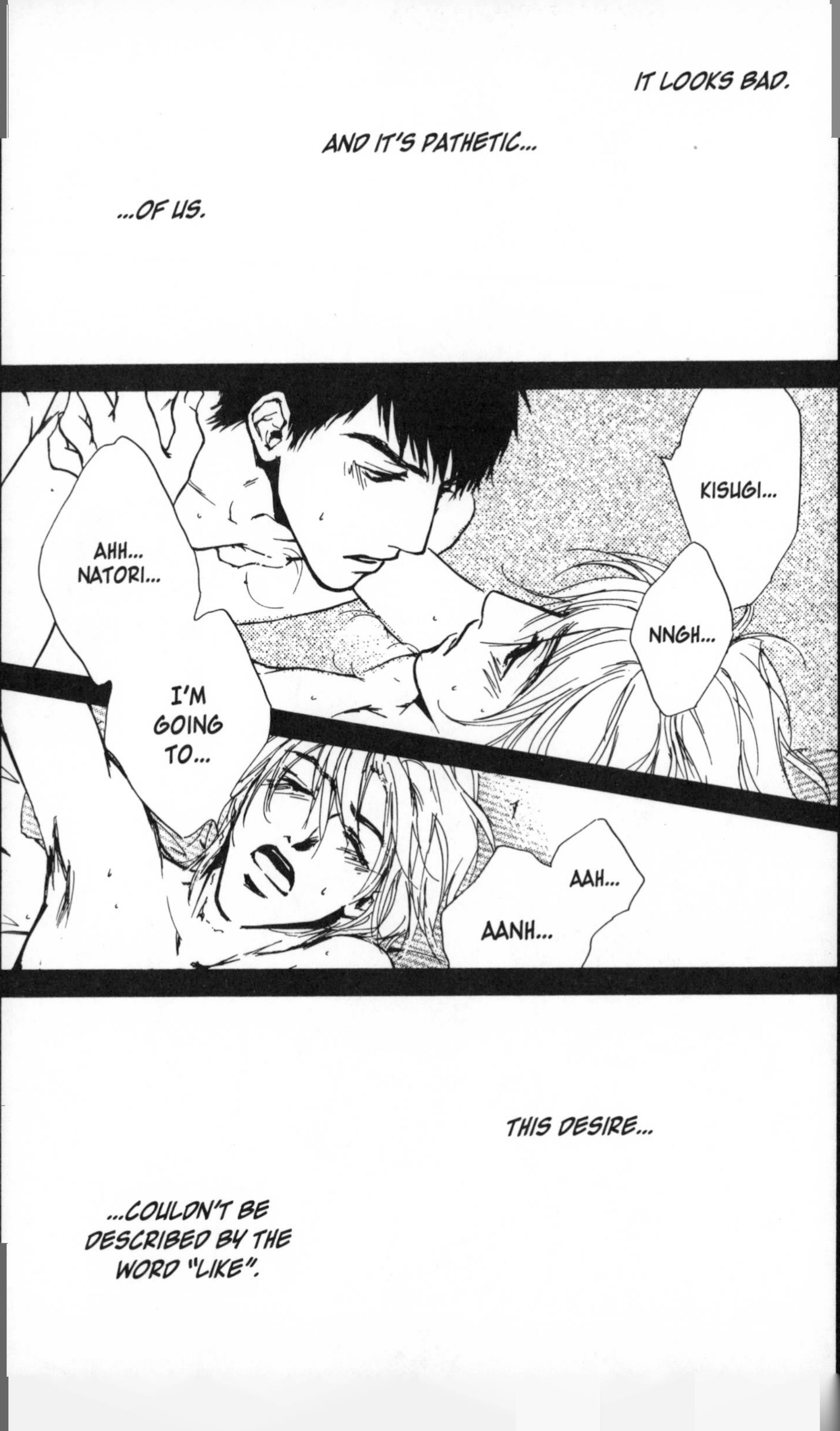
IT LOOKS BAD.
AND IT'S PATHETIC...
...OF US.
KISUGI...
NNGH...
AHH... NATORI...
I'M GOING TO...
AAH...
AANH...
THIS DESIRE...
...COULDN'T BE DESCRIBED BY THE WORD "LIKE".

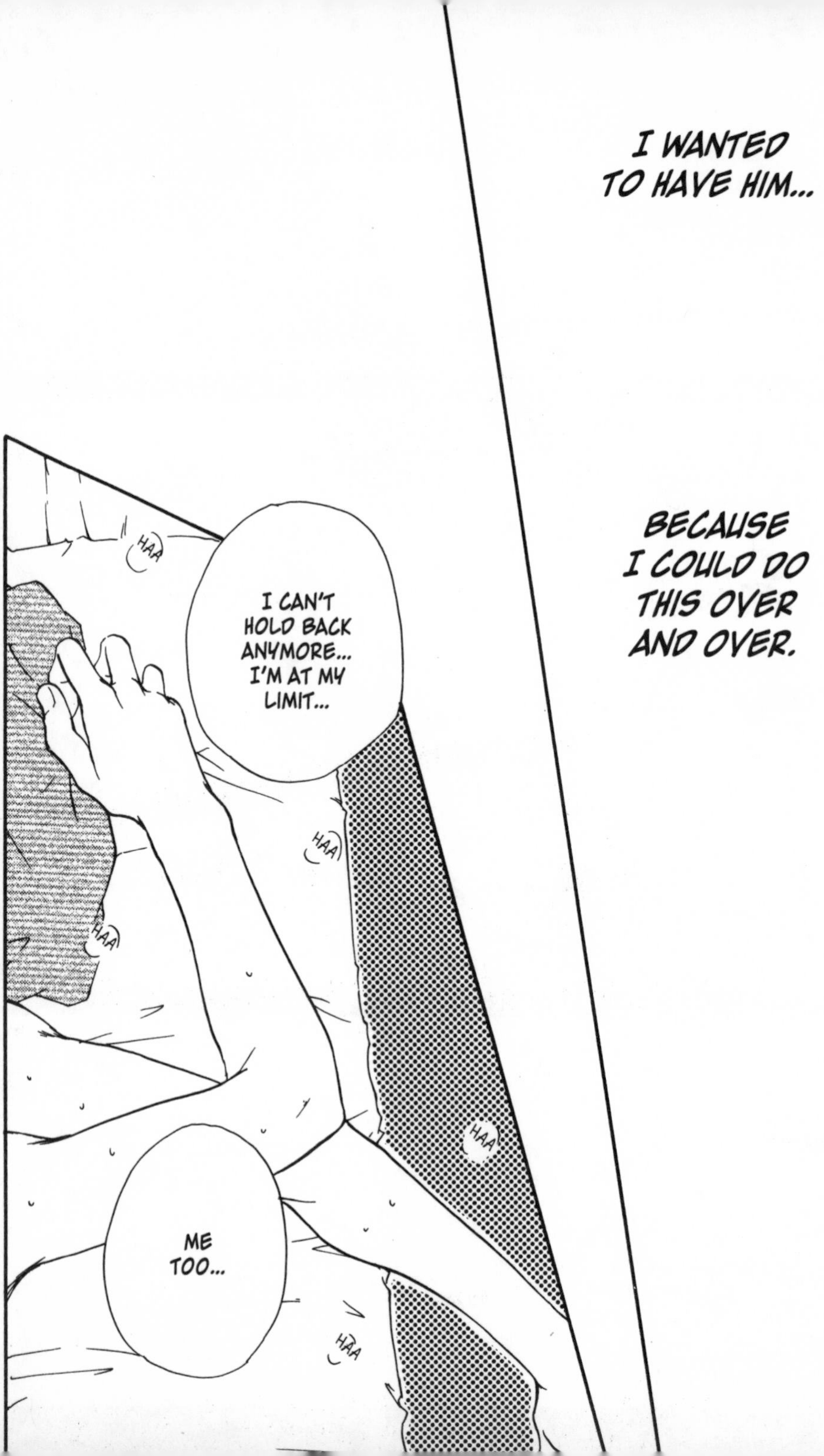
I WANTED TO HAVE HIM...
BECAUSE I COULD DO THIS OVER AND OVER.
HAA
I CAN'T HOLD BACK ANYMORE... I'M AT MY LIMIT...
HAA
HAA
HAA
ME TOO...
HAA

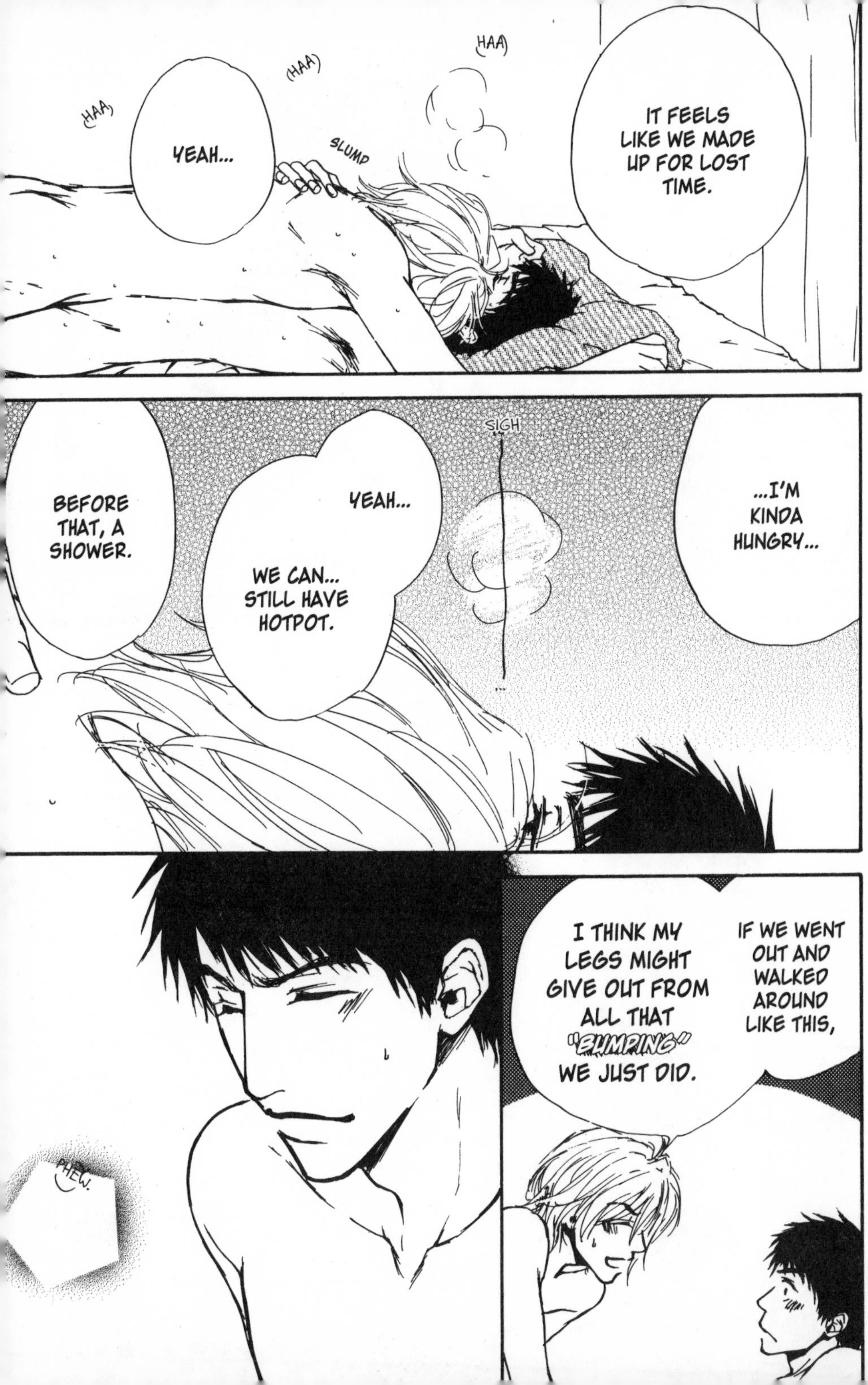
IT FEELS LIKE WE MADE UP FOR LOST TIME.
HAA
HAA
SLUMP
YEAH...
HAA
...I'M KINDA HUNGRY...
SIGH
YEAH...
WE CAN... STILL HAVE HOTPOT.
BEFORE THAT, A SHOWER.
IF WE WENT OUT AND WALKED AROUND LIKE THIS,
I THINK MY LEGS MIGHT GIVE OUT FROM ALL THAT "BUMPING" WE JUST DID.
PHEW.

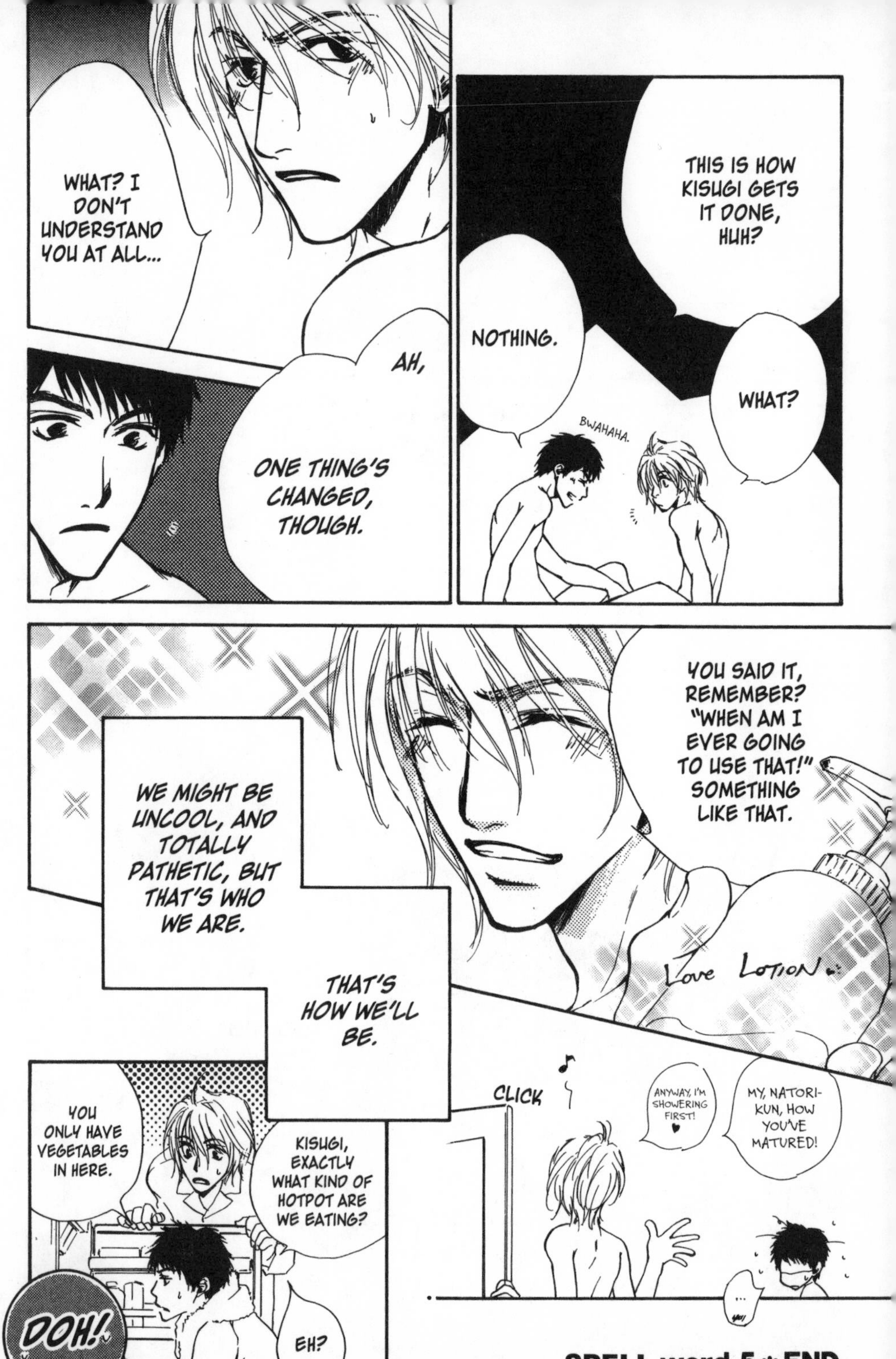
THIS IS HOW KISUGI GETS IT DONE, HUH?
WHAT?
NOTHING.
BWAHAHA.
WHAT? I DON'T UNDERSTAND YOU AT ALL...
AH,
ONE THING'S CHANGED, THOUGH.
YOU SAID IT, REMEMBER? "WHEN AM I EVER GOING TO USE THAT!" SOMETHING LIKE THAT.
WE MIGHT BE UNCOOL, AND TOTALLY PATHETIC, BUT THAT'S WHO WE ARE.
THAT'S HOW WE'LL BE.
Love Lotion
MY, NATORI-KUN, HOW YOU'VE MATURED!
ANYWAY, I'M SHOWERING FIRST!
CLICK
...
KISUGI, EXACTLY WHAT KIND OF HOTPOT ARE WE EATING?
YOU ONLY HAVE VEGETABLES IN HERE.
EH?
DOH!

SPELL word. 5 * END

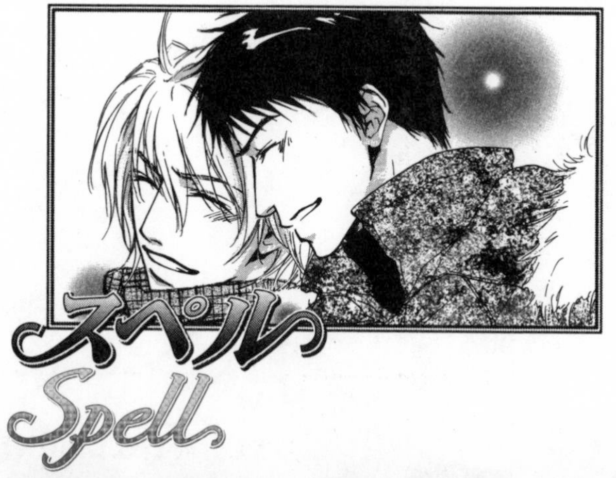

スペル

Spell

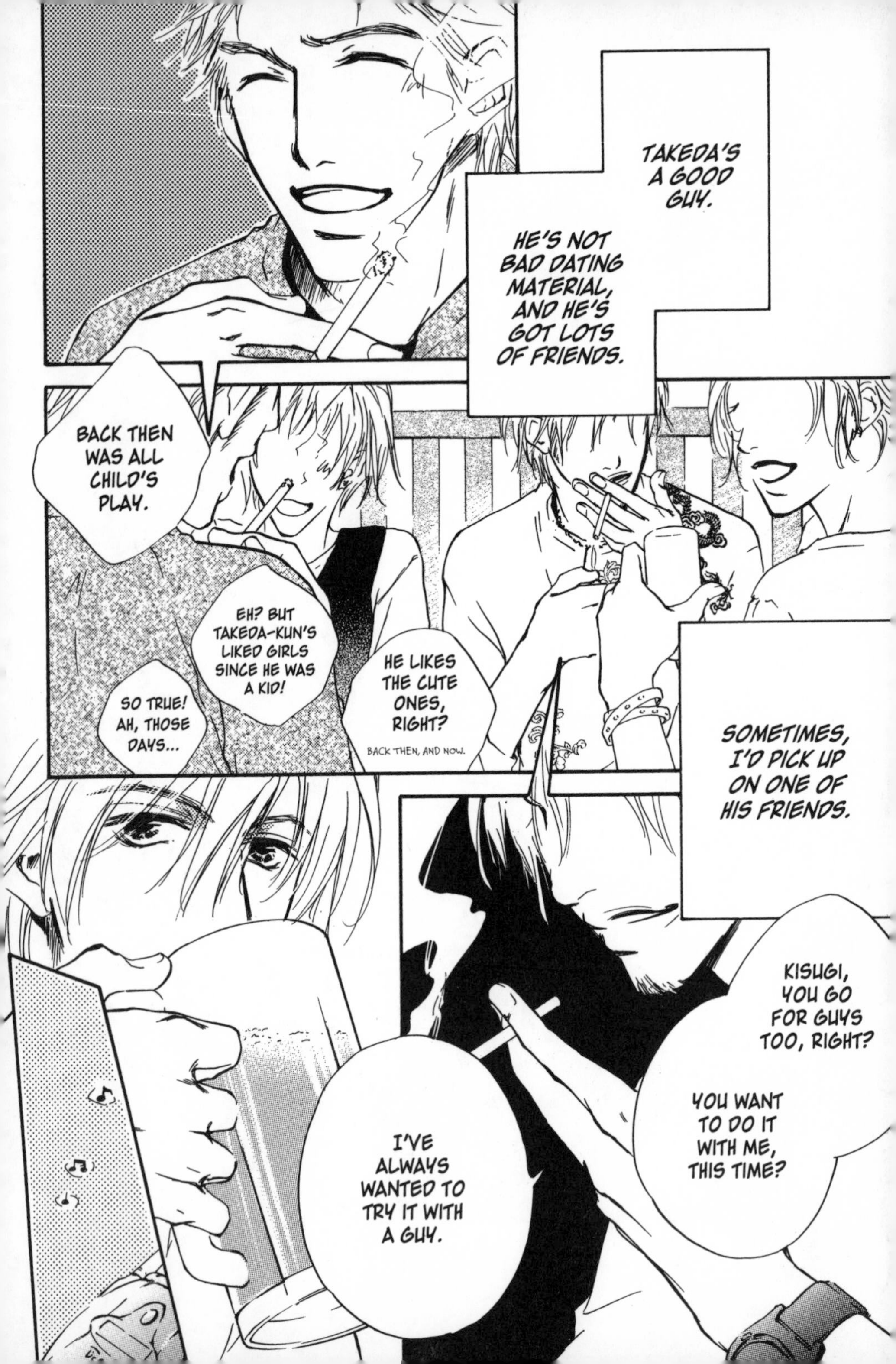
TAKEDA'S A GOOD GUY.
HE'S NOT BAD DATING MATERIAL, AND HE'S GOT LOTS OF FRIENDS.
BACK THEN WAS ALL CHILD'S PLAY.
EH? BUT TAKEDA-KUN'S LIKED GIRLS SINCE HE WAS A KID!
HE LIKES THE CUTE ONES, RIGHT?
BACK THEN, AND NOW.
SO TRUE! AH, THOSE DAYS...
SOMETIMES, I'D PICK UP ON ONE OF HIS FRIENDS.
KISUGI, YOU GO FOR GUYS TOO, RIGHT?
YOU WANT TO DO IT WITH ME, THIS TIME?
I'VE ALWAYS WANTED TO TRY IT WITH A GUY.

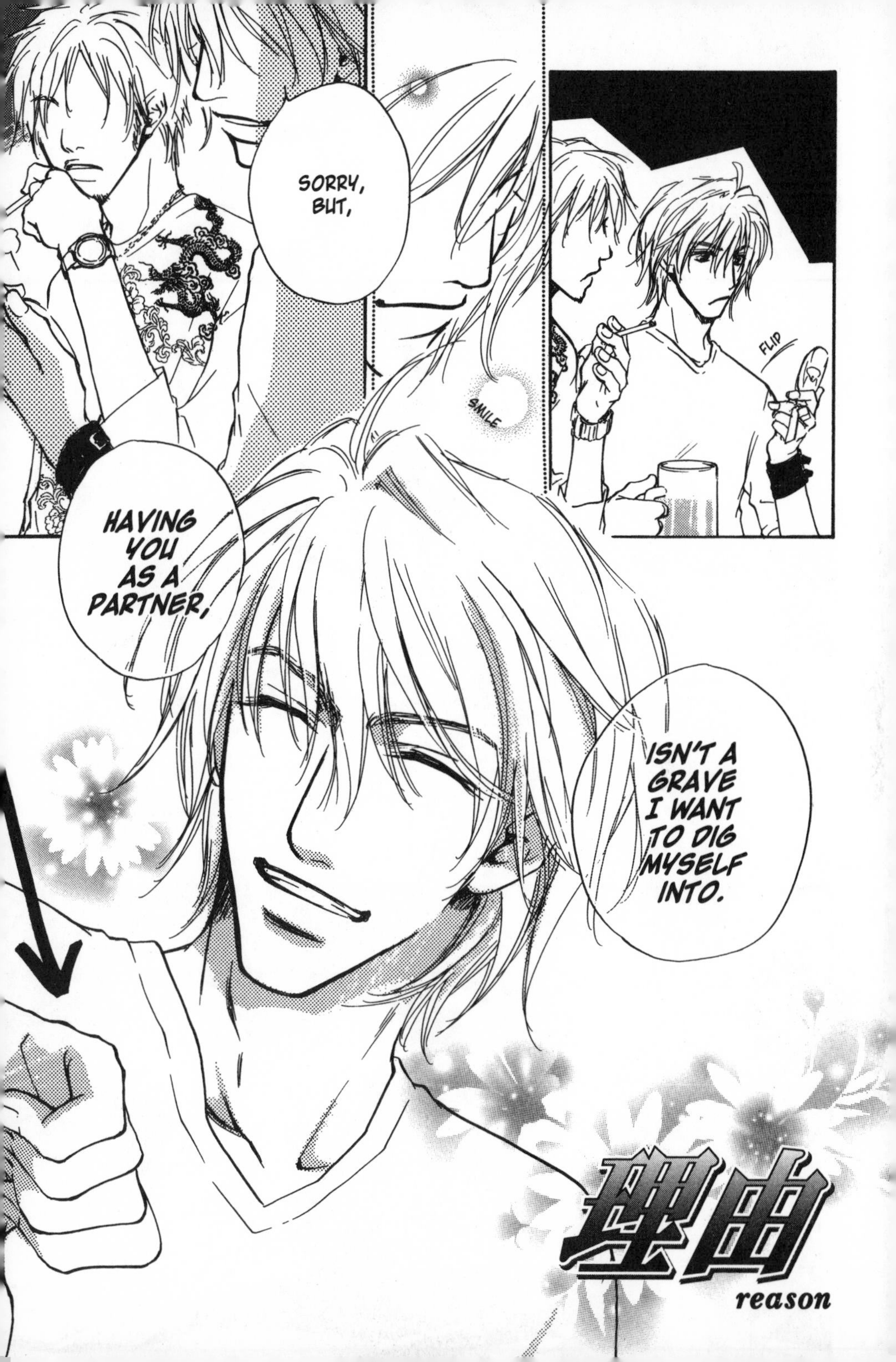
FLIP
SORRY, BUT,
SMILE
HAVING YOU AS A PARTNER,
ISN'T A GRAVE I WANT TO DIG MYSELF INTO.
理由
reason

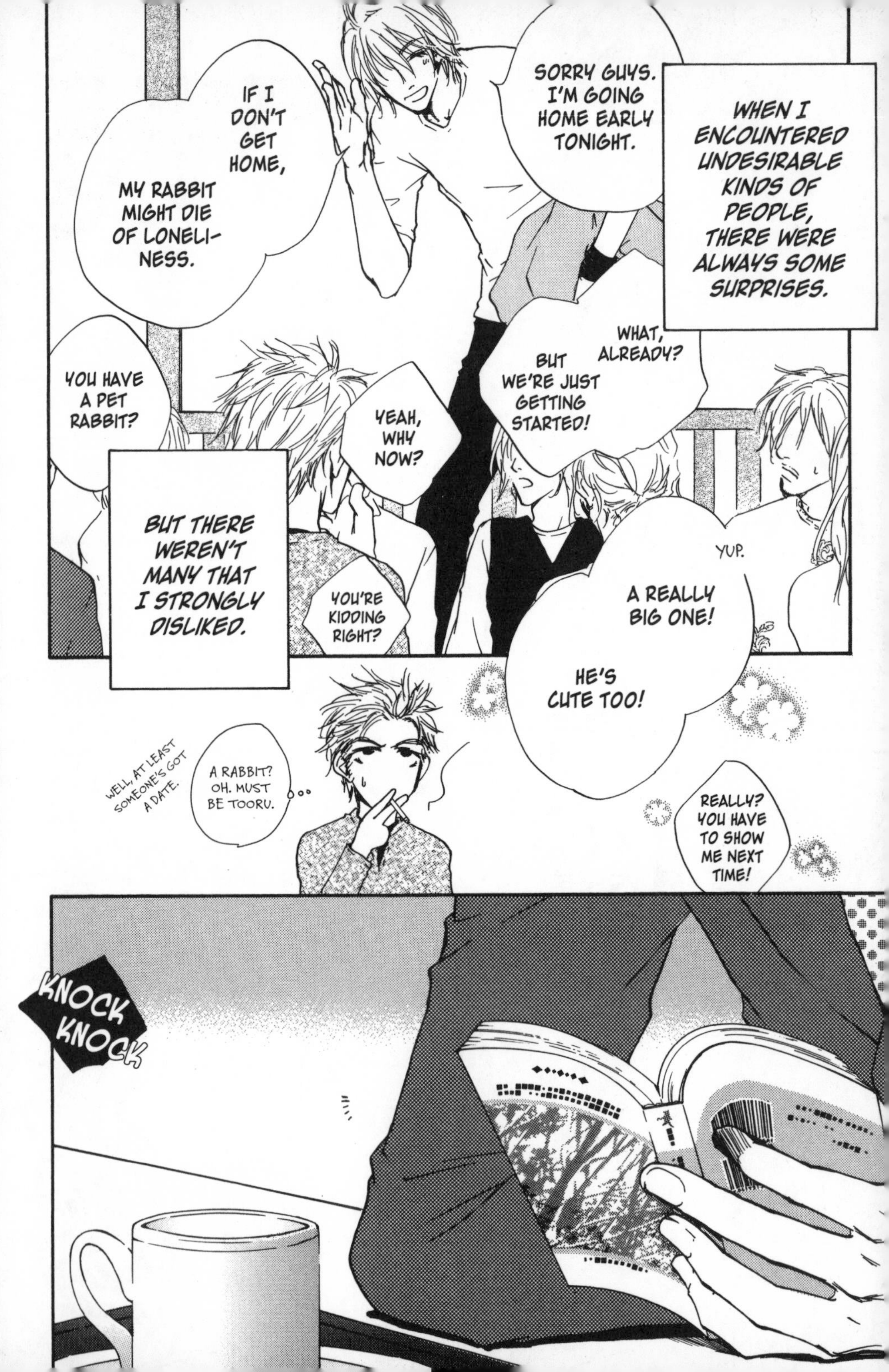
WHEN I ENCOUNTERED UNDESIRABLE KINDS OF PEOPLE, THERE WERE ALWAYS SOME SURPRISES.
SORRY GUYS. I'M GOING HOME EARLY TONIGHT.
IF I DON'T GET HOME, MY RABBIT MIGHT DIE OF LONELI-NESS.
WHAT, ALREADY?
BUT WE'RE JUST GETTING STARTED!
YEAH, WHY NOW?
YOU HAVE A PET RABBIT?
YUP.
A REALLY BIG ONE!
HE'S CUTE TOO!
YOU'RE KIDDING RIGHT?
BUT THERE WEREN'T MANY THAT I STRONGLY DISLIKED.
REALLY? YOU HAVE TO SHOW ME NEXT TIME!
A RABBIT? OH. MUST BE TOORU.
WELL, AT LEAST SOMEONE'S GOT A DATE.
KNOCK KNOCK

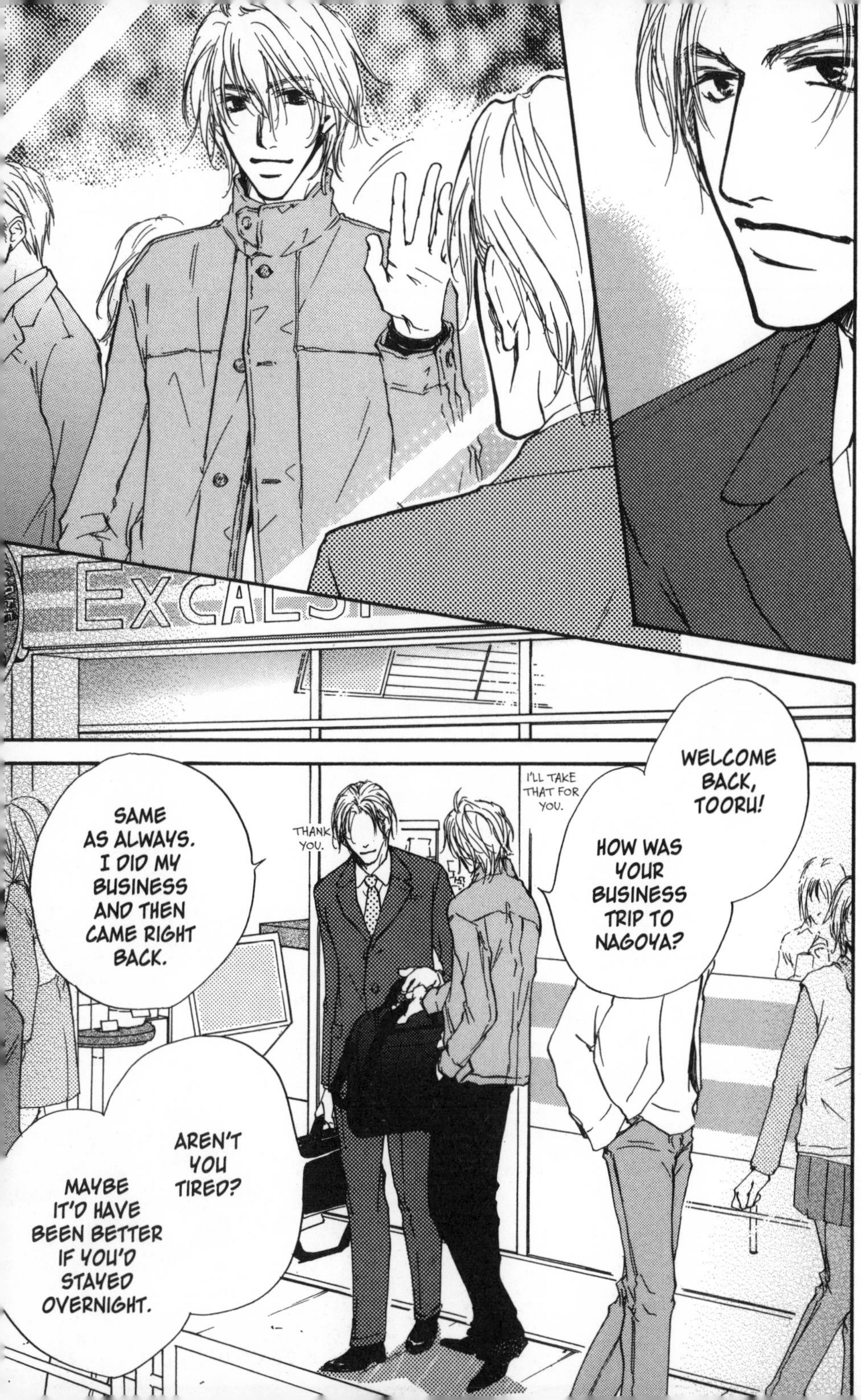
WELCOME BACK, TOORU!
HOW WAS YOUR BUSINESS TRIP TO NAGOYA?
I'LL TAKE THAT FOR YOU.
THANK YOU.
SAME AS ALWAYS. I DID MY BUSINESS AND THEN CAME RIGHT BACK.
AREN'T YOU TIRED?
MAYBE IT'D HAVE BEEN BETTER IF YOU'D STAYED OVERNIGHT.

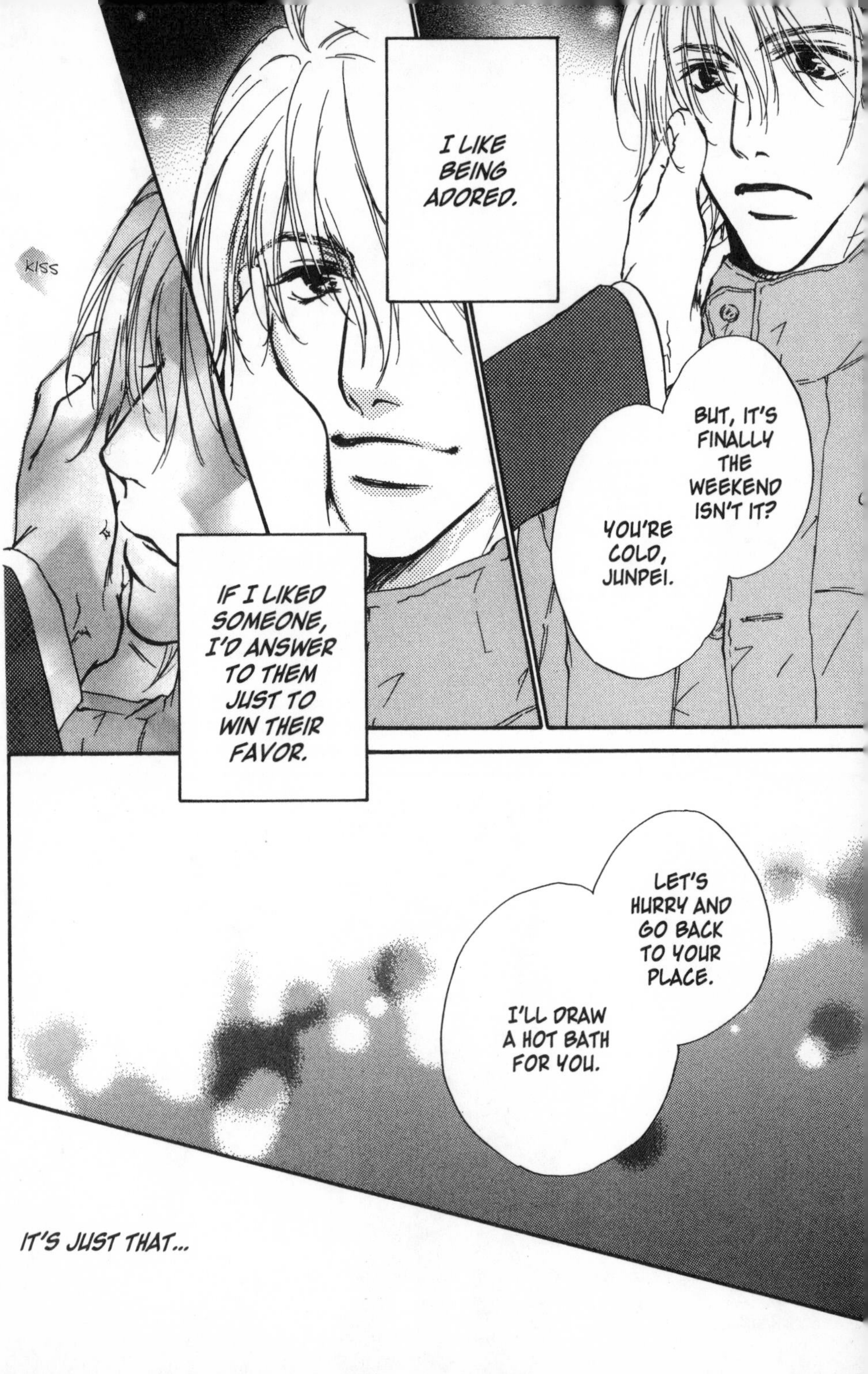
BUT, IT'S FINALLY THE WEEKEND ISN'T IT?
YOU'RE COLD, JUNPEI.
I LIKE BEING ADORED.
IF I LIKED SOMEONE, I'D ANSWER TO THEM JUST TO WIN THEIR FAVOR.
KISS
LET'S HURRY AND GO BACK TO YOUR PLACE.
I'LL DRAW A HOT BATH FOR YOU.
IT'S JUST THAT...

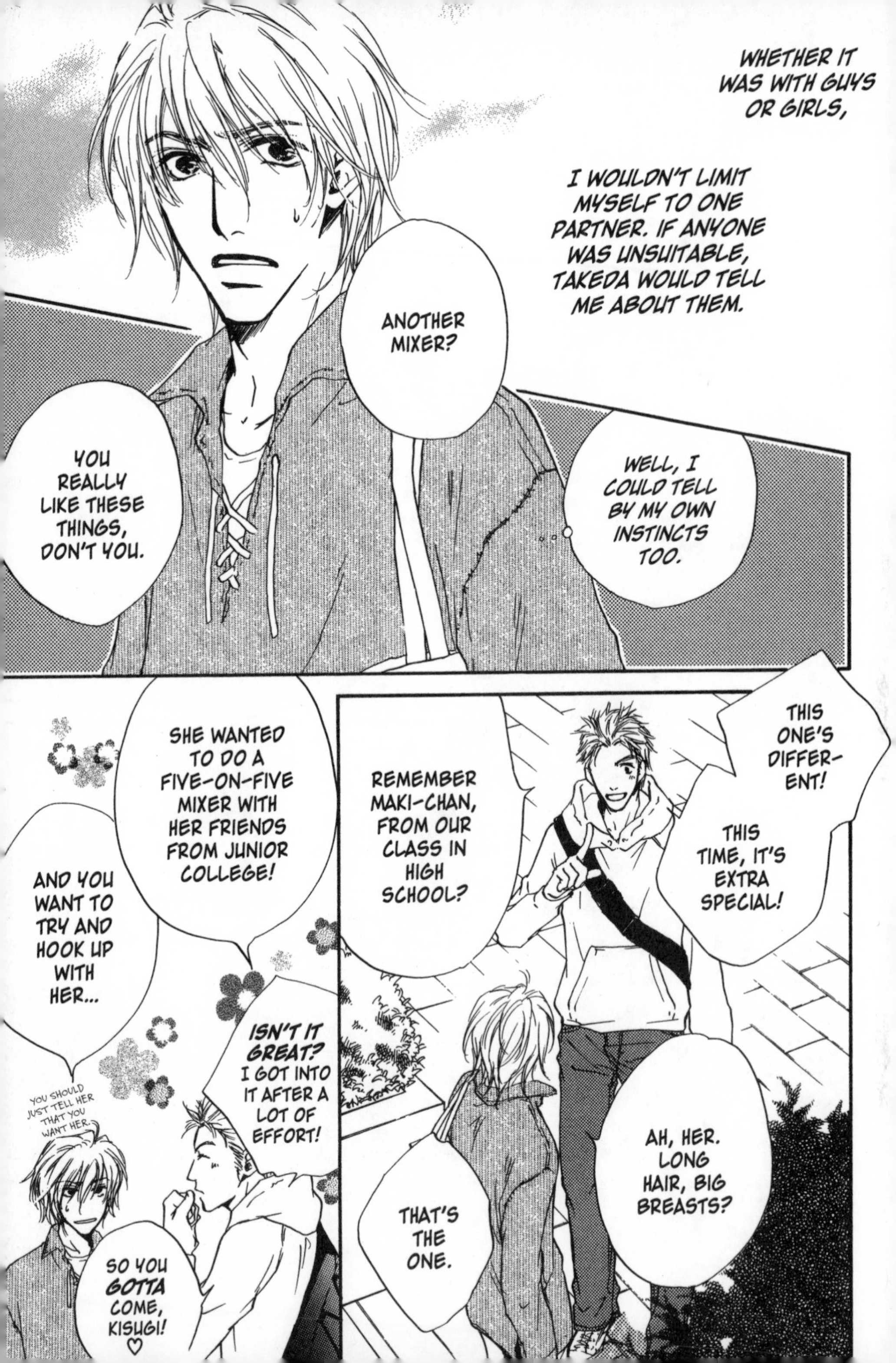
WHETHER IT WAS WITH GUYS OR GIRLS,
I WOULDN'T LIMIT MYSELF TO ONE PARTNER. IF ANYONE WAS UNSUITABLE, TAKEDA WOULD TELL ME ABOUT THEM.
WELL, I COULD TELL BY MY OWN INSTINCTS TOO.
ANOTHER MIXER?
YOU REALLY LIKE THESE THINGS, DON'T YOU.
THIS ONE'S DIFFER-ENT!
THIS TIME, IT'S EXTRA SPECIAL!
REMEMBER MAKI-CHAN, FROM OUR CLASS IN HIGH SCHOOL?
AH, HER. LONG HAIR, BIG BREASTS?
THAT'S THE ONE.
SHE WANTED TO DO A FIVE-ON-FIVE MIXER WITH HER FRIENDS FROM JUNIOR COLLEGE!
ISN'T IT GREAT? I GOT INTO IT AFTER A LOT OF EFFORT!
AND YOU WANT TO TRY AND HOOK UP WITH HER...
YOU SHOULD JUST TELL HER THAT YOU WANT HER.
SO YOU GOTTA COME, KISUGI! ♡

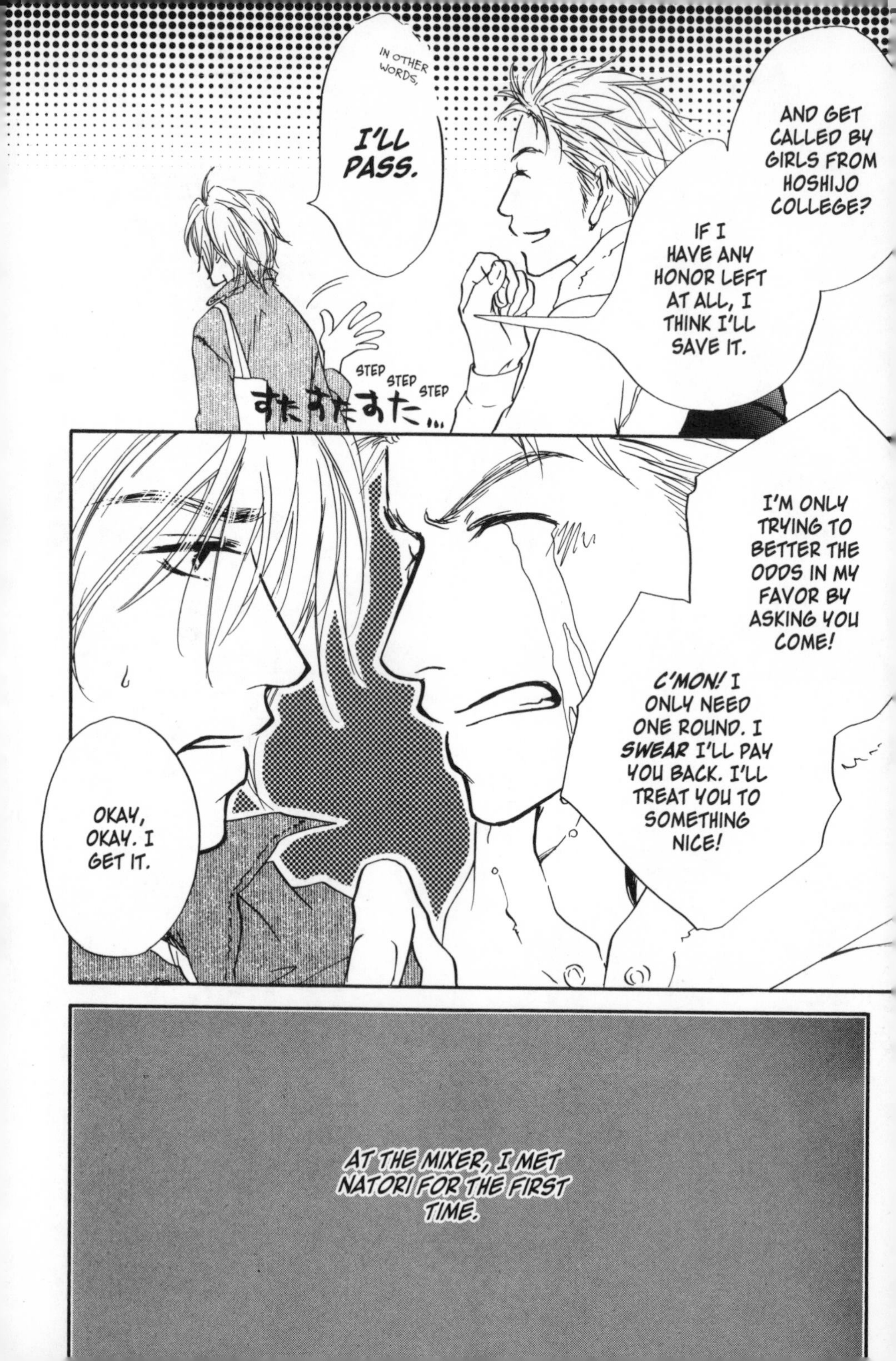
AND GET CALLED BY GIRLS FROM HOSHIJO COLLEGE?
IF I HAVE ANY HONOR LEFT AT ALL, I THINK I'LL SAVE IT.
IN OTHER WORDS,
I'LL PASS.
STEP STEP STEP
すたすたすた…
I'M ONLY TRYING TO BETTER THE ODDS IN MY FAVOR BY ASKING YOU COME!
C'MON! I ONLY NEED ONE ROUND. I SWEAR I'LL PAY YOU BACK. I'LL TREAT YOU TO SOMETHING NICE!
OKAY, OKAY. I GET IT.
AT THE MIXER, I MET NATORI FOR THE FIRST TIME.

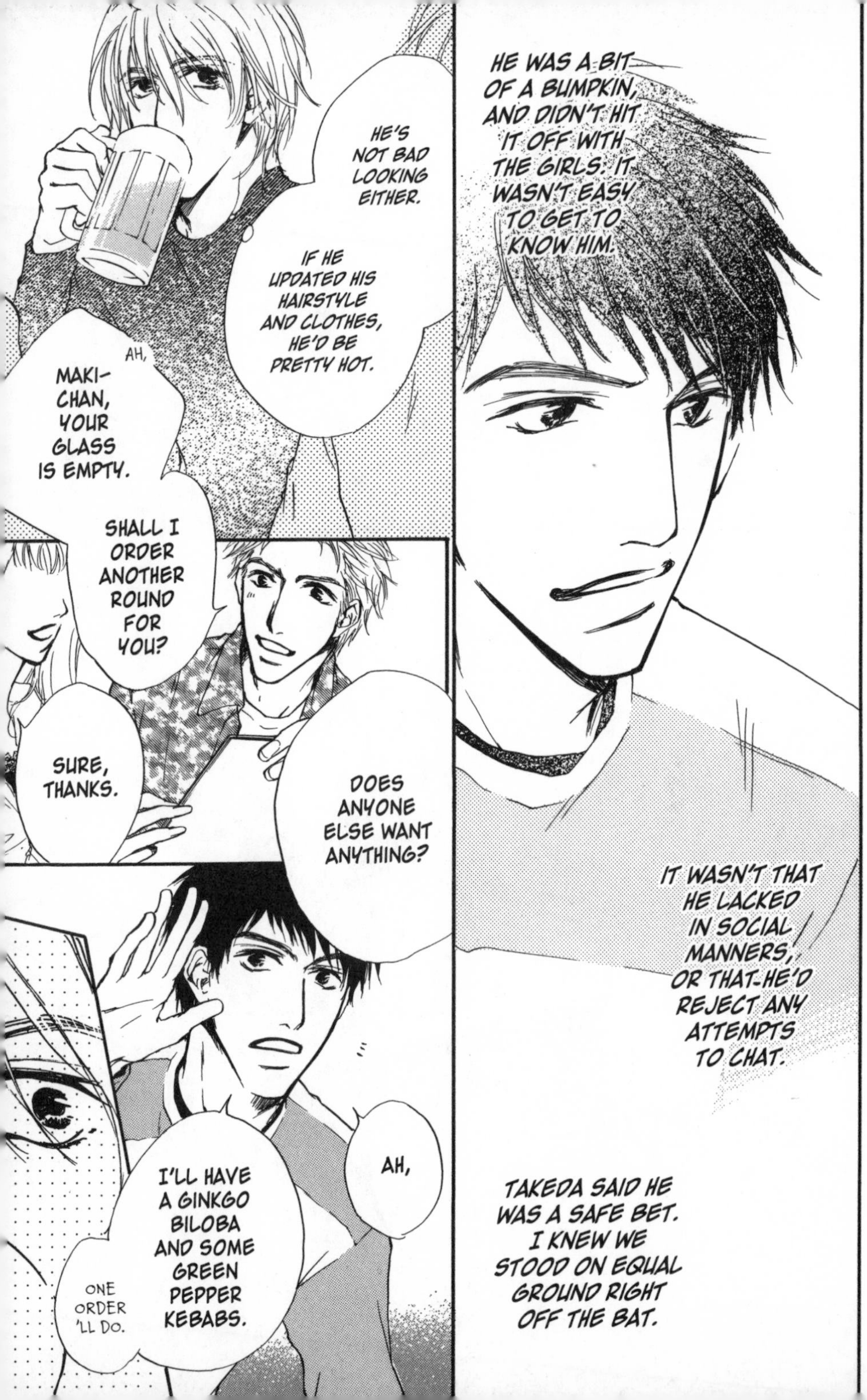
HE WAS A BIT OF A BUMPKIN, AND DIDN'T HIT IT OFF WITH THE GIRLS. IT WASN'T EASY TO GET TO KNOW HIM.
IT WASN'T THAT HE LACKED IN SOCIAL MANNERS, OR THAT HE'D REJECT ANY ATTEMPTS TO CHAT.
TAKEDA SAID HE WAS A SAFE BET. I KNEW WE STOOD ON EQUAL GROUND RIGHT OFF THE BAT.
HE'S NOT BAD LOOKING EITHER.
IF HE UPDATED HIS HAIRSTYLE AND CLOTHES, HE'D BE PRETTY HOT.
AH,
MAKI-CHAN, YOUR GLASS IS EMPTY.
SHALL I ORDER ANOTHER ROUND FOR YOU?
SURE, THANKS.
DOES ANYONE ELSE WANT ANYTHING?
AH,
I'LL HAVE A GINKGO BILOBA AND SOME GREEN PEPPER KEBABS.
ONE ORDER 'LL DO.

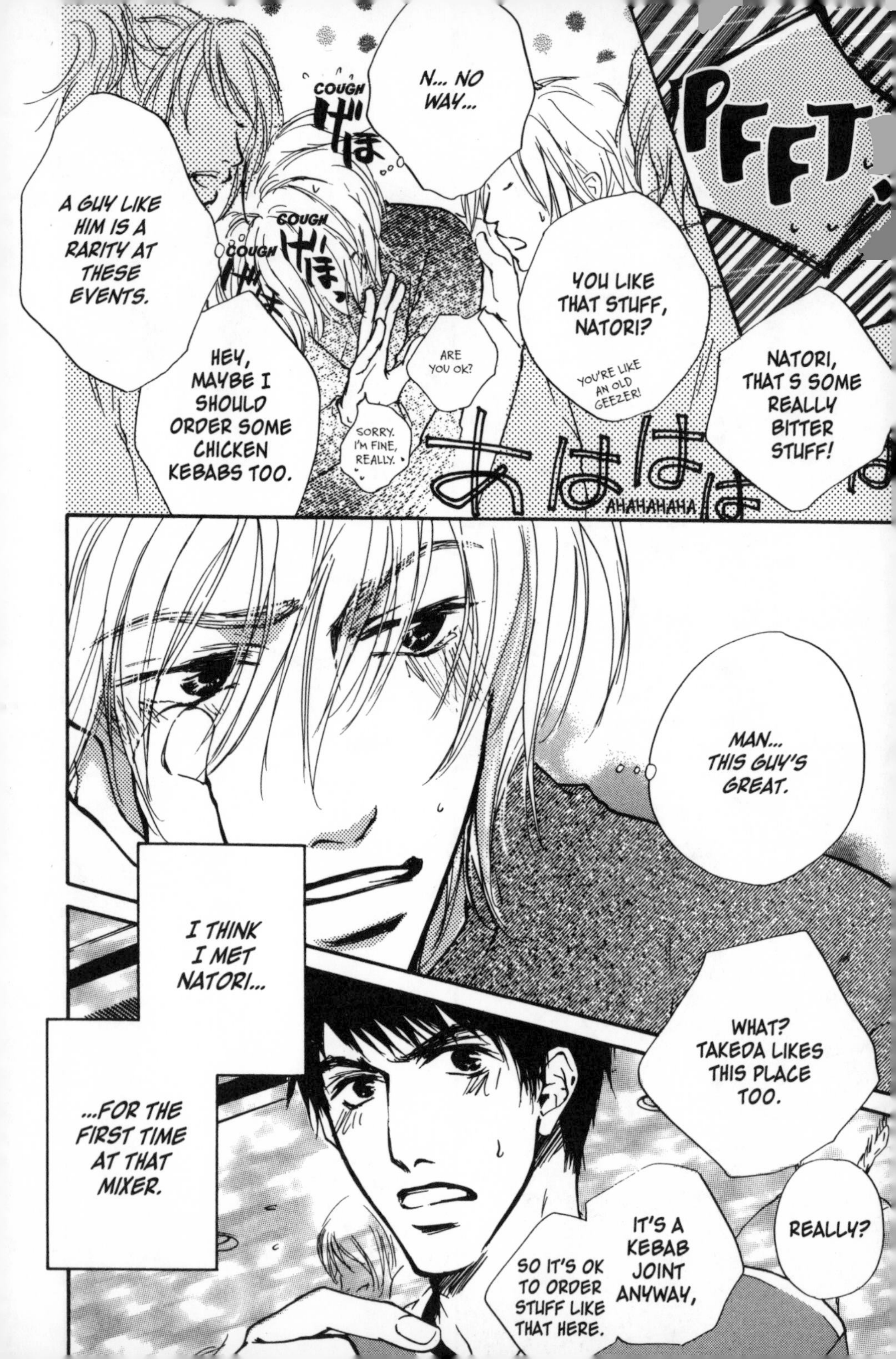
PFFT
NATORI, THAT S SOME REALLY BITTER STUFF!
YOU LIKE THAT STUFF, NATORI?
YOU'RE LIKE AN OLD GEEZER!
N... NO WAY...
COUGH
COUGH
COUGH
ARE YOU OK?
SORRY. I'M FINE, REALLY.
あははは
AHAHAHAHA
A GUY LIKE HIM IS A RARITY AT THESE EVENTS.
HEY, MAYBE I SHOULD ORDER SOME CHICKEN KEBABS TOO.
MAN... THIS GUY'S GREAT.
I THINK I MET NATORI...
...FOR THE FIRST TIME AT THAT MIXER.
WHAT? TAKEDA LIKES THIS PLACE TOO.
REALLY?
IT'S A KEBAB JOINT ANYWAY,
SO IT'S OK TO ORDER STUFF LIKE THAT HERE.

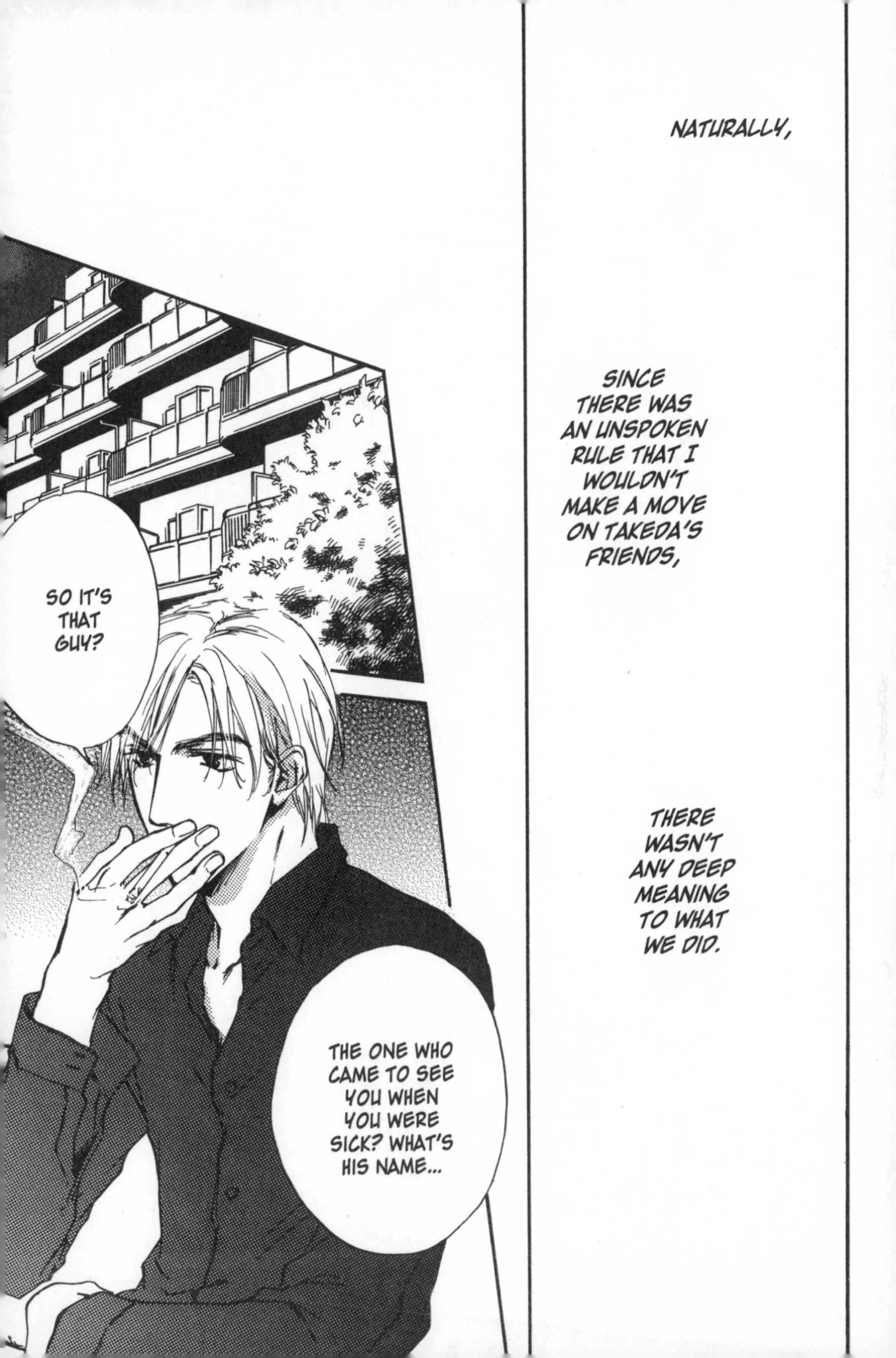
NATURALLY,
SINCE THERE WAS AN UNSPOKEN RULE THAT I WOULDN'T MAKE A MOVE ON TAKEDA'S FRIENDS,
THERE WASN'T ANY DEEP MEANING TO WHAT WE DID.
SO IT'S THAT GUY?
THE ONE WHO CAME TO SEE YOU WHEN YOU WERE SICK? WHAT'S HIS NAME...

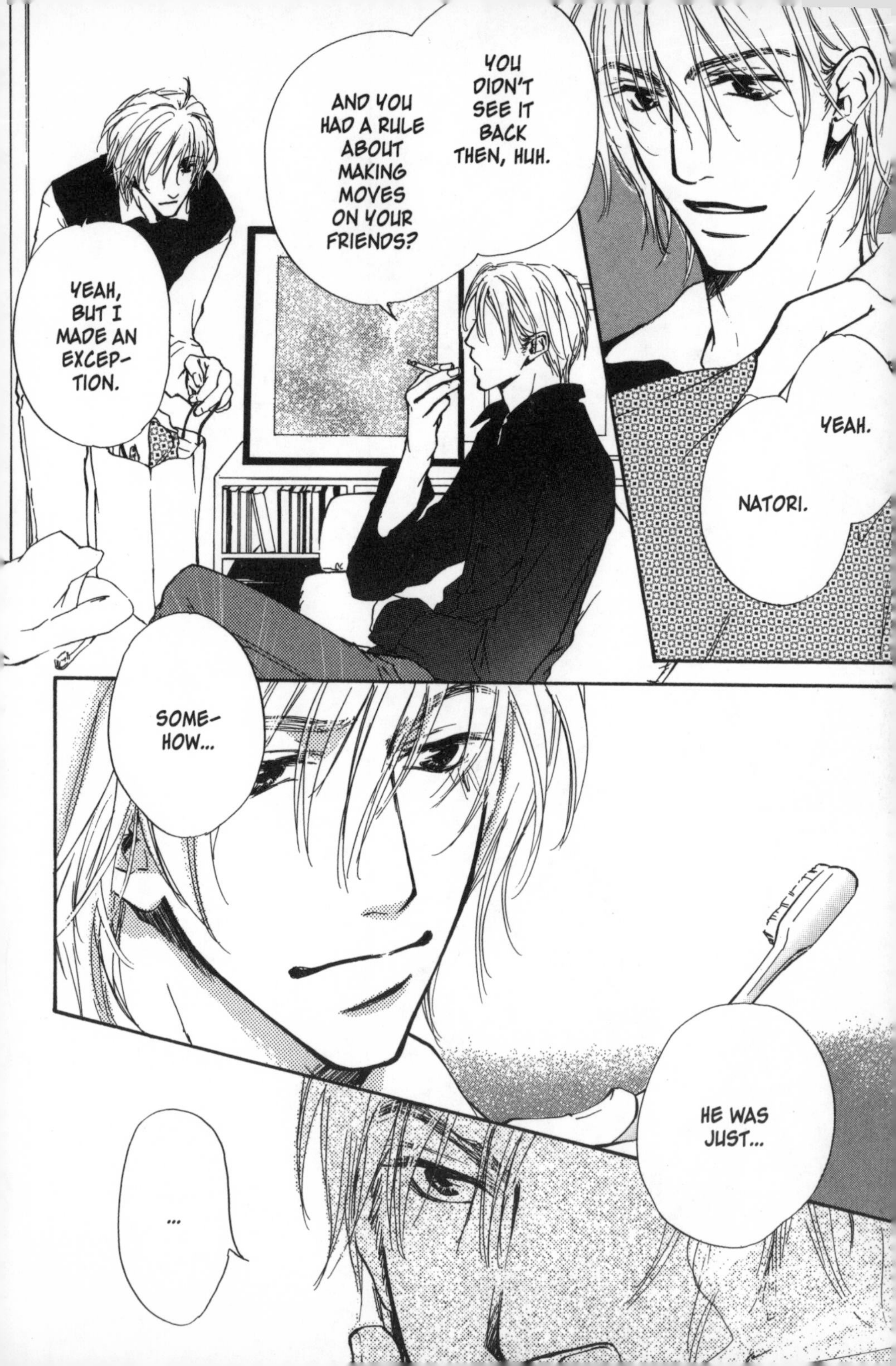
YEAH.
NATORI.
YOU DIDN'T SEE IT BACK THEN, HUH.
AND YOU HAD A RULE ABOUT MAKING MOVES ON YOUR FRIENDS?
YEAH, BUT I MADE AN EXCEPTION.
SOME-HOW...
HE WAS JUST...
...

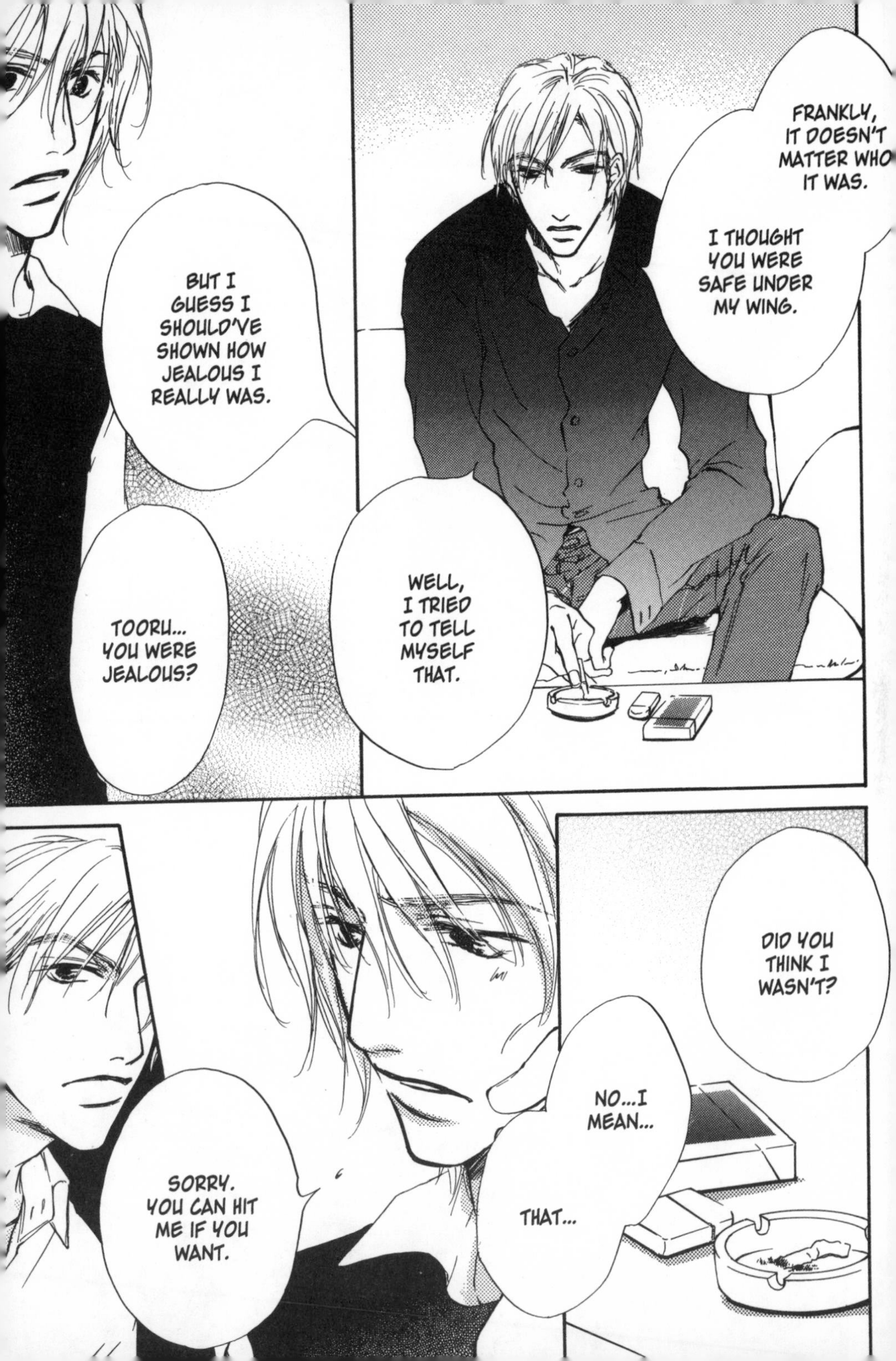
FRANKLY, IT DOESN'T MATTER WHO IT WAS.
I THOUGHT YOU WERE SAFE UNDER MY WING.
WELL, I TRIED TO TELL MYSELF THAT.
BUT I GUESS I SHOULD'VE SHOWN HOW JEALOUS I REALLY WAS.
TOORU... YOU WERE JEALOUS?
DID YOU THINK I WASN'T?
NO...I MEAN...
THAT...
SORRY. YOU CAN HIT ME IF YOU WANT.

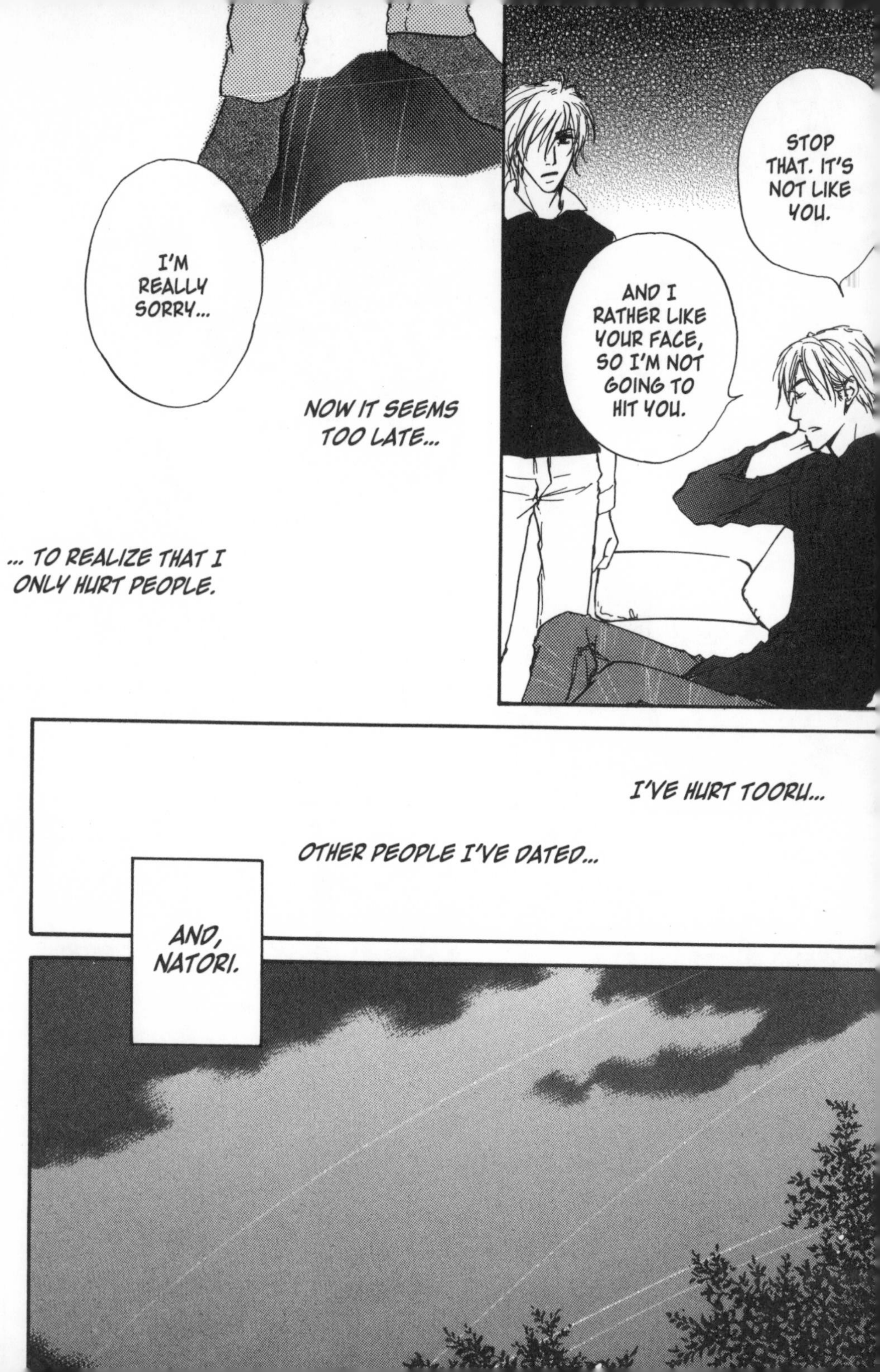
STOP THAT. IT'S NOT LIKE YOU.
AND I RATHER LIKE YOUR FACE, SO I'M NOT GOING TO HIT YOU.
I'M REALLY SORRY...
NOW IT SEEMS TOO LATE...
... TO REALIZE THAT I ONLY HURT PEOPLE.
I'VE HURT TOORU...
OTHER PEOPLE I'VE DATED...
AND, NATORI.

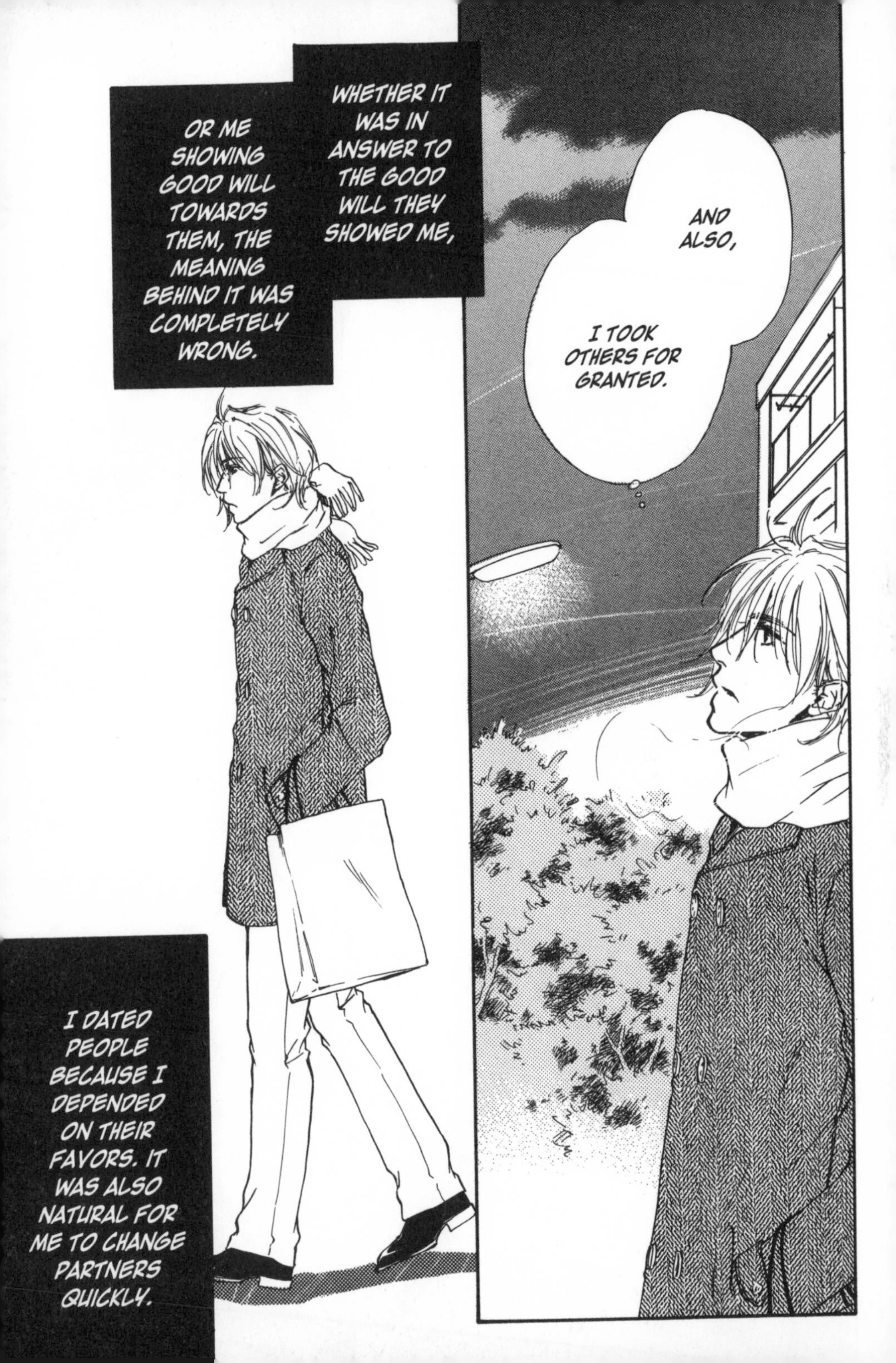
AND ALSO,
I TOOK OTHERS FOR GRANTED.
WHETHER IT WAS IN ANSWER TO THE GOOD WILL THEY SHOWED ME,
OR ME SHOWING GOOD WILL TOWARDS THEM, THE MEANING BEHIND IT WAS COMPLETELY WRONG.
I DATED PEOPLE BECAUSE I DEPENDED ON THEIR FAVORS. IT WAS ALSO NATURAL FOR ME TO CHANGE PARTNERS QUICKLY.

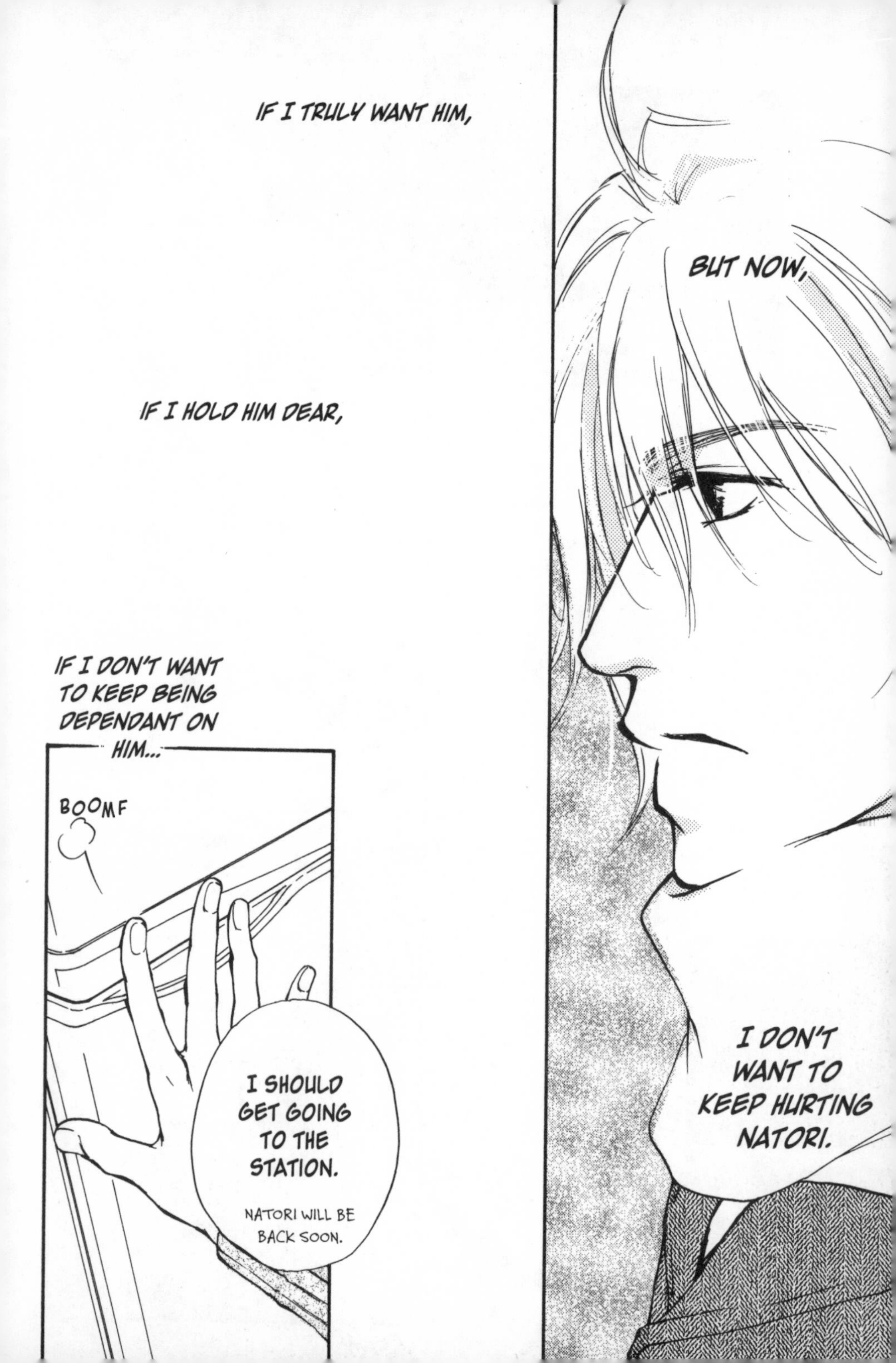
BUT NOW,
I DON'T WANT TO KEEP HURTING NATORI.
IF I TRULY WANT HIM,
IF I HOLD HIM DEAR,
IF I DON'T WANT TO KEEP BEING DEPENDANT ON HIM...
BOOMF
I SHOULD GET GOING TO THE STATION.
NATORI WILL BE BACK SOON.

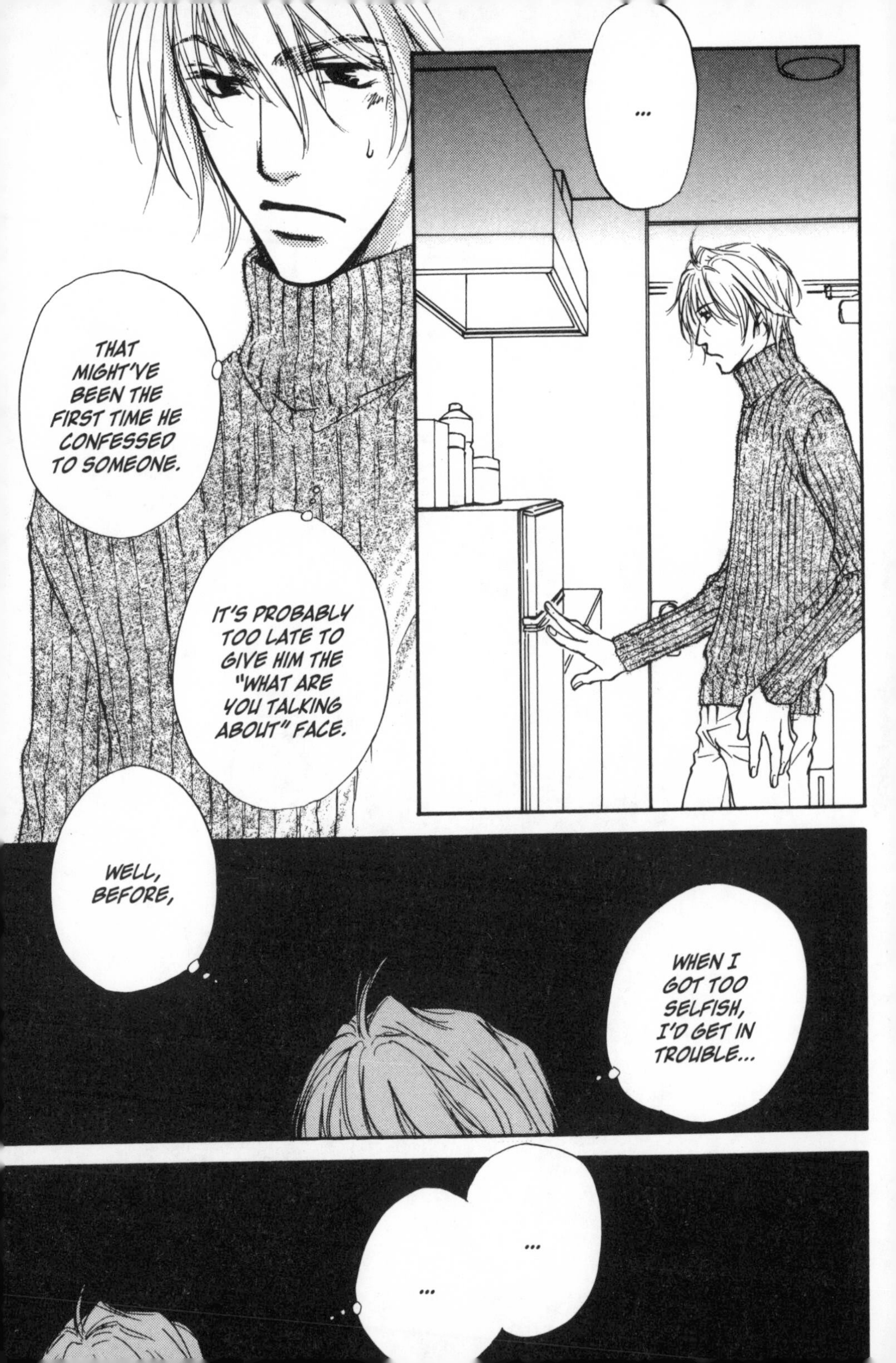
...
THAT MIGHT'VE BEEN THE FIRST TIME HE CONFESSED TO SOMEONE.
IT'S PROBABLY TOO LATE TO GIVE HIM THE "WHAT ARE YOU TALKING ABOUT" FACE.
WELL, BEFORE,
WHEN I GOT TOO SELFISH, I'D GET IN TROUBLE...
...
...

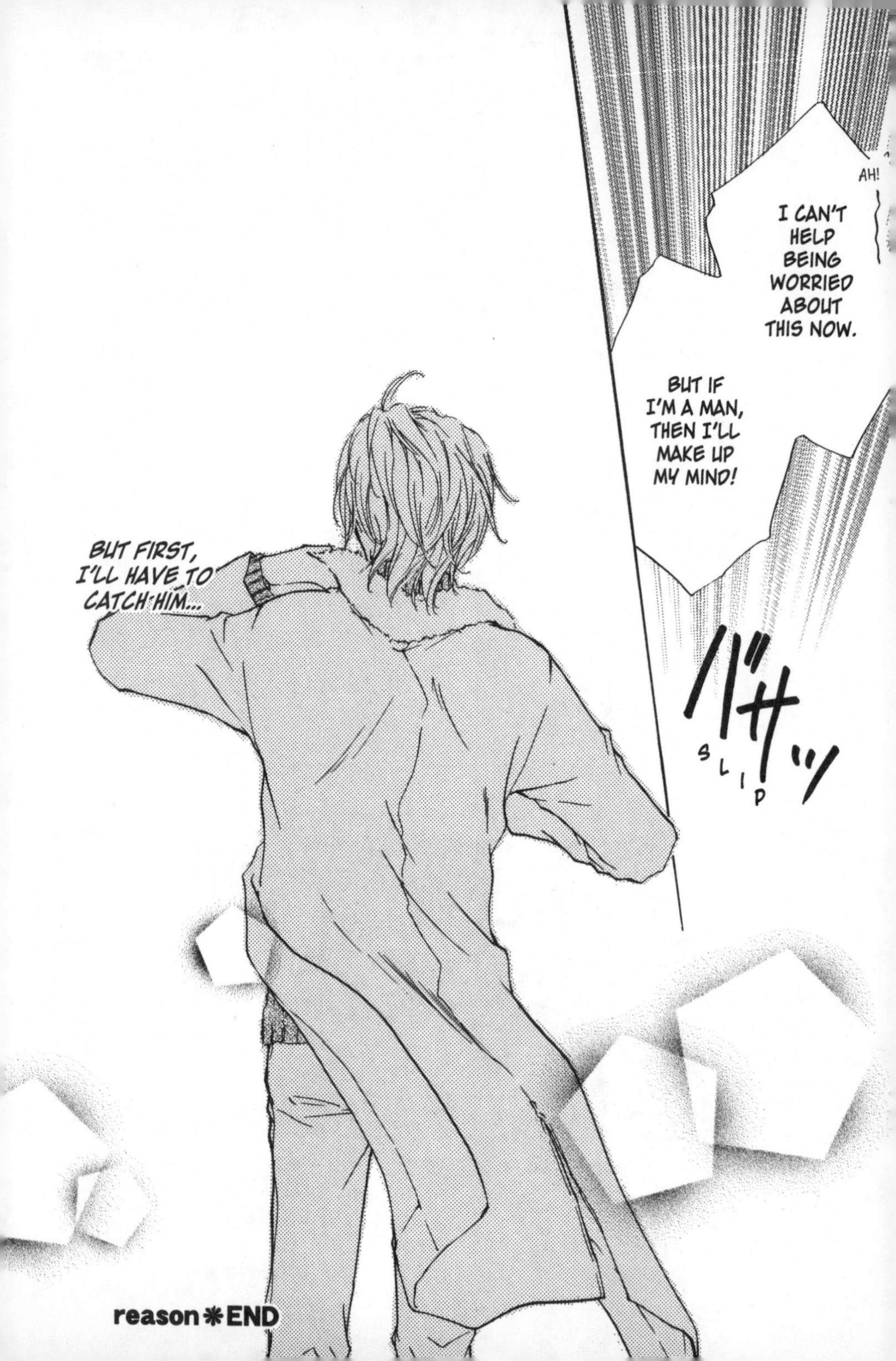
AH!
I CAN'T HELP BEING WORRIED ABOUT THIS NOW.
BUT IF I'M A MAN, THEN I'LL MAKE UP MY MIND!
バサッ
SLIP
BUT FIRST, I'LL HAVE TO CATCH HIM...

reason ✱ END

• AFTERWORD •

FOR ME, THIS MANGA WAS MY FIRST SERIAL TITLE. (IT WAS PUBLISHED EVERY OTHER MONTH). SO I MADE IT A POINT TO INCLUDE EVERYTHING I'D BEEN THINKING OF WRITING ABOUT:

1. INCLUDE THE GIRLS IN THE STORY. ← IT'S SOMETHING I'LL PROBABLY ALWAYS STRUGGLE WITH. I HAD FUN THOUGH.
2. WRITE THE WHOLE STORY FROM THE SEME'S POINT OF VIEW. ← ALTHOUGH I DID SUCCEED, I WAS DISSATISFIED AND ENDED UP WRITING A BUNCH OF FOLLOW-UP STORIES. SO I SORT OF FELL SHORT...
3. MAKE THE SEME'S CHARACTER SAPPY AND HELPLESS LIKE THOSE GUYS FROM ROMANTIC COMEDIES.

SOMEHOW NATORI TURNED OUT TO BE EVEN MORE PATHETIC THAN THE GUYS IN ROMANTIC COMEDIES... SORRY NATORI! (LAUGH)

↑ TRYING TO LAUGH IT OFF.

EPISODE MEMO 1
KISUGI'S BOAST ABOUT THE LOTION IS ACTUALLY A TRUE STORY FROM ONE OF MY GAY FRIENDS. (LAUGH) ONLY, THE PART ABOUT IT BEING ONLY FOR MEN'S PERSONAL USE MIGHT HAVE BEEN SOMETHING I JUST MADE UP...

I RATHER PREFER THE SAPPY, PATHETIC SEME, BUT I GUESS THE SEME IN A BOY'S LOVE STORY NEEDS TO BE ABLE TO DO HIS THING AND CAPTURE THE HEARTS OF THE READERS... SO HE NEEDS THAT STRENGTH AS WELL, I THINK.

THERE ARE OTHER POINTS TO REFLECT UPON LIKE THE ONES I MENTIONED ABOVE (LIKE HOW I STRAYED A LOT WHILE DRAWING, SO THERE WERE A LARGE QUANTITY OF ADJUSTMENTS TO BE MADE), BUT I JUST HOPE THAT I MADE THIS STORY FUN AND INTERESTING TO READ.

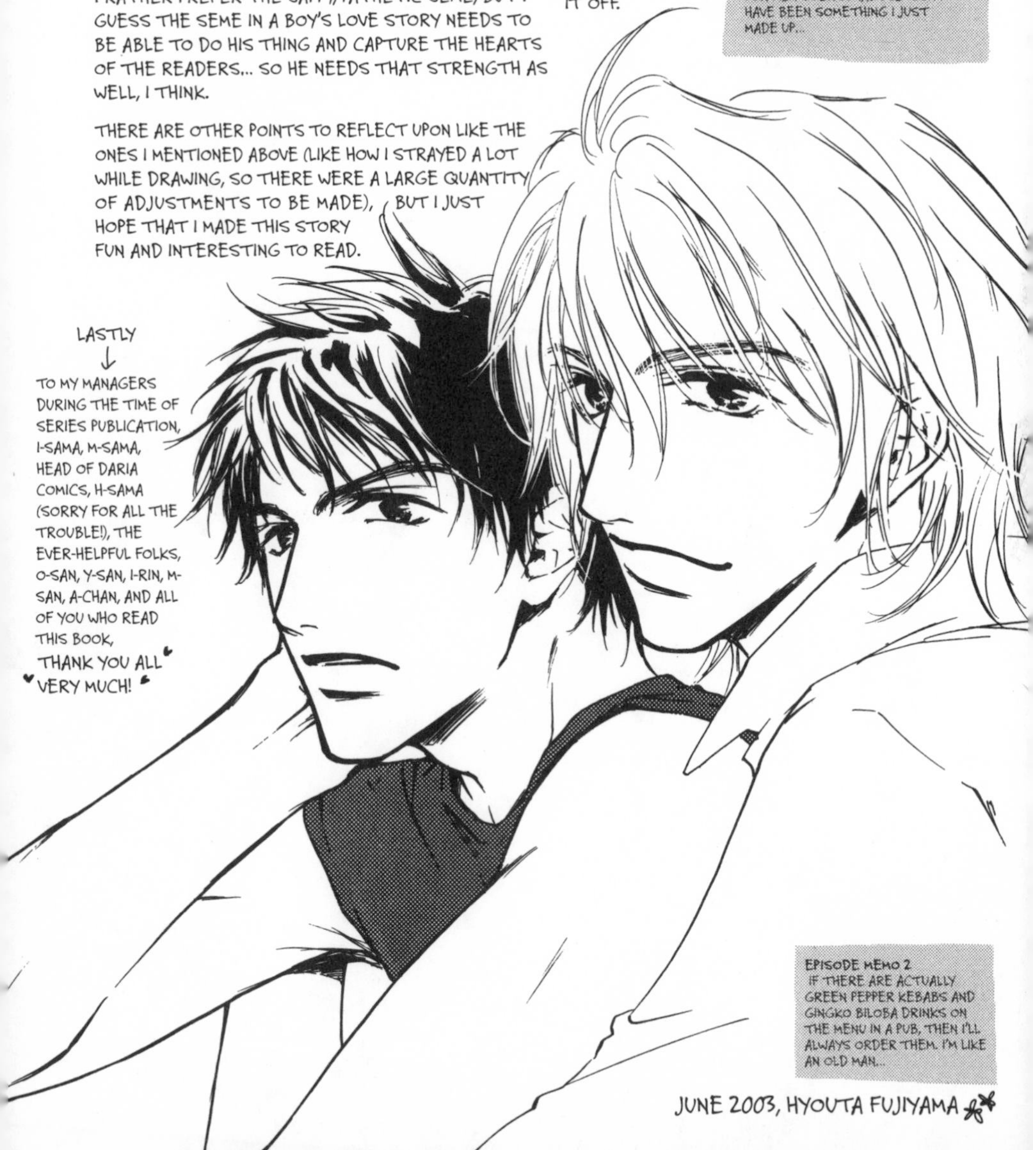

LASTLY ↓

TO MY MANAGERS DURING THE TIME OF SERIES PUBLICATION, I-SAMA, M-SAMA, HEAD OF DARIA COMICS, H-SAMA (SORRY FOR ALL THE TROUBLE!), THE EVER-HELPFUL FOLKS, O-SAN, Y-SAN, I-RIN, M-SAN, A-CHAN, AND ALL OF YOU WHO READ THIS BOOK, THANK YOU ALL VERY MUCH!

EPISODE MEMO 2
IF THERE ARE ACTUALLY GREEN PEPPER KEBABS AND GINGKO BILOBA DRINKS ON THE MENU IN A PUB, THEN I'LL ALWAYS ORDER THEM. I'M LIKE AN OLD MAN...

JUNE 2003, HYOUTA FUJIYAMA

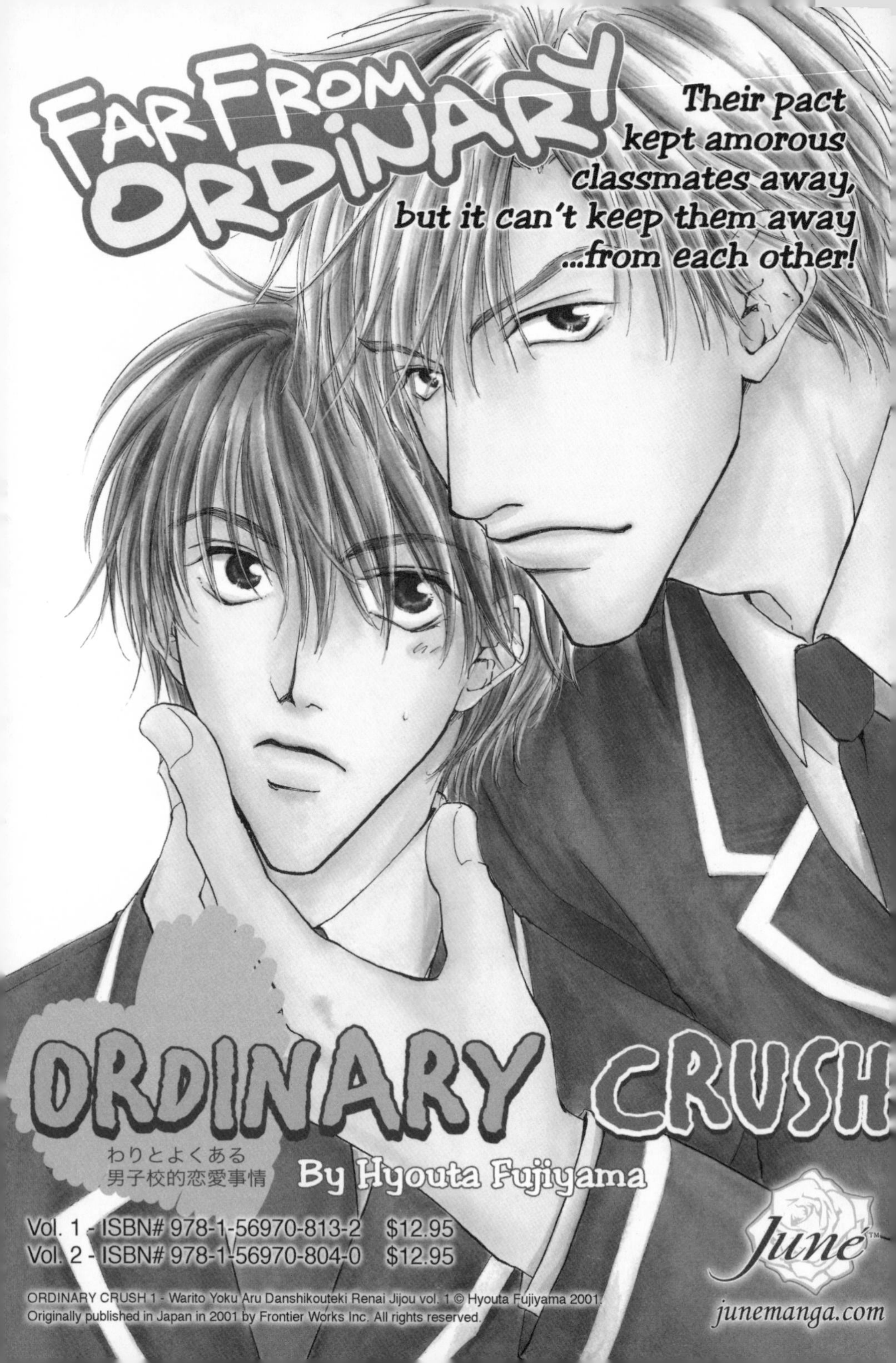
FAR FROM ORDINARY
Their pact kept amorous classmates away, but it can't keep them away ...from each other!
ORDINARY CRUSH
わりとよくある
男子校的恋愛事情
By Hyouta Fujiyama
Vol. 1 - ISBN# 978-1-56970-813-2 $12.95
Vol. 2 - ISBN# 978-1-56970-804-0 $12.95
June™
ORDINARY CRUSH 1 - Warito Yoku Aru Danshikouteki Renai Jijou vol. 1 © Hyouta Fujiyama 2001.
Originally published in Japan in 2001 by Frontier Works Inc. All rights reserved.
junemanga.com

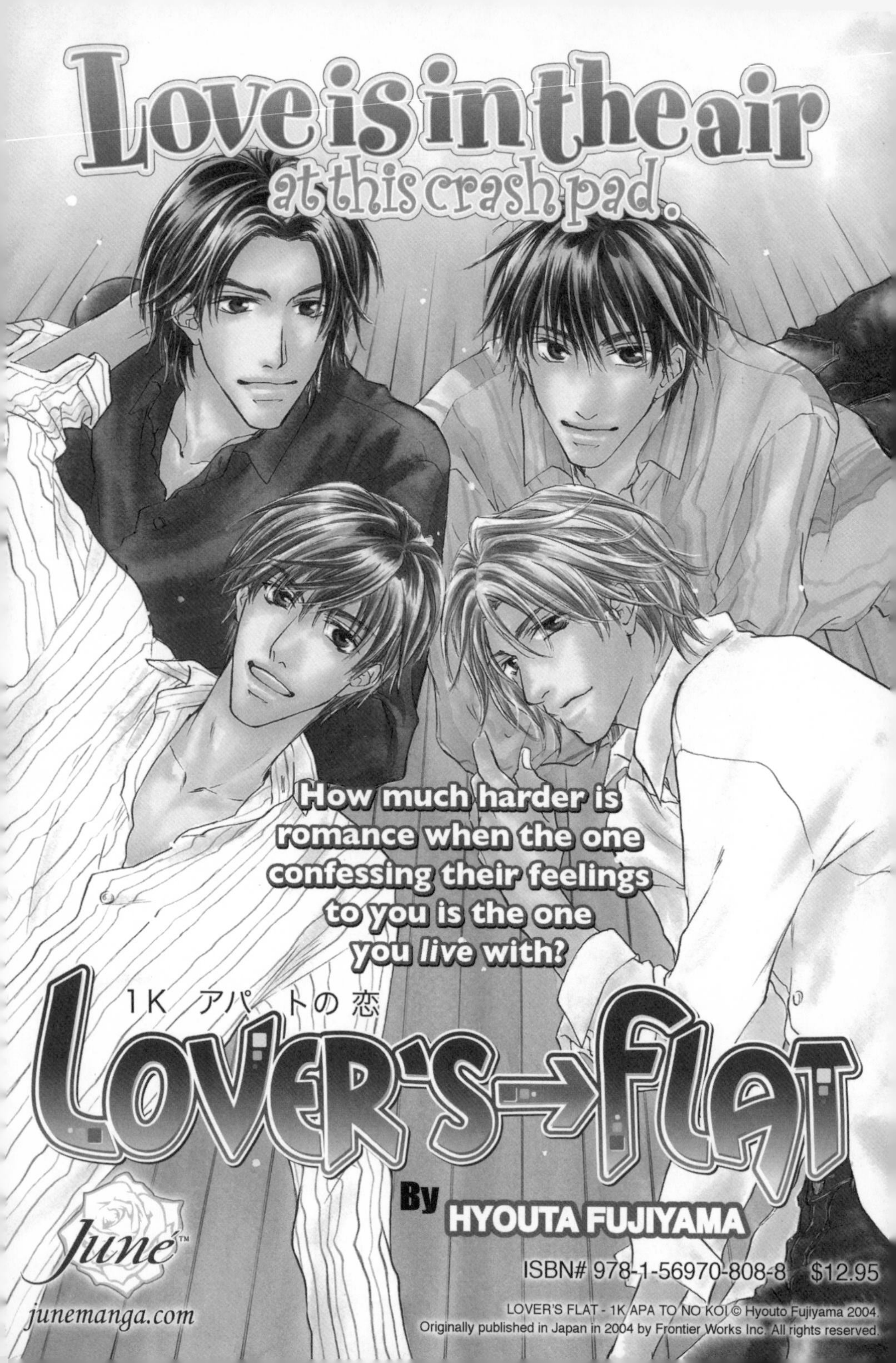
Love is in the air
at this crash pad.
How much harder is romance when the one confessing their feelings to you is the one you *live* with?
1K アパートの恋
LOVER'S FLAT
By HYOUTA FUJIYAMA
June™
junemanga.com
ISBN# 978-1-56970-808-8 $12.95
LOVER'S FLAT - 1K APA TO NO KOI © Hyouto Fujiyama 2004.
Originally published in Japan in 2004 by Frontier Works Inc. All rights reserved.

by Hyouta Fujiyama

Sunflower
てっぺんのひまわり

Sowing the Seeds of Love ♥

ISBN# 978-1-56970-807-1 $12.95

June

junemanga.com

If you can't
Beat them, Join them

From the artist of

RIN!

When a country-bumpkin becomes landlord of the school, it's time for a whole new set of rules!

CAN'T WIN WITH YOU!

きみには
勝てない

SATOSUMI TAKAGUCHI   **YUKINE HONAMI**

Vol. 1 - ISBN# 978-1-56970-812-5 $12.95
Vol. 2 - ISBN# 978-1-56970-819-4 $12.95
Vol. 3 - ISBN# 978-1-56970-821-7 $12.95

June™

junemanga.com

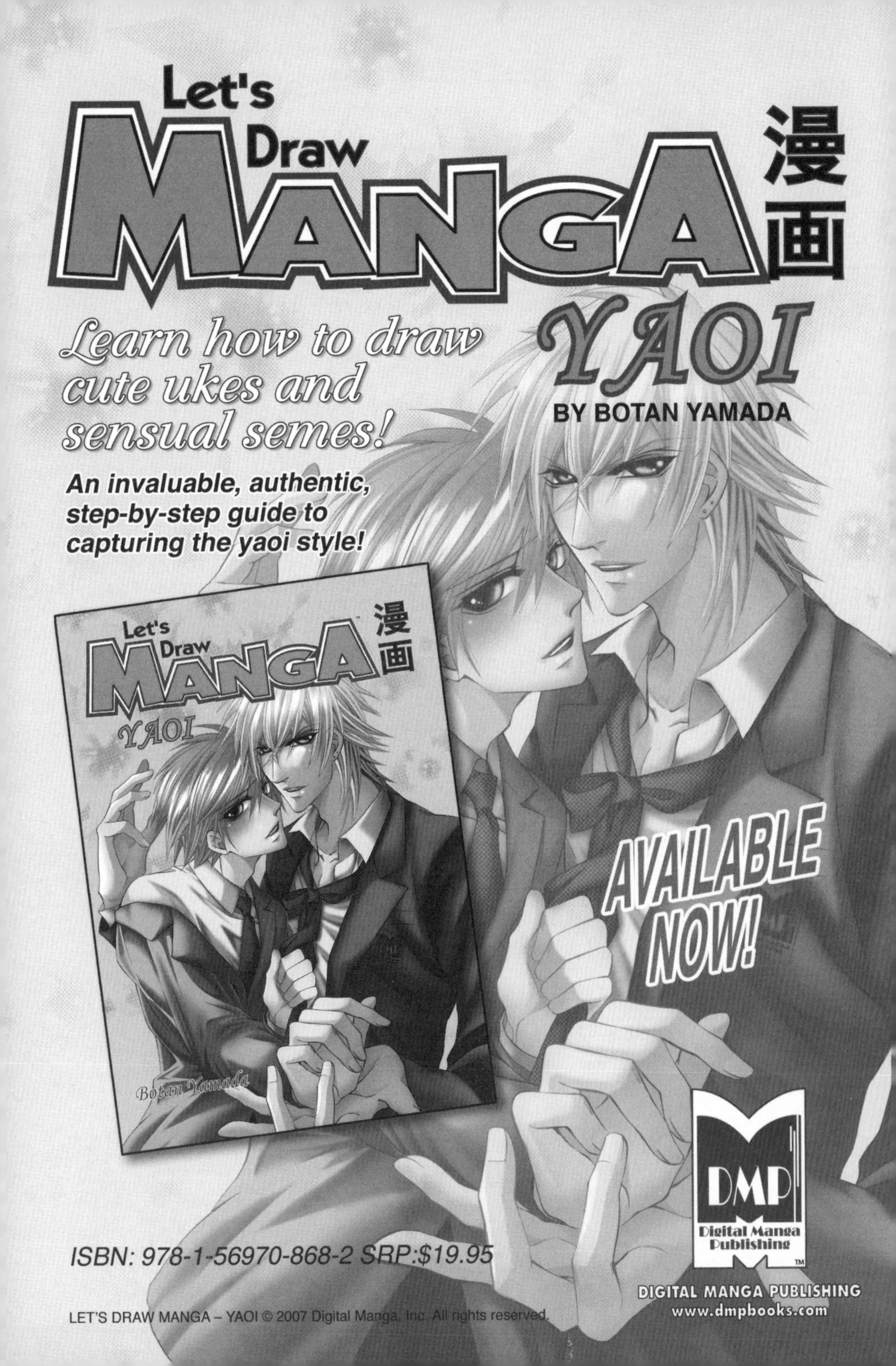
Let's Draw MANGA 漫画
YAOI
BY BOTAN YAMADA
Learn how to draw cute ukes and sensual semes!
An invaluable, authentic, step-by-step guide to capturing the yaoi style!
Let's Draw MANGA 漫画
YAOI
Botan Yamada
AVAILABLE NOW!
DMP Digital Manga Publishing
ISBN: 978-1-56970-868-2 SRP:$19.95
DIGITAL MANGA PUBLISHING
www.dmpbooks.com
LET'S DRAW MANGA – YAOI © 2007 Digital Manga, Inc. All rights reserved.

STOP

This is the back of the book!
Start from the other side.

NATIVE MANGA readers read manga from *right to left*.

1
2
1
3
2
3
5
4
4
6
5
8
7
6

If you run into our ***Native Manga*** *logo on any of our books... you'll know that this manga is published in it's true original native Japanese right to left reading format, as it was intended. Turn to the other side of the book and start reading from right to left, top to bottom.*

Follow the diagram to see how its done.
Surf's Up!

NATIVE MANGA
READ RIGHT TO LEFT